HUMAN MOTOR CONTROL

HUMAN MOTOR CONTROL

David A. Rosenbaum

Department of Psychology
University of Massachusetts
Amherst, Massachusetts

Academic Press, Inc.
Harcourt Brace Jovanovich, Publishers
San Diego   New York   Boston
London   Sydney   Tokyo   Toronto

Copyright © 1991 by Academic Press, Inc.
All Rights Reserved.
No part of this publication may be reproduced or transmitted in any
form or by any means, electronic or mechanical, including photocopy,
recording, or any information storage and retrieval system, without
permission in writing from the publisher.

Academic Press, Inc.
San Diego, California 92101

United Kingdom Edition published by
Academic Press Limited
24–28 Oval Road, London NW1 7DX

Library of Congress Cataloging-in-Publication Data

Rosenbaum, David A.
    Human motor control / David A. Rosenbaum.
        p.   cm.
    Includes index.
    ISBN   0-12-597300-4   (alk. paper)
        1. Movement, Psychology of. 2. Motor learning.   I. Title.
BF295.R67   1991
152.3--dc20   90-1063
                                                      CIP

Printed in the United States of America
91 92 93 94   9 8 7 6 5 4 3 2 1

for Judy

■ CONTENTS IN BRIEF

■ CONTENTS

CHAPTER 3
PSYCHOLOGICAL FOUNDATIONS

■ PART II
THE ACTIVITY SYSTEMS

CHAPTER 4
WALKING

CHAPTER 5
LOOKING

CHAPTER 8
KEYBOARDING

CHAPTER 9
SPEAKING AND SINGING

CHAPTER 10
SMILING

PART III
PRINCIPLES AND PROSPECTS

CHAPTER 11
CONCLUSIONS

 PREFACE

Imagine what life would be like if you couldn't move. Unable to speak, activate your arms, walk, or even glance around, it would be impossible for you to gesture, transport yourself from one location to another, reach for objects, communicate with others, or see. The prospect of being paralyzed is terrifying. But by considering paralysis, even briefly, one recognizes how vital movement is for all that we do.

Movement is just one of the functions of the motor system. The other is stability. Maintaining balance and resisting mechanical disturbances are prime examples of stabilizing behaviors. When the motor system is impaired, stabilization becomes difficult. In the worst case, behaviors that we take for granted—the ability to ride a subway, walk through a thickly weeded forest, or hold an upset baby—are all but impossible.

This book is an introduction to research on human motor control. The volume is mainly written for students still gaining an introduction to behavioral science. In teaching about motor control to a wide range of students, I have been struck by the fact that many important and interesting topics have so far been presented only in highly technical terms. The sight of frustrated students struggling to read this material has convinced me that they need an approachable, friendly introduction to the field.

To help you feel comfortable with the material at hand, I have organized the book in a modular fashion. Chapter 1, "Introduction," sets the stage for the field at large, stressing the main questions to be addressed, the types of answers to be sought, and the methods used to pursue them. Chapter 2, "Physiological Foundations," describes the physiological approach to motor control, emphasizing neural substrates. Chapter 3, "Psychological Foundations," is concerned with a more abstract level of analysis—one not explicitly concerned with the physical basis of performance. In my teaching, I have found that students unfamiliar with scientific psychology somtimes have difficulty seeing that a psychological model can be a *bona fide* scientific explanation. Chapter 3 shows how serious research can be done, and important advances can be made, using psychological techniques.

The next seven chapters contain the bulk of the book's material. Each chapter is devoted to a distinct set of activities in which motion and stability are key. The chapters are titled "Walking," "Looking," "Reaching and Grasping," "Writing and Drawing," "Keyboarding," "Speaking and Singing," and "Smiling." These titles are meant to exemplify rather than encompass the behaviors they suggest. Thus, the chapter on walking includes a discussion of running, the chapter on smiling includes a discussion of scowling, and so forth. I have organized the chapters by activities because much of the work in human motor control has been compartmentalized this way. Devoting separate chapters to distinct activities allows attention to be given to the unique methods and concerns that have arisen in each area. Treating each activity separately also makes it easy to look for similarities among subsystems while scouting for differences.

The last chapter, "Conclusions," wraps things up. It also describes two integrative activities (hand-eye coordination and hitting approaching balls), the nature of individual differences, and several new approaches that are likely to play an increasingly important role in the years ahead.

Although this book is primarily meant for students, it should also be useful for nonstudents whose work or recreation touches on motor control or its ramifications. Motor control impinges on a large number disciplines. Some are defined almost entirely with respect to movement and stability: Physical education, physical therapy, occupational therapy, prosthetics, dance, kinesiology, and biomechanics. Other disciplines have vested interests in understanding motor performance, even if movement and stability are not their sole province: Medicine, sports, musical performance, the fine arts, psychology, physiology, human factors, ergonomics, robotics, engineering. Because I want this book to be an approachable introduction to the entire field of motor control, I hope it will be useful to people in all these areas.

I am a psychologist, and as such want to comment briefly on the special importance that this book may have for my colleagues. Psychology is the science of mental life and behavior. Yet psychologists have paid remarkably little attention to the physical substrates of behavior (by which I mean the control of bodily motion and stability). The reasons for this neglect are not entirely obvious. I have heard it said that motor control can only be studied with highly technical appratus (not true), that one should start studying stimulus-response connections by studying stimulus processing (a view that assumes that we *react* to the world but do not *act* on it), and that when one studies motor performance, one is at the whim of the experimental participant (not if one is a skillful experimenter). In my view, the neglect of motor control by psychologists ultimately derives from a belief that motor control takes very little intelligence, even viewing intelligence in broad computational terms. Moving and stabilizing the body are, after all, done as well by animals as by people. If one wants to understand how humans differ from animals (an aim bequeathed by Descartes and embraced by many psychologists), then one might as well focus on those aspects of behavior (such as language) which clearly demarcate our species from others.

One message I want to communicate to psychologists is that motor control requires highly sophisticated computational and cognitive machinery. Were this not true, modern robots might now be able to pick berries, put band-aids on scraped knees, climb trees, or amble over rocky terrains. These tasks, which most 5-year-olds can do reasonably well, cannot be achieved by robots today. This outcome is ironic when one recalls that contemporary computer systems can play chess at nearly grand-master level, can give credible legal advice, and can diagnose illnesses as well as skilled physicians (within particular domains of medical practice). So it is not the case that motor performance, or perceptual-motor integration, is computationally undemanding. On the contrary, it is so demanding that we are only beginning to develop the tools to understand it.

I might add that it is incorrect to assume that motor performance provides no lines of demarcation between human and nonhuman species. Besides speech, movements with purely symbolic functions like pointing or drawing appear to be exclusively human. Likewise, physical behaviors which are defined relatively arbitrarily by human culture and which usually take enormous amounts of time to learn well—such as playing the piano, performing pirouettes, or weaving—appear to have no counterparts in the animal kingdom.

There is an excellent chance that the computational machinery underlying perception and action predated the evolution of human language and "high-level" intellectual competence. If this assumption is correct, then understanding the computational basis of perception and action should help us understand the higher mental capacities as well as perception and action themselves. Psychology should therefore benefit from the study of motor control and in turn contribute to the explication of motor function.

Like any book, this one has limitations. First, it contains relatively little information about anatomy or biomechanics. Historically, motor control has been pursued without much attention to these topics, though this situation is now changing. To reflect the way the field has been pursued, and to present what I know best, I have concentrated on the psychological and neural aspects of motor control.

Second, though the book is mainly organized by activity, some activities are not covered. Digestion, copulation, and excretion are omitted, for example, not because they are unsavory, but because their analysis has been off-stage. Some other activities are omitted or discussed only in passing because they probably are assembled out of more basic motor elements. Bowling, somersaulting, pole-vaulting, and flipping pizzas are all wonderful maneuvers to watch and try, but until their constituent actions are understood, their holistic control will likely remain unappreciated.

Third, this book is not meant to be an exhaustive treatment of motor control. Exhaustive treatments are exhausting for readers and (especially) for authors. I have omitted a number of studies that make points that I feel are too detailed, too uncertain, or too technical for this kind of text. (Some of the studies on this list are my own). The currency of some of the material may also be less than what one would ideally like. In preparing a volume of this kind, one finds oneself between a rock and hard place with respect to the inclusion of new material. On the one hand, one wants to present the latest word on everything. On the other hand, doing so keeps the book from ever being completed. One of my most frustrating experiences has been to discover in the library or in a package mailed from a helpful colleague some exciting new theory or experimental result which bears on a topic I have just written about and sent to the publisher. In such circumstances, I have often had to grit my teeth and move on. At the same time, I have been reassured by the hope that you may be motivated to seek out new references and learn about the new results yourself. An even fonder hope is that in the future, if you are so inclined, you will add to the literature yourself.

A final word about the text is that it is neither a textbook nor a monograph in the traditional senses of those terms. I have tried to review the field without attempting a global new theory (as in a textbook), but I have also expressed a number of opinions and proposed some new models (as in a monograph). In particular, I have suggested a new model for aspects of speech production (in Chapter 9) and for two-hand coordination phenomena (in Chapter 11). Because I have been engaged in motor-control research for over a decade, I have come to believe in the value of a certain perspective (that has changed in some important respects in recent years), and I have taken the liberty of using this book as a vehicle for defending that perspective. The field of motor control is a dynamic one, with some radically different approaches being trumpeted by various factions. This is a healthy state for a field to be in, but it also leaves one feeling unable to stand dispassionately on the sidelines.

It is in the nature of such a treatise that the material one presents does not come tidied up, presented as if everyone agrees on the meaning of the work that has been done. Good scientists criticize and argue, and part of learning to do science is becoming familiar with scientific debate. There is a good deal of debate in this book, because I believe in the value of critical thinking. What this implies for you is that you should be prepared for occasional "nonanswers" to questions that are posed, or admissions of division among the experts. Such is the state of this field (like most). If everyone in motor control agreed on everything, the field would be much less stimulating than it is, though of course some would probably disagree with that appraisal!

My last prefatory remark is that I welcome your input. Please feel free to contact me with suggestions, comments, or questions. My address is Department of Psychology, University of Massachusetts, Amherst, Massachusetts 01003. My electronic-mail address is ROSENB@UMASS.BITNET.

■ ACKNOWLEDGMENTS

One of my main reasons for writing this book has been to study the field of human motor control in a disciplined way. As part of this educational process, I have taken the liberty of asking a number of people to comment on parts of the manuscript. For their valuable feedback, I thank Neil Carlsmith, Charles Clifton, Rachel Clifton, William Cooper, Mark Feinstein, Claude Ghez, Herbert Heuer, Michael Jordan, Steven Keele, Eileen Kowler, James Lackner, Keith Rayner, William Rinn, Herbert Schriefers, Henry Shaffer, Neil Stillings, Piet van Wieringen, Jonathan Vaughan, Alan Wing, and Howard Zelaznik. Any errors that have slipped into the final product belie their expertise and bespeak my fallibility.

I owe thanks too to a number of people who provided valuable background stimulation and support. Gordon Bower, my graduate advisor at Stanford, was an important intellectual influence, as was Saul Sternberg, my supervisor for four years at Bell Laboratories. While at Hampshire College (Amherst, Massachusetts) from 1981-1987, I benefited especially from the erudition and unstinting support of my fellow cognitive psychologist, Neil Stillings. My colleagues at the University of Massachusetts, where I have worked since 1987, have been equally helpful; I especially thank Dan Anderson, Sy Berger, Chuck Clifton, Rachel Clifton, Jim Chumbley, Stan Moss, Jerry Myers, Sandy Pollatsek, Keith Rayner, and Arnie Well.

The individuals with whom I have collaborated also played central roles in my thinking about motor control: Janey Barnes, Ron Calvanio, Andy Gordon, Albrecht Inhoff, Michael Jordan, Matt Jorgensen, Bill Hazelett, Van Hindorff, Abby Kingman, Frank Marchak, Ed Munro, Dick Pew, Jacob Reider, Ed Saltzman, Jim Slotta, Erika Stewart, Jonathan Vaughan, Bob Weber, and Howard Zelaznik. Some of these individuals were soulmates as well as collaborators.

Throughout preparation of the book, I was fortunate to have several grants and fellowships. Early planning of the book occurred in 1984-85 when I was a fellow at MIT's Center for Cognitive Science. Starting in 1985, it became possible for me to devote five full years to research and writing through a Research Career Development Award from the National Institutes of Health. I was also fortunate to receive continued grant support from the Human Cognition and Perception Program (formerly, Memory and

Cognitive Processes) of the National Science Foundation, under the direction of Dr. Joseph L. Young. The book was completed while I was a fellow at the Netherlands Institute for Advanced Study (Professor Dirk van de Kaa, Director), where I was a member of the Human Movement Nucleus. I learned a great deal from the other members of the Nucleus, and thank them here: Gerard van Galen, Denis Glencross, Herbert Heuer, Wouter Hulstijn, Réjean Plamondon, Jeff Summers, Ar Thomassen, and Piet van Wieringen.

Completing a large project like this depends to a large extent on the skill of the editor. Joe Ingram at Academic Press deserves a medal for the way he handled me and my work. It was Joe's honesty and care that led me to sign with Academic Press in the first place. I never regretted the decision. Sabine Teich, Joe's colleague, did a terrific job in finalizing matters prior to publication. Melinda Provenza's excellent copyediting and Toni Dillon's artistry in preparing the figures are also appreciated.

At a personal level, I have been blessed with a full complement of parents and parents-in-law who were always there for me. The three people who were most important to me during preparation of the book were my wife, Professor Judith Kroll (who usually does not insist that I call her "Professor" or even "Judith"), and our two daughters, Nora and Sarah Kroll-Rosenbaum (who usually don't insist that I use their last name). They supplied me with limitless emotional and intellectual support. Without them, the book might have been completed sooner, but thanks to them I found myself doing things other than reading about motor control and staring at the Macintosh screen. For their help in allowing me to preserve my humanity during the seemingly endless writing process, I express my deepest love and appreciation. For the beauty she has cast on the world we have shared, I dedicate this book to Judy.

PART I

PRELIMINARIES

 INTRODUCTION

How do we move? How do we walk, talk, sing, and smile? How do we perform on the athletic field, play musical instruments, craft tools and works of art? How do we learn to carry out these activities, and why are some of us better at them than others? What goes wrong when, through accident or disease, the ability to move is impaired? How can movement disabilities be restored or, better yet, prevented? And how can machines be made to carry out the tasks that most people (and animals) perform effortlessly?

As this list of questions suggests, understanding human motor control can have significant effects in a wide range of endeavors. This is hardly surprising given that movement occurs in virtually all walks of life. In sports, where rapid coordinated action can make the difference between victory and defeat, an understanding of motor control can allow for more victories or heightened levels of competition. In the fine arts, where performance on the stage or in the studio allows for aesthetic expression, understanding how we control the movements of our bodies can enhance the quality of expression as well as the training that leads to it. In medicine, where paralysis, lack of coordination, or weakness can sabotage the quality of life, rehabilitation can be improved through a deeper appreciation of the means by which the motor system functions. Finally, at home and in the workplace, the use of machines or appliances can be made safer or more efficient through the application of principles gained through motor control research.

Two fundamental questions lie at the heart of this field of study. One is how we control our movements; the other is how we maintain stability. Holding an object steady in changing wind conditions or standing still in a subway are tasks that demand stabilization. Without muscular control, such tasks would be hopeless—as hopeless, in fact, as moving. Because stabilization as well as movement must be achieved by the system we will be studying, we will not refer to it as the *movement* system or the *stabilization* system, but rather the *motor* system.

The word *motor* has some unfortunate connotations. One is that of machinelike rigidity. Conventional motors churn away monotonously, performing the same motions over and over again. By contrast, behavior is endlessly novel, at least under normal conditions. The novelty of behavior could only occur if the motor system allowed for the generation of continually changing patterns of muscle activity. It does so by relying on a rich configuration of neuromuscular assemblages that have evolved over millions of years. If you doubt the sophistication of the motor system, consider modern robots. These devices embody much of what we currently know about motor control, yet they can barely walk across uneven surfaces without toppling over, or engage in such mundane activities as tying a Boy Scout knot. Given the relatively mediocre performance of state-of-the-art robots, our ignorance of motor control is painfully obvious. A robot may run with motors—the other connotation of "motor" control—but the human body does not, at least not with conventional motors made of axles and magnetic coils. The motive forces for behavior are controlled in more subtle and sophisticated ways. Understanding how these forces are governed and physically realized can help us develop more effective robots. In addition, and perhaps more importantly, it can help us appreciate how we function as active, intelligent agents.

■ PHYSIOLOGICAL AND PSYCHOLOGICAL EXPLANATION

What does it mean to understand human motor control? What is to be understood, and what form should the understanding take? The answers to these questions are not obvious, for under normal circumstances movement and stability just seem to happen. When things work well, it is often unclear what their underlying components are. A hallmark of skilled performance, in fact, is that it occurs effortlessly. Thinking about motor skills can often prevent them from happening.

In *abnormal* circumstances skills may be disrupted. As a result of accident or disease, one's ability to move or stabilize the body may be drastically impaired. A wide range of motor disorders afflict people; many will be discussed here. Considering these disorders and the factors that cause them helps illuminate the substrates of normal performance.

It is possible to study the motor system in many ways. Understanding the physical components of the system is a task of *physiologists*—people who investigate the functions served by the physical structures of the body. Physiologists interested in motor control focus on *muscles, bones,* and *joints,* as well as the *nervous system,* the neural network that governs how muscles act. The practitioners who apply this information in the clinic include *neurol-*

ogists, who diagnose and treat ailments of the nervous system, *orthopedists,* who diagnose and treat disorders of bones and joints, *physical therapists,* who help restore motion and stability through behavioral rehabilitation, and *prostheticians,* who design and fit artificial limbs (*prostheses*) for people with amputations. Rudiments of motor physiology will be described in Chapter 2, Physiological Foundations.

Besides analyzing motor control in physical terms, another useful approach is *psychological.* This approach is described in Chapter 3, Psychological Foundations. Theories in psychology are not restricted to effects of personality, mental illness, or conscious thought. They also focus on mental *functions*—conscious or unconscious—underlying performance. Psychologists do not usually deny physical causes of behavior; in fact, they are usually pleased if their models find physiological support. However, the explanations that psychologists pursue usually do not require one-to-one mappings of identified biological mechanisms to behavioral or mental phenomena. Psychologists accept the fact that perception, thought, and action may emerge from the collective effects of many biological mechanisms. Identifying those mechanisms or the way they work is of less concern than understanding the emergent properties of the system as a whole.

Both for psychologists and for physiologists, four major problems occupy the core of motor control research. These are (1) the *degrees-of-freedom* problem, (2) the *serial-order* problem, (3) the *perceptual–motor integration* problem, and (4) the *skill-acquisition* problem. The next sections introduce each of these problems in turn.

■ THE DEGREES-OF-FREEDOM PROBLEM

Most physical tasks can be performed in an infinite number of ways. This has some advantages. One is obstacle avoidance (Cruse, 1986). If you need to reach for an object and there are obstacles in the way, it is helpful to have more than one way to reach for it. Another advantage is that the limbs that normally perform the task may not always be available for doing so. Holding a heavy package, for example, may make it impossible for you to turn on a light switch the way you usually do (with your hand). Nevertheless, you can turn on the light switch with your chin, even if you have never done so before. Similarly, if you need to write with a pencil held between your teeth (for example, to write a rescue note if you are held captive), chances are you can do so, and even preserve your normal writing style (see Figure 1.1). Students of motor behavior call the capacity to perform a given task in a variety of ways *motor equivalence.*

The capacity for motor equivalence is made possible by the many degrees of freedom within the motor system. The degrees of freedom in a system are the number of dimensions in which the system can independently vary. The joints of the arm have seven degrees of freedom. The shoul-

A *Able was I ere I saw Elba*

B *Able was I ere I saw Elba*

C *Able was I ere I saw Elba*

D *Able was I ere I saw Elba*

E *Able was I ere I saw Elba*

Figure 1.1 Handwriting achieved through different means: (A) With the right (dominant) hand; (B) with the right arm but with the wrist immobilized; (C) with the left hand; (D) with the pen gripped between the teeth; and (E) with the pen attached to the foot. (Reprinted from Raibert, 1977.)

der has three (it can move up and down, from side to side, and it can twist), the elbow has two (it can bend and it can twist), and the wrist has two (it can move up and down and it can turn from side to side).

If the degrees of freedom of the motor system bestow the advantages of obstacle avoidance and motor equivalence, why speak of a degrees-of-freedom *problem*? To see why, consider the simple act of touching the tip of your nose with the end of your right index finger. Perform this act before reading on.

In all likelihood, you touched your nose in a relatively efficient way. It is unlikely, for example, that you snaked your arm around the back of your head or that you extended your arm straight in front of you and then brought your finger back toward your face. These would have been odd ways of touching your nose, although they are possible. The fact that you selected a more efficient trajectory suggests that you somehow eliminated from consideration awkward or inefficient movement paths. This seems unremarkable until you recall that the joints of the arm have seven degrees of freedom, but the tip of your nose (or its location) has three degrees of freedom—its x, y, and z position in Cartesian coordinates. Thus without even considering the finger, which adds still more degrees of freedom, a problem arises in determining how to bring the tip of your finger to the tip of your nose. There are more degrees of freedom in the arm than in the target location. Consequently, there are an infinite number of ways of bringing the tip of your finger to the tip of your nose. Thus the problem of selecting a path that brings the tip of your finger to the tip of your nose is mathematically underdetermined. Still, you instantly and effortlessly picked just one path. Understanding how you did this, and how you regularly perform other related feats (however mundane they may seem), is the degrees-of-freedom problem.

Efficiency

How can the degrees-of-freedom problem be solved? One kind of solution relies on movement efficiency. As I mentioned before, it is unlikely that you brought your finger to the tip of your nose by wrapping your arm around the back of your head. Apart from the fact that this would have taken longer than a more direct path, this indirect path would have gotten your arm into an awkward final position. Your wrist and shoulder joints would have been in extreme angles at the end of the movement. As a result, your ability to make a second, unanticipated response would have been impaired. In general, it is not a good idea to end a movement with the limb adopting extreme joint angles, just as it is generally not a good idea to remain near the edge of a tennis court after returning a shot to your opponent. By returning to mid-court in tennis, you are in the best possible position for returning the next shot that may come your way. Similarly, by having your arm in the middle of its range of motion at the end of a motor act, the movements you can perform with it next are maximally diverse (Cruse, 1986; Rosenbaum, 1989).

Another possible efficiency constraint is to move as smoothly as possible. One way to do this is to minimize jerk, the rate of change of acceleration. To understand what this means, consider Figure 1.2, which plots acceleration as a function of time. The slope of the curve is steep when jerk is high but shallow when jerk is low. Correspondingly, when jerk is high, curves relating velocity to time are highly peaked, but when jerk is low, curves relating velocity to time are bell shaped. (Recall that acceleration is the time rate of change of velocity, and velocity is the time rate of change of position.) Measuring the velocities of aimed hand movements shows that they are usually bell shaped, as would be expected if jerk (or more properly, mean squared jerk integrated over movement duration) were minimized. Based on this fact, it has been proposed that minimizing mean squared jerk is a constraint on motor control (Hogan & Flash, 1987). If the constraint is used, it helps reduce the number of movements that can be performed. In addition, it can boost efficiency because when jerk is high, large forces must be generated, and these can place high demands on muscle metabolic energy.

Minimizing mean squared jerk and avoiding extreme joint angles are just two possible constraints for movement selection. Other possible constraints include minimizing changes in muscle torque (Uno, Kawato, & Suzuki, 1989) and minimizing a variable related to muscle stiffness (Hasan,

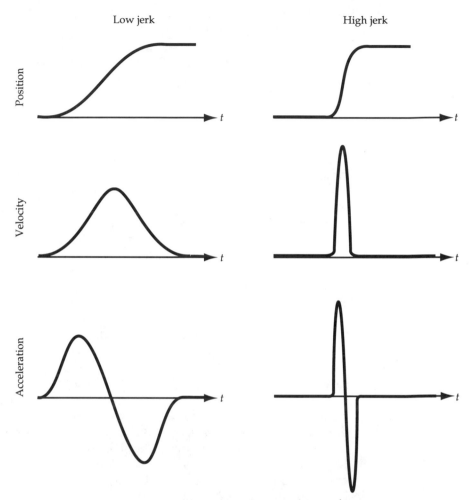

Figure 1.2 Position, velocity, and acceleration as a function of time, t, for a movement produced with low jerk and a movement produced with high jerk. Note that the absolute amplitudes of the velocity and acceleration profiles are higher for the high-jerk movement than for the low-jerk movement.

1986). Though there is debate about which constraints are actually used, the important point for now is that constraints for efficiency may help solve the degrees-of-freedom problem (Nelson, 1983).

Synergies

Another approach to the degrees-of-freedom problem is to suppose that there are dependencies between components of the motor system. Having such dependencies reduces the degrees of freedom that must be indepen-

A

Right pectoral fin   a

Left pectoral fin

2 sec

Dorsal fin

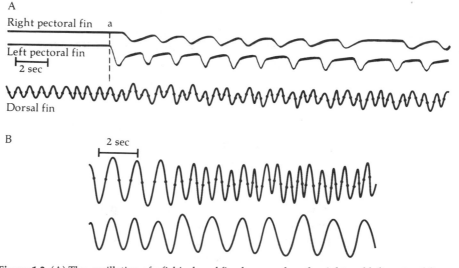

B

2 sec

Figure 1.3 (A) The oscillation of a fish's dorsal fin changes when the right and left pectoral fins begin to oscillate. (B) In a person, when the right arm (*upper curve*) is supposed to oscillate at increasing frequencies, the left arm is affected. In both panels, the dots superimposed on the curves occupy equal time intervals. Thus variations in the dot positions along the vertical dimension indicate that the limb does not occupy the same position at the same time in the cycle. (From von Holst, 1939/1973b.)

dently controlled. This was the strategy advocated by Nicolai Bernstein (1967), the Russian physiologist who first identified the degrees of freedom problem.

A commonplace, if homely, example of a synergy is the tendency to blink during sneezing. This is a "hard-wired" motor interaction, in the sense that it occurs without our ability to control it. It illustrates how one kind of motor activity automatically dictates which other activities can or cannot occur.

Another example of a synergy is the difficulty encountered while rubbing the stomach and patting the head. In a formal experiment designed to evaluate this familiar difficulty, it was found that when people make rhythmic movements with two hands simultaneously, the frequency of one hand's movement influences the frequency of movement by the other hand (Gunkel, 1962). Dependencies between simultaneous movements also exist within individual limbs. The ability to flex and extend the wrist is aided if the elbow flexes when the wrist flexes and if the elbow extends when the wrist extends. If the elbow extends while the wrist flexes or if the elbow flexes while the wrist extends, the task is considerably more difficult (Kots & Syrovegin, 1966).

Such interactions have ancient evolutionary origins, for the fins of a fish, like the arms of a person, are also coupled. Figure 1.3 shows interactions between the fins of a fish and interactions between the arms of a person engaged in comparable activities (von Holst, 1939). For both organisms, the activity of one extremity has a pronounced effect on the activity of the other. Having dependencies like these frees us from having to "worry about" all the degrees of freedom that ultimately must be controlled.

Relying on Mechanics

The interactions just described are most likely based on the way nerve fibers are connected to one another. Recently it has been proposed that biomechanical factors alone can also simplify the degrees-of-freedom problem (Bizzi & Mussa-Ivaldi, 1989; Thelen, Kelso, & Fogel, 1987). A simple example is swinging the leg forward during walking—the so-called *swing phase* of locomotion. Detailed modeling of the behavior of the leg during the swing phase suggests that it can be achieved without concurrent muscle activation (McMahon, 1984). In other words, the trajectory of the leg during the swing phase need not be planned or controlled in detail but rather can be produced by taking advantage of the physical properties of the leg within the gravitational field. Thus the exact trajectory of the leg need not be planned explicitly, which implies further that the degrees of freedom that must be dealt with can be considerably reduced.

Muscle alone has mechanical properties that can be exploited to simplify the degrees of freedom problem. As will be seen in Chapter 6 (Reaching and Grasping), it has been useful to view muscles as springs whose resting lengths or stiffnesses can be set by the nervous system. (The resting length of a spring is the length to which it returns when no external force stretches or compresses it; the stiffness of a spring is the ratio of the tension it produces to the length it is stretched or compressed.)

An experiment in my laboratory (Rosenbaum, 1989) shows how the elastic properties of muscle may simplify movement planning. University students reached for a handle and turned it from each of a number of starting orientations to each of a number of target orientations. In analyzing how subjects chose to grab the handle just before turning it, we found that a simple "rule of thumb" accounted for their behavior (Figure 1.4). Subjects adopted relatively awkward arm postures when first grabbing the handle, but these postures ensured that by the end of the handle rotation the subjects' arms were always at or close to the resting position—with the right thumb pointing toward 11 o'clock. Thus subjects may have controlled their movements by treating their muscles (and tendons) like springs that could be "wound up" prior to movement and released to produce the needed movement. This strategy would have allowed elastic energy, stored in the muscles and tendons prior to the handle rotation, to be converted into kinetic energy during the rotation phase. If this is indeed what subjects did (albeit unconsciously), then they simplified the movement-planning problem by exploiting the mechanical properties of the muscles and tendons of their upper extremities.

A

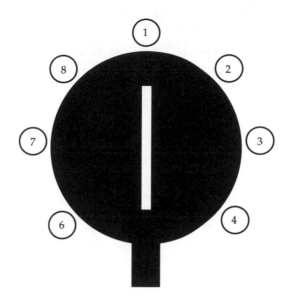

B

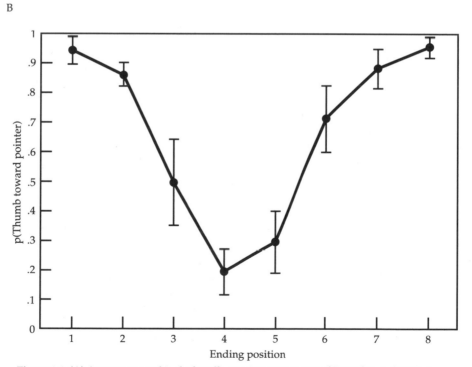

Figure 1.4 (A) Apparatus used in the handle-turning experiment of Rosenbaum (1989). A representative task was turning the handle so a tab initially covering target 5 would cover target 1 at the end of the rotation. (B) Probability of grabbing the handle with the thumb toward the tab as a function of the tab's ending position. The estimate of variability (±1 standard error of estimate of the mean) for each point is based on *starting* position variability. (From Rosenbaum, 1989.)

Path Planning, Inverse Kinematics, and Inverse Dynamics

A final remark about the degrees-of-freedom problem is that it is a problem at several levels (Jordan & Rosenbaum, 1989). At the highest level is the problem of *path planning*. A representative path-planning problem is deciding whether to reach to the right or left of a milk bottle to take hold of a cereal box. At a lower level is the *inverse kinematics* problem. This is the problem of converting the selected path into a time-varying set of joint angles. At a still lower level is the *inverse dynamics* problem—determining the forces to be produced in order to generate the desired joint angles. A considerable amount of work has been done on these problems in robotics and human motor control (Craig, 1986; Jordan & Rosenbaum, 1989; Saltzman & Kelso, 1987).

One of the most intriguing results from path-planning research is that people have a preference for straight-line hand motions. When asked to move the hand from one point to another on a horizontal surface, people are likely to move the hand in a straight line (Morasso, 1981). Even when people are asked to draw curved lines (which of course they can do), detailed analysis of their movements suggests that the curves they produce consist of series of straight-line segments (Abend, Bizzi, & Morasso, 1982). The finding that hand paths are often linear was first taken to suggest that path planning is done with respect to the Cartesian coordinates in which the hand moves, not with respect to joint coordinates. Later it was suggested that minimizing mean squared jerk could also give rise to straight-line hand trajectories (Hogan & Flash, 1987). Most recently, it has been suggested that minimizing torque changes at the joints can also yield straight-line hand paths and that this constraint accurately predicts deviations from straight-line paths (Uno *et al.*, 1989).

These three proposals have interesting implications for a general theory of motor control. The first proposal assumes that path planning is determined primarily by *geometric* constraints, the second proposal assumes that path planning is determined primarily by *kinematic* constraints, and the third proposal assumes that path planning is determined primarily by *dynamic* constraints. (*Kinematics* is concerned with motions without regard to the forces producing or preventing them. *Dynamics* is concerned with forces as well as motions.) The recognition that kinematics and even dynamics can affect path planning suggests that high-level aspects of movement planning do not occur in ignorance of the means by which plans must be executed. Apparently, low levels of control influence higher levels.

■ THE SERIAL-ORDER PROBLEM

Another major issue in the study of human motor control is how we control the serial order of our behaviors. The serial order of a set of elements is simply the sequence in which those elements occur. Thus *abc* has a differ-

Figure 1.5 Professor William Archibald Spooner. (Reprinted from Potter, 1980.)

ent serial order than *acb*. When we engage in behaviors that have distinct elements, such as speaking, typing, or walking, the elements of the behaviors must be ordered correctly. Otherwise the behavioral outcomes would be maladaptive.

Speech Errors

As a case in point, consider Professor William Archibald Spooner, who taught at Oxford University in the late nineteenth and early twentieth century (see Figure 1.5). Professor Spooner made frequent speech errors. Typical examples were "The queer old dean" instead of "The dear old queen" and "You hissed all my mystery lectures" instead of "You missed all my history lectures." Although there is some question about the authenticity of these reports (Potter, 1980), there is no doubt that all of us make such mistakes from time to time. The errors mentioned above, which involve exchanging two speech sounds, are examples of *Spoonerisms*, named after the hapless professor.

What do speech errors tell us about the control of serial order? Suppose you said "We're going to the bootfall game" instead of the intended "We're going to the football game." Speech errors like this have been recorded in spontaneous conversation (Garrett, 1982) and in the laboratory (Motley, 1980). The error suggests that before you said the "f" that normally goes with "football," the "b" sound was available. Moreover, since the "b" sound exchanged with the "f" rather than, say, with the long "e" in "We're," the switch occurred in a nonarbitrary way. It is a general rule, in fact, that consonants only exchange with other consonants and vowels only exchange with other vowels. Relatedly, though at a higher level of linguistic analysis, nouns tend only to exchange with other nouns and verbs tend only to exchange with other verbs.

Regularities of this sort suggest that there are distinct levels of representation in the planning and production of speech (Fromkin, 1973, 1980). For example, there is a level involving whole words, which respects their syntactic status (nouns versus verbs), and there is a level involving individual phonemes (see Chapter 9), which respects the distinction between consonants and vowels. Understanding how these levels of representation are used in speech production has been a topic of considerable interest among psycholinguists (Dell, 1986). More will be said about the modeling of speech errors in Chapter 9 (Speaking and Singing). For now, the important point is that the kinds of speech errors that people make indicate that speech is not simply produced by planning an utterance and then executing it, planning the next utterance and then executing it, and so on. Rather, there is usually a *plan* for an extended series of utterances and the words of which they are a part (Lashley, 1951).

Errors analogous to those in speech also occur in other domains of performance. Perhaps you have made the error of accidentally throwing a pair of dirty socks into a trash can rather than a clothes hamper (where you intended it). Or perhaps you accidentally poured catsup into your coffee rather than on the hamburger you wanted to flavor. Errors like these tend to occur when we are distracted, but they indicate that our bodily actions, like our speech, are based on plans that may have distinct functional levels. Pouring the catsup into the coffee indicates that part of the plan for pouring catsup includes the goal of emptying the contents into a suitable receptacle. The catsup-pouring error is not based on an inability to visually distinguish coffee cups from hamburgers. Instead, the problem arises because there is an abstract description of the task to be achieved (pouring) but the specifics of the task situation are momentarily misdefined. Analyses of such *action slips* suggest, therefore, that complex action patterns are assembled out of more basic schemas for action (Norman, 1981).

Coarticulation

Inferences about serial order are not only based on mistakes. Look into a mirror and say (rather deliberately) the word *tulip*. If you look closely, you will notice that your lips round before you say "t." Speech scientists call this phenomenon *anticipatory lip rounding*. Like the speech errors described above, anticipatory lip rounding suggests that a plan for the entire word is available before the word is produced. If "tulip" were produced in a piecemeal fashion, with each sound planned only after the preceding sound was produced, the rounding of the lips required for "u" would only occur *after* "t" was uttered.

Anticipatory lip rounding illustrates a general tendency that any theory of serial ordering must account for—the tendency of effectors to coarticulate. The term *coarticulation* refers to the simultaneous motions of effectors that help achieve a temporally extended task. In speech production, coarticulation occurs in anticipatory lip rounding, as we have seen, and in other aspects of speech as well. For example, *nasalization*, the passage of air from the lungs through the nasal cavity, often occurs before production of the consonant for which nasalization is required. In saying "freon," for example, nasalization often occurs during the first vowel, even though it is required only for the /n/. (Nasalization is made possible by lowering the *velum*, a fold separating the oral and nasal cavities.)

It does not suffice to say that coarticulation is simply governed by "low-level" physiological mechanisms, such as the activity of other articulators, for coarticulatory events are language dependent. In French, for example, where some words are distinguished by nasalization alone, nasalization occurs before /n/ but never so early that vowel identities (or word identities) are affected. By contrast, in English, where vowels typically are not distinguished by nasalization, lowering the velum often occurs in vowels (such as those in "freon") where it would not occur in French (Jordan, 1986). Results like these indicate that a theory of coarticulation (and so a theory of serial order) must account for psychological as well as physiological constraints.

Two final comments are in order about coarticulation. One is that coarticulation is not restricted to speech. Films of typists' hands reveal that both hands move continually during typewriting (see Figure 1.6). The fingers of each hand move toward their respective keyboard targets, even while other keys are being struck (Rumelhart & Norman, 1982). More will be said about this in Chapter 8.

Second, no matter how difficult coarticulation may be to explain, it is a blessing for us as behaving organisms. Think about a typist who could move only one finger at a time. Lacking the capacity for finger coarticulation, the person's typing speed would be very slow. Simultaneous movements of the fingers allow for rapid responding, just as concurrent movements of the tongue, lips, and velum allow for rapid speech. Coarticulation is an effective method for increasing response speed given that individual effectors (body parts used for movement) may move relatively slowly.

■ THE PERCEPTUAL–MOTOR INTEGRATION PROBLEM

Feedback and Feedforward

Consider once again the task of bringing the tip of your index finger to the tip of your nose. You may have noticed that, when you performed this task, your hand moved rapidly at first and then slowed down dramatically.

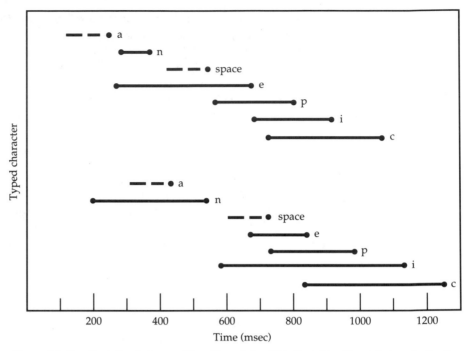

Figure 1.6 Coarticulation in typewriting. Though the "i" in "epic" is ultimately typed after the "e" and "p," it is initiated before either letter. Similarly, the first time "epic" is typed, the "e" is initiated before the "n" in the preceding word ("an"). The data were obtained from film records. (From Gentner, Grudin, & Conway, 1980.)

Virtually all aiming movements proceed in this two-stage fashion, with a *ballistic* phase followed by a *corrective* phase (Woodworth, 1899). Ballistic movements cannot be altered once they have been initiated. (Ballistic missiles, for example, cannot be steered once they are launched.) Ballistic movements are typically fast and cover most of the distance to the target. If the target has not been reached, corrective movements may then follow, using feedback to indicate the discrepancies to be overcome. Corrective movements, when they are effective, allow the distance between the effector and the target to be minimized.

When feedback is relied on effectively, corrective movements bring the effector closer and closer to the target until the distance to the target is acceptably small. This process is an instance of a negative feedback loop or *servomechanism* (see Figure 1.7). Servomechanisms have several components. The *reference* signal provides input to the loop about the target or goal state. In the case of bringing the hand to a target, the reference signal is a representation of the hand at the target. The *plant* is responsible for converting control signals into real outputs (for example, moving the hand). The *comparator* (the circled X in Figure 1.7) indicates the discrepancy between the sensed position of the effector and the reference signal. The *gain* (not shown in Figure

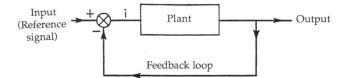

Figure 1.7 A negative feedback loop. (From Legge & Barber, 1976.)

1.7) transforms the discrepancy into a control signal that works to bring the sensed position closer to the reference signal, thus negating the error (hence the term *negative* feedback loop).

If bringing the hand closer and closer to a target illustrates the operation of a *negative* feedback loop, what is a *positive* feedback loop? If you have ever tried to cut your own hair, you probably have a good sense of what a positive feedback loop is. You may have tried to cut the hair on the back of your head while looking into a hand-held mirror in which you saw the reflection of your head in another mirror. Working in this miniature hall of mirrors, you may have discovered that every time you tried to bring the scissors closer to where you wanted them, they only moved farther away. This is an example of a positive feedback loop. The defining feature of such a loop is that errors increase rather than decrease when attempts are made to correct them.

Why is it so difficult to control one's movements when observing them through a double mirror? The answer is that the normal mappings between movements and their visual consequences are reversed. Even under such drastically changed conditions, we are nonetheless able to adjust our behavior, often in a relatively short amount of time (see Chapter 6). One of the most interesting problems in motor control research is how such compensations occur and why they occur as readily as they do.

Some additional terms are useful in connection with feedback processing. These are *closed-loop* control, *open-loop* control, and *feedforward*. Closed-loop control occurs when feedback can return to the comparator to be used for error correction. Seeing your hand as it approaches a visible target is an instance of closed-loop control. Here you can see where your hand is in relation to the target and make the necessary corrections based on vision.

Open-loop control occurs when feedback is unavailable. In open-loop situations, you get no information about the success or failure of your performance. As a result, your performance may fail dismally. Pointing at a moving target may be impossible, for example, if the position of the target cannot be seen, heard, or felt. Without feedback, the servo loop that normally allows you to point at the target has been opened (hence the term *open-loop control*).

There is an open-loop condition in which you can track a moving target reasonably successfully, however. This is when the target's motion is predictable. For example, if your task is to point to a target that moves from one fixed location to another at a constant rate, it may be possible to point to the target quite well. The reason is that you can anticipate the target's position; your reference signal changes as a function of time. Such anticipation is called *feedforward*. Whenever performance is accurate though feedback is removed, it can be inferred that feedforward is being used.

Under open-loop conditions, a surprising number of movement sequences can be performed reasonably well. For example, monkeys deprived of sensory feedback from their limbs can walk and climb, though less gracefully than monkeys with sensory feedback (Taub & Berman, 1968). Similarly, a man who could not feel his body (shudder the thought!) because of a disease affecting his sensory pathways but not his motor pathways could draw complex figures on command, could sequentially touch his thumb with each finger of the same hand, and could touch his nose, all without the aid of vision (Marsden, Rothwell, & Dell, 1984). Abilities like these indicate that the gross features of some movements can be performed entirely under feedforward control. When these same movements are performed with feedback, they are performed more precisely.

Spatial Coordinates

Let us consider for one last time the task of bringing the fingertip to the tip of the nose. As we have seen, this task, when performed under normal feedback conditions, illustrates the operation of a negative feedback loop. Considering the nature of the error correction necessary for this task reveals another important aspect of the perceptual–motor integration problem. If your eyes are closed and your finger is not yet in contact with your nose, the error being reduced is the discrepancy between the felt position of your finger and the felt position of your nose. In order for this distance to be reduced, the felt positions of your finger and your nose must be referred to some common spatial coordinate system. Without such a common spatial coordinate system, your finger would wander aimlessly toward or away from the target, perhaps eventually touching it, but only by chance.

One of the issues to be resolved in the analysis of perceptual–motor integration is which spatial coordinate system is used for any given task. For the task of bringing the finger to the nose, it can be assumed that errors are defined with respect to a *body-centered* spatial coordinate system. That is, the "map" that must be used need not take into account where the body is situated in the external environment. On the other hand, the map must take into account the relative positions of the hand and nose. It would not suffice, for example, merely to know how far the finger is from the nose along the length of the arm, neck, and face, because this distance (measured along the skin) remains constant during the movement.

For other tasks, it may be necessary to assume that the spatial coordinates that are relied on are defined with respect to the external environment. As an illustration, consider a study reported in 1938 by Wickens (reviewed in Gallistel, 1980). Subjects in this experiment held the hand palm-side down on a device that transmitted an electric shock to the fingertip. The shock was regularly preceded by a tone, and after a few exposures to the tone–shock pair, subjects withdrew their fingers from the shocker as soon as the tone was presented (but before the shock came on); to make the withdrawal response, subjects *extended* their fingers. The critical experimental manipulation occurred when subjects were asked to turn their hands over, leaving the palm up rather than down on the shocker. The question was what response subjects would now display after hearing the warning tone. Would they *extend* the finger, the muscle response they had previously displayed, or would they *flex* the finger, the muscle response that would bring the finger to the spatial position it had been brought to before? The answer was that they *flexed* the finger—the response that was muscularly opposite the earlier withdrawal response. Flexing the finger in the palm-up orientation was clearly adaptive given the unpleasantness of the shock. Evidently, the response that was learned was defined with respect to the spatial layout of the experimental apparatus, not with respect to the muscle movements that happened to be made in the first part of the experiment.

Another study leading to the same kind of conclusion involved a reaction-time procedure. Subjects in this experiment (Wallace, 1971) were asked to press a left or right button with their right or left hand (see Figure 1.8). The signals for the button presses were lights that appeared on the left or right side of a panel placed directly in front of the subject. In one condition (the *compatible* condition), when the left light came on, the left button was to be pressed, and when the right light came on, the right button was to be pressed. In the *incompatible* condition, the right light signaled the left button press and the left light signaled the right button press. Subjects were slower to respond in the incompatible condition than in the compatible condition.

In another set of experimental conditions, subjects crossed their hands, so instead of pressing the left button with the left hand and the right button with the right hand, they pressed the right button with the left hand and the left button with the right hand. The question was which relations would give rise to fast responses—the relations between the positions of the lights and the positions of the *buttons*, or the relations between the positions of the lights and the positions of the *hands*? The answer was that the locations of the buttons mattered more than the locations of the hands (Wallace, 1971; see also Brebner, Shephard, & Cairney, 1972; Reeve & Proctor, 1984). Subjects were faster to respond with the left button when the signal appeared on the left than when the signal appeared on the right and subjects were faster to respond with the right button when the signal appeared on the right rather than on the left. This was true even though the right hand pressed the left button and the left hand pressed the right button. Thus subjects behaved as if the important feature determining the speed of their responses was where the responses were made in space, not which part of the body happened to make the response.

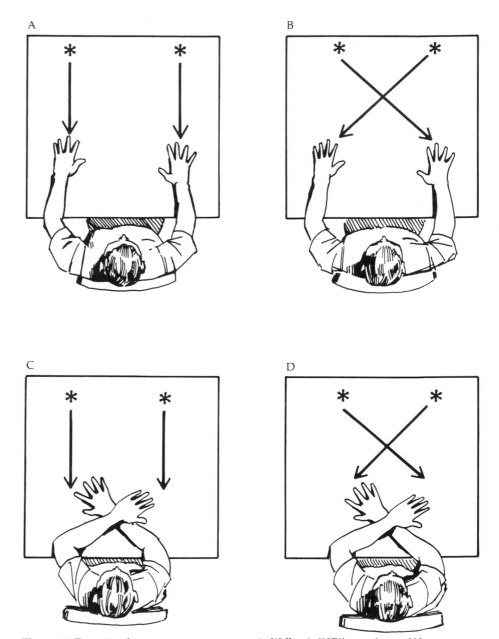

Figure 1.8 Four stimulus–response arrangements in Wallace's (1971) experiment. (A) Compatible mappings between stimulus locations and button locations and also between stimulus locations and effector (hand) locations; (B) incompatible mappings between stimulus locations and button locations and also between stimulus locations and effector locations; (C) compatible mappings between stimulus locations and button locations but not between stimulus locations and effector locations; and (D) compatible mappings between stimulus locations and effector locations but not between stimulus locations and button locations. Choice reaction times were faster in conditions (A) and (C) than in conditions (B) and (D).

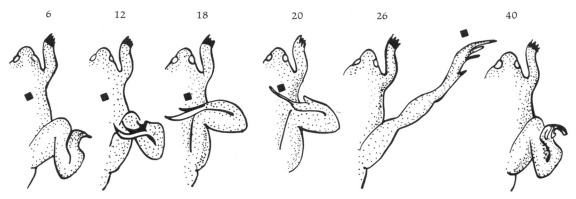

Figure 1.9 Wiping reflex in the spinal frog evoked by chemical stimulation (black square). The numbers at the top are film frame numbers. The movement was filmed at 48 frames per second. (From Berkenblit, Fel'dman, & Fucson, 1986.)

Results like these, which highlight the importance of spatial coding, will turn up throughout this book. One other study (Fucson, Berkenblit, & Fel'dman, 1980) is worth mentioning on this theme because of how beautifully it shows the fundamental nature of spatial coordinates in motor control. This study was done with frogs whose brains were surgically disconnected from their spinal cords (Figure 1.9). The experimenters applied a bit of irritating chemical to the skin of the frog and filmed the reactions that followed. Normally, frogs display a "wiping" reflex when treated in this manner. They reach for and whisk the irritated spot, just as they would wipe away a blade of grass or a fly that happened to land on their skin. Fucson *et al.* observed that the performance of the experimentally treated frogs was essentially the same as that of frogs with intact connections between the brain and spinal cord. As in normal frogs, even when the initial position of the frog's hindlimb varied and the location of the touch was unpredictable, the hindlimb maneuvered so it approached the irritation site from a propitious angle. The wiping motion that followed was remarkably accurate.

The coordination required for the wiping reflex is similar to that required for bringing the fingertip to the nose. The frog's ability to bring the end of its hindlimb directly to the irritated skin patch implies that within the frog's spinal cord are mechanisms capable of relating body positions within a single spatial map. Attributing this capability to the frog's spinal cord is not to trivialize the computations. The fact that brainless frogs can perform the wiping reflex implies that the transformations of sensory signals from the skin and limb into a spatial map, and the subsequent translation of those spatial coordinates into motor commands, are phylogenetically ancient capabilities.

Movement Enhances Perception

So far in this section on perceptual–motor integration, I have discussed the importance of feedback and feedforward for successful movement as well as

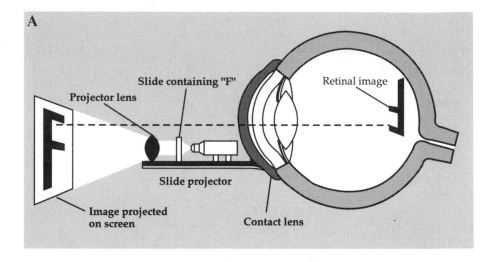

Figure 1.10 Retinal stabilization. (A) Overview of the method. (From Hilgard, Atkinson, and Atkinson, 1979.) (B) Disintegration of a retinally stabilized image over the course of time (*left* to *right*). From *Cognitive psychology and its implications*, by John R. Anderson. Copyright © 1980 by W. H. Freeman and Company. Reprinted by permission.

the significance of spatial coordinates. A common feature of the studies I have mentioned is that they demonstrate that movement benefits from perception. In this section, I show that perception also benefits from movement.

Movement never occurs in a behavioral vacuum. We move to be able to perceive, just as we perceive to be able to move. (Arguing which is more important, as some authors have, strikes me as a "red herring.") One reason perception benefits from movement is that movement allows for the transport of sensory receptors. We turn our eyes and our heads so we can take in visual information from a wide range of locations. We walk to new locations to see and hear what is going on there. We use our hands to feel objects or bring the objects to locations where we can inspect them further.

There are more subtle ways in which movement affects perception. Consider the visual effects of *retinal stabilization*. Here an image is projected onto the back of the eye (the retina) so that when the eye moves, the image goes with it (Pritchard, 1961). Usually when the eye moves, the image of a stationary object shifts across the retina. Images of moving objects also undergo some retinal slippage since visual tracking (following an object with the eye) tends to be imperfect (see Chapter 5). The question of interest in the retinal stabilization study is what happens when retinal slippage is eliminated.

The apparatus used to study retinal stabilization is shown in Figure 1.10. It consists of a contact lens attached to the cornea (the clear layer in the front of the eye) with a tiny projection system attached to the lens. The projection system allows different images to be cast on the retina. It might be expected that with the image continually projected onto the same part of the retina, perception of the image would be clearer than usual. In fact, the opposite is the case. Within a few seconds, subjects see parts of the figure disappear. In the case of a letter, for example, first one stem disappears, then another, and then another (see Figure 1.10). Ultimately, the letter vanishes completely, though when a new letter is projected onto the retina, it can be seen, though it too fades in a piecewise fashion after a short time. These results indicate that people become functionally blind to retinally stabilized images.

The fact that retinally stabilized images fade from view shows that the light-sensitive cells in the retina (photoreceptors) fatigue or adapt rapidly if they are continually stimulated in an unchanging fashion. The motion of the eye prevents this fatigue or adaptation.

Movement aids perception through means other than refreshing sensory receptors. People are more likely to identify a felt object correctly if they can explore the object actively with their hands than if the object is made to slide passively over the fingers (Gibson, 1962). Similarly, if people are asked to recall where their hands were positioned on a bar, they can recall the position better if they placed their hands in the position than if their hands were placed there by an experimenter (Paillard & Brouchon, 1968). These results indicate that the opportunity to move actively facilitates perceptual identification and memory.

Suppression Effects

Whereas the examples just described show that movement enhances perception, movement can also have the opposite effect. Look into a mirror and try to watch your eyes move. You cannot see them do so (Dodge, 1900). If you have a friend look at your eyes while you move them, he or she will be able to see them move. This shows that eye movements are not simply too quick to be seen.

Why can't you see your own eyes move? Perhaps the most intriguing hypothesis is that your brain suppresses the visual inputs that occur when your eyes move rapidly from one place to another (Volkmann, 1976; see Chapter 5). There could be a distinct functional advantage of such *saccadic suppression*. (Saccades are the "jumps" of the eye that occur when you visually inspect a static scene or text.) Since the retinal image is smeared during saccades, the smear might not serve a useful purpose for perception and in fact could mask visual percepts obtained just before or just after saccades occur. Saccadic suppression could help reduce the damage to visual perception caused by such retinal smearing. (Chapter 5 provides a more extensive discussion and critical evaluation of this proposal.)

Suppression effects are not limited to eye movements. Chewing sounds are loud, yet we barely hear them. The reason is that during chewing there is internal suppression of auditory feedback (Rosenzweig & Lehman, 1982). Similarly, during active hand movements (but not passive hand movements), sensitivity to brief tactile stimuli is reduced (Coquery, 1978; Garland & Angel, 1972). Finally, though it is a lighthearted example, it is noteworthy that we cannot tickle ourselves. To get a good tickle, you must be tickled by a friend!

Suppression of sensory inputs during movement helps the nervous system filter out movement-based sensory changes. As will be seen in Chapter 5, the filtering helps us distinguish perceptual changes due to motion of the environment from perceptual changes due to motion of the self. The disambiguation occurs by "subtracting" perceptual changes from motor commands.

This subtraction process was first discovered through a remarkable experiment with flies (von Holst & Mittelstaedt, 1950; see Figure 1.11). The experiment was prompted by the observation that when a fly stands still and a drum with vertical stripes is turned around it, the fly turns with the drum, presumably to keep itself stationary with respect to the external world; this behavior is known as the *optomotor reflex*. However, when the stripes are stationary the same fly moves freely in front of them. The paradox is that the visual stimulus is approximately the same when the fly moves and the stripes are stationary as when the fly is stationary and the stripes move, yet only in the latter case does the fly reposition itself with respect to the stripes. Why does the fly turn with the stripes when the stripes turn but disregard the stripes when the stripes are stationary?

To find out, von Holst and Mittelstaedt twisted the fly's head 180° with respect to the longitudinal axis of its body and glued the head in this new position. The effect was to spatially interchange the left and right eyes. Under this condition, the fly's behavior was, to say the least, strange. When the fly stood still and the vertical stripes turned to the right, the fly turned to the left, but when the fly stood still and the vertical stripes turned to the left, the fly turned to the right. When the fly attempted to move on its own, it took a step one way or the other and then stood stock still, frozen!

How can these results be explained? The answer ascribes more intelligence to the fly than one might expect. According to von Holst (1973a), the fly "expects a quite specific retinal image displacement, which is neutralized when it occurs" (p. 179). In other words, when the fly turns to the right, it has a reference signal for a retinal displacement to the left, and when it turns to the left, it has a reference signal for a retinal displacement to the right. Obtaining the expected retinal displacement indicates to the moving fly that the world has in fact remained stationary. However, if the fly is stationary and the retinal image moves, the shift of the retinal image indicates just as clearly that the world has moved so, to keep its bearings, the fly makes a compensatory movement to realign itself with its surroundings. Finally, if

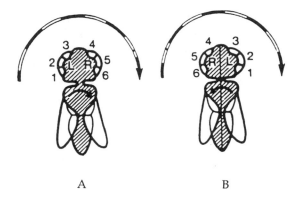

A   B

Figure 1.11 The behavior of a fly whose left and right eyes are in normal position (A) and whose left and right eyes have been interchanged by twisting its head 180° about the longitudinal axis of the body (B). Numbers designate eye segments. The arrow on the fly indicates the direction in which the fly is most likely to rotate given that the vertical stripes in front of it rotate to the right. (From Gallistel, 1980.)

the eyes are spatially interchanged, the expected and obtained retinal image displacements are reversed and the result, as von Holst and Mittelstaedt (see von Holst, 1973a, p. 179) put it colorfully, is a "central catastrophe."

Considering this behavior of the fly shows again how sophisticated the perceptual–motor system can be and at how early a stage of evolution this sophistication took hold. Not surprisingly, similar subtraction processes have been attributed to higher animals, including people (Sperry, 1950; von Holst & Mittelstaedt, 1950). More will be said about this process in Chapter 5.

■ THE SKILL-ACQUISITION PROBLEM

I have now discussed three of the four problems at the heart of motor control research: the degrees-of-freedom problem, the serial-order problem, and the perceptual–motor integration problem. One other problem remains to be summarized in this introductory chapter: how motor skills are acquired.

The problem of skill acquisition consists of several subproblems: (1) To what extent are motor skills innate and to what extent are they learned? (2) For those skills that are learned, how are they acquired? (3) Once a motor skill has been acquired, what is the nature of its underlying memory representation? More specific questions can also be added to this list: (4) As a motor skill develops, what changes in performance can be observed? (5) What is the role of feedback in learning motor skills? (6) What practice schedule is optimal? (7) How does the ability to learn or retain motor skills depend on the state of the learner, such as his or her age, neurological status, and motivation? (8) Is there an upper limit on the level of skill that can be achieved? (9) Is continued practice required to maintain skill levels? (10)

What factors determine how well one can transfer from one skill to another?

A section of Chapter 3 (Psychological Foundations) will be devoted to skill acquisition, so I will refrain from providing a detailed treatment now. Instead, I will describe one limited body of research that illustrates how skill acquisition can be studied effectively. This research captures some of the ideas about feedback processing that I have already introduced, although it concerns a relatively microscopic aspect of perceptual–motor behavior. Analyzing skill acquisition in detail is a formidable task because of the complexity of the problem. Therefore, it can be profitable to study "miniature" skills.

Modification of the Vestibulo-Ocular Reflex

Before reading further, perform the following task. Hold your hand straight in front of you, holding your thumb straight up. Keep your eyes on your thumb and rotate your head back and forth in the horizontal plane. As you do this, you will most likely notice that the visual image of your thumb remains crystal clear.

Now perform a complementary task. Hold your head still and swing your hand back and forth, holding your thumb erect. If you try to keep your eyes on your thumb, you will probably discover that you cannot see it clearly unless you rotate your arm rather slowly.

Why can you see your thumb more clearly when you turn your head than when you turn your arm? The answer is that different sources of information regulate your eye movements in the two situations. When your head is still and your eyes track your moving thumb, your eyes rely solely on visual error to keep the image of your thumb centered on your fovea (the part of the retina best adapted for fine pattern perception). By contrast, when you turn your head and try to keep your eyes on a stationary target, nonvisual feedback as well as visual feedback provide signals that help you maintain visual fixation.

The evidence for nonvisual feedback comes from experiments in which the head is passively rotated in the dark and the positions of the eyes are recorded. (Passive head rotation is usually achieved with a motor that turns an axle to which the head, or a helmet over the head, is attached.) Under these conditions, the eyes remain straight ahead when the head is rotated. Thus, the eyes counterrotate while the head turns, so the gaze is directed to the same location in the external environment. Since the eyes remain straight ahead even in complete darkness, their counterrotation is not based on visual feedback, but instead is based on *vestibular* feedback. Feedback mediated by the vestibular system concerns the orientation of the body or parts of the body. The vestibular system consists of structures within the inner ear that mechanically register accelerations in each of the three perpendicular dimensions (see Chapter 5, Looking). When the vestibular system is damaged, counterrotation of the eyes during head-turning is disrupted (Bizzi, 1974). When the vestibular system is intact, the eyes begin counterrotating within 14 milliseconds (msec), or 14 thousandths of a second, of the start of head turning. This is too short for the eye movement to be based on visual feedback; the time needed for the eye to move in response to a visual stimulus is at least 100 msec (Lisberger, 1988). The eye's response to head rotation is therefore mediated by the vestibular system. The eye's response to head rotation is called the *vestibulo-ocular reflex* (VOR).

What does the VOR have to do with motor learning? First, it remains exquisitely precise over the course of growth and aging. A measure of the precision of the VOR is its *gain*, the speed of eye movement divided by the speed of head movement. A gain of 1.0 indicates perfect compensation, and this is the value that is normally recorded. Because gains of 1.0 are obtained in organisms whose nerve and muscle tissue have grown and undergone normal wear and tear, the VOR must change as a result of experience.

Just how changeable the VOR is has been demonstrated in experiments where magnifying or minifying lenses are placed over the eyes, causing images appearing on the retina to expand or contract. The lenses alter the speed at which visual images appear to move when the head turns. Magnifying lenses increase the apparent speed of image displacement, and minifying lenses reduce the apparent speed of image displacement. The consequence of magnification or minification is that the normal gain of the VOR is initially too small or too large. For example, when lenses double the image size, the speed of image displacement doubles, so the optimal gain for the VOR becomes 2.0 rather than the normal 1.0. After a few days of wearing such magnifying lenses under conditions of normal illumination, monkeys tested in the dark have gains close to 2.0, implying that the VOR adapts fully to the new relation between eye movement and image displacement. When minifying lenses are worn, the opposite effect is obtained. After wearing lenses that shrink images to one-quarter their normal size, the gain of the VOR approaches .25 (Lisberger, 1988).

For the gain of the VOR to change, the subject must be exposed to visual input and head rotations simultaneously. Wearing the lens with the head held stationary does not lead to adaptation, nor does moving the head in the dark. It is as if the nervous system learns to *correlate* head rotations with eye movements, based on the retinal image displacements that accompany head rotations. If the head rotations and retinal image displacements do not occur simultaneously, the correlations between them cannot be reevaluated (Lisberger, 1988).

What mechanism allows for changes of VOR gain? One way to find out is to study the times during eye counterrotations when recalibration effects appear. The first response to head-turning occurs 14 msec after the head starts to turn, as noted earlier. This delay remains unaffected by lens exposure. However, by 19 msec after the start of head-turning, experience-based changes in compensatory eye movements can be detected (see Figure 1.12). These results suggest that there are three components to VOR adaptation: (1)

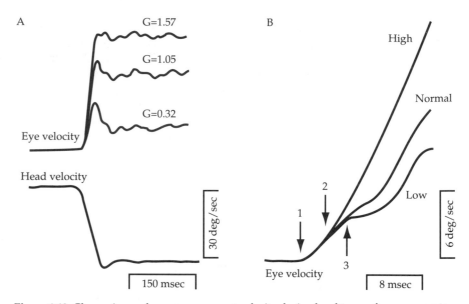

Figure 1.12 Change in monkey eye-movement velocity during head turns after exposure to *magnifying* lenses that increase the gain from 1.05 (the pretraining value) to 1.57 or after exposure to *minifying* lenses which decrease the gain from 1.05 to 0.32. (A) Slow-sweep records, showing the relation of the eye movements to head movements. (B) Fast-sweep records, showing the initial, immutable eye-movement trajectory, which begins at time 1, followed by the experience-based change in gain, first apparent at time 2 for the high-gain state and at time 3 for the low-gain state. (From Lisberger, 1988.)

an immediate, unchanging response; (2) a delayed, changing response; and (3) a capacity for introducing changes to subsequent responses based on the outcome of previous eye–head movements. Detailed work on the neurophysiological underpinnings of the VOR has shown that distinct neural pathways are responsible for these three functions and that the three pathways work in parallel. (It would be premature to identify these pathways now, since the rudiments of neuroanatomy have not yet been introduced.) The broader lesson is that even for a response system as simple and "mechanistic" as the VOR, complex neural subsystems come into play, with distinct functional responsibilities associated with each of them. One system acts automatically and immutably. Another acts rapidly but can be changed through learning. A third tunes the second based on feedback. As will be seen later, similar three-part schemes for motor learning and control have been identified in other, more complex skill-learning systems.

■ ORGANIZATION OF THE BOOK

Just as it is useful to have a plan for a series of movements, it is useful to have a plan for reading a book. The organization of this book is as follows.

As I have already indicated, Chapters 2 and 3 (which conclude Part

I) are concerned with physiological and psychological foundations, respectively. The bulk of the book (Part II) is organized by activity. Chapter 4 is concerned with walking and related forms of locomotion. Chapter 5 is concerned with looking and the control of eye and head movements. Chapter 6 focuses on reaching and grasping. Chapter 7 treats the control of writing and drawing. Chapter 8 covers the control of typewriting, piano playing, and other finger-movement tasks, which I refer to collectively as keyboarding. Chapter 9 pertains to the control of speaking and singing. Chapter 10, the last chapter in Part II, is concerned with smiling and other forms of facial expression.

Devoting a separate chapter to each of these classes of activity has several advantages. One is that research in motor control, like research in most fields today, has become rather specialized. It is not really a caricature of the field to say that there are people who work entirely on eye movements, others who work entirely on reaching and grasping, others who work entirely on speech, and so on. Judging from the specialized journals and meetings that exist for these subdisciplines, one might be led to conclude that the questions pursued in one have little or nothing to do with the questions in another.

The proliferation of subspecialties within motor control derives partly from the practical and theoretical interests of workers in the field. Practical concerns with particular tasks sometimes compel investigators to pursue those tasks at the expense of others. A researcher working for a typewriter company, say, is naturally more interested in keyboarding than singing. Theoretical interests also place some investigators on circumscribed research paths. Students of vision, for example, are naturally more interested in oculomotor control than in speech, just as researchers concerned with linguistics are more concerned with speech than with the control of eye movements. Because particular tasks rather than motor control as a whole may continue to interest many individuals, I have organized Part II so that any given chapter can be read on its own.

My second reason for devoting separate chapters to separate activities is that many specialty areas have developed their own problems and methodologies. The twists and turns within one area do not always map easily onto the issues in another. Rather than risk losing the richness of particular areas of study, I have decided to pay each area its due by considering it on its own.

In treating the subsystems separately, it is critical that the treatment not become too parochial. Therefore, areas of common concern will be highlighted as such, as will work focusing on coordination of different motor tasks. Being on the lookout for similarities among motor subsystems also puts us in an advantaged position for detecting differences among them. That there might be significant differences is a real and intriguing possibility, given that some information-processing functions may be controlled by independent modules with their own rules of operation (Fodor, 1983). If modularity applies to the motor system, different motor activities might be controlled in wholly different ways. Treating the motor activities separately should allow us to identify these differences if they exist or to note their absence when they might be expected. (There are other defining features of modularity which need not concern us at this time.)

The final part of the book (Part III) is concentrated into a single chapter (Chapter 11, Conclusions). Here I offer some generalizations about motor control based on the preceding chapters, I consider in some detail two tasks that require coordination of several motor activities (eye–hand coordination and hitting an oncoming ball), I briefly review work on individual differences, and I discuss some promising new lines of investigation.

A final comment about the organization of the book concerns its title, *Human Motor Control.* Most but not all of the studies that I will describe have been done with humans, and many but not all of the activities that I will discuss can only be carried out by people. I have therefore included the word *human* in the title, though I will introduce animal research throughout the volume because of its enormous importance for the field at large.

My reason for using the term *motor control* also requires some justification, for some may feel it is a mistake to claim there is a system responsible for motor activity, separate from the systems responsible for perception or cognition. I make no such claim, however. What I do believe is that the control of movement and the control of stability can be properly viewed as distinct *functions*, or sets of functions, achieved by the nervous system. Demarcating neural control systems for analytic purposes does not imply a belief that the systems are isolated from one another. It is reasonable, and I believe helpful, to regard motor control as a topic for study in its own right, just as it is helpful to analyze perceptual function (for example, vision or audition) on its own.

Considering what we know about motor control is both gratifying and humbling. It is gratifying because great strides have been made in the past few years and hopefully will continue to be made in the near future. It is also humbling because so many challenges lie ahead. For all that we know about motor control, many questions remain. My fondest hope is that as you read this book, you will feel inspired to answer the questions that I raise as well as the questions you raise yourself.

■ SUMMARY

1. Motor control is essential for virtually all aspects of life. It allows us to communicate, manipulate objects, transport ourselves from place to place, eat, breathe, and reproduce. The central issues in motor control research are twofold: (1) How do we make movements, and (2) How do we maintain stability?

2. Two principal kinds of analyses have been pursued in the study of human motor control. One is tied to the physical mechanisms responsible for movement and stability. This sort of analysis has been pursued chiefly by physiologists. The other kind of analysis is concerned with functional aspects of motor control and can be carried out without necessary regard for the physical underpinnings of behavior. This sort of analysis has been pursued chiefly by psychologists.

3. One of the major issues in the field of human motor control is the *degrees-of-freedom* problem. The question is how particular movements are selected given that there are more degrees of freedom in the muscles and joints than in the description of the task to be performed. One way of solving the degrees-of-freedom problem has been to propose that *efficiency* is taken into account in selecting movements. One possible efficiency constraint is minimizing mean squared jerk. (Jerk is the time rate of change of acceleration.) Another approach has been to identify motor *synergies*—dependencies among effector elements, seen, for example, in the functional coupling of the two arms. These dependencies effectively reduce the degrees of freedom that must be controlled. A third approach is to rely on the *biomechanical* properties of the motor system. By relying on the effects of gravity, for example, or on the effects of the elasticity of the muscles and tendons, it may be unnecessary to compute detailed aspects of movement trajectories.

4. The *serial-order* problem—determining how movements are sequenced —is another central issue in motor control research. Errors in speech and other activities indicate that movement sequences are governed by complex plans with distinct levels of representation. The existence of plans is suggested as well by analyses of *coarticulation*—the concurrent activity of distinct effectors subserving temporally extended tasks such as speaking and typewriting. An example of coarticulation is anticipatory lip rounding during pronunciation of the word *tulip*.

5. Understanding how we coordinate motor activity and perception lies at the core of the *perceptual–motor integration* problem. Feedback processing provides an important illustration of perceptual–motor integration. When feedback loops are closed, it is possible to respond to feedback, but when feedback loops are open, behavior is ballistic and can be controlled only as well as feedforward (anticipation) allows. A negative feedback loop allows for error reduction based on feedback, whereas attempts at error correction in a positive feedback loop generally result in increased rather than decreased error.

6. Much of motor performance is organized with respect to the spatial coordinates of the body or the spatial coordinates of external space. The importance of spatial coordinates has been demonstrated in studies of learning and in studies of stimulus–response compatibility. The motor system aids perception by moving the sensory receptors. Eliminating the visual effects of eye movement by stabilizing retinal images causes visual percepts to vanish. The motor system also aids perception by serving as a vehicle for active exploration of the environment, as when one actively explores an object with the hands. Perception can also be *suppressed* by motor activity, as in saccadic suppression. Some suppression effects are achieved by "subtracting" expected perceptual consequences from the perceptual consequences that occur when movements are actively generated. Even flies behave in ways consistent with this hypothesis.

7. The *skill-acquisition* problem is the fourth major issue in the study of motor control. A system that has been used to study this problem is the vestibulo-ocular reflex (VOR), which is manifested in the tendency of the eyes to maintain their line of sight as the head turns. After wearing magnifying or minifying lenses for a few days, the *gain* of the VOR (the ratio of eye speed to head speed) changes. Three subsystems seem to underlie the adaptation. One is rapid and unchangeable. The second is a bit slower and can be modified. The third brings about major gain changes based on feedback.

■ REFERENCES

Abend, W., Bizzi, E., & Morasso, P. (1982). Human arm trajectory formation. *Brain*, **105**, 331–348.

Anderson, J. R. (1980). *Cognitive psychology and its implications*. San Francisco: Freeman.

Berkenblit, M. B., Fel'dman, A. G., & Fucson, O. J. (1986). Adaptability of innate motor patterns and motor control. *Behavioral and Brain Sciences*, **9**, 585–638.

Bernstein, N. (1967). *The coordination and regulation of movements*. London: Pergamon.

Bizzi, E. (1974). The coordination of eye-head movements. *Scientific American*, No. 10, 100–106.

Bizzi, E., & Mussa-Ivaldi, F. A. (1989). Geometrical and mechanical issues in movement planning and control. In M. I. Posner (Ed.), *Handbook of cognitive science* (pp. 769–792). Cambridge, MA: MIT Press.

Brebner, J., Shephard, M., & Cairney, P. (1972). Spatial relations and S-R compatibility. *Acta Psychologica*, **36**, 1–15.

Coquery, J.-M. (1978). Role of active movement in control of afferent input from skin in cat and man. In G. Gordon (Ed.), *Active touch*. Oxford: Pergamon.

Craig, J. J. (1986). *Introduction to robotics*. Reading, MA: Addison-Wesley.

Cruse, H. (1986). Constraints for joint angle control of the human arm. *Biological Cybernetics*, **54**, 125–132.

Dell, G. S. (1986). A spreading activation theory of retrieval in sentence production. *Psychological Review*, **93**, 283–321.

Dodge, R. (1900). Visual perception during eye movement. *Psychological Review*, **7**, 454–465.

Fodor, J. A. (1983). *The modularity of mind*. Cambridge, MA: MIT Press.

Fromkin, V. A. (Ed.) (1973). *Speech errors as linguistic evidence*. The Hague: Mouton.

Fromkin, V. A. (Ed.) (1980). *Errors in linguistic performance*. New York: Academic Press.

Fucson, O. I., Berkenblit, M. B., & Fel'dman, A. G. (1980). The spinal frog takes into account the scheme of its body during the wiping reflex. *Science*, **209**, 1261–1263.

Gallistel, C. R. (1980). *The organizaton of action*. Hillsdale, NJ: Erlbaum.

Garland, H. T., & Angel, R. W. (1972). Modulation of tactile sensitivity during movement. *Neurology*, **24**, 361.

Garrett, M. F. (1982). Production of speech: Observations from normal and pathological language use. In A. W. Ellis (Ed.), *Normality and pathology in cognitive functions* (pp. 19–76). London: Academic Press.

Gentner, D. R., Grudin, J., & Conway, E. (1980). *Finger movements in transcription typing* (Tech. Rep. No. 8001). La Jolla: University of California, San Diego, Center for Human Information Processing.

Gibson, J. J. (1962). Observations on active touch. *Psychological Review, 69*, 477–491.

Gunkel, M. (1962). Über relative Koordination bei willkürlichen menschlichen Gliedbewegungen. *Pflügers Archiv für die Gesamte Physiologie des Menschen und der Tiere, 215*, 472–477.

Hasan, Z. (1986). Optimized movement trajectories and joint stiffness in unperturbed, inertially loaded movements. *Biological Cybernetics, 53*, 373–382.

Hilgard, E. R., Atkinson, R. L., & Atkinson, R. C. (1979). *Introduction to psychology.* New York: Harcourt Brace Jovanovich.

Hogan, N., & Flash, T. (1987). Moving gracefully: Quantitative theories of motor coordination. *Trends in the Neurosciences, 10*(4), 170–174.

Jordan, M. I. (1986). Attractor dynamics and parallelism in a connectionist sequential machine. In C. Clifton, Jr. (Ed.), *Proceedings of the 8th Annual Meeting of the Cognitive Science Society* (pp. 531–545). Hillsdale, NJ: Erlbaum.

Jordan, M. I., & Rosenbaum, D. A. (1989). Action. In M. I. Posner (Ed.), *Foundations of cognitive science* (pp. 727–767). Cambridge, MA: MIT Press.

Kots, Y. M., & Syrovegnin, A. V. (1966). Fixed set of variants of interactions of the muscles of two joints in the execution of simple voluntary movements. *Biophysics, 11*, 1212–1219.

Lashley, K. S. (1951). The problem of serial order in behavior. In L. A. Jeffress (Ed.), *Cerebral mechanisms in behavior* (pp. 112–131). New York: Wiley.

Legge, D., & Barber, P. J. (1976). *Information and skill.* London: Methuen.

Lisberger, S. G. (1988). The neural basis for learning of simple motor skills. *Science, 242*, 728–735.

Marsden, C. D., Rothwell, J. C., & Dell, B. L. (1984). The use of peripheral feedback in the control of movement. *Trends in the Neurosciences, 7*, 253–257.

McMahon, T. A. (1984). *Muscles, reflexes, and locomotion.* Princeton, NJ: Princeton University Press.

Morasso, P. (1981). Spatial control of arm movements. *Experimental Brain Research, 42*, 223–227.

Motley, M. T. (1980). Verification of "Freudian slips" and semantic prearticulatory editing via laboratory-induced spoonerisms. In V. A. Fromkin (Ed.), *Errors in linguistic performance* (pp. 133–147). New York: Academic Press.

Nelson, W. L. (1983). Physical principles for economies of skilled movements. *Biological Cybernetics, 46*, 135–147.

Norman, D. A. (1981). Categorization of action slips. *Psychological Review, 88*, 1–15.

Paillard, J., & Brouchon, M. (1968). Active and passive movements in the calibration of position sense. In S. J. Freedman (Ed.), *The neuropsychology of spatially oriented behavior* (pp. 37–55). Homewood, IL: Dorsey.

Potter, J. M. (1980). What was the matter with Dr. Spooner? In V. A. Fromkin (Ed.), *Errors in linguistic performance* (pp. 13–34). New York: Academic Press.

Pritchard, R. M. (1961). Stabilized images on the retina. *Scientific American, 204*, 72–78.

Raibert, M. H. (1977). *Motor control and learning by the state-space model* (Tech. Rep. AI-TR-439). Cambridge, MA: Artificial Intelligence Laboratory, MIT.

Reeve, T. G., & Proctor, R. W. (1984). On the advance preparation of discrete finger responses. *Journal of Experimental Psychology: Human Perception and Performance, 10*, 541–553.

Rosenbaum, D. A. (1989). On the selection of physical actions. *Five College Cognitive Science Paper,* #89-4.

Rosenzweig, M. R., & Lehman, A. L. (1982). *Physiological psychology.* Lexington, MA: D.C. Heath.

Rumelhart, D. E., & Norman, D. A. (1982). Simulating a skilled typist: A study of skilled cognitive-motor peformance. *Cognitive Science, 6*, 1–36.

Saltzman, E., & Kelso, J. A. S. (1987). Skilled actions: A task-dynamic approach. *Psychological Review, 94*, 84–106.

Sperry, R. W. (1950). Neural basis of the spontaneous optokinetic response produced by visual inversion. *Journal of Comparative and Physiological Psychology, 43*, 482–489.

Taub, E., & Berman, A. J. (1968). Movement and learning in the absence of sensory feedback. In S. J. Freeman (Ed.), *The neuropsychology of spatially oriented behavior* (pp. 173–192). Homewood, IL: Dorsey.

Thelen, E., Kelso, J. A. S., & Fogel, A. (1987). Self-organizing systems and infant motor development. *Developmental Review, 7*, 39–65.

Uno, Y., Kawato, M., & Suzuki, R. (1989). Formation and control of optimal trajectory in human multijoint arm movement: Minimum torque-change model. *Biological Cybernetics, 61*, 89–101.

Volkmann, F. C. (1976). Saccadic suppression: A brief review. In R. A. Monty & J. W. Senders (Eds.), *Eye movements and psychological processes* (pp. 73–84). Hillsdale, NJ: Erlbaum.

Volkmann, F. C., Riggs, L. A., & Moore, R. K. (1980). Eyeblinks and visual suppression. *Science, 207*, 900–902.

von Holst, E. (1939). Die relative Koordination als Phänomenon und als Methode zentralnervöser Funktionsanalyse. *Ergebnisse der Physiologie, Biologischen Chemie und Experimentellen Pharmakologie, 42*, 228–306. (English translation in von Holst, 1973b)

von Holst, E. (1973a). The reafference principle. In R. Martin (Trans.), *The behavioral physiology of animals and man: The collected papers of Erich von Holst* (Vol. 1). London: Methuen.

von Holst, E. (1973b). Relative coordination as a phenomenon and as a method of analysis of central nervous functions. In R. Martin (Trans.), *The behavioral physiology of animal and man: The collected papers of Erich von Holst* (Vol. 1). London: Methuen.

von Holst, E., & Mittelstaedt, H. (1950). Das Reafferenzprinzip. Wechselwirkungen zwischen Zentralnervensystem und Peripherie. *Naturwissenschaften, 37*, 464–476. (English translation in von Holst, 1973a)

Wallace, R. J. (1971). Stimulus-response compatibility and the idea of a response code. *Journal of Experimental Psychology, 88*, 354–360.

Wickens, D. (1938). The transference of conditioned excitation and conditioned inhibition from one muscle group to the antagonistic group. *Journal of Experimental Psychology, 22*, 101–123.

Woodworth, R. S. (1899). The accuracy of voluntary movement. *Psychological Review Monograph Supplements, 3*, No. 3.

2 PHYSIOLOGICAL FOUNDATIONS

■ INTRODUCTION

Movements are made in response to a variety of signals—external ones (a traffic light changing from red to green, the sound of a car horn, a thumb tack stepped on accidentally) and internal ones (a suddenly remembered appointment, an impulsive thought, a deep sentiment). Some movements are automatic whereas others are deliberate. Withdrawing the hand from a hot stove is usually an automatic act. Giving a downbeat to a symphony orchestra is usually carried out with more deliberate control.

No matter what the signal or the context for movement, virtually all movements involve the participation of large numbers of muscles (see Figure 2.1). If we had to think about all the muscles involved in motor performance, we would probably be unable to move skillfully or with enough time or energy left over for other tasks. The main challenge in the study of motor physiology is to understand how, from a physical standpoint, we can move as adaptively and effortlessly as we do.

The principal way that the nervous system allows for skilled motor performance is with special-purpose mechanisms. At the lowest levels are sensory receptors and muscle fibers. These structures are connected through a variable number of synapses (gaps between neurons). Some of the connections involve only a single synapse (*monosynaptic* connections). Others involve many synapses. Because only a few synapses are required for some connections, some responses to perceptual inputs are extremely rapid and automatic. The patellar tendon tap, in which the physician taps on the tendon just below the knee and the leg lifts, is a familiar example.

Pathways running through the spinal cord allow for communication between the peripheral and central nervous systems. Ascending spinal

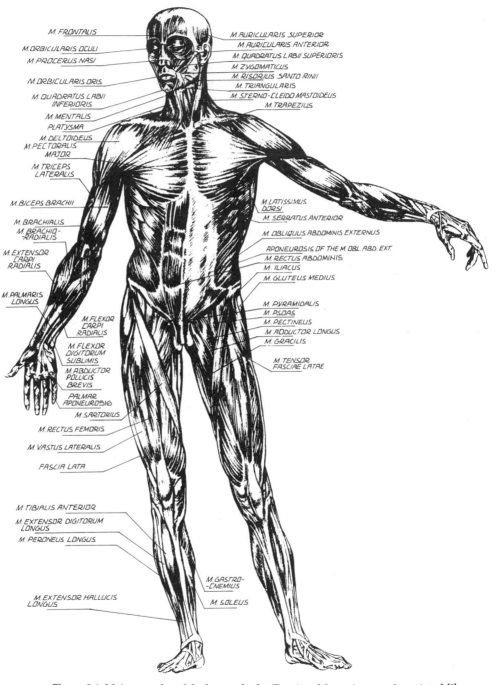

Figure 2.1 Major muscles of the human body. (Reprinted from *Anatomy for artists*. Milan: Vinciana.)

pathways allow afferent (incoming) signals from the periphery to reach the brain. Descending pathways from the brain allow efferent (outgoing) signals from higher centers to reach the periphery, where they excite or inhibit motor neurons and excite or inhibit interneurons (neurons synapsing onto other neurons).

The brain itself is an extraordinary network of neural elements consisting of 10^{12} to 10^{14} neurons, each of which may have as many as 10^4 synaptic connections. The brain is not anatomically homogeneous. Even to the naked eye, distinct regions can be discerned (see Figure 2.2) and, through dissection and other neuroanatomical techniques, a number of cell types and patterns of connection can be seen.

By recording the activity of neurons in different brain regions and by studying the effects of lesions in various brain sites, it has been demonstrated that there are important *functional* distinctions among brain centers. Some centers are primarily devoted to hearing, others to vision, others to smell, and so forth. In the domain of motor control, some centers are involved in relatively low-level aspects of the control of movement and posture, such as the direction and force of single limb movements, whereas others are involved in

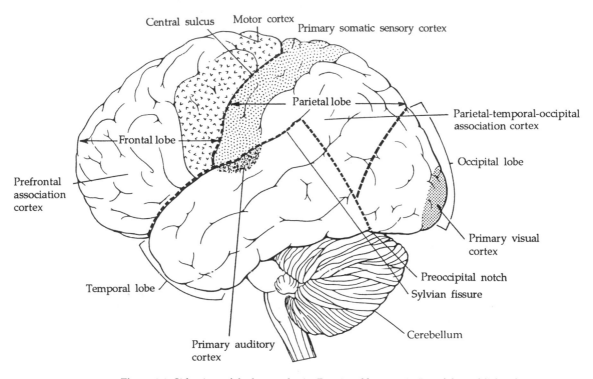

Figure 2.2 Side view of the human brain. Reprinted by permission of the publisher from E. R. Kandel & J. H. Schwartz (eds.), *Principles of neural science* (2d ed.), p. 214. Copyright © 1985 by Elsevier Science Publishing Co., Inc.

higher-level aspects, such as planning extended sequences of actions. The notion that different parts of the nervous system provide different levels of control will be a recurrent theme throughout this chapter.

Some cautions should be given about the review. First, it is not meant to be an exhaustive treatment of motor physiology. For example, I will not explain why many of the structures have the names they do; the reasons are often obscure and, in the present context, unimportant. Second, I will not attempt to provide a detailed overview of the neuroanatomical subdivisions within the nervous centers to be described, nor an account of all the connections among them. Knowing these facts is important for a complete theory of motor physiology, but such a theory is not the goal of this chapter. The more modest aim is to convey a sense of the major principles of motor physiology. References at the end of the chapter can be pursued for more information.

■ MUSCLE

Muscles produce force by contracting. They contract in response to a neurotransmitter, *acetylcholine*, released by motor nerves at the *neuromuscular junction*. When a muscle's receptors for acetylcholine are damaged, as in the disease *myesthenia gravis*, muscle contraction is impaired and severe weakness can result (Drachman, 1983).

Whereas muscles *contract* in response to nerve impulses, they *stretch* (or lengthen) only mechanically, through the action of opposing muscles or external loads.

It was not always known that muscles contract. An ancient Greek, Erasistratus, proposed in the third century B.C. that muscles fill with spirits sent through the nerves (McMahon, 1984). According to this theory, when muscles fill up, their girth expands but their length decreases, much as a balloon changes shape when it fills with air. Not until 1663 was it established that muscles simply shorten. In the decisive experiment, a frog's muscle was placed in an air-filled tube and the nerve running to the muscle was pinched. The muscle contracted in response to the nerve stimulation, but the volume of air in the tube did not decrease (Needham, 1971).

It took nearly 300 years to appreciate how muscle contraction works. With the evelopment of the electron microscope and the polarizing light microscope, it became possible to see that when muscle shortens, two types of protein filaments, *actin* and *myosin*, slide past each other, forming tiny interlocking cross-bridges. The cross-bridges allow for the buildup of muscle force (Pollack, 1983).

The Length–Tension Relation

Formation of cross-bridges between actin and myosin affects macroscopic as well as microscopic features of muscle performance. If a single muscle (excised from an animal) is stretched to different lengths, it resists the stretch with more tension the more it is stretched (see Figure 2.3A). This is a result of the passive mechanical properties of the muscle; the muscle responds this way even when it receives no nerve stimulation. (A mechanical spring behaves in roughly the same way; see Chapter 6.)

If the experiment is repeated and the nerve to the muscle is stimulated, the total tension the muscle produces is greater than the tension produced when the muscle is stretched but not stimulated (the "passive" condition). The total tension curve ("active + passive") has a somewhat different shape from the passive tension curve. The passive tension curve rises monotonically, but the total tension curve has a dip. The difference between the two curves provides an estimate of the amount of actively developed tension in the muscle—the amount of tension resulting from neurally driven contraction. As shown in Figure 2.3A the active tension curve is an inverted U-shaped function of length.

What accounts for the inverted U shape of the active tension curve? It most likely reflects the strength of actin–myosin cross-bridges formed at different muscle lengths (Figure 2.3B). When muscle is very short, there is too much overlap among the filaments to allow much tension to build up, and when muscle is very stretched, there is too little overlap for the development of appreciable tension. At intermediate muscle lengths, many cross-bridges can be formed and tension can be great (Huxley, 1974; McMahon, 1984).

Length–tension relations have effects on everyday activities. At extreme joint angles, when the muscles tend to be maximally stretched or contracted, the forces that can be produced are smaller than at intermediate joint angles. This is why greater force can be generated when the joint is in the middle of its range of motion. A practical consequence of this fact has been described colorfully by Rothwell (1987, p. 24):

> As every hero in a gangster movie knows, the way to make the villain release his grip on the gun is to flex the wrist forcibly to reduce the power of the finger flexors. The gun will thereupon fall dramatically to the floor, to be kicked neatly away by the hero's foot. The importance of this example is that the nervous system must somehow take into account the length–tension relationship of muscle during normal movement, in this instance by extending the wrist when a maximal flexor force is required.

Motor Units and Recruitment

Muscles are composed of muscle fibers. The muscle fibers within a muscle group are innervated by several *motor neurons*. Any given muscle fiber is innervated by just one motor neuron. A motor neuron and the muscle fibers it innervates form what is called a *motor unit*.

The muscle fibers within a motor unit usually have similar mechanical properties. Such mechanical homogeneity simplifies the job of recruiting motor units. For a given task, the motor units to be recruited can be the ones that are mechanically best suited to the task. For tasks with different

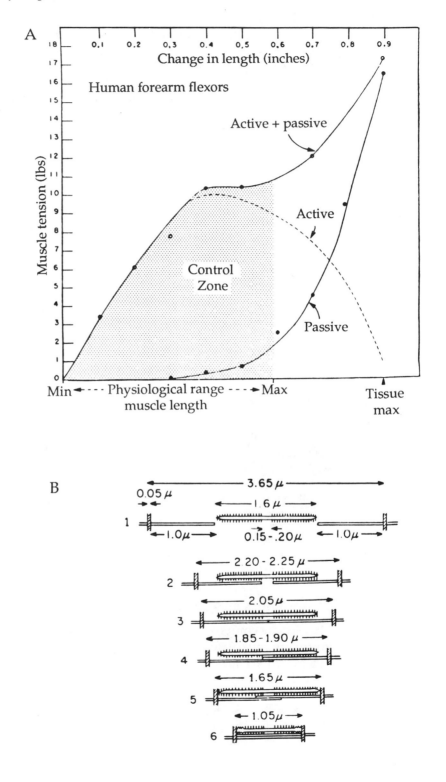

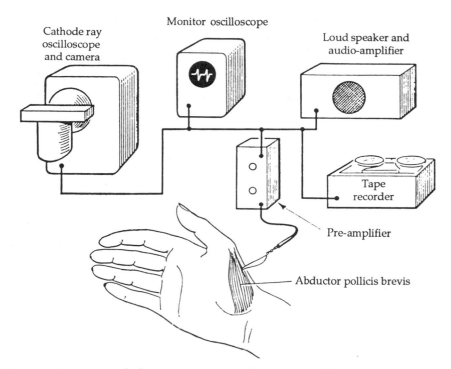

Figure 2.4 Arrangement for learning to activate single motor units. (From J. V. Basmajian, *Muscles alive: Their functions revealed by electromyography* (3d ed.). Copyright © by Williams and Wilkins, 1974.

mechanical demands, different motor units can be recruited. Swinging the leg or maintaining stance, for example, are carried out with different motor units (Loeb, 1985).

The number of muscle fibers in a motor unit varies from effector to effector. In the hand and eye fewer than 100 muscle fibers occupy a motor unit, but in the lower leg a single motor unit may contain as many as 1000 muscle fibers (Buchthal & Schmalbruch, 1980). Generally, the larger the number of muscle fibers in a motor unit, the less precise the movements it allows.

It is impossible to activate voluntarily some but not all of the muscle fibers within a motor unit. In this sense, the motor unit is the most basic unit of motor control. However, it is possible voluntarily to recruit some motor units but not others. With feedback, such as visual or auditory signals about

Figure 2.3 (*Opposite page*) The length–tension relation. (A) Tension developed by muscle contraction ("Active") estimated by subtracting tension in passively stretched muscle ("Passive") from tension in driven muscle ("Active + Passive"). (From Brooks, 1981.) (B) Presumed basis for the relation. Active tension is greatest when there is maximum overlap between filaments (2 and 3) and decreases if the overlap is less (worst case in 1) or if the filaments collide (worst case in 6). 1 corresponds to the right side of the graph in (A); 6 corresponds to the left side. (From Rothwell, 1987.)

the activity of single motor units, people can learn to activate one motor unit at a time (Figure 2.4). In more natural situations, when movements are produced without overt feedback about the activity of single motor units, motor units still tend to be recruited in an orderly fashion (see Figure 2.5). The first activated motor units are usually the ones whose muscle fibers are smallest and least forceful. As recruitment continues, the motor units that turn on have larger and more forceful muscle fibers. This orderly relation is called the *size principle* (Henneman, Somjen, & Carpenter, 1965).

What is the physiological basis of the size principle? The answer is related to thresholds of action potentials (neural firing). Motor units with small muscle fibers have small motor neurons, whereas motor units with large muscle fibers have large motor neurons. Small motor neurons have low thresholds for generating action potentials (neural "firings"), but large motor neurons have high thresholds for generating action potentials. Thus weak inputs to the motor neuron pool can produce action potentials in small motor neurons. As the strength of input grows, larger motor neurons begin to fire.

The size principle has several functional advantages for motor control. One is that large forces are not produced when they are unnecessary; recruitment can stop when the appropriate force has been generated. The size principle also confers a computational benefit. Because hundreds or even thousands of motor units may be involved in the activation of a muscle group, the number of possible recruitment orders can become very large—larger in fact than the number of neurons in the brain (Enocka & Stuart, 1984). Thus a regular recruitment order based on size helps reduce

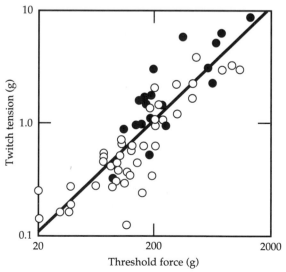

Figure 2.5 The size principle of Henneman, Somjen, & Carpenter (1965). Open and filled circles correspond to data obtained from the same subject at different times. (Adapted from Brooks, 1986.)

the degrees-of-freedom problem at this low level of control. [For discussion of some exceptions to the size principle, see Desmedt (1981).]

■ PROPRIOCEPTION

Information about the position and motion of the limbs is provided both by the overt consequences of our actions, perceived primarily through the eyes and ears, and also from sensory receptors within the muscles, tendons, joints, and skin. Information provided by the latter receptors is called *proprioception*. Proprioceptive information specifically related to movement is sometimes called *kinesthesis*.

Muscle Spindles

Only some of the muscle fibers within a muscle group are powerful enough to move or stabilize a limb. These large-diameter muscle fibers are called *extrafusal* fibers (or extrafusals). Lying in parallel with extrafusals, and attached to them, are *muscle spindles*. Muscle spindles contain small muscle fibers called *intrafusal* fibers (or intrafusals). As shown in Figure 2.6, the intrafusals making up a muscle spindle are connected to a single extrafusal. The midsection of the muscle spindle contains the spindle's cell nuclei, housed in a *nuclear bag* or *nuclear chain* fiber.

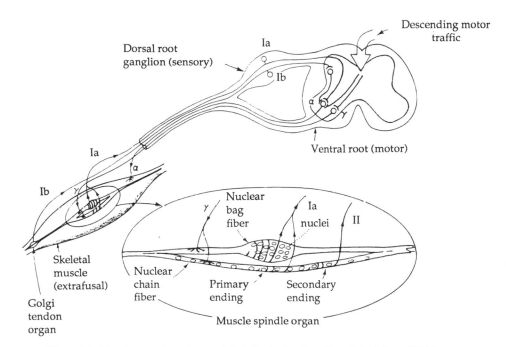

Figure 2.6 Muscle proprioceptors and their basic circuitry. (From McMahon, 1984.)

A sensory nerve fiber—the *Ia afferent*—is wrapped around the central region of the nuclear bag fiber as well as the central region of the nuclear chain fiber; the part of the Ia afferent surrounding the spindle is called the *primary ending*. The Ia afferent responds primarily to differences between the length of the extrafusal and the length of the intrafusal as well as changes in this length difference over time (Matthews, 1972). When an extrafusal fiber contracts relative to an intrafusal fiber, Ia activity diminishes, but when an extrafusal fiber stretches relative to an intrafusal, Ia activity increases. The increase in Ia activity results in signals being sent to the spinal cord, where they can trigger reflex responses.

Another sensory fiber—the *group II afferent*—is wrapped around the peripheral region of the nuclear chain fiber, in what is called the *secondary ending*. Like the Ia, the activity of the group II afferent diminishes when the extrafusal contracts relative to the intrafusal and increases when the extrafusal stretches relative to the intrafusal. The group II afferent is less sensitive than the Ia (Matthews, 1972; Rothwell, 1987).

For some time, it was believed that muscle-spindle discharge does not contribute to conscious perception of muscle stretch. The belief was prompted by a report (Gelfan & Carter, 1967) that awake patients undergoing routine operations on the ankle literally could not tell when someone was pulling their leg. In this study, an investigator pulled on the long tendon of the toe muscles to determine whether patients could tell their tendons were being pulled. They could not. The same result was obtained for the wrist, where the long tendons of the finger muscles were tugged. Again patients seemed unaware that this manipulation was being carried out. The findings seemed to rule out a contribution of muscle-spindle activity to the perception of muscle stretch.

Matthews and Simmons (1974) later repeated the procedure and found that patients could in fact detect muscle and tendon stretch quite well. In another study, not involving surgery, Goodwin, McCloskey, and Matthews (1972) applied vibration to the biceps muscle. Vibration applied to muscle stimulates muscle spindles. Goodwin *et al.* reasoned that the vibration would activate muscle stretch receptors. Therefore, if subjects sensed muscle stretch, they would perceive the limb as being more extended than it really was. The prediction was confirmed. As shown in Figure 2.7, when subjects (with eyes closed) positioned the other arm so it matched the perceived position of the stimulated arm, they overestimated the angle of the elbow joint. In a control condition, when subjects were asked simply to match the position of the unvibrated arm with the other arm, they could do so nearly perfectly. Thus subjects could accurately match the positions of the two arms. The systematic errors observed in the vibration condition suggest that muscle stretch is consciously perceived.

Golgi Tendon Organs

Muscles attach to bone through tendons. Sensory receptors in the tendons—*Golgi tendon organs*—have distinct afferent fibers (Ib fibers) whose response characteristics are, to a first approximation, opposite those of muscle spin-

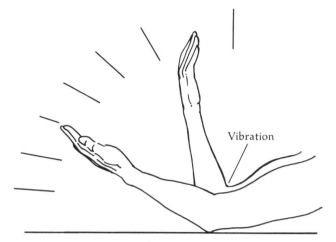

Figure 2.7 Effect of vibration applied to the biceps of the right arm. The subject tried to match the felt position of the right arm with the position of the left arm. The scale marks 10° divisions. (Adapted from Rothwell, 1987.)

dles (see Figure 2.8). When a muscle twitches (undergoes a rapid, single contraction), its muscle stretch receptors usually fire less than before the twitch, as stated earlier. Golgi tendon organs, in contrast, fire *more* when the twitch begins and usually stop firing when the twitch is over (Matthews, 1972).

For some time, it was believed that the exclusive role of Golgi tendon organs is to signal dangerously high muscle tensions. This belief arose because Golgi tendon organs appeared to have high thresholds for firing. Apparently, it took a great deal of muscle tension to activate Ib afferents

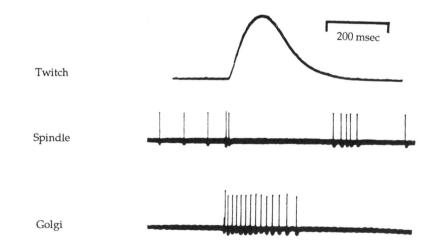

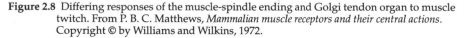

Figure 2.8 Differing responses of the muscle-spindle ending and Golgi tendon organ to muscle twitch. From P. B. C. Matthews, *Mammalian muscle receptors and their central actions.* Copyright © by Williams and Wilkins, 1972.

(Rothwell, 1987). More detailed study revealed that tendon organs are in fact quite sensitive to muscle tension. For example, Ib afferents actually respond to induced muscle tensions of a tenth of a gram or less (Binder, Kroin, Moore, & Stuart, 1977; Houk & Henneman, 1967). In view of these data, Golgi tendon organs are now viewed as being highly sensitive to muscle tension.

Joint Receptors

Sensory endings in the joint provide another source of proprioceptive information. In 1956, it was reported that individual joint receptors respond preferentially to different joint angles (Skoglund, 1956) (see Figure 2.9). It also appeared that joint receptors adapt slowly, that is, continue to fire for a long time after a joint angle is assumed. Joint receptors were therefore assumed to supply information about static limb position. More recent work has called this view into question. Clark and Burgess (1975) and Grigg (1976) found that most joint receptors fire only at extreme joint angles and that joint receptors adapt quickly.

 The exact role of joint receptors remains to be articulated. In view of the Clark and Burgess findings, it has been suggested that joint receptors may provide the sort of signal that Golgi tendon organs were once assumed to provide—a danger signal about extreme joint angles (Rothwell, 1987).

Cutaneous Receptors

When movements are made, the skin surface deforms. Standing creates pressure sensations in the soles of the feet, for example. Rubbing one's hand on a table produces sensations of displacement over the skin surface. The sensory

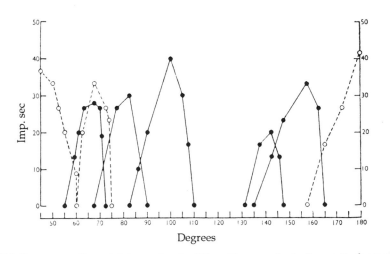

Figure 2.9 Responses of knee-joint receptors to different knee angles in the cat. Each set of connected points corresponds to a single receptor. First cat (○–○); second cat (●–●). (From Skoglund, 1956.)

receptors that respond to mechanical deformation of the skin are called *mechanoreceptors*. Other skin receptors respond to temperature and pain.

Damage to cutaneous mechanoreceptors can have disruptive effects on performance. Patients with damage to pressure sensors in the soles of the feet have difficulty maintaining balance if their eyes are closed (*Romberg's sign*). Similarly, fine manipulations with the hands and fingers, performed without visual feedback, become difficult or even impossible if the cutaneous mechanoreceptors of the hand are destroyed (Rothwell, 1987).

An indication of the tightness of the coupling between mechanoreceptor activity and motor control is the rapidity with which people can respond to tactile stimuli. In lifting a small object with the fingers, the grip may tighten 80 msec after the object has slipped very slightly (Johansson & Westling, 1988).

There has been relatively little research on the role of cutaneous receptors in motor control. In the area of robotics, however, increasing attention has been paid to touch because of the need for precise sensing of mechanical disturbances in machine assembly and related tasks. For example, robots that place nuts on screws display improved performance if equipped with sensitive touch sensors (Brady, Hollerbach, Johnson, Lozano-Perez, & Mason, 1982). The Steinway piano company recently began to explore the use of robots for polishing pianos. Equipping robot polishers with tactile sensors enhances polishing performance (Amato, 1989).

■ SPINAL REFLEXES

As was shown in Figure 2.4, Ia and Ib afferents project to the spinal cord. The Ib afferent, from the Golgi tendon organ, synapses onto an interneuron, which synapses onto a motor neuron, which in turn stimulates the extrafusal muscle to which the tendon is attached. Thus the Ib afferent from the Golgi tendon organ ultimately has an inhibitory effect on the extrafusal muscle to which the tendon is attached. The inhibitory effect reduces the muscle tension sensed by the tendon organ.

In contrast to the Ib afferent from the tendon organ, the Ia afferent from the muscle spindle synapses directly onto the motor neuron for the spindle's extrafusal fiber. This monosynaptic connection allows for the most famous of all reflexes—the simple *reflex arc*. When impulses arrive from the Ia, the motor neuron for the extrafusal is excited. This causes the extrafusal to contract, which in turn relieves the stretch on the spindle. When the stretch is relieved, the Ia quiets down and the reflex contraction subsides.

Servo Theory

Recall that the muscle spindle contains a muscle fiber—the intrafusal. The intrafusal has a dedicated motor neuron, the so-called γ (gamma) motor neuron. The extrafusal has a dedicated motor neuron called the α (alpha) motor neuron. Why does the muscle spindle contain a contractile fiber with its own motor neuron (the γ)?

A provocative answer was suggested by Merton (1972). According to his model, the entire spindle–extrafusal system works like a servo device (see Chapter 1). Suppose an intrafusal fiber is made to contract through the effect of a γ motor neuron, but the adjacent extrafusal fiber does not contract because its α motor neuron has been activated. The intrafusal shortens, but because the intrafusal is small, its contraction is too weak to move the limb. Because the intrafusal shortens while the extrafusal does not, the central, noncontractile portion of the muscle spindle stretches, causing the Ia to fire. The firing of the Ia causes the α motor neuron to fire, and the α motor neuron then causes the extrafusal fiber to contract. In essence, the signal from the γ motor neuron to the intrafusal fiber becomes amplified. The entire system acts as a servo, much like the system that enables a driver to turn a 2-ton automobile by rotating the steering wheel with one finger.

What is the advantage of this method of control? Amplifying the effect of the intrafusal does not reduce effort, for the same degree of effort must ultimately be expended regardless of whether the extrafusal is turned on directly, via immediate stimulation of the α motor neurons, or indirectly, via the γ loop. The main advantage of the γ loop is that it can promote efficient load compensation. If the extrafusal is stretched during a contraction by the imposition of an unexpected load (for example, if the arm bumps against an object), there will be a discrepancy between the length of the intrafusal and the length of the extrafusal. When such a discrepancy occurs, the stretch receptor will fire, causing the extrafusal immediately to contract to counteract the stretch. Having the γ loop therefore provides an effective means of compensating rapidly for load disturbances.

Despite the attractiveness of Merton's (1972) servo hypothesis, it ran into an obstacle. The damage came from a study in which fine electrodes were used to record the activity of muscle-spindle afferents as well as extrafusals during isometric flexion of the index finger (Vallbo, 1970). (During an isometric flexion, there is muscle contraction that would allow flexion to occur, but the limb is prevented from moving by an external force.) As shown in Figure 2.10, action potentials from the spindle afferents occurred *after* the onset of electromyographic (EMG) activity in the extrafusal muscle. The result directly contradicts the prediction of the servo model that spindles should become active *before* extrafusals.

In hindsight, there may be a good reason why the servo model was disproved. If α motor neurons could only be activated after γ motor neurons turned on, delays would always occur before extrafusal contraction began (Vallbo, 1970). Such delays would not be adaptive when rapid responses are required.

α–γ Coactivation

Why did spindle afferents fire at all in Vallbo's (1970) experiment? Contraction of the extrafusal should have relieved stretch on the muscle spindle, so spindle afferents should have *stopped* firing, not *started* firing,

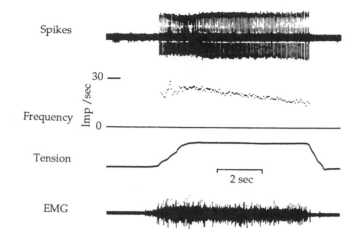

Spikes

Frequency   Imp /sec   30 —

0

Tension

2 sec

EMG

Figure 2.10 Muscle-spindle discharge during weak voluntary isometric flexion of the index finger. *Top trace:* Directly recorded spindle afferent activity. *Second trace:* Instantaneous frequency of spindle afferent action potentials (in impulses per second). *Third trace:* Muscle tension. *Fourth trace:* Muscle EMG. (From Vallbo, 1970.)

when the extrafusal contracted. The firing of the spindle afferents implies that the length of the muscle spindle relative to the extrafusal decreased, which means in turn that the spindle contracted. Spindle contraction is caused by γ motor neuron activity, whereas extrafusal contraction is caused by α motor neuron activity. The simultaneous activation of the spindle afferent and extrafusal must have come about, therefore, because the α and γ motor neurons came on at about the same time. This phenomenon is called *α–γ coactivation.*

Why does the nervous system turn on α s and γ s simultaneously? Perhaps the simplest reason is that turning them on at different times would require a mechanism to select and control the delays. The cost of such a mechanism, in terms of number of neurons or neural connections, might be prohibitive. Moreover, having α s and γ s come on together may allow for rapid compensation for imposed loads. Delaying α activation would introduce a period when the capacity for compensation is eliminated.

Recurrent Inhibition

As was shown in Figure 2.6, the spinal cord is the site of communication between Ia afferents and α motor neurons as well as between Ib afferents and α motor neurons. A number of other spinal circuits allow for communication among neural elements involved in muscle activation and proprioception. One circuit allows motor neurons to inhibit themselves—a phenomenon called *recurrent inhibition.* Recurrent inhibition is achieved with a neuron (the *Renshaw* cell) that inhibits the motor neuron that excites it (see Figure 2.11). The inhibitory effect of the Renshaw cell also extends to nearby motor neurons (Baldissera, Hultborn, & Illert, 1981).

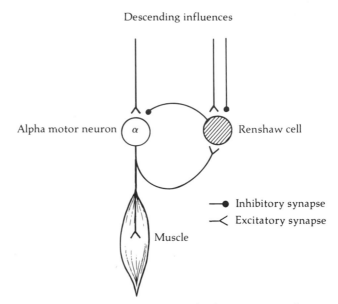

Descending influences

Alpha motor neuron

Renshaw cell

Inhibitory synapse
Excitatory synapse

Muscle

Figure 2.11 The Renshaw cell and its connections with other neuromotor elements. (Adapted from Rothwell, 1987.)

A likely reason for recurrent inhibition is that modulating the activity of Renshaw cells can affect the sensitivity of motor neurons. If Renshaw cells are activated by supraspinal centers, the Renshaw cells have a greater inhibitory effect on motor neurons. Consequently, more activation must be supplied to the motor neurons to get them to produce a desired level of activity. On the other hand, if Renshaw cells receive little or no activation from supraspinal centers (or if they are inhibited by supraspinal centers), relatively little excitation is needed to drive the motor neurons. Modulating the level of Renshaw cells therefore influences the level of excitation needed to drive motor neurons. This can be a useful tool for moving at the slightest provocation or for refraining from moving unless it is essential.

Inhibiting Renshaw cells may also allow coarsely graded descending signals to have more finely graded motor effects (Baldissera *et al.*, 1981). Suppose for the sake of argument that descending signals can only take on the values of 10, 30, 50, 70, and 90 (arbitrary units). If Renshaw cells reduce these signals by a factor of 2, the possible signal strengths are 5, 15, 25, 35, and 45. If the Renshaw cell reduces the signals by a factor of 10 rather than 2, the possible signal strengths are 1, 3, 5, 7, and 9. Greater resolution of signal strengths is therefore possible within the range 5 to 15 when the Renshaw cell reduces signals by a factor of 10 rather than 2 (or 1).

Reciprocal Inhibition

Another form of interaction within the spinal cord, *reciprocal inhibition*, can be demonstrated as follows (McMahon, 1984). Flex your elbow and stiffen it, as in Figure 2.12A. Place your other hand around your upper arm. You should be able to feel the biceps and triceps muscles harden, reflecting their contracted state. Now ask a friend to push upward against your hand (Figure 2.12B). You should feel your biceps briefly "soften" as the upward force is applied. When this occurs, the biceps is momentarily inactive.

The spinal circuit underlying this effect is shown in Figure 2.12C. When the upward force is applied to the hand, the triceps stretches and stretch receptors within the triceps are activated. Afferent fibers from stretch receptors in the triceps project to interneurons in the spinal cord which inhibit motor neurons of the opposing muscle (the biceps).

Reciprocal inhibition is not restricted to the biceps and triceps of the human arm. It is a general phenomenon in which the stretch of one muscle inhibits the activity of the opposing muscle. Reciprocal inhibition prevents muscles from working against each other when external loads are encoun-

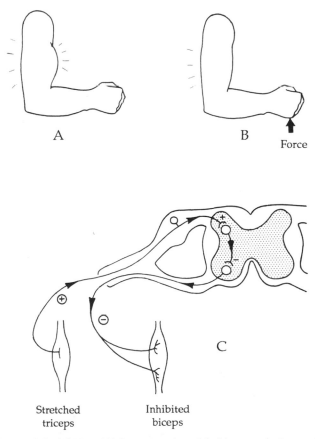

Figure 2.12 Reciprocal inhibition. (A) Co-contraction of the biceps and triceps while holding the elbow at 90°. (B) The biceps is deactivated when an upward force is applied to the forearm. (C) The underlying mechanism. Plus sign denotes an excitatory effect. Minus sign denotes an inhibitory effect. (From McMahon, 1984.)

tered. The physiological properties of reciprocal inhibition have been studied in detail (Jankowska & Lindstrom, 1971).

It is worth emphasizing that reciprocal inhibition does not occur between motor neurons directly. Biceps motor neurons do not inhibit triceps motor neurons, for example. If inhibition existed between motor neurons of opposing muscle groups, it would be difficult to activate the opposing muscles simultaneously, as in the first part of this exercise. Co-contraction of opposing muscles is widespread (Marsden, Obeso, & Rothwell, 1983). It allows joints to stiffen, which is an effective means of resisting perturbations (for example, when preparing to catch a heavy object dropped from overhead).

Stiffening a joint by contracting the muscles around it can be a more efficient means of resisting load perturbations than activating only a single muscle and relying on stretch reflexes to counteract loads that may be encountered (Hasan, 1986). Keeping a medium level of stiffness may also be an optimal means of moving a limb through an entire trajectory. Small changes in the relative stiffnesses of the muscles can create a series of equilibrium positions to which the limb is driven over time (Hasan, 1986). (More will be said about relative stiffnesses and equilibrium positions in Chapter 6.)

■ CEREBELLUM

In the preceding sections, I focused on spinal mechanisms. In the sections to follow, I will "look up" to the brain. The brain's principal roles in motor control are to govern motor output based on perceptual information and intentional states, and to acquire perceptual–motor skills. In the sections to follow, I will concentrate on the roles that six brain centers play in human motor control. These are the cerebellum, the basal ganglia, the motor cortex, the premotor cortex, the supplementary motor cortex, and the parietal cortex (see Figure 2.2). This section is concerned with the cerebellum.

More than half the neurons in the human brain are located in the cerebellum (Ito, 1984). Cerebellar anatomy has been studied in great detail, but it is not essential for present purposes to review the anatomy here; information about it can be found in Ito (1984) or Llinas (1981). Instead I will consider the main motor-control functions served by the cerebellum, with only brief reference to cerebellar anatomy. The main motoric functions of the cerebellum are regulation of muscle tone, coordination, timing, and learning.

Regulation of Muscle Tone

The cerebellum receives input from muscle spindles and Golgi tendon organs as well as centers for vision, hearing, touch, and balance. When the cerebellum is damaged, muscle tone (the slight tension continually present in the muscles) is adversely affected. In cats, disconnecting the cerebellum from the spinal cord results in *decerebrate rigidity*, a syndrome in which the

Figure 2.13 Decerebrate rigidity in the cat. From L. J. Pollock & L. Davis (1927).

limbs become extremely rigid (see Figure 2.13). The source of rigidity is elevated sensitivity of the muscle-spindle system. The stretch receptors become highly sensitive to extrafusal stretch, causing extrafusals to contract more than usual (Matthews & Rushworth, 1958).

In human and nonhuman primates damage to the cerebellum results in abnormally low rather than abnormally high muscle tone (*hypotonia*). Anatomical differences between the feline and the primate nervous systems account for the fact that cerebellar damage leads to rigidity in cats and flaccidity in primates (Gilman, Bloedel, & Lechtenberg, 1981).

Coordination

Cerebellar damage often takes the form of coordination deficits (*ataxia*). The incoordination can take several forms. Maintaining steady balance while standing can be compromised (Nashner, 1976) (see also Chapter 4). Walking heel-to-toe may become all but impossible. Speech may become slurred (*dysarthria*), and *nystagmus* eye movements (see Chapter 5) can be adversely affected. Visually guided hand movements may also deteriorate. In attempting to point to a target, cerebellar patients may significantly overshoot the target (*hypermetria*) and then perform a series of "homing-in" movements. Once the arm comes to rest, it may oscillate noticeably. Because this oscillation usually occurs just before or after purposeful movements, it is sometimes called intention tremor.

Cerebellar insult can also impair the production of sequences of movements. Alternating between palm-up and palm-down hand gestures, for example, may break down (see Figure 2.14). The mental effort required for such tasks may also increase. Normally, a task like turning the hand back and forth between a palm-up and palm-down posture (*supinating* and *pronating* the hand) can occur automatically. It takes much more concentration in cerebellar patients. One cerebellar patient, while carrying out this

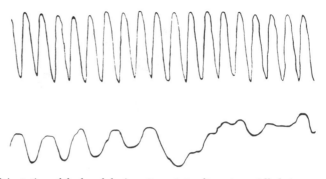

Figure 2.14 Orientation of the hand during attempts to alternate rapidly between a palm-up and a palm-down position in a patient with unilateral cerebellar damage. *Top trace:* Performance by the unaffected hand. *Bottom trace:* Performance by the affected hand. (From Holmes, 1939.)

task, reportedly said, "I have to think out each movement ... I come to a dead stop in turning and have to think before I start again" (Holmes, 1939).

Timing

Closely related to difficulties in sequencing are difficulties in timing. Overshooting targets during aiming movements (*hypermetria*) can be viewed as a timing problem (Eccles, 1977). The timing of muscle contractions is also impaired after cerebellar damage. A situation in which such impairment has been observed is step-input tracking. Here a target jumps from one position to another, typically on a computer screen, and the subject is supposed to keep another object (the cursor) aligned with the target.

Hallet, Shahani, and Young (1975a,b) set up a step-input tracking task in which subjects made flexion movements about the elbow to keep the cursor aligned with the target. Elbow angle was recorded electronically and was then represented by the cursor's position on the screen. The subject's task was to keep the cursor aligned with the target by flexing or extending the elbow. In normal individuals (Hallet, Shahani, & Young, 1975a), a characteristic pattern of EMG activity was recorded from the biceps and triceps (see Figure 2.15). First the agonist became active, then the antagonist became active, and then the agonist became active again. (An *agonist* is a muscle that promotes a movement; an *antagonist* is a muscle that opposes it.) This pattern of EMG activity was not present in cerebellar patients (Hallet, Shahani, & Young, 1975b). For them, the first agonist burst was prolonged, or the first agonist burst and antagonist burst were prolonged.

Alcohol produces similar effects in normal individuals. Like patients with cerebellar damage, normal individuals who have ingested large amounts of alcohol show elevated reaction times, behaviors reminiscent of hypermetria and intention tremor, and abnormally timed EMG patterns in step-input tracking tasks (Marsden, Merton, & Morton, 1977). Perhaps it is

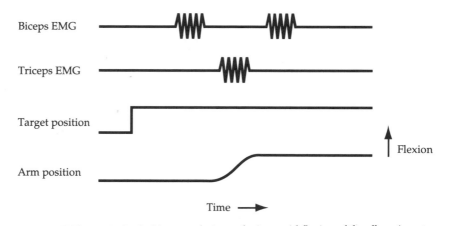

Figure 2.15 EMG activity in the biceps and triceps during rapid flexion of the elbow in a step-tracking task. (Adapted from Hallet, Shahani, & Young, 1975a.)

no wonder, then, that cerebellar patients appear to the untrained eye to be intoxicated. The similarities between the effects of alcohol and the effects of cerebellar damage suggest that the cerebellum may be a brain center which is especially strongly affected by alcohol.

A recent study has suggested that different parts of the cerebellum may affect different stages in the production of timed responses. Ivry, Keele, and Diener (1988) investigated rhythmic finger tapping in patients with presumed lesions in the lateral or intermediate regions of the cerebellum. The patients were asked to tap at a rate of about 2 cycles/sec. By recording the timing of patients' finger taps, Ivry *et al.* (1988) used the statistical properties of times between taps to estimate the temporal variability associated with two basic processes underlying tapping performance: (1) briefly waiting to initiate each response, and (2) executing each response when the brief waiting period was over. Ivry *et al.* (1988) found that patients with damage in the *lateral* region of the cerebellum exhibited higher-than-normal variability in the timing process but essentially normal variability in the execution process. By contrast, patients with primary damage in the *intermediate* region exhibited higher-than-normal variability in the execution process but essentially normal variability in the timing process. (More will be said about the dissociation of timing and response execution in Chapter 8.)

Other studies corroborate the view that the lateral and intermediate regions of the cerebellum are associated with different aspects of motor control. Neurons in lateral cerebellum become active well in advance of EMG activity, but neurons in the more medial zones become active only during or shortly after movements have been performed (Schwartz, Ebner, & Bloedel, 1987). This finding fits with the hypothesis that the lateral region is primarily involved in aspects of motor control that pertain to the planning or programming of movement, whereas intermediate or medial regions are primarily involved in movement execution.

Learning

The cerebellum is not only important for *performing* behaviors. It is also important for *learning* them. Damage to the cerebellum interferes with motor learning. For example, cerebellar damage interferes with adaptation of the vestibular ocular reflex (VOR). Recall from Chapter 1 that when one looks at a stationary object, movements of the head give rise to automatic compensatory eye movements that keep the eyes on the visual target. Adaptation of the VOR has been studied by fitting volunteer subjects with prisms that reverse the right and left visual fields. Over time, the direction of eye rotation relative to head rotation reverses. In animals with lesions of the cerebellum this reversal never occurs, though in animals without lesions of the cerebellum it does (Robinson, 1976).

The cerebellum also appears to be involved in learning skillful *limb* movements. Gilbert and Thach (1977) recorded the electrical activity of fibers within the cerebellum (climbing fibers) in monkeys trained to resist loads applied to the wrist. As the resistive movements became more coordinated during learning, there was an accompanying change in the firing patterns of the cerebellar fibers.

Learning to anticipate visual stimuli in reaction-time tasks also appears to be based on cerebellar changes (Sasaki, Gemba, & Mizuno, 1982). Cerebellar neurons fire before movements are made in response to anticipated visual signals, and lesions of the cerebellum reduce the capacity for visuomotor anticipation.

Results like these have encouraged the development of detailed computational models of cerebellar leanring (Albus, 1971; Ito, 1984; Llinas, 1981; Marr, 1969). Analysis of the cerebellum as a perceptual–motor learning device has become one of the most active research areas in neural and cognitive science (Churchland, 1986; McCormick & Thompson, 1984).

■ BASAL GANGLIA

The basal ganglia are a set of interconnected structures in the forebrain. The roles played by the basal ganglia in motor control are suggested by the behavioral disruptions following basal ganglia damage.

Huntington's Disease

A dramatic behavioral syndrome attributable to damage of the basal ganglia is *Huntington's disease*. This disease manifests itself initially as occasional clumsiness and forgetfulness. Gradually, the patient falls prey to uncontrollable ballistic movements (*chorea*), an inability to reason (*dementia*), and finally death. The choreiform movements of Huntington's disease can be grotesque. The patient's arms and legs may flail about wildly. The face can become a mask of contorted expressions. In the late stages of the disease, the patient must be confined to a wheelchair.

The physiological change that occurs in Huntington's disease is damage to the dendrites responsible for the production and uptake of a neurotransmitter, gamma-aminobutyric acid (GABA). The cause of this physiological change is genetic. This was established through a study of the family histories of Huntington's patients on the East Coast of the United States. Almost all the patients descended from a single family that had migrated to Salem, Massachusetts, from England in 1630 (Côté & Crutcher, 1985). Seventeenth-century Salem was known for its "witches"— individuals whose bizarre behavior led to their being accused of possession by the devil. Of course, most of these people were just victims of Huntington's disease.

The growth of expertise in genetics in the twentieth century has made it possible to determine the specific chromosomal defect that causes Huntington's disease. It has become possible to identify the defect in still-healthy individuals. For individuals in families with a history of the disease, determining whether or when to be tested for the chromosomal abnormality can be an agonizing personal decision (Brody, 1988).

Parkinson's Disease

Another motor disorder associated with damage to the basal ganglia is *Parkinson's disease*. Named after James Parkinson, a London physician who described the syndrome in 1817, Parkinson's disease has several signs. One is a shuffling gait. Another is shaking motion at rest (*resting tremor*). Others are slowness in the initiation of movements on command (*akinesia*) and slowness in the completion of movements that are finally under way (*bradykinesia*). In clinical examination, Parkinson's patients often display high resistance to tugging on the limb. Normal individuals demonstrate moderate resistance to passive manipulation (a sign of normal muscle tone), but Parkinson's patients remain stiff, both in flexor and extensor muscles (*rigidity*).

The cause of Parkinson's disease is a deficit of a neurotransmitter, *dopamine*. Lower-than-normal amounts of dopamine have been found in autopsy studies of the brains of Parkinson's patients. A drug (L-DOPA) which elevates brain dopamine levels can help Parkinson's patients, but only temporarily and sometimes with unpleasant side effects. A new drug, *deprenyl*, appears to be significantly more effective. Rather than boosting dopamine levels directly, it retards the action of enzymes that break down dopamine too rapidly. Administration of deprenyl can delay the onset of Parkinson's disease by several months (Fackelmann, 1989). Another new treatment for Parkinson's disease is transplantation of dopamine-producing tissues (for example, from the adrenal gland) into the basal ganglia. The effectiveness of this procedure remains controversial (Lewin, 1988).

Theories of Basal Ganglia Function

Exactly what functions are served by the basal ganglia? From the outset, it is important to observe that while the basal ganglia are clearly involved in motor control, they may serve other functions as well. Patients with basal ganglia disease have difficulty recalling sequences of symbolic events as well as performing sequences of motor acts (Côté & Crutcher, 1985; Gunilla, Öberg, & Divac, 1981) and, as I mentioned earlier, one symptom of Huntington's disease is dementia.

One hypothesis about the role of the basal ganglia in motor control is that they contribute to the activation or retrieval of movement plans (Marsden, 1982). Consistent with this hypothesis, neurons in some basal ganglia structures (the *globus pallidus* and the *zona reticulata* of the *substantia nigra*) have been found (in monkeys) to discharge before voluntary movements of the arm or leg and before chewing or licking movements (Iansek & Porter, 1980). Parkinson's patients have difficulty beginning voluntary movements. For example, it may be hard for them to start walking when asked to do so. Paradoxically, they may start walking with no difficulty in a different intentional context—when asked simply to leave the room. Visual stimuli can help Parkinson's patients start to walk. Figure 2.16 shows that the placement of markers on the floor at regularly spaced intervals can help Parkinson's patients locomote in a nearly normal fashion. Providing the markers can be nearly as effective as L-DOPA medication (Forssberg, Johnels, & Steg, 1984).

Besides serving to retrieve or initiate movement plans, the basal ganglia may serve to scale the amplitudes of movements. According to Brooks (1986), basal ganglia disease may disrupt the overall size and timing of movements in such tasks as handwriting, reaching, grasping, and manual positioning. (The *pallidum* appears to be the basal ganglia structure primarily responsible for this scaling function, according to Brooks.)

A final function served by the basal ganglia pertains to perceptual–motor integration. Cells in the caudate nucleus of the basal ganglia have been found, in sedentary cats, to respond to light brushing of the face, but to respond at different levels if the same stimulus is applied during mouth or head movements (Manetto & Lidsky, 1989). Conceivably, then, the basal ganglia may allow for the gating of perceptual inputs during motor activity.

■ MOTOR CORTEX

So far in this chapter, I have "moved up" from the lowest, or most primitive, levels of the motor system to the higher, more phylogenetically advanced levels. Now I wish to consider the phylogenetically highest levels—those occupying the cerebral cortex. First, I consider the motor cortex. Then I consider the premotor cortex. Next I look at the supplementary motor cortex. Finally, I discuss the parietal association area.

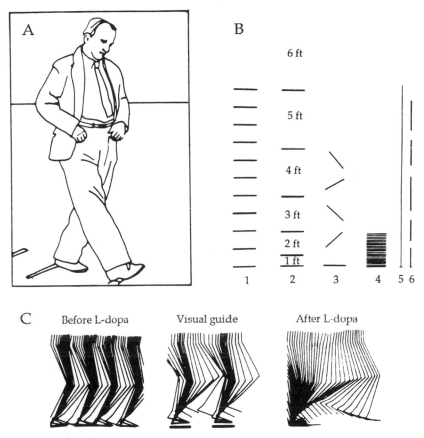

Figure 2.16 Walking in Parkinson's patients can be improved with visual cues for stepping. (A) Parkinson's patient walking on a floor with stripes. (B) Positions of stripes that are most helpful (1), somewhat helpful (2), and unhelpful (3–6). (C) Time-lapse diagrams of shuffling gait before medication, after medication, and with visual guidance but no medication. (From Brooks, 1986.)

The motor cortex was the first brain area in which evidence was obtained for localization of brain function. In the mid-nineteenth century the British neurologist, Hughlings Jackson, suggested that there might be an orderly representation within the brain of muscle groups from different parts of the body. Jackson arrived at this conclusion by watching the gradual spread of focal epileptic seizure activity from one part of the body to the other. He hypothesized that during an epileptic attack, one brain site after the other falls prey to an electric "storm." By observing the orderly spread of epileptic activity, Jackson reasoned that distinct areas of the brain control the musculature of distinct body parts and that adjacent body parts are represented in adjacent brain sites.

Jackson's inference was confirmed in 1870 by two German physiologists, Fritsch and Hitzig, working with dogs. They applied voltage to the area now known as the motor cortex and observed muscle twitches immediately after the electrical stimulation was delivered. The muscles that twitched depended on where the stimulating electrodes were placed. When an electrode was turned on in one spot, muscle activity occurred in the lower part of a leg; when an electrode was turned on in a nearby site, muscle activity occurred in the upper part of the same leg, and so forth. Based on these observations, Fritsch and Hitzig suggested that muscles are represented discretely and *topographically* within the brain. (A topographic representation is one that preserves the spatial organization of the objects being represented, even if the relative sizes of the objects are not preserved.) The conclusion of Fritsch and Hitzig therefore agreed with Jackson's conjecture.

It remained to be shown that electrical stimulation of the *human* brain would directly confirm Jackson's hypothesis. The critical test was provided by two Canadian neurosurgeons, Penfield and Rasmussen (1950). They treated severe epilepsy in the principal way available at their time—cutting nerve tracts within the brain to reduce the spread of seizure activity. Before lesioning a brain site, Penfield and Rasmussen determined whether the site was vital for cognitive and behavioral functions. To test an area that was a candidate for lesioning, Penfield and Rasmussen placed stimulating electrodes in that area and observed what happened when the electrode was turned on. Like Fritsch and Hitzig, they stimulated one area, observed any muscle response that occurred, then stimulated a neighboring region, observed the resulting muscle activity, and so on. By repeating this procedure, Penfield and Rasmussen developed a "motor map" of the body (see Figure 2.17). The map revealed that neighboring parts of the musculature are controlled by neighboring sites in the motor cortex and that some body regions are more amply represented than others. The fingers and lips, for example, take up a larger portion of motor cortex than do the thighs or torso. Presumably, the great precision with which the mouth and hands can move is attributable to the larger amount of motor cortex dedicated to the oral and manual regions.

Elicitation of muscle twitches by stimulation of the motor cortex is what one might expect from a center that activates muscles but is not involved in higher-level aspects of motor preparation, such as organizing complex programs for extended movement sequences. If the motor cortex were a site for high-level motor programming, stimulation of the motor cortex would be expected to result in complex movement patterns. A way to test this hypothesis is to determine when the motor cortex becomes active relative to the onset of movement. If the motor cortex becomes active immediately before movement occurs, but other areas become active significantly earlier, this would support the idea that the motor cortex is a *trigger* center rather than a *planning* center for movement.

Recordings of the electrical activity of the brain from the scalp bear out the trigger interpretation. Deecke, Scheid, and Kornhuber (1969) recorded brain potentials from people asked to move the right index finger at will. By recording when various brain areas became active before the

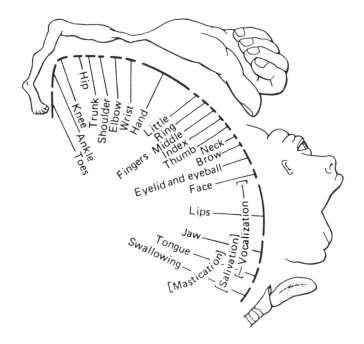

Figure 2.17 The motor map of Penfield and Rasmussen (1950). Reprinted by permission of the publisher from Voluntary movement by C. Ghez, in *Principles of neural science* (2d ed.), pp. 487–501. Copyright © 1985 by Elsevier Science Publishing Co., Inc.

movement, Deecke *et al.* found that there was a reliable increase of electrical activity in the motor cortex about 50 msec before the first sign of electrical activity in the finger muscles. Earlier activity was recorded elsewhere. (Deecke *et al.* called the burst of electrical activity in the motor cortex the *motor potential*.) Insofar as 50 msec is a very short delay prior to EMG activity, the outcome supports the hypothesis that the motor cortex is one of the last sites in the brain to be active before movements begin.

Why, from a neuroanatomical perspective, are such short delays observed between motor-cortex activity and EMG activity? In primates, many neurons of the motor cortex make monosynaptic connections with spinal motor neurons, especially motor neurons of the finger muscles (Phillips & Porter, 1977). Such connections presumably allow for the precision of hand and finger movements. Some motor-cortex neurons also synapse onto only one motor unit (Asanuma, 1981), suggesting that at least some motor-cortex neurons control individual muscles rather than entire movements (Evarts, 1967).

Force and Direction Control

Although the motor cortex is primarily related to muscle activity rather than to more global aspects of movement, it has been possible to relate motor-cortex activity to two features of movement, *force* and *direction*. In a classic series of studies on force and direction control, Evarts and his colleagues (see Evarts, 1981) showed that neurons of the motor cortex discharge selectively depending on the direction and force of forthcoming movements. In one experiment, monkeys turned a handle back and forth, and a weight attached to the handle assisted or resisted one of the directions of movement. Recordings of individual neurons in the motor cortex showed that the cells' discharge frequency increased with the force required to turn the handle. If flexion was *assisted* by the weight (so low force was required), the discharge frequency was low, but if flexion was *resisted* by the weight (so high force was required), the discharge frequency was high. The cells began to discharge before movement-related EMGs were observed, indicating that the cells were involved in some aspect of the preparation or triggering of movement. Moreover, the cells' activity depended on whether the forthcoming movement required flexion or extension, suggesting that the cells were tuned to movement direction.

A recent series of experiments has shed more light on the control of direction by the motor cortex (Georgopoulos, Schwartz, & Kettner, 1986; Georgopoulos, Lurito, Petrides, Schwartz, & Massey, 1989; Georgopoulos, 1990). In these experiments, monkeys made manual movements to each of a number of targets spaced around a starting point (see Figure 2.18). Discharge rates of individual neurons were found to depend on the direction of movement, but none of the neurons fired uniquely to a *particular* direction. Thus one motor-cortex neuron fired the most when the monkey's paw moved in the 45° direction, less in the 35° or 55° direction, and still less in the 25° or 65° direction. Another motor-cortex neuron fired most when the monkey's paw moved in the 55° direction, less in the 45° or 65° direction, still less in the 35° or 75° direction, and so on. Every direction studied was found to have a cell that fired most vigorously to it. Interestingly, none of the cells responded differentially according to the *amplitude* of movement. This outcome supports the view that direction and amplitude are separable components of motor control (Rosenbaum, 1980; Soechting & Terzuolo, 1990).

Given that none of the cells studied by Georgopoulos *et al.* (1986) uniquely coded a particular direction, how could movements be made in specific directions? The answer, according to Georgopoulos *et al.* (1986), is embodied in the *population coding* hypothesis. According to this hypothesis (as applied to the control of movement direction), the direction in which a limb is commanded to move represents a weighted sum of the directions signaled by the population of cells in the motor cortex. The commanded direction of movement is the direction with the largest weighted sum.

This computational scheme is surprisingly powerful and may be used in other brain systems as well—for example, in systems underlying visual perception (Erickson, 1984). An advantage of population coding is that it leaves the behaving organism relatively untarnished by localized brain damage. Suppose a cell in the motor cortex responds with strength

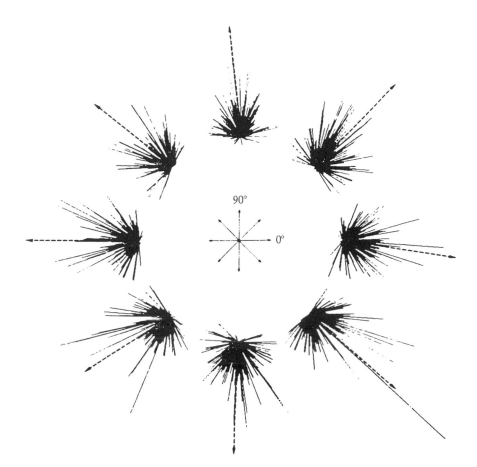

Figure 2.18 Population coding in the motor cortex. The "sunburst" at each of the eight positions displays the amount of activity of over 200 neurons when a monkey made a movement toward a target at a radial position corresponding to the radial position of the sunburst (for example, toward 4 o'clock in the case of the sunburst at the 4 o'clock position). The length of each sunburst line corresponds to the amount of activity from one neuron. The arrow extending from each sunburst indicates the population vector of the entire ensemble. (From Georgopoulos, Caminiti, Kalaska, & Massey, 1983.)

100 (arbitrary units) when receiving a signal calling for a movement in that cell's preferred direction, but it responds with one less unit of strength for each degree of angular departure from that preferred direction. Thus a cell might respond with strength 100 for a 90° movement, 99 for a 91° or 89° movement, 98 for a 92° or 88° movement, and so on. Another cell, specialized for an 80° movement, might respond with strength 100 to a signal calling for an 80° movement, 99 to a signal calling for a 79° or 81° movement, 98 to a signal calling for a 78° or 82° movement, and so on. Suppose a signal to the motor cortex calls for a movement of 85°. Each of the cells described above would respond with strength 95, yielding a net output of 95 + 95 =

190. If another direction were called for, say 90° rather than 85°, the cell specialized for 90° would respond with strength 100 and the cell specialized for 80° would respond with strength 90, so the net output would again be 190. Thus the same strength of output would be possible for the 85° movement and the 90° movement, even though the 85° direction had no specialized cell. There is some price for having missing cells, however. Directional accuracy is compromised when cells are missing (Sahrmann & Norton, 1977).

One of the most exciting possibilities afforded by the population coding hypothesis is that, by recording from many neurons of the motor cortex simultaneously, it is possible to determine where, at any moment, the population vector "points." The direction implied by the summed activity of motor-cortex neurons can be estimated at successive times to find out how the implied direction changes. Georgopoulos *et al.* (1989) exploited this possibility in an ingenious experiment where a monkey learned that if a light appeared at a point along the perimeter of a circle, the movement that would have to be performed (to obtain a sip of fruit juice) would be directed to a point 90° counterclockwise from the original stimulus. Remarkably, the direction of the neuronal population vector shifted steadily from the original stimulus location to the final target location. It was as if the monkey performed a "mental rotation" (Shepard & Metzler, 1971).

Long-Loop Reflexes

The motor cortex not only plays a role in triggering movements. It also gets feedback from the movements it helps trigger. Neurons of the motor cortex receive sensory feedback from the muscle fibers they innervate (Asanuma, 1981). This allows for tight coupling between efferent and afferent functions.

Some of the earliest evidence for such coupling came from an experiment in which people were asked either to resist or not resist a tug on the wrist (Hammond, 1956). Depending on the instruction, the EMG response was either large or small. However, the instructionally influenced component of the EMG came *after* another EMG response, which was essentially unaffected by instruction. The early response was likely to be based entirely on spinal circuits, in view of how quickly it occurred. By contrast, the delayed response was likely to have been mediated by pathways between the spinal cord and the motor cortex, given that it occurred much later. Consistent with the latter hypothesis, the delayed response was seldom seen in patients with lesions in spinal pathways that allow sensory signals to be relayed from the muscles to the cerebral cortex (Marsden, Merton, & Morton, 1973). In addition, neural firing rates in the motor cortex have been found to increase immediately after external loads are imposed on cortically driven muscles (Cheney & Fetz, 1984).

A feedback loop involving the motor cortex has functional utility. With such a "long-loop reflex," the responsiveness of cortically driven muscles to external loads can be modulated by altering motor cortex excitability, depending on the actor's "set." A number of studies have supported the hypothesis that responsiveness within the motor cortex can be significantly affected by set or expectancy (Bonnet & Requin, 1982; Evarts & Tanji, 1976). In Evarts and Tanji's experiment, monkeys were trained either to resist or assist an externally imposed muscle stretch. If the movement was primarily achieved with the triceps, then when the triceps was stretched by the external load, there was an immediate increase in the firing rate of triceps-related motor-cortex neurons. The magnitude and latency of the response were approximately the same, regardless of the instructed response stretch. However, about 40 msec later, the same neurons discharged differently depending on the instructional context. Either the rate increased when the stretch was to be assisted (with increased triceps activity) or it decreased when the stretch was to be resisted (with increased biceps activity). The first response was automatic and was triggered by pathways running directly from the muscle spindles to the motor cortex. The second response was affected by the animal's volitional state. Because the second response as well as the first influenced the muscle response, the set effect, established in the motor cortex, had an overt functional effect.

■ PREMOTOR CORTEX

Whereas the motor cortex mainly projects to the distal musculature (especially the fingers), the area just anterior to the motor cortex, the *premotor cortex*, mainly projects to the proximal musculature. Efferent fibers from the premotor cortex primarily serve to innervate motor neurons of the trunk and shoulders (Wiesendanger, 1981). The premotor cortex receives inputs from the posterior parietal cortex, an area important for spatial orientation. These anatomical features suggest that the premotor cortex plays a role in orienting the body and readying the postural muscles for forthcoming movements.

Recordings from neurons in the premotor cortex corroborate this hypothesis. Weinrich and Wise (1982) recorded from premotor cortex cells in monkeys performing a task in which a warning light indicated the likely (but not guaranteed) direction of a forthcoming movement. During the interval between the warning signal and the go signal a number of cells in the premotor cortex fired vigorously, and they stopped firing after the go signal appeared. The cells may have helped establish the postural set for the forthcoming task, providing input to the postural muscles to allow those muscles to remain poised for the movement that would probably be required.

Another function of the premotor cortex is to help select movement trajectories. In monkeys, lesions of premotor cortex often result in an inability to redirect the paw around the back of a transparent object to reach a food reward. Even with visual feedback indicating that the object is in the way, monkeys with premotor cortex lesions do not recognize the possibility of guiding the paw through an alternative, indirect route (Wiesendanger, 1981).

■ SUPPLEMENTARY MOTOR CORTEX

Located just above and anterior to the motor cortex (in the standing human) is the supplementary motor cortex. This structure appears to be involved in the planning and production of complex sequences of movements (Wiesendanger, 1987). Monkeys with damage to the supplementary motor cortex have difficulty carrying out complex finger sequences and tasks requiring bimanual coordination, such as pushing a morsel of food from a hole and catching it with the other hand (Brinkman, 1984) (see Figure 2.19).

When electrical activity of the brain is monitored during periods preceding spontaneously generated movement, significant levels of activity can be detected over the supplementary motor area as long as 1 sec before movement begins (Deecke *et al.*, 1969). Assuming that centers responsible for high levels of control become activated long before the inception of movement, this outcome suggests that the supplementary motor cortex plays a role in planning rather than in triggering movements. (Recall that the motor cortex usually becomes active only 50 msec before movement.)

Another source of evidence for the planning role of the supplementary motor cortex comes from studies in which blood flow in the brain is monitored through the use of positron emission tomography (PET) scans. In this technique, volunteers are injected with radioactive xenon (dissolved in a saline solution) which is then carried through the bloodstream. The procedure is carried out for diagnostic purposes (for example, to determine the location of a suspected brain tumor). Areas of the brain that are metabolically active tend to draw more blood than areas that are less metabolically active. Therefore, the amount of blood flow in a given area, as indexed by the amount of radioactive xenon carried to it, reveals how active that brain region is.

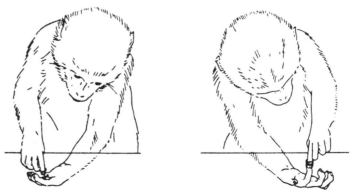

Normal animal   5 months after right SMA lesion

Figure 2.19 Unilateral lesion of the supplementary motor area disrupts cooperative behavior of the two hands, even when the monkey receives visual feedback. Normally the monkey can push a morsel of food out of the hole and catch it with the other hand, but not after the lesion. From C. Brinkman, Lesions in supplementary motor area interfere with a monkey's performance of a bimanual co-ordination task, *Neuroscience Letters*, **27**, 267–270. Copyright © by Williams and Wilkins, 1981.

Finger movement sequence (performance)

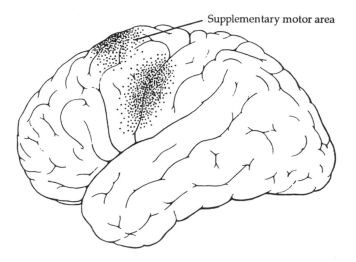

Finger movement sequence (mental rehearsal)

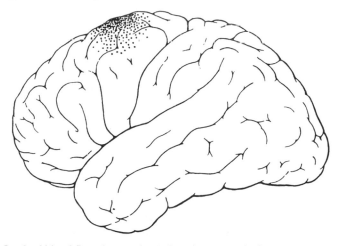

Figure 2.20 Cerebral blood flow during physical performance of a finger sequence (*top panel*) and during mental rehearsal of the same finger sequence (*bottom panel*). Reprinted by permission of the publisher from Voluntary movement by C. Ghez, in *Principles of neural science* (2d ed.), pp. 487–501. Copyright © 1985 by Elsevier Science Publishing Co., Inc.

PET scans show that the supplementary motor cortex as well as the motor cortex are highly active when people carry out sequences of finger movements (see Figure 2.20). When the finger sequences are only *imagined*, blood flow to the supplementary motor cortex remains high but blood flow to the motor cortex returns to normal levels (Roland, Larsen, Lassen, & Skinhoj, 1980). This remarkable finding confirms the hypothesis that the supplementary motor cortex is a site for high-level movement planning or the maintenance of already developed plans for movement sequences (Wiesendanger, 1987).

■ PARIETAL CORTEX

The three parts of the cerebral cortex that I have discussed so far—the motor cortex, the premotor cortex, and the supplementary motor cortex—occupy the frontal lobes. These are cerebral structures lying anterior to the Sylvian fissure (see Figure 2.2). The parietal cortex, the brain region considered in this section, lies posterior to the Sylvian fissure and anterior to the parietal–occipital sulcus (see Figure 2.2). Damage to the parietal cortex often results in deficits of spatial attention and an inability to perform activities requiring spatial facility, such as drawing diagrams or building three-dimensional block structures (Luria, 1973). Cells in this region respond selectively to signals presented at locations to which movements will be made. The same cells may be quiet when stimuli are presented at the same locations and no movements are made to them or when the same movements are made in an apparently purposeless way (Mountcastle, Lynch, Georgopoulos, Sakata, & Acuna, 1975). Thus the cells seem to code spatially relevant behavioral intentions.

Apraxia

Damage to the parietal cortex results in the syndrome *apraxia*. First identified in the early twentieth century by the neurologist Hugo Liepmann, apraxia is a "disturbance of motor behavior that cannot be attributed to muscular weakness, incoordination, or sensory loss, or to lack of attention or the incomprehensibility of directions to act" (Freeman, 1984, p. 30). Apraxic patients have difficulty carrying out tasks such as lighting a cigar, putting on a hat, or opening a lock with a key. Because they can carry out the individual components of these acts and can understand verbal instructions (as demonstrated through independent tests), the difficulties these patients experience stem from a breakdown in the retrieval of movement plans or the enactment of those plans once they are retrieved.

Liepmann identified two kinds of apraxia. One, *ideational* apraxia, is a breakdown in the ability to access the "ideas" or "memory representations" for motor acts. A patient with ideational apraxia cannot pantomime the use of an object when asked to do so but can manipulate the object successfully when it is physically present (Heilman & Roth, 1985). Such a patient cannot swing an imaginary hammer when asked to demonstrate hammering, but when given a hammer can handle it properly. Another symptom of ideational apraxia is the inability to sequence complex chains of acts. Preparing a cup of coffee or opening a can and emptying its contents may become impossible. The inability to sequence tasks correctly can have dire consequences. One ideationally apraxic patient almost lost her life when she misordered the tasks of turning on a gas stove, lighting a match, and blowing out the match (Miller, 1986).

Difficulties like these result from an inability to access *concepts* for sequencing, not just an inability to perform the sequences. That the difficulty is conceptual and not just motoric was demonstrated in a study in which ideational apraxics were asked to arrange photographs of related tasks in correct order. A representative task was ordering pictures of someone looking up a telephone number, picking up the receiver, and dialing the number. The patients could not perform this task correctly (Lehmkuhl & Poeck, 1981).

Another kind of apraxia identified by Liepmann is *ideomotor* apraxia. This form of apraxia represents a breakdown in the translation of memory representations into motor commands. The problem is not that the memories cannot be accessed, but rather that once they have been accessed they cannot be realized. A symptom of ideomotor apraxia is the inability to imitate what someone else is doing, though the patient can say (or otherwise indicate) what action he or she is supposed to perform (DeRenzi, Motti, & Nichelli, 1980).

Liepmann ventured a hypothesis about the neurological disconnections that give rise to apraxia. In arriving at the hypothesis, he was struck by the fact that apraxia was far more common in people with right-side hemiplegia (paralysis of the right side of the body) than in people with left-side hemiplegia (paralysis of the left side of the body). Because each side of the body is primarily controlled by the contralateral (opposite) hemisphere, Liepmann surmised that the left hemisphere houses the plans that cannot be accessed or realized in apraxia.

Liepmann had another insight as well. He saw that if the plans for movement are in the left hemisphere, and the left hand is activated by the right hemisphere, then the plans must somehow be passed from the left hemisphere to the right. He proposed that the *corpus callosum*, a pathway linking the left and right hemispheres, might be the conduit for this information. According to this model, instructions from the left hemisphere pass through the corpus callosum to the right hemisphere and from there to the right side of the body (Figure 2.21). Post-mortem examinations of apraxic patients have largely confirmed this hypothesis (Freeman, 1984; Heilman & Roth, 1985; Miller, 1986).

■ CONCLUDING REMARKS

Motor physiology is a dynamic field in which many breakthroughs have been made and will, in all likelihood, continue to be made. I have merely skimmed the surface of this exciting area of study and, to keep the major points in focus, have had to omit a great deal of material. More detailed reviews can be found in Brooks (1981, 1986), Jeannerod (1988), Kandel and Schwartz (1985), and Rothwell (1987), as well as other sources cited in the Reference section.

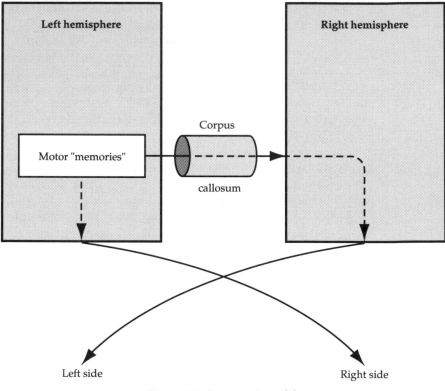

Figure 2.21 Liepmann's model.

Before ending the chapter, I wish to introduce some ideas that were not broached earlier and to reinforce some ideas that were only intimated. First, it is important to realize that any given motor act is made possible by the collective effects of many brain centers, acting simultaneously and sequentially. As indicated in the foregoing review, at different times relative to the production of a single motor act, different brain areas become active (Deecke *et al.*, 1969). Thus a motor act is the product of the orchestrated activity of many brain centers.

There is some redundancy in the roles served by different brain areas. Sometimes an area that reliably becomes active when a particular act is performed is not active when that act is performed in other contexts. For example, though the motor cortex projects to the arms, the arms can sometimes move when the motor cortex is silent. This point became apparent in a laboratory where a monkey was trained to make a controlled lever movement (Fetz, cited in Ghez, 1985). One day the monkey became agitated and banged the lever back and forth. In this emotional state, the monkey's motor cortex became *less* active than normal. This surprising result implies that the monkey's arm could be driven by structures other than the motor cortex.

Thus there are multiple routes to the production of arm movements. A multiplicity of paths exists for other movements as well. The notion of multiple paths for the production of a single motor act was recognized as long ago as 1906, when Sherrington, one of the first physiologists to study reflexes in detail (see Chapter 4), referred to the motor unit as the *final common pathway* (Sherrington, 1906).

The second general point about motor physiology is that the centers I have discussed are not the only ones involved in motor control. The centers considered here are often regarded as major centers for diverse aspects of motor function. Other centers also come into play, however, and virtually all areas of the brain, when stimulated strongly enough, give rise to some form of overt behavior. This means that a complete theory of motor physiology will probably amount to a complete theory of the brain. By the same token, studying the neural basis of motor control is likely to shed light on brain organization at large.

The final item to be discussed in this chapter concerns the source of intentions. Movements are made in response to perceptual input and intentional states. But where do intentional states come from? The question is a profound one; possibly it is unanswerable. Nonetheless, if any area of study can isolate the source of intentions, it may be the study of the physiological substrates of voluntary performance. Two studies provide an indication of the sort of answer that may emerge.

One study was an investigation that I have already discussed—the study by Deecke *et al.* (1969)—on the electrical activity of the human brain prior to voluntary movement. Recall that Deecke *et al.* (1969) found that, over the motor cortex, motor potentials occur 50 msec prior to the first sign of finger EMGs. However, as long as 1.5 sec before the same EMGs diffuse activity was recorded over virtually the entire cerebral cortex. As the time of finger movement approached, the recorded brain activity became more and more focused, concentrating ultimately in the motor cortex. The timing of the early brain activity (the *premovement* potential) gives a hint of when intentions arise—at least 1.5 sec before simple movements. As for *where* intentions arise, the topography of the premovement potential suggests that intentions originate out of the collective activity of many thousands or even millions of neurons, widely dispersed throughout the brain (or alternatively, from a single source that has not yet been found).

Another study yielded a similar result. Here people were asked to estimate when they first decided to produce a simple voluntary movement (Libet, Gleason, Wright, & Pearl, 1983). The time estimates that subjects gave were consistently late. They estimated the initial decision as occurring a half-second *after* premovement potentials were recorded from their own brains. A possible interpretation of this result is that people are poor at estimating when things happen inside their heads. But in a control condition, Libet *et al.* (1983) found that the same subjects accurately estimated when a sensory stimulus was presented. Apparently, people *can* accurately estimate times of brain events. They become aware of their own intentions only after a significant amount of neurological activity allows those intentions to coalesce.

■ SUMMARY

1. The central aim of motor physiology is to understand how the physical makeup of the nervous system and the musculoskeletal system allows for the adaptive control of posture and movement. Specialized mechanisms allow motor control to be carried out such that attention to the detailed properties of muscle activity is generally unnecessary.

2. Muscles contract when stimulated at neuromuscular junctions and stretch when subjected to mechanical loads.

3. The tension developed by muscle during active contraction is an inverted U-shaped function of muscle length. The shape of the function is due to the strength of actin–myosin bridges at different muscle lengths.

4. A motor neuron and the muscle fibers it innervates comprise a motor unit, the most basic element of motor control. It is impossible to contract voluntarily some, but not all, of the muscle fibers within a motor unit. With feedback, however, it is possible to activate a single motor unit. Motor units tend to be recruited in an orderly size-dependent fashion. Units containing small muscle fibers are generally activated before units containing large muscle fibers.

5. Muscle spindles are attached to the large muscle fibers (extrafusals) that produce adequate force to move a limb. Muscle spindles contain small fibers (intrafusals) that also contract. The sensory nerve fibers attached to muscle spindles respond to differences in the length of the muscle spindle and the length of the extrafusal. These sensory fibers serve as muscle stretch receptors. The signals they produce can be consciously perceived.

6. Sensory receptors in muscle tendons (Golgi tendon organs) tend to fire when muscle tension increases. The response properties of Golgi tendon organs are roughly opposite the response properties of muscle spindles: Golgi tendon organs fire when muscles contract, whereas stretch receptors fire when muscles lengthen.

7. Sensory receptors in the joints fire primarily at extreme joint angles. They may provide a warning signal about awkward or dangerous postures.

8. Sensory receptors in the skin (cutaneous receptors) are vital for precise manipulation, particularly when other forms of feedback, such as vision, are absent. They may also be important for balance.

9. Spinal circuits provide the neurological basis for perceptual–motor communication in the peripheral motor system. The simplest spinal circuit is the reflex arc. Here a muscle contracts immediately in response to its own stretch.

10. According to one theory (servo theory), it was hypothesized that extrafusals contract via a stretch reflex triggered by the earlier activation of intrafusals. The timing of muscle-spindle discharge and extrafusal activity suggests, however, that intrafusals and extrafusals generally become active simultaneously. Such coactivation permits rapid correction for unexpected loads when movements are in progress.

11. Motor neurons not only activate muscles. They also excite Renshaw cells, which in turn inhibit the motor neurons themselves. This seemingly paradoxical effect has functional advantages. It provides a way of modulating the amount of input sufficient to activate motor neurons, and it increases the resolution of motor neuron activation.

12. Reciprocal inhibition exists between stretch receptors from one muscle and motor neurons for opposing muscles. Reciprocal inhibition prevents muscles from working against each other during response to muscle stretch.

13. The cerebellum regulates muscle tone, coordination, timing, and learning. If the cerebellum is disconnected from the spinal cord, muscle tone is adversely affected. Coordination deficits following cerebellar damage take the form of poor balance (*ataxia*), slurred speech (*dysarthria*), reaching too far (*hypermetria*), and oscillation in conjunction with purposeful movements (*intention tremor*). The sequencing of repetitive movements becomes difficult and requires more attention than usual. Timing difficulties associated with cerebellar damage take the form of abnormal durations and phase relations of EMG patterns as well as abnormal variability of rhythmic tapping behavior. The cerebellum's role in learning is suggested by the inability of animals with cerebellar damage to adapt eye–head coordination after wearing reversing prisms, by changes in cerebellar activity related to the development of limb coordination, and by the need for the cerebellum in learning visuomotor anticipation.

14. The roles of the basal ganglia in motor control are suggested by behavioral consequences of basal ganglia disease. In Huntington's chorea, patients make wild, uncontrollable movements. In Parkinson's disease, patients exhibit shuffling gait, shaking motion at rest (*resting tremor*), slow movement initiation (*akinesia*), slow movement execution (*bradykinesia*), and muscle rigidity. The basal ganglia appear to play a role in initiating movements, modulating the global scale of movements, and regulating perceptual–motor interactions.

15. Localized electrical stimulation of the motor cortex elicits muscle twitches. The muscles that twitch depend on where the stimulation is applied. Varying the stimulation site allows investigators to develop "motor maps." These are organized topographically, with neighboring regions representing neighboring musculature.

16. Cells of the motor cortex generally fire just before movements are made, especially before manual movements. The discharge of motor-cortex cells is related to the force and direction of movement. Different cells are tuned to different directions of movement, but individual cells respond to a range of directions. Outputs of the entire population of motor-cortex neurons lead to particular commanded directions (population coding).

17. Motor-cortex neurons receive sensory feedback from the muscles they drive, allowing for cortically mediated responses to muscle stretch. Because these responses have relatively long latencies, they are called long-loop reflexes. The immediate responses of motor-cortex neurons to muscle stretch are independent of volitional state, but later responses are influenced by expectancies.

18. The premotor cortex is primarily involved in readying postural muscles for forthcoming movements. It also plays a role in selecting movement trajectories.

19. The supplementary motor cortex is involved in the planning of extended movement sequences. Regardless of whether a person performs a finger sequence or imagines it, the supplementary motor cortex "lights up" in positron emission tomography (PET) scans of the brain.

20. The parietal cortex contains cells whose discharge properties are related to the behavioral relevance of spatial locations. In general, this brain region is crucial for spatially directed behavior. Damage to the parietal cortex can result in apraxia, an inability to perform purposeful motor acts when one's perceptual, cognitive, and motor faculties are otherwise intact. The incidence of apraxic symptoms in the left and right hand suggests that the memory representations for learned movement sequences are generally stored in the left hemisphere. The right hand receives motor commands directly from the left hemisphere, whereas the left hand receives motor commands from the right hemisphere after the right hemisphere has received signals from the left hemisphere via the corpus callosum.

21. Every motor act is the product of the collective activity of many brain centers. The brain centers discussed in this chapter are only some that contribute to motor control.

22. The study of motor physiology may provide insight into the physical sources of intentions. Thus far a single origination point for volitions has not been identified.

■ REFERENCES

Albus, J. S. (1971). *Brains, behavior, and robotics*. Peterborough, NH: BYTE Books.

Amato, I. (1989). The finishing touch: Robots may lend a hand in the making of Steinway pianos. *Science News*, **135,** 108–109.

Asanuma, H. (1981). The pyramidal tract. In V. B. Brooks (Ed.), *Handbook of physiology* (Sec. 1, Vol. II, pp. 703–733). Bethesda, MD: American Physiological Society.

Baldissera, F., Hultborn, H., & Illert, M. (1981). Integration in spinal neuronal systems. In V. B. Brooks (Ed.), *Handbook of physiology* (Sec. 1, Vol. II, pp. 509–597). Baltimore: Williams & Wilkins.

Basmajian, J. V. (1974). *Muscles alive: Their functions revealed by electromyography* (3rd ed.). Baltimore: Williams & Wilkins.

Binder, M. D., Kroin, J. S., Moore, G. P., & Stuart, D. G. (1977). The response of Golgi tendon organs to single motor unit contractions. *Journal of Physiology, 271,* 337–349.

Bonnet, M., & Requin, J. (1982). Long loop and spinal reflexes in man during preparation for directional hand movements. *Journal of Neuroscience, 2,* 90–96.

Brady, M., Hollerbach, J. M., Johnson, T. L., Lozano-Perez, T., & Mason, M. T. (Eds.) (1986). *Robot motion: Planning and control.* Cambridge, MA: The MIT Press.

Brinkman, C. (1981). Lesions in supplementary motor area interfere with a monkey's performance of a bimanual co-ordination task. *Neuroscience Letters, 27,* 267–270.

Brinkman, C. (1984). Supplementary motor area of the monkey's cerebral cortex: Short- and long-term deficits after unilateral ablation and the effects of subsequent callosal section. *Journal of Neuroscience, 4,* 918–929.

Body, J. E. (1988). Personal health: For those at risk of developing Huntington's, an anguished decision on testing for the disorder. *The New York Times,* August 25, B17.

Brooks, V. B. (Ed.) (1981). *Handbook of physiology* (Sec. 1, Vol. II) Baltimore: Williams & Wilkins.

Brooks. V. B. (1986). *The neural basis of motor control.* New York: Oxford University Press.

Buchthal, F., & Schmalbruch, M. (1980). Motor unit of mammalian muscle. *Physiological Reviews, 60,* 90–142

Cheney, P. D., & Fetz, E. E. (1984). Corticomotoneuronal cells contribute to long-latency stretch reflexes in the rhesus monkey. *Journal of Physiology, 349,* 249–272.

Churchland, P. S. (1986). *Neurophilosophy.* Cambridge, MA: MIT Press.

Clark, F. J., & Burgess, P. R. (1975). Slowly adapting receptors in the cat knee joint: Can they signal joint angle? *Journal of Neurophysiology, 38,* 1448–1463.

Côté, L., & Crutcher, M. D. (1985). Motor functions of the basal ganglia and diseases of transmitter metabolism. In E. R. Kandel & J. H. Schwartz (Eds.), *Principles of neural science* (2d ed., pp. 523–535). New York: Elsevier.

Deecke, L., Scheid, P., & Kornhuber, H. H. (1969). Distribution of readiness potential, pre-motion positivity, and motor potential of the human cerebral cortex preceding voluntary finger movements. *Experimental Brain Research, 7,* 158–168.

DeRenzi, E., Motti, F., & Nichelli, P. (1980). Imitating gestures: A quantitative approach to ideomotor apraxia. *Archives of Neurology, 37,* 6–10.

Desmedt, J. E. (1981). *Motor unit types, recruitment and plasticity in health and disease (Progress in clinical neurophysiology,* Vol. 9). Basel: Karger.

Drachman, D. B. (1983). Myasthenia gravis: Immunobiology of a receptor disorder. *Trends in the Neurosciences, 6,* 446–451.

Eccles, J. (1977). Cerebellar function in the control of movement. In F. Rose (Ed.), *Physiological aspects of clinical neurology* (pp. 157–178). Oxford: Blackwell.

Enocka, R. M., & Stuart, D. G. (1984). Henneman's size principle: Current issues. *Trends in the Neurosciences, 7,* 226–227.

Erickson, R. P. (1984). On the neural bases of behavior. *American Scientist, 72,* 233–241.

Evarts, E. V. (1967). Representation of movement and muscles by pyramidal tract neurons of the precentral motor cortex. In M. D. Yahr & D. P. Purpura (Eds.), *Neurophysiological basis of normal and abnormal motor activities.* New York: Raven Press.

Evarts, E. V. (1981). Role of motor cortex in voluntary movements in primates. In V. B. Brooks (Ed.), *Handbook of physiology* (Sec. 1, Vol. II, pp. 1083–1120). Bethesda, MD: American Physiological Society.

Evarts, E., & Tanji, J. (1976). Reflex and intended responses in motor cortex pyramidal tract neurons of monkey. *Journal of Neurophysiology, 39,* 1069–1108.

Fackelmann, K. A. (1989). Drug slows Parkinson's progression. *Science News, 136* (6), 84.

Forssberg, H., Johnels, B., & Steg, G. (1984). Is parkinsonian gait caused by a regression to an immature walking pattern? *Advances in Neurology, 40,* 375–379.

Freeman, R. N. (1984). The apraxias, purposeful motor behavior, and left-hemisphere function. In W. Prinz & A. F. Sanders (Eds.), *Cognition and motor processes* (pp. 25–50). Berlin: Springer-Verlag.

Gelfan, S., & Carter, S. (1967). Muscle sense in man. *Experimental Neurology, 18,* 469–473.

Georgopoulos, A. P. (1990). Neurophysiology of reaching. In M. Jeannerod (Ed.), *Attention and performance XIII* (pp. 227–263). Hillsdale, NJ: Erlbaum.

Georgopoulos, A. P., Caminiti, R., Kalaska, J. F., & Massey, J. T. (1983). Spatial coding of movement direction by motor cortical populations. In J. T. Massion, J. Paillard, W. Schultz, & M. Wiesendanger (Eds.), Neural coding of motor performance. *Experimental Brain Research, Supplement 7,* 327–336.

Georgopoulos, A. P., Lurito, J. T., Petrides, M., Schwartz, A. B., & Massey, J. T. (1989). Mental rotation of the neuronal population vector. *Science, 243,* 234–236.

Georgopoulos, A. P., Schwartz, A. B., & Kettner, R. E. (1986). Neuronal population coding of movement direction. *Science, 233,* 1416–1419.

Ghez, C. (1985). Voluntary movement. In E. R. Kandel & J. H. Schwartz (Eds.), *Principles of neural science* (2d ed., pp. 487–501). New York: Elsevier.

Gilbert, P. F. C., & Thach, W. T. (1977). Purkinje cell activity during motor learning. *Brain Research, 128,* 309–328.

Gilman, S., Bloedel, J. R., & Lechtenberg, R. (1981). *Disorders of the cerebellum.* Philadelphia: Davis.

Goodwin, G. M., McCloskey, D. J., & Matthews, P. B. C. (1972). The contribution of muscle afferents to kinaesthesia shown by vibration-induced illusions of movement and by the effect of paralysing joint afferents. *Brain, 95,* 705–748.

Grigg, P. (1976). Responses of joint afferent neurons in cat medial articular nerve to active and passive movements of the knee. *Brain Research, 118,* 482–485.

Gunilla, R., Öberg, E., & Divac, I. (1981). Cognition and the control of movement. *Trends in Neuroscience, 4,* 122–124.

Hallett, M., Shahani, B. T. & Young, R. R. (1975a). EMG analysis of stereotyped voluntary movements in man. *Journal of Neurology, Neurosurgery, and Psychiatry, 38,* 1154–1162.

Hallett, M., Shahani, B. T. & Young, R. R. (1975b). EMG analysis of patients with cerebellar deficits. *Journal of Neurology, Neurosurgery, and Psychiatry, 38,* 1163–1169.

Hammond, P. H. (1956). The influences of prior instruction to the subject on an apparently involuntary neuro-muscular response. *Journal of Physiology, 132,* 17–18P.

Hasan, Z. (1986). Optimized movement trajectories and joint stiffness in unperturbed, inertially loaded movements. *Biological Cybernetics, 53,* 373–382.

Heilman, K. M. & Roth, L. J. (1985). Apraxia. In K. M. Heilman & E. Valenstein (Eds.), *Clinical neuropsychology* (2d ed., pp. 131–150). New York: Oxford.

Henneman, E., Somjen, G., & Carpenter, D. (1965). Excitability and inhibitability of motoneurons of different size. *Journal of Neurobiology, 28,* 599–620.

Holmes, G. (1939). The cerebellum of man. *Brain, 62,* 1–30.

Houk, J., & Henneman, E. (1967). Responses of Golgi tendon organs to active contractions of the soleus muscle of the cat. *Journal of Neurophysiology, 30,* 466–481.

Huxley, A. F. (1974). Review lecture: Muscular contraction. *Journal of Physiology, 243,* 1–43.

Iansek, R., & Porter, R. (1980). The moneky globus pallidus: Neuronal discharge properties in relation to movement. *Journal of Physiology (London), 301,* 439–455.

Ito, M. (1984). *The cerebellum and neural control.* New York: Raven Press.

Ivry, R. I., Keele, S. W., & Diener, H. C. (1988). Dissociation of the lateral and medial cerebellum in movement timing and movement execution. *Experimental Brain Research, 73,* 167–180.

Jankowska, E., & Lindstrom, S. (1971). Morphology of interneurones mediating Ia reciprocal inhibition of motoneurones in the spinal cord of the cat. *Journal of Physiology, 226,* 805–823.

Jeannerod, M. (1988). *The neural and behavioral organization of goal-directed movements.* Oxford: Oxford University Press.

Johansson, R. S., & Westling, G. (1988). Programmed and triggered actions to rapid load changes during precision grip. *Experimental Brain Research*, **271**, 1–15.

Kandel, E. R., & Schwartz, J. H. (Eds.) (1985). *Principles of neural science* (2d ed.). New York: Elsevier/North-Holland.

Lehmkuhl, G., & Poeck, K. (1981). A disturbance in the conceptual organization of actions in patients with ideational apraxia. *Cortex*, **17**, 153–158.

Lewin, R. (1988). Disappointing brain graft results. *Science*, **241**, 1407.

Libet, B., Gleason, C. A., Wright, E. W., & Pearl, D. K. (1983). Time of conscious intention to act in relation to onset of cerebral activity (Readiness-Potential). *Brain*, **106**, 623–642.

Llinas, R. (1981). Electrophysiology of the cerebellar networks. In V. B. Brooks (Ed.), *Handbook of physiology* (Sec. 1, Vol II, pp. 831–875.) Bethesda, MD: American Physiological Society.

Loeb, G. E. (1985). Motorneurone task groups: Coping with kinematic heterogeneity. *Journal of Experimental Biology*, **115**, 137–146.

Luria, A. R. (1973). *The working brain*. New York: Basic Books.

Manetto, C., & Lidsky, T. I. (1989). The effects of movements on caudate sensory responses. *Neuroscience Letters*, **96**, 295–299.

Marr, D. (1969). A theory of cerebellar cortex. *Journal of Physiology (London)*, **202**, 437–470.

Marsden, C. D. (1982). The mysterious functions of the basal ganglia: The Robert Warternberg Lecture. *Neurology*, **32**, 514–539.

Marsden, C. D., Merton, P. A., & Morton. H. B. (1973). Is the human stretch reflex cortical rather than spinal? *Lancet*, **1**, 759–761.

Marsden, C. D., Merton, P. A., & Morton, H. B. (1977). Disorders of movement in cerebellar disease in man. In F. C. Rose (Ed.), *Physiological aspects of clinical neurology*. Oxford: Blackwell.

Marsden, C. D., Obeso, J. A., & Rothwell, J. C. (1983). The function of the antagonist muscle during fast limb movements in man. *Journal of Physiology (London)*, **335**, 1–13.

Marsden, C. D., Rothwell, J. C., & Day, B. L. (1983). Long-latency automatic responses to muscle stretch in man: Origin and function. In J. E. Desmdt (Ed.), *Advances in Neurology*, **39**, 509–539.

Matthews, P. B. C. (1972). *Mammalian muscle receptors and their central actions*. London: Arnold.

Matthews, P. B. C., & Rushworth, G. (1958). The discharge from muscle spindles as an indicator of γ efferent paralysis by procaine. *Journal of Physiology*, **140**, 421–426.

Matthews, P. B. C., & Simmons, A. (1974). Sensations of finger movement elicited by pulling upon flexor tendons in man. *Journal of Physiology*, **239**, 27–28.

McCormick, D. A., & Thompson, R. F. (1984). Cerebellum: Essential involvement in the classically conditioned eyelid response. *Science*, **223**, 296–299.

McMahon, T. A. (1984). *Muscles, reflexes, and locomotion*. Princeton, NJ: Princeton University Press.

Merton, P. A. (1972). How we control the contraction of our muscles. *Scientific American*, **226** (5), 30–37.

Miller, N. (1986). *Dyspraxia and its management*. London: Croom Helm.

Mountcastle, V. B., Lynch, J. C., Georgopoulos, A., Sakata, H., & Acuna, C. (1975). Posterior parietal association cortex of the monkey: Command functions for operations within extrapersonal space. *Journal of Neurophysiology*, **38**, 871–908.

Needham, D. M. (1971). *Machina Carnia: The biochemistry of muscular contraction in its historical development*. Cambridge: Cambridge University Press.

Penfield, W., & Rasmussen, T. (1950). *The cerebral cortex of man: A clinical study of localization of function*. New York: MacMillen.

Phillips, C. G., & Porter, R. (1977). *Corticospinal neurones: Their role in movement*. London: Academic Press.

Pollack, G. H. (1983). The cross-bridge theory. *Physiological Reviews*, **63**, 1049–1130.

Pollack, L. J., & Davis, L. (1927). The influence of the cerebellum upon the reflex activities of the decerebrate animal. *Brain*, **50**, 277–312.

Robinson, D. A. (1976). Adaptive gain control of vestibulo-ocular reflex by the cerebellum. *Journal of Neurophysiology*, **39**, 954–969.

Roland, P. E., Larsen, B., Lassen, N. A., & Skinhoj, E. (1980). Supplementary motor area and other cortical areas in organization of voluntary movements in man. *Journal of Neurophysiology, 43,* 118–136.

Rosenbaum, D. A. (1980). Human movement initiation: Specification of arm, direction, and extent. *Journal of Experimental Psychology: General, 109,* 444–474.

Rothwell, J. C. (1987). *Control of human voluntary movement.* London: Croom-Helm.

Sasaki, K., Gemba, H., & Mizuno, N. (1982). Cortical field potentials preceding visually initiated hand movements and cerebellar actions in the monkey. *Experimental Brain Research, 46,* 29–36.

Sahrmann, S. A., & Norton, B. J. (1977). The relationship of voluntary movement to spasticity in the upper motor neuron syndrome. *Annals of Neurology, 2,* 460–465.

Schwartz, A., Ebner, T., & Bloedel, J. (1987). Responses of interposed and dentate neurons to perturbations of the locomotor cycle. *Experimental Brain Research, 67,* 323–338.

Shepard, R. N., & Metzler, J. (1971). Mental rotation of three-dimensional objects. *Science, 171,* 701–703.

Sherrington, C. S. (1906). *Integrative action of the nervous system.* New York: Scribner.

Skoglund, S. (1956). Anatomical and physiological studies of knee joint innervation in the cat. *Acta Physiologica Scandinavica, 36,* (Supplement 124), 1–101.

Soechting, J. F., & Terzuolo, C. A. (1990). Sensorimotor transformations and kinematics of arm movements in three-dimensional space. In M. Jeannerod (Ed.), *Attention and performance XIII* (pp. 479–494). Hillsdale, NJ: Erlbaum.

Vallbo, A. B. (1970). Slowly adapting muscle receptors in man. *Acta Physiologica Scandinavica, 78,* 315–333.

Weinrich, M., & Wise, S. (1982). Premotor cortex of the monkey. *Journal of Neuroscience, 2,* 1329–1345.

Wiesendanger, M. (1981). Organization of secondary motor areas of cerebral cortex. In V. B. Brooks (Ed.), *Handbook of physiology* (Sec. 1, Vol. II, pp. 1121–1147). Bethesda, MD: American Physiological Society.

Wiesendanger, M. (1987). Initiation of voluntary movements and the supplementary motor area. In H. Heuer & C. Fromm (Eds.), *Generation and modulation of aciton patterns* (pp. 3–13). Berlin: Springer-Verlag.

PSYCHOLOGICAL FOUNDATIONS

◼ INTRODUCTION

This chapter, in contrast to the last, presents a level of description somewhat removed from the physical basis of movement. The level of description is "psychological" in the sense that the structures and processes of interest are discussed without necessary reference to their physical realization. In physiology, by contrast, one is interested in functional relations among *physical* elements.

The chapter has three parts. The first is concerned with theories of serial order. Historically, the serial-order problem has been a focus of research for two main groups—psychologists working outside the field of motor control and researchers working on motor control not identified primarily as psychologists. This dual approach makes serial order an ideal starting point for the discussion.

The second part of the chapter is concerned with theories of skill learning. Again, this topic has been pursued by investigators both inside and outside the field of motor control. Diverse approaches have been taken to the skill-learning problem, and theorists have themselves become more and more adroit at explaining the facts of skill acquisition.

The third part of the chapter is concerned with topics related to the "information-processing" approach to performance. Some theoretical constructs from this framework have become controversial. Understanding the controversies provides useful background for the remaining chapters. It also gives a sense of the passion that many researchers have brought to bear in arguing for and against alternative approaches to motor control.

◼ THEORIES OF SERIAL ORDER

Much of the work in psychology that bears on motor control has been concerned with the serial-order problem. Recall from Chapter 1 that the essence of this problem is to discover how the elements of a movement sequence are chronologically sequenced. When one says "Happy birthday," for example, what is the nature of the memory representation that allows the sounds of this phrase to be arranged as they are? In this section, I review four historically important theories of serial order: response chaining, element-to-position associations, interelement inhibition, and hierarchies.

Response Chaining

The oldest proposed solution to the serial-order problem is that the feedback produced by a movement triggers the next movement in the sequence. This hypothesis was popularized by William James (1890), who suggested that as connections between feedback and responses become stronger in the course of practice, movement sequences can be produced more and more rapidly and smoothly.

It is difficult to introduce response-chaining theory without appearing to treat it as a straw man. So many arguments have been leveled against it that the amount of space devoted to its destruction usually exceeds the amount of space devoted to its introduction. Nevertheless, it is worth discussing the arguments against the theory because a considerable amount of work by experimental psychologists (and physiologists) has been incited by the theory. Moreover, a critical review of the arguments provides a potentially enlightening introduction to psychological argumentation.

One problem with response chaining concerns *timing*. Suppose it takes 100 msec to initiate a movement in response to feedback from the immediately preceding movement. Then if movements can be produced faster than once every 100 msec, response-chaining theory can be rejected. This argument was presented in a famous article on the serial-order problem by the American physiologist Karl Lashley (1951). The article is worth reading today because of its historical importance as a manifesto for cognitive psychology. Lashley argued that the high speed of many movement sequences rules out response chaining. For example, pianists produce arpeggios so quickly that one cannot take seriously the proposition that each keystroke is produced in response to feedback from the keystroke before it.

There is a difficulty with this argument, however: it is hard to know how long it takes to respond to feedback. Suppose it takes 80 msec rather than 100 msec. Then if responses can be produced at a rate of once every 80 msec, response-chaining theory need not be rejected. No matter how quickly responses can be produced, a proponent of chaining theory might argue that feedback works more quickly than was previously suspected (see Adams, 1976, for an example of this kind of argument).

Another difficulty with Lashley's (1951) timing argument is that one can imagine that a movement may not be produced in response to feedback from the *immediately* preceding movement but rather in response to feedback from an earlier movement. Even if the delay between movement $n - 1$ and movement n is too short, movement n might be produced in response to movement $n - 2$ or $n - 3$. Thus the argument against response-chaining theory based on high response rates need not be devastating to the theory, provided one allows that the links in the response chain pass over immediately adjacent responses.

Another challenge to response-chaining theory pertains to a logical problem. Suppose that instead of saying "Happy birthday," one says "Happy birth*right*." According to response-chaining theory, when one says "birth," the next syllable should be uniquely triggered. However, the same utterance can be followed by different outputs, as this example shows. The capacity to follow one response with different ones is problematic for response-chaining.

A counterargument can be proposed, however. There might be subtle differences in the first syllable of "birthday" and "birthright." The difference might be great enough to trigger "day" or "right" selectively. If one's measure were sensitive enough, then one would be able to identify these differences; not being able to find them doesn't mean they don't exist. This is a weak counterargument because it can never be rejected with data. Still, it is logically admissible and therefore relevant to the evaluation of the theory.

Let us therefore try another argument against response-chaining. The argument concerns the effects of interrupting feedback. If feedback is artificially eliminated, then according to chaining theory, it should be impossible to carry out well-ordered sequences of movement. A number of studies have shown, however, that movement sequences can be performed reasonably well even if sensory feedback is interrupted. For example, Lashley (1917) found that a man with damage to the sensory nerves leading from his legs (caused by a gunshot wound) was still able to make voluntary leg movements. (Other examples will be presented in Chapter 4.) Results like these appear devastating to response-chaining theory.

But are they? The problem with the feedback-interruption studies is that they rule out a particular version of response-chaining theory—a version which assumes that *peripheral* feedback provides the necessary trigger for forthcoming movements. If one does not interpret the theory this way, then the ability to move when feedback is eliminated limits the *scope* of the theory but not its basic assumptions (Adams, 1984). Chaining theory can be viewed more abstractly as simply implying a series of "forward associations": Response n triggers response $n + 1$, which triggers response $n + 2$, and so on. Each trigger is made possible by an associative link. The physical basis of the link need not be specified. (Remember that psychological theories need not make commitments about physical implementation.) If the theory is viewed in these abstract terms (or if the forward associations are assumed to occur entirely within the central nervous system), then the fact that movements can be carried out without peripheral feedback is not devastating.

An abstract chaining theory was once proposed for the serial ordering of speech (Wickelgren, 1969). It held that a word like *pin* is represented by elements with information about each of its linguistically distinct sound elements, or *phonemes* (see Chapter 8). According to the theory, *pin* is represented as $\{_{\#}p_i, _pi_n, _in_\#\}$, where the subscripts denote preceding and following elements and $_\#$ denotes a word boundary. The ordering of phonemes for production is given by the subscripts. Thus once $_{\#}p_i$ has been activated, the next element to be called for is $_pi_n$, because its core element, i, is designated by the right-hand subscript of $_{\#}p_i$. Furthermore, the left-hand subscript of $_pi_n$ indicates that p is the preceding phoneme.

The chief problem with this theory is the logical one raised earlier. Why wouldn't *pin* be replaced by *pit*, for example? The string for *pit*, $\{_{\#}p_i, _pi_t, _it_\#\}$, has the same initial element as the string for *pin*. Activating $_{\#}p_i$, therefore, does not uniquely specify the following element. A second problem is that there are rules for pronunciation which generalize beyond familiar utterances. When children are presented with a picture of a novel creature with an unfamiliar name (a "wug") and are asked to say what they see when presented with a picture of two such creatures, they say "wugs," pronouncing the final "s" as a "z" rather than as a hard "s" in accord with English phonology (Berko, 1958). How can children produce phonologically lawful utterances for words they have never heard? According to chaining theory, or the version of it proposed by Wickelgren (1969), a distinct string for "wugs" would be needed. Where this string comes from would be mysterious. More worrisome, distinct strings would be needed for every possible utterance, which would surely tax the storage capacity of human memory (MacNeilage, 1970).

A way around this problem, as intimated earlier, is to posit *rules* for speaking or other kinds of behavior. It has been shown, in fact, that rule-governed behavior is not limited to language production; it is displayed by people in nonlinguistic contexts and by animals. In one demonstration of rule-governed behavior in animals (Hulse, 1978), rats were trained on a maze-running task where, in successive experimental trials, they received more and more reinforcement or less and less reinforcement, no matter how well or how poorly they performed. In blocks of trials where more reinforcement was given, running speed increased, but in blocks of trials where less reinforcement was given, running speed decreased. When the rats were transferred to a new maze, similar either to the one in which reinforcement grew more generous or similar to the one in which reinforcement grew less generous, running times were faster or slower, respectively. Thus the rats seemed to induce a *rule*. Similar results with other species (and with rats in other experimental contexts) support the conclusion that animals pick up lawful relations among events, even if the relations are not realized physically in the environment (Hulse, Fowler, & Honig, 1978). This capacity for apprehending rules and behaving according to them is difficult to accommodate with chaining theory—so hard in fact that no one has been able to resurrect chaining theory in the face of it. For this reason, even the most ardent defenders of response-chaining theory have come to admit that "response chaining ... is dead" (Adams, 1984, p. 20).

Element-to-Position Associations

Other theories of serial order have done only marginally better than response-chaining theory. It is worth mentioning these other theories to provide a sense of the range of theories that have been proposed. Also, it happens that one of the theories has recently been incorporated into a modern (and quite impressive) theory of typewriting performance (Rumelhart & Norman, 1982) (see Chapter 8).

One of these theories holds that serial order is represented by associations between response elements and serial-position tags. "Happy birthday," for example, might be represented by a link between /ha/ and 1, a link between /pi/ and 2, and so forth. The theory can account for the fact that when people try to recall previously learned lists of words, they accidentally substitute words from similar list positions. For example, when trying to recall the second word from one list, they may substitute the second word from another list (Fuchs & Melton, 1974). The phenomenon is easy to account for with element-to-position associations: The correct position association is activated, but not the correct element.

An appealing feature of element-to-position theory is that it can be generalized to include *time* tags. Suppose one wants to play three notes on the piano, but with different rhythms. The timing as well as the serial ordering of notes can be defined by associating the notes with tags for different times (Rosenbaum, 1985). An $F^\sharp$ played as a half note followed by a G played as a quarter can be represented by associating $F^\sharp$ with Time 1 and G with Time 3 (arbitrary time units), but if $F^\sharp$ is to be played as a *quarter* note followed by G played as a quarter, then $F^\sharp$ can be associated with Time 1 and G can be associated with Time 2.

The problem with this theory is that, like chaining theory, it fails to account for rule-governed behavior. In addition, the question arises of how times or serial positions should be marked. What is "Time 1," for example? When one is born? Another problem is that it is unclear how to speed up or slow down rates of performance. Modulation of response rates seems to require a separate representation of serial order and timing, which is what this theory was designed to avoid.

Interelement Inhibition

Whereas element-to-position theory assumes that there are abstract elements (serial-position tags) to which response elements are associated, the next theory to be discussed holds that serial order is represented solely in terms of connections among the elements of the sequence itself (Estes, 1972). In this respect, the theory is like response-chaining theory. However, in contrast to response-chaining theory, it assumes that there are inhibitory as well as excitatory connections between elements.

The main ideas in this *interelement inhibition* theory are illustrated in Figure 3.1 for a sequence of four elements. Element 4 receives inhibitory connections from all the other elements. Element 3 receives inhibitory connections from only two other elements (1 and 2). Element 2 receives inhibitory input only from element 1. The labels are presented only for expository purposes; no labels are assumed in the theory. All the elements are activated simultaneously by a high-order element. The element that is produced first is the one with the least inhibition (Element 1). Once Element 1 has been produced, it no longer inhibits the other elements, leaving Element 2 as the element with the least inhibition, so it is produced next. Once Element 2 is produced, it stops inhibiting the remaining elements, allowing Element 3 to be produced next. Finally, Element 4 remains and it is the last element to be produced.

This theory has much to recommend it. By relying on inhibitory connections among elements, it does not beg the question of how serial position is represented (unlike the element-to-position model). Moreover, inhibitory connections are physiologically plausible. The utility of the theory has been demonstrated in a rather successful model of typewriting control (Rumelhart & Norman, 1982), discussed in some detail in Chapter 8.

Nevertheless, several concerns can be expressed about interelement inhibition (Rosenbaum, 1985). One is that it is unclear how a sequence can be initiated. When the elements of a sequence receive excitatory input, why don't all the elements fire at once? Inhibition must build up among the elements to ensure that they are produced in the order implied by their inhibitory connections. This means that some additional mechanism must delay simultaneous production of the elements until enough inhibition has built up.

A second concern is that the same elements are sometimes produced in different orders. It is possible to say "villain" and "anvil," for example, or "bad" and "dab." In the theory, to allow for reversals, one would

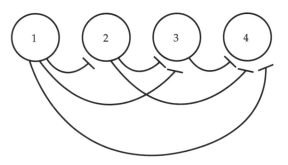

Figure 3.1 The interelement inhibition model of Estes (1972).

have to invert inhibitory connections between sequence elements. Thus inhibition from "d" to "b" in "dab" would be replaced with inhibition from "b" to "d" in "bad." But then some other mechanism would be needed to determine how the inhibitory connections should be set up. One would be left with the underlying questions of how the determination should be made, what mechanism should achieve the reordering, and so forth. A way around this problem is to allow for multiple representations of sequences containing the same elements. There would be a "dab" sequence apart from a "bad" sequence, for example. Since "dab" and "bad" mean different things, this might be tolerable. However, one would ultimately need as many representations of a phoneme as there are words containing it. Every word with a "b," for instance, would need its own inhibitory pattern. Thus the "b" representation would be replicated thousands or even millions of times, which seems uneconomical.

A final problem with the interelement inhibition theory is the one that bedevils the other theories as well: It cannot account easily for rule-based behavior.

Hierarchies

The final theory of serial order that I will review is the one that has fared the best. It assumes that elements of response sequences are organized hierarchically. The distinguishing feature of hierarchical organization, for present purposes, is the notion of distinct levels of control.

A company may be hierarchical in that there is a president at the highest level, vice presidents at a lower level, department heads at a still lower level, and so forth. When the president issues a command, it is interpreted by the vice presidents, who delegate authority to department heads, and so on. In some hierarchies the president issues commands directly to department heads or workers at lower levels. Likewise, feedback to someone at a given level may come only from individuals at the next lower level or, in a more freewheeling institution, from individuals one or more than one level down. In all such cases, the system can be considered hierarchical in the sense that it has distinct levels or tiers of control.

A considerable amount of evidence suggests that hierarchical models are useful for understanding motor control. In the context of the serial-order problem, a hierarchical model does much better than any other model I have discussed so far.

Consider the finding that has been most troublesome for the other models—the importance of rules. In hierarchical models, a rule can be viewed as a function applying to any of a large number of possible instances. The function can be assumed to occupy a high level in the hierarchy, and the sequences to which the rule applies can be assumed to occupy (or be represented at) lower levels.

To make this more concrete, consider the task of learning a sequence of numbers, such as 3, 2, 4, 3, 5, 4, 6, 5, and so on. This sequence is easy to learn, particularly if it is presented in chunks—[3,2], [4,3], [5,4], [6,5]. A simple set of rules describes this sequence: Start with an input number, $n = 3$, subtract 1 to get an output number, then repeat this procedure again, incrementing the last input number by 1 each time the procedure is repeated. Note that the description refers to a repeated procedure. In models of sequence learning, such procedures have been represented hierarchically (for example, with tree diagrams). It has been found that when sequences are easy to describe hierarchically they are easy to learn, but when they are hard to describe hierarchically they are harder to learn (Jones, 1981; Restle, 1970; Simon, 1972).

A corollary of this finding is that when people are asked to recall previously learned material, their recall indicates that they use hierarchical codes. Consider the following list of letters: FB, ICI, AKG, BTW, A. This list is hard to learn. But if the boundaries between the letters are shifted, the list suddenly becomes much easier to learn: FBI, CIA, KGB, TWA (Bower, Clark, Lesgold, & Winzenz, 1969). In the second segmentation, the sequences are familiar. In terms of a hierarchical model, each sequence makes contact with an already-learned high-level unit (a familiar three-letter sequence). The availability of these already-learned units facilitates learning the new sequence.

A study of chess players supports this interpretation. Expert and novice chess players were shown displays of chess pieces. Later they were asked to recall the positions. When the pieces were organized randomly, there was no difference between the recall levels of the experts and those of the novices, but when the pieces were organized sensibly, as in a game, the experts recalled the positions better than the novices (deGroot, 1965). Apparently, the experts benefited from exposure to previously learned configurations. The experts had in memory hierarchically structured representations of chess-piece configurations. When they recalled the chess configurations by placing pieces on the board, pieces belonging to meaningful groups were usually set down in rapid succession. After a meaningful configuration was completed, there was often a long delay until the next configuration began (Chase & Simon, 1972). These results are consistent with a hierarchical model. They suggest that information is accessed or "unpacked" in groups or "chunks" (Miller, 1956). Similar timing effects have been observed in studies of rapid motor performance (see Chapter 8), suggesting that access to hierarchically organized information applies to motor control as well as to more "symbolic" behaviors.

■ SKILL ACQUISITION

In the preceding section I discussed the memory representations underlying the serial ordering of behavior. In this section, I turn to the question of how movement sequences are learned. Before beginning the section, I wish to emphasize that the treatment will be brief, owing to my primary interest in motor *control*. Learning cannot be ignored in the study of motor control, of course, because what is learned must be suited to the kinds of movements that can be made, and the movements that can be made are largely determined by what can be learned. Trying to provide a comprehensive treatment of motor learning would result in a section as long as one of the volumes already written on this important topic (Holding, 1989; Magill, 1989; Schmidt, 1988).

Closed-Loop Theory

Adams (1971) proposed that motor learning proceeds through the refinement of perceptual–motor feedback loops. Consider the task of reaching for a glass. According to Adams, when one has little experience with this task, a crude first movement is made toward the glass, perceptual feedback indicates that the movement was not effective, and then subsequent movements are performed to reduce the error between the perceived position of the hand and the perceived position of the glass. As practice continues, the perceptually defined reference condition for each hand position along the trajectory toward the glass becomes better suited to successful completion of glass grabbing. Adams called this perceptually defined reference condition the *perceptual trace*. He argued that learning reflects the development of more adaptive perceptual traces as well as more adaptive capacities for generating movements that reduce errors between perceptual traces and actual outcomes. Adams used the term *closed loop* to underscore this error-correction property. (Recall from Chapter 1 that closed-loop control relies on feedback-based correction.)

According to closed-loop theory, feedback should help people perform tasks more effectively. Feedback does, in general, aid skill acquisition. People learning new tasks who are explicitly told about their peformance usually do better than people not told how they have done. Such explicit, verbal feedback is called *knowledge of results* (KR). In one of the earliest demonstrations of KR, Thorndike (1927) showed that blindfolded subjects could learn to draw a line of fixed length if they were told "right" or "wrong" after each trial but not if they were told nothing (the no-KR condition). Closed-loop theory accounts for this rather unsurprising result by saying that subjects developed a well-formed perceptual trace in the KR condition but not in the no-KR condition.

Although closed-loop theory seems to provide a reasonable account of skill acquisition, it runs into problems. That it does so is not to undermine the importance of Adams' (1971) contribution, for had he not proposed closed-loop theory, many important findings in the field of motor learning, sought at first to test his theory, might not have been obtained.

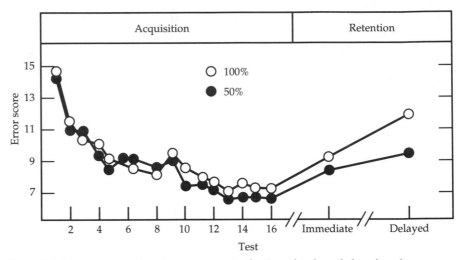

Figure 3.2 Average error in target movement reproduction when knowledge of results was given on 100 or 50% of the trials. Each data point corresponds to a 12-trial block. From Sensorimotor feedback by C. J. Winstein & R. A. Schmidt, in *Human skills* (2d ed.), pp. 17–47. Copyright © 1989. Reprinted by permission of John Wiley & Sons, Ltd.

One problem with closed-loop theory is that it ultimately reduces to a response-chaining theory. Each movement, or component of a movement, is assumed to be triggered by a perceived error. Yet many movement sequences can be performed effectively when feedback is removed. As will be seen in Chapter 4 (Walking) and Chapter 6 (Reaching and Grasping), complex movements can often be performed effectively without proprioceptive, visual, or other forms of feedback. This implies that not all movements are controlled as Adams assumed.

A second difficulty with closed-loop theory is that it applies almost uniquely to simple, unidimensional movements. In bringing one's hand toward a glass, for example, it is plausible that the distance between the hand and the glass is reduced over time through an error-correction strategy. But if the task is to say "Happy birthday," it stretches credulity to think that each utterance is initiated for the sake of correcting an error. Thus the scope of the theory is limited (Schmidt, 1988).

A third difficulty with closed-loop theory is that it predicts incorrectly that the more KR a learner receives, the more effectively he or she will perform. In fact, this is not always the case. Consider the data in Figure 3.2, which come from an experiment in which people were trained to reproduce target movements with the arm (Winstein, 1987; Winstein & Schmidt, 1989). For some subjects, KR was given on 100% of the trials, but for other subjects KR was given on every other trial (50% of the time). During training, the performance levels of the two groups did not differ and, in an immediate retention test in which KR was withheld, there was hardly any difference between the groups. However, in a delayed retention test, given a day later, the 50%

group did *better* than the 100% group. This surprising result constitutes disappointing KR for Adams (1971). Also disappointing for closed-loop theory is the fact that similar results have been obtained by others (Ho & Shea, 1978; Johnson, Wicks, & Ben-Sira, 1981, cited in Winstein & Schmidt, 1989).

Generalized Programs

A theory that does a better job of accounting for these results is that learners form *schemas* or *generalized programs* while acquiring new skills. A schema is a knowledge structure that can be instantiated in different ways depending on the values of its underlying variables or parameters. A generalized program is a schema for a procedure. Its parameters affect the specific form that the procedure takes.

An advantage of the schema or generalized-program view is that it provides a way of accounting for the endless variability and novelty of performance (Bartlett, 1932). It also provides a way of accounting for consistency in the movement patterns that are produced—for example, the consistency of a person's handwriting style (Glencross, 1980). In the theory, consistency derives from the use of the same generalized program in different circumstances. Variability derives from the modifiability of parameters within the same generalized program. The capacity for setting parameters in a generalized program reduces the number of distinct programs that must be held in memory (Schmidt, 1975, 1976). Instead of storing a memory for every possible sequence—an uneconomical approach, as suggested earlier—only a core set of programs needs to be maintained. Setting the parameters of the programs allow them to be tailored to the demands of the moment.

An experiment in my laboratory indicates how parameter setting might work (Rosenbaum, Inhoff, & Gordon, 1984). College students were asked to perform a finger-tapping sequence with the left or right hand, where the hand to be used was indicated by a visual signal (an X or an O) appearing on a computer screen. In one condition, the left- and right-hand sequences were mirror images. For example, the subject was required to tap, with either the left or the right hand, the index finger, then the middle finger, and then the middle finger again. The choice was between *imm* and *IMM*, where *i* denotes the left index finger, *m* denotes the left middle finger, *I* denotes the right index finger, and *M* denotes the right middle finger. In another condition, the two sequences were not mirror images of one another. The second tap was performed with the middle finger of one hand or with the index finger of the other hand. Thus the choice was *imm* versus *IIm* or, in another condition, *iim* versus *IMM*. The time to perform the first response in the required sequence (always an index-finger tap) was shorter when the sequences were mirror images than when they were not (see Table 3.1).

This result can be explained with a parameter-setting model. Suppose the choice between mirror-image sequences is achieved with a gen-

■ **Table 3.1** Mean Choice Reaction Times to Select Each of Two Types of Finger Sequence When the Other Possible Finger Sequence Was a Mirror Image or a Nonmirror Image of the Sequence to Be Performed[a, b]

Relation	Finger sequence	
	Index, index, middle	Index, middle, middle
Mirror	434 ± 15	441 ± 15
Nonmirror	492 + 10	491 + 7

[a]Times are in milliseconds, as are estimates of ±1 standard error of estimate of the mean.
[b]From Rosenbaum, Inhoff, and Gordon (1984).

well as a parameter corresponding to the left or right hand. A verbal statement of such a program might be:

1. Sequence = *Hand* (Index, Middle, Middle)
2. If the signal is X, then *Hand* = Left;
   if the signal is O, then *Hand* = Right.
3. Perform the sequence.

Statement 2 denotes the decision to be made to choose the right- or left-hand sequence. The decision cannot be made until the choice signal is identified.

If the choice is between two sequences that are not mirror images, an additional decision is required:

1. Sequence = *Hand* (Index, *Finger*, Middle)
2. If the signal is X, then *Hand* = Left and *Finger* = Middle;
   if the signal is O, then *Hand* = Right and *Finger* = Index.
3. Perform the sequence.

Note that in this instance, the value of a finger parameter as well as the value of a hand parameter must be specified. If specifying the extra parameter takes extra time, then choice times for mirror-image sequences should be shorter than choice times for non-mirror-image sequences, as was observed.

Other experiments support the conclusion that choices between movement sequences speed up when the sequences can be distinguished by a small number of parameters. Heuer (1982) showed that choosing between left- and right-hand movements is quicker if the movements have the same spatiotemporal form than if they have different spatiotemporal forms. These results, and others like them, are most easily explained in terms of parameter-setting models, some of which can be developed to a considerable level of detail (Rosenbaum, 1987a,b, 1990).

Besides making predictions about choice reaction times, generalized program theory also makes a rather surprising prediction about skill learning. It predicts that variable practice can lead to better transfer to new tasks than consistent practice (Schmidt, 1975). Consistent practice is practice on just one task. Variable practice is practice on a range of related tasks.

Suppose one practiced equally on Tasks 1, 2, 4, and 5, where the tasks vary along some continuum, such as the required duration of a lever movement. If Task 3 were tested for the first time, then according to generalized-program theory, it would be performed well because it is the average of the other tasks that were practiced. Suppose, on the other hand, that one practiced on Task 2 only. Performance on Task 3 would then be worse according to the theory because the task average was centered on 2 rather than 3. This prediction is surprising because more practice occurred close to 3 when only 2 was practiced than when the *range* of tasks was practiced. All practice was one step away from 3 in the consistent-practice condition (2 only), but only two out of four practice experiences were one step away from 3 in the variable-practice condition.

The data on the effects of consistent versus variable practice have, in several cases, upheld the prediction that variable practice should lead to better performance than consistent practice. [For reviews, see Johnson (1984), Newell (1985), and Schmidt (1988).] However, there have also been failures to support the prediction (van Rossum, 1990).

In one successful study (Carson & Wiegand, 1979), children either practiced throwing a bean bag of a *single* weight to a target or practiced throwing bean bags of *different* weight to the same target. Later, when the children threw a bean bag with a weight that had not been previously experienced, the group exposed to several bean bags did better than the group exposed to only one.

In another study, subjects were trained on a task in which a tennis ball had to be grabbed, then several barriers had to be knocked down with the hand, and then the ball had to be placed in a final location (Shea & Morgan, 1979). The goal was to minimize the time for the entire series of actions. One group of subjects (the *blocked* group) practiced the task with the barriers occupying a fixed set of locations within a block of trials. Another group of subjects (the *random* group) practiced the task with the barriers occupying a number of different locations within a block. As seen in Figure 3.3, during acquisition, the blocked group outperformed the random group, but in a later transfer test the random group outperformed the blocked group. This result is similar to the "bean-bag" results described earlier. Both studies suggest that exposure to a range of tasks leads to better long-term retention than exposure to only a single version of the task.

What caused the benefit of variable practice? One possibility is that subjects formed an "average" representation of the experiences they had and that the average was generally more stable when the instances were randomly presented than when they were not. Suppose one is supposed to learn the average of a series of numbers from 1 to 8. If the numbers are presented in random order (without replacement) such that the first eight numbers are 7, 2, 4, 6, 3, 8, 1, 5, the running average for this series is 7, 4.5, 4.3, 4.75, 4.4, 5.0, 4.43, 4.5. (A running average is simply the average of the numbers up to that

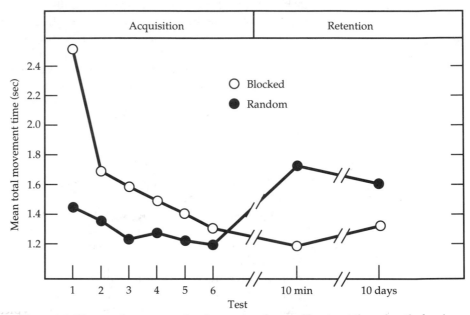

Figure 3.3 Mean total movement time for a series of manual barrier strikes when the barriers were either in a single set of locations in each block of acquisition trials (Blocked) or in varied locations (Random). From J. B. Shea & R. L. Morgan (1979). Contextual interference effects on acquisition, retention, and transfer of a motor skill. *Journal of Experimental Psychology: Human Learning and Memory,* **5,** 179–187. Copyright © 1979 by the American Psychological Association. Adapted with permission.

point.) By contrast, suppose the numbers are presented in blocked fashion, and only 1 and 8 are presented in the first eight positions: 1, 1, 1, 1, 8, 8, 8, 8. The running average for this series is 1, 1, 1, 1, 2.4, 3.33, 4.0, 4.5. Note that the running average ends up the same (4.5) in the two cases. However, the running average is less stable in the second (blocked) series than in the first (the random case). The greater stability of the running average for the random series could lead to its being better learned.

Hierarchical Learning

Schemas and generalized programs are intuitively attractive concepts, but they are hard to identify and their internal structure is difficult to probe. Hierarchical structures, on the other hand, are, by their very nature, structured in a clearly defined way. Furthermore, it is easy to image how a hierarchy might emerge in the course of skill acquisition. Low-level units could promote formation of higher-level units, which in turn could promote formation of still higher-level units.

The earliest proposal about hierarchical skill learning appeared in the late nineteenth century (Bryan & Harter, 1897). Curious about the training of telegraph operators, Bryan and Harter suggested that students of Morse code first put dots and dashes together to form letters, and then put letters together to form words. Early in practice, only dots and dashes are heard automatically, then letters are heard automatically, and then words are heard automatically. A similar course of development presumably also applies to the *sending* of Morse code (Leonard & Newman, 1964; Povel & Collard, 1982; Rosenbaum, Kenny, & Derr, 1983), although Bryan and Harter did not explicitly study this aspect of telegraphy.

It is possible to formalize Bryan and Harter's description to allow it to make quantitative predictions. Suppose one must be exposed to a sequence of events a minimal number of times to have it form a memory unit. Because there are 26 letters in the alphabet but more than 26 words, any given letter is likely to be experienced more often than any given word. It should therefore take longer to form word units than letter units. Furthermore, if having units in memory speeds up the processing of their constituent elements, then as more units are formed, and as units are formed at higher levels, the time needed to process the elements should decrease.

This line of reasoning, with more detailed assumptions, can be used to account for the change in performance speed that typically occurs with continued practice on a task. A representative curve is shown in Figure 3.4A which shows how the rate of rolling cigars in a factory changed over the course of years at the job. The time needed to roll cigars decreased and then appeared to level off (Crossman, 1959).

These data points can be fitted with a curve described by the equation

$$T = \frac{a}{P^b} \qquad (3.1)$$

where T denotes the time to complete the task, P denotes the number of practice trials, and a and b are empirical constants. This equation is sometimes called the *Power Law of Learning* (Newell & Rosenbloom, 1981), because P is raised to a power (b). Equation 3.1 can be converted to the equation for a straight line by converting to logarithms:

$$\log T = \log (a/P^b) = \log (aP^{-b}) = \log a - b(\log P) \qquad (3.2)$$

Because log a and b are constants, Eq. 3.2 describes a straight line, as shown in Figure 3.4B. The linear and curvilinear representations are mathematically equivalent. However, the straight-line representation helps one see that improvement never stops. Based on this derivation, one can say that an old dog *can* learn new tricks, or at least get faster on the tricks it has learned, provided it continues to practice.

Another way that hierarchical skill learning can be demonstrated is to show that people benefit from accessing high-level memory units during the course of practice (MacKay, 1982, 1987). An experiment by MacKay and Bowman (1969) illustrates this approach. Subjects fluent in both English and

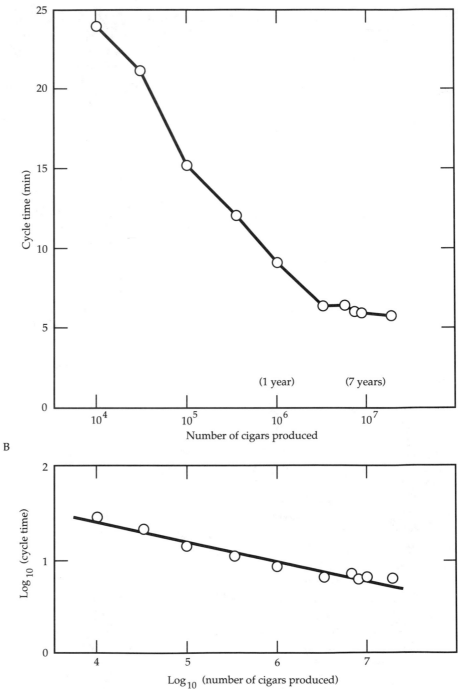

Figure 3.4 Time to roll cigars as a function of practice. (A) Cycle time versus number of cigars produced. (B) Same data plotted on log–log coordinates. (Adapted from Fitts & Posner, 1967.)

German recited a sentence in one language, attempting to say it more and more quickly with practice. Speaking rate increased as practice continued. The subjects then switched to a sentence in the other language. Recitation speed continued to improve, but only if the new sentence had the same meaning as the sentence recited before. If the new sentence had a different meaning, improvement was less rapid, regardless of whether the new sentence was in the same language as the first sentence or in a different language.

MacKay and Bowman (1969) explained this remarkable result by suggesting that learning proceeds much as Bryan and Harter (1897) assumed, through the formation of higher-level units. The highest-level unit for a sentence is its meaning. If subjects practice saying a sentence over and over again, a unit corresponding to the meaning of the sentence may be formed. Later, when subjects switch to another sentence, if the same meaning can be activated, the new sentence can be learned quickly because its meaning has already been acquired.

Mental Practice

If learning is hierarchical, it should be possible to improve on a task by practicing it mentally. The reason is that mental practice should help form or refresh high-level units activated when the task is later carried out. Partly to test this prediction, and partly because it may be useful for skill learning, mental practice has become a popular research topic. In general, mental practice has been found to be more effective than no practice, but less effective than physical practice (Feltz & Landers, 1983; Richardson, 1967a,b). A judicious mixture of mental and physical practice can significantly reduce the amount of physical practice needed to achieve a given level of performance, however (McBride & Rothstein, 1979).

MacKay (1981) directly tested the value of mental practice in his speeded-recitation task (see Figure 3.5). Besides asking subjects to recite sentences overtly, he also asked them to do so covertly. While beginning each covert recitation, subjects pressed a button, recited the sentence silently, and then pressed the button when the sentence was over. When the times between button presses were later compared with the times to say the same sentences aloud, they declined with practice in almost the same way. This is what would be expected if practice strengthened high-level units as well as low-level units. Had there been no high-level units (or if only low-level units could be strengthened by practice), practice on the covert task would not have led to the improvements that were observed.

Although the idea of mental practice is enticing to many, it is not palatable to everyone—especially those who feel that explaining behavioral data with mental states begs the question how the behavior came to be learned or controlled in the first place. Can MacKay's results be explained without appealing to mental practice?

Suppose MacKay's subjects made small, inaudible movements with

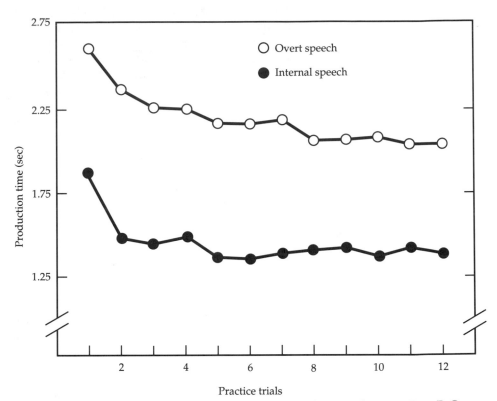

Figure 3.5 Time to produce sentences overtly or covertly as a function of practice. From D. G. MacKay (1982). The problem of flexibility, fluency, and speed-accuracy trade-off in skilled behavior. *Psychology Review,* **89,** 483–506. Copyright © 1982 by the American Psychological Association. Adapted with permission.

their mouths (subvocal movements). The improvements they showed could then be attributed to low-level effects rather than to learning at high levels of the skill hierarchy (if one exists). It has been found in fact that when people are asked to imagine making movements, significant electromyographic (EMG) activity occurs in the associated musculature (Hale, 1982; Jacobson, 1931).

MacKay (1981) did not measure articulatory EMGs, but it is doubtful that subvocal speech accounted for his results. As mentioned earlier, MacKay found that subjects exhibited perfect transfer from one language to another only if the meaning of the sentence was preserved; this is a high-level effect *par excellence*. Furthermore, one must be skeptical of "demand characteristics" in experiments where EMGs are recorded and subjects are asked to imagine making movements with the body parts to which electrodes are attached. To please the experimenter, the subject may purposely make small movements. Finally, other studies of mental practice have yielded results which do not support the view that muscle activity is essential for learning. Minas (1978) examined the effects of mental practice in a task where balls of different weight were to be thrown into a sequence of bins. Mental practice facilitated sequencing (getting the balls into the right bins at the right times) but not force modulation (propelling balls of different weight into the correct bins). If subjects had made subtle arm movements during the rehearsal period, they would have been able to control the forces of their throws as well as the sequencing. The fact that only sequencing benefited from mental practice suggests that mental practice was not just an artifact of muscular change. Recall too from Chapter 2 that during mental rehearsal of motor tasks, the supplementary motor cortex but not the motor cortex is active, while during overt performance the supplementary motor cortex *and* motor cortex are active (Roland, Larsen, Lassen, & Skinhoj, 1980). Thus the brain respects the difference between mental practice and physical practice, suggesting that brain *theorists* should as well.

Fitts' Stage Theory

When one learns a new skill, one has the sense of progressing through distinct stages. Paul Fitts (1964), a pioneer in the field of skilled performance, suggested that there are three principal stages of skill acquisition. Initially, during the *cognitive* stage, one learns the basic procedures to be followed, often using verbal cues. Talking to oneself is not uncommon at this early stage. A considerable amount of attention is also usually required during this early period.

The second stage represents a transition from reliance on verbal, conscious control to more automatic control. Fitts (1964) called this the *associative* phase. He chose this term because he believed that during this stage the learner tries out various task components and associates them with the success or failure that follows. Through this associative process, task components that contribute to success are preserved, whereas task components that contribute to failure are eliminated. Feedback about performance is especially important during this phase (Johnson, 1984).

In the third stage, the *autonomous* or *automatic* stage, behavior can be performed quickly and consistently with little conscious involvement. Performance at this stage is possible even when one engages in other tasks. Skilled typists, for example, can repeat what is said to them while typing (Shaffer, 1975) and, with enough training, college students can read intelligently while writing down and even categorizing other words presented to them at the same time (Spelke, Hirst, & Neisser, 1976).

Another important feature of automatization is that the performer shifts from continual to intermittent reliance on feedback. This shift was demonstrated in a tracking study (Pew, 1966). Subjects tried to keep a dot in the middle of a screen (see Figure 3.6). The dot moved unpredictably to the left or right. Subjects learned that pressing a left button caused the dot to move to the left, and pressing a right button caused the dot to move to the right. At first, subjects made one button press and waited to observe its effect, then made another button press, waited to observe its effect, and so on. Later,

EARLY PRACTICE

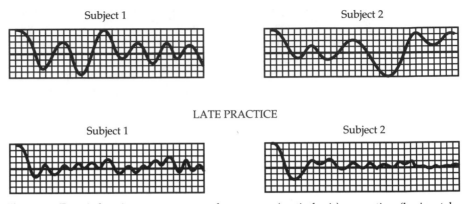

Figure 3.6 Error in keeping a cursor centered on a screen (vertical axis) versus time (horizontal axis) for two subjects, early and late in practice. From R. W. Pew (1966). Acquisition of hierarchical control over the temporal organization of a skill. *Journal of Experimental Psychology,* **71,** 764–771. Copyright © 1966 by the American Psychological Association. Reprinted with permission.

they produced rapid sequences of responses, with delays between button presses that were too short to allow for corrective responses to individual button presses. Evidently, subjects learned to anticipate the effects of their responses. As they did so, the dot stayed closer to the center of the screen for longer periods.

Physical Changes

So far in this discussion of skill learning, I have concentrated on theories that emphasize changes in memory representations and cognitive strategies for perceptual–motor coordination. The only measures I have discussed have been response speed and accuracy. Of course, performance also becomes more graceful and efficient with learning. Moreover, not all changes associated with skill development are cognitive or even neural. Figure 3.7 shows a tennis champion's two arms. The arm used for hitting the ball became larger than the other arm because of the stresses placed on the muscles and bones through years of play. (I assume the player's arms were not different before he started to play.) The illustration shows that adaptation to ongoing, repetitive movement demands can occur in muscle and bone.

Other skill-related changes can be attributed to improvements in muscle timing, tuning, and coordination. Figure 3.8 summarizes the results of a study of gymnastic performance in novice and skilled gymnasts (Kamon & Gormley, 1968). With practice, the movements of the gymnast become more refined, and the efficiency of muscle activity improved. Strong bursts of activity generally had shorter and shorter durations, and the number of times that a given muscle reached maximum levels of activity diminished. Findings such as these suggest that greater skill means greater efficiency.

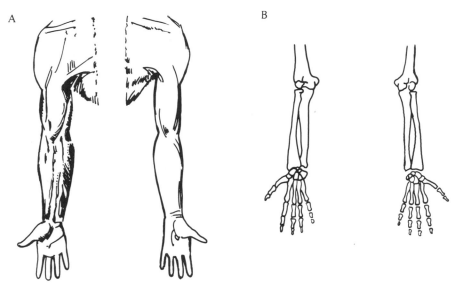

Figure 3.7 Right and left arms of a Davis Cup tennis champion. [Adapted from E. Jokl (1981). The human hand. *International Journal of Sport Psychology,* **12,** 140–148.]

Counterproductive or unnecessary movements tend to fall away (Sparrow, 1983; Sparrow & Irizarry-Lopez, 1987).

Besides varying the timing of muscle events, skill learners also alter patterns of interlimb coordination. Recall from Chapter 1 that one of the central problems for the motor system is the degrees-of-freedom problem—the problem of regulating the many degrees of freedom responsible for achieving a given task. Bernstein (1967) suggested that novice performers try to reduce the complexity of the problem by locking joints, and then, with experience, letting the joints move more freely. The transition that Bernstein (1967) predicted was observed by a team of Russian investigators (Arutyunyan, Gurfinkel, & Mirskii, 1968) analyzing the motion and stability of people learning to shoot hand-held pistols. They found that novice shooters first held their wrists and elbows rigid. Later, the shooters unlocked their wrists and elbows, and firing accuracy improved. Unlocking the wrist and elbow allowed the arm to compensate for motion in the hand, and vice versa. Thus variability in the position of the gun barrel was reduced even though *more* motion occurred in the arm and hand than before. A recent study of dart throwing has revealed a similar developmental trend (McDonald, van Emmerick, & Newell, 1989).

Thus far no cognitive model has been developed for freeing up degrees of freedom during skill development, and doubts have been expressed about how and whether such a model can ever be developed (Fowler & Turvey, 1978). My view is that there is no reason why such a model cannot emerge. An obvious possibility is to pursue a hierarchical model. One would assume that the limb segments are first controlled independently and then a higher-level control element is formed which enables

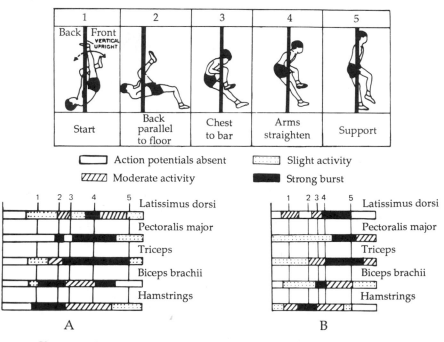

Figure 3.8 Changes in the amount and timing of muscle activity in novice gymnasts (A) and practiced gymnasts (B) while performing the five maneuvers shown in the top panel. Numbers in the bottom panels correspond to the five maneuvers. (From Kamon & Gormley, 1968.)

motion in one segment to be compensated for by motion in other segments. Fowler and Turvey proposed that *coordinative* structures serve this function. How and whether coordinative structures differ from hierarchical structures (in the broad sense in which I have used the latter term) is unclear. An advantage of pursuing a hierarchical model of limb coordination is that one might then have a model which applies to all of skilled behavior—not just to interlimb coordination.

■ STORAGE, ACCESS, AND CODES

Let us turn now from skill acquisition to the information-processing system that allows skilled performance to occur. I will not attempt to review the vast literature on the architecture of the human information-processing system, for much of it has been concerned with topics quite removed from motor control. Useful reviews can be found in Anderson (1985), Best (1986), Cowan (1988), and Stillings *et al.* (1987), among others. A theme emerging from these reviews is that the information-processing system can be conceptualized as having distinct subsystems for storing and coding information. A similar picture emerged from neurophysiology (Chapter 2), adding weight to the generalization.

Stored information occupies different memorial states. On the one hand, it may be permanent and not currently attended to (*long-term* memory). On the other hand, it may be the subject of current awareness (*working* memory). It may also be in a somewhat fragile state soon after assimilation by the perceptual system (*short-term* memory) or in an even more fragile state immediately after entry into the senses. The latter form of storage has been called *iconic* memory for visual information (Neisser, 1967) and *echoic* memory for auditory information (Darwin, Turvey, & Crowder, 1972). A tactile form of sensory storage has also been proposed (Bliss, Hewitt, Crane, Mansfield, & Townsend, 1966).

The memory states just referred to need not be equated with distinct storage compartments. It need not be the case, for example, that there is a separate "box" corresponding to working memory. Rather, the contents of working memory may simply be those parts of long-term memory that are most highly active. Likewise, the contents of iconic memory may simply be the parts of long-term memory most recently activated by visual inputs.

Most of the work that has led to these claims about the information-processing system has been concerned with information *intake* rather than information *output*. Research into the structure of the information-processing system has largely ignored motor function, motor control often being added as an afterthought (if at all) in many models. The reasons for this neglect are not entirely clear (see Whiting, 1989, and the Preface to this volume). Nevertheless, a major question for students of motor control is whether the sorts of models that have been proposed for information *intake* also apply to information *output*. This will be a central question in the discussion to follow.

Codes

Although stored information is ultimately represented in the form of neural activity, it is experienced in distinct *codes*. These representational formats are subjective memory qualities. They turn out to have important functional consequences for memory and performance.

A first demonstration of memory codes was the finding that people make different sorts of mistakes when recalling information to which they were exposed either a short or long time previously. Shortly after seeing letters, people tend to substitute letters that *look* like the letters they were shown, but later they substitute letters that *sound* like the letters (Conrad, 1965). This pattern of results suggests that the information is first represented in visual form and is then represented in acoustic form.

A great deal of research has been done on memory codes (Posner, 1978). Codes have been identified for most of the sensory modalities (see

Posner, 1978) and for more abstract features of space (Baddeley & Lieberman, 1980) and meaning (Kroll & Potter, 1984). Whether there are distinct *motor* codes is a question taken up later in the chapter.

Procedural and Declarative Knowledge

Perhaps the most fundamental distinction that has been drawn in the study of memory representations is between *procedural* and *declarative* knowledge (Squire, 1987). Insofar as motor control involves the physical enactment of procedures, it is worth considering this distinction in some detail. A way to do so is to review the case of a neurological patient known in the literature by his initials, H. M.

When H. M. was a young man he had severe epilepsy. To alleviate his seizures, he underwent a surgical procedure involving removal of the hippocampus, a structure in the forebrain. Soon after H. M.'s surgery, it became apparent that, as a result of the operation, he had suffered a significant memory impairment. H. M. could not learn new facts. For example, he could not learn new lists of words. When he was later asked to recall the lists or indicate whether he recognized them, his performance was no better than chance. H. M. was unable to recognize the people who visited him each day to test him on the word lists he had been taught. A convenient interpretation of H. M.'s difficulty was that he was unable to form new memories. According to this view, the regions of H. M.'s brain that were lesioned were the areas that allow for the transformation of information from a short-term, fragile state to a long-term, permanent state.

This interpretation came into question when it was found that H. M. could learn new perceptual–motor skills. For example, he could learn mirror tracing—a task in which one traces a complex path while viewing the path through a mirror. The task is hard at first, but with practice gets better. H. M. improved at the normal rate, yet each day when the task was presented to him, he denied ever having seen it before!

This strange phenomenon suggests that the human brain is organized in such a way that it stores different kinds of information in different ways (or perhaps in different locations). It is as if there is a distinction between "knowing how" and "knowing that," or what has been called *procedural* and *declarative* knowledge (Squire, 1987). Declarative knowledge consists of facts that can be stated verbally, such as propositions about persons, places, things, and events. An example is the proposition "Christopher Columbus discovered America in 1492." Procedural knowledge consists of instructions for the performance of series of operations. As often as not, procedural knowledge is difficult or even impossible to verbalize. An example is the knowledge one has for riding a bicycle.

The fact that information is coded in procedural form does not mean it can never be articulated. Otherwise, it would be a vain hope for researchers concerned with skill to think they could ever articulate the nature of skill knowledge. Physicists know, for example, that the rule for riding a bicycle is to turn the handlebars so the curvature of the bike's trajectory is proportional to the angle of its imbalance divided by the square of its speed (Polanyi, 1964). Most bicyclists do not know this proposition, stated as such. However, at some level, the information summarized in the proposition is embodied in the neural networks that allow cyclists to stay erect while cycling.

Long-Term Memory

Let us consider the parallels that have been observed between characteristics of the information-processing systems underlying motor production and characteristics of the information-processing systems underlying symbolic inputs. First consider long-term memory. Recall that long-term memory is the relatively permanent repository of previously learned material, where material can reside without being attended to. Although there is debate as to how much information can be held in long-term memory and over how long a period of time (Penfield & Roberts, 1959; Loftus & Loftus, 1980), there is no question that its capacity is vast.

One form of long-term memory that is said to be especially resistant to forgetting is motor-skill information. Once one learns how to ride a bicycle, one never forgets how to do so—at least according to popular lore. Surprisingly, there has been little research on the long-term retention of motor skills, though the studies that have been done accord with what is generally believed. In one study (Fleishman & Parker, 1962) it was reported that subjects who learned a three-dimensional tracking task retained their ability to perform the task, even over a 2-year period (see Figure 3.9). Whatever decrement there was upon returning to the task after 2 years was overcome within the first two trials!

The few other studies that have been reported on long-term retention of motor skills have been concerned with shorter lags between initial learning and later testing. Little or no skill loss has been observed in tasks to which subjects return after intervals of 21 days (Ryan, 1962), 12 weeks (Meyers, 1967), or 1 year (Ryan, 1965). A personal anecdote from an authority on skill learning and retention is also worth quoting:

> My father started me skiing when I was 4 years old, and I skied every winter until I was 15, whereupon I stopped completely for 14 years. When I returned after this retention interval ... it seems safe to say that I was skiing as well as I ever did, and that by the end of the day I was skiing better. [Schmidt, 1988, p. 500]

Short-Term or Working Memory

The retention of just-experienced movement information may be similar to the retention of just-experienced symbolic information. Posner (1967) investigated the codes used in short-term memory for movement. His subjects traced a straight line with one hand, moving from a home position to a final

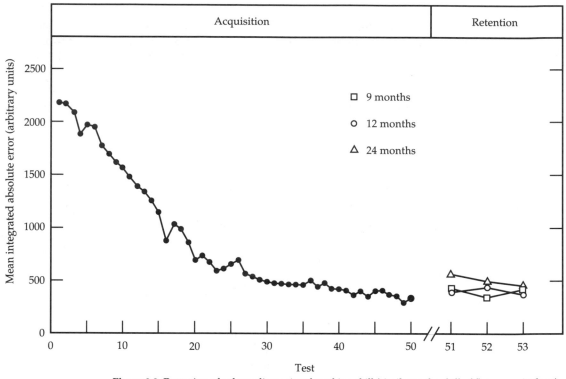

Figure 3.9 Retention of a three-dimensional tracking skill (similar to the skill of flying an airplane) 9 months, 12 months, or 24 months after a series of fifty 6-minute practice periods. From E. A. Fleischman & R. F. Parker, Jr. (1962). Factors in the retention and relearning of perceptual motor skill. *Journal of Experimental Psychology,* **64,** 215–226. Copyright © 1962 by the American Psychological Association. Adapted with permission.

target position. The movement was performed with or without visual feedback; in both conditions kinesthetic feedback was available. After the movement was completed, subjects tried to reproduce the movement either immediately or after a delay. Two delay conditions of equal duration were used. In one, subjects had no specific instructions (an "unfilled interval"). In the other, subjects classified numbers (a "filled interval"). Posner found that when visual feedback was not available, accuracy of reproduction was worse following the filled interval than following the unfilled interval; reproduction was best when there was no delay prior to testing. When visual feedback was available, accuracy of reproduction was as good following unfilled intervals as in the immediate-test condition (though it was worse when the interval was filled than unfilled). Having visual information therefore helped safeguard the information from forgetting. This outcome supports the hypothesis that there are distinct codes for motor information.

What aspect of movement was most important in this experiment? Was it the *distance* to be covered or the *location* of the final position? Efforts to tease apart these two variables have yielded dramatic results. Laabs (1973) found that location reproduction was relatively unaffected by the duration of an unfilled retention interval but that distance reproduction was substantially affected by the duration of the retention interval. Distance and location were experimentally dissociated by independently varying the amplitude of the movement and its starting and ending locations. Other investigators have replicated Laabs' findings (see Smyth, 1984, for review).

What accounts for the superiority of location reproduction over distance reproduction? An intriguing possibility is that movements may be *produced* with reference to location rather than distance. This would help explain the superiority of location reproduction, provided one assumes that recall improves if it recreates the means by which information is stored. Consistent with this idea, it has been found that people are better at recalling verbal information they previously generated than at recalling information they were simply told to learn (Slamecka & Graf, 1978). Similarly, memory for positioning movements is better when subjects select the movements they will later reproduce than when their hands are passively manipulated by someone else (Kelso & Stelmach, 1976; Paillard & Brouchon, 1968).

Kelso and Holt (1980) provided evidence for the view that movements are produced through location specification. In their study, subjects were temporarily deprived of proprioceptive feedback from the fingers of one hand. The blockage of feedback was achieved with a child's blood-pressure cuff. At the start of each trial, the subject rotated the extended index finger to a location (or orientation) of his or her choosing. The finger was then returned either to the original starting position or to a different starting position. The subject's task was to bring the finger back to the *location* that was reached before or to cover the same *distance* as was reached before. Subjects reproduced locations more accurately than distances.

How could subjects bring the finger to the correct final location when feedback was eliminated? Answering this question would distract us from the questions at hand; in Chapter 6, in the section on the *mass-spring* model, an extended discussion will be provided. The important point for now is that movements appear to be *generated* with respect to target locations rather than target distances. This may explain why reproduction of location is generally better than reproduction of distance. With respect to codes for motor memory, the results of Kelso and Holt (1980) support the view that the motor system does indeed use distinct codes for representing information.

A more recent study of memory for movement (Smyth & Pendelton, 1989) provides additional support for this view. The question posed by Smyth and Pendelton was whether movement information and spatial information are represented differently. *A priori* the answer is not obvious, for movements usually have spatial components, and spatial tasks, such as pointing to a series of locations, have motor elements. To test for a dissociation of spatial and motor codes, Smyth and Pendelton asked subjects to watch someone perform a sequence of hand gestures that would have to be reproduced immediately thereafter. In one condition, while watching the hand gestures, subjects repeatedly squeezed a hand-held tube. In another condition, while watching the hand gestures, subjects continually tapped four plates in a clockwise order. In a control condition, subjects watched the gestures without performing a concurrent task. Reproduction of the hand gestures was as accurate following the finger-tapping task as in the control condition but was worse following the squeezing task.

How can this result be explained? A straightforward explanation is that the squeezing task drew upon a motor code whereas the finger-tapping task drew upon a spatial code. The selective interference between squeezing and learning hand gestures may have occurred because the hand gestures were coded primarily in motoric form.

A challenge to this interpretation is that the squeezing task simply may have been more demanding than the tapping task. The difficulty of squeezing may have been sufficient to impair learning of any kind. To test this possibility, Smyth and Pendleton (1989) conducted a second experiment in which subjects watched someone tap out a spatial pattern with a finger. While watching, subjects performed the same concurrent tasks as in the first experiment—simply watching the to-be-performed movements while squeezing a tube or tapping in a clockwise order. This time, reproduction of the observed pattern was adversely affected by the tapping task, not by the squeezing task. Thus there was selective interference depending on the nature of the task. These results, taken as a whole, suggest that spatial codes and motor codes are distinct. If one considers other movement tasks, such as belly dancing, this conclusion appears sensible.

Parameter Remapping

The studies I have just reviewed tell us about people's abilities to reproduce movements they have just *learned*. Another approach to the study of short-term motor memory is to ask how well people remember movements they have just *performed*. My colleagues and I studied how well people perform sequences of repetitive motor responses, where the responses to be performed within a production cycle were either identical to or somewhat different from responses in previous production cycles (Rosenbaum, Weber, Hazelett, & Hindorff, 1986). One task was repeating the first n letters of the alphabet over and over again as quickly as possible for 10 sec. This task was performed under the requirement that speakers always alternate between stressed and unstressed utterances. As shown in Figure 3.10, the mean number of letters that speakers produced was higher when n was even than when n was odd.

What accounts for this suprising result? The likely source of difficulty in the odd-n case was related to the fact that a given letter was produced with varying stress levels in successive production cycles. When n equaled 3, for instance, the sequence to be produced was AbCaBcAbCa ..., where capital letters denote stressed letters and lower-case letters denote unstressed letters. Note that each letter alternates between stressed and un-stressed form. By contrast, when *n* equaled 4, the sequence to be produced was AbCdAbCd.... In this condition, each letter was always stressed or al-ways unstressed. The greater difficulty encountered in the odd-*n* case can be explained by supposing that each time the subject got ready to produce a letter, he or she accessed a still-active memory trace from its last production. If the stress level from the last production matched the stress level of the next production, the trace could serve as a "ready-to-run" program. However, if the necessary stress of the letter did not match its previous value, then the stress level had to be altered which, by hypothesis, took extra time. According to this model, mapping a new parameter (such as a new stress level) to a letter name slowed performance. As the delay be-tween successive productions of a letter increased, the strength of the asso-

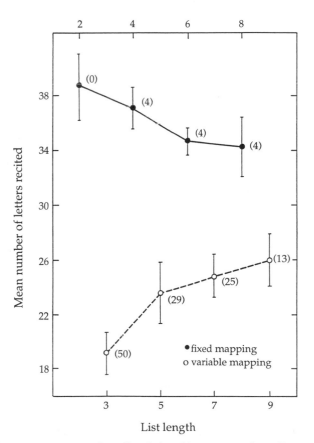

Figure 3.10 The parameter remapping effect, indexed by mean number of letters recited in 10 sec as a function of list length (number of letters recited from the beginning of the alphabet). Number of errors is given in parentheses. (From Rosenbaum, Weber, Hazelett, & Hindorff, 1987.)

ciation between the stress level and the letter name diminished. This can explain why as n increased, the difference between odd and even values of n grew smaller. My colleagues and I called the slowing of performance in this context the *parameter remapping* effect.

The parameter remapping effect is a robust phenomenon that can be demonstrated in a number of production tasks, including speech, finger tapping, and violin bowing (Rosenbaum *et al.*, 1987). From the perspective of short-term or working memory, it suggests that the information guiding production of a motor response remains active in memory for some time after the response has been produced. If this were not the case, it would not matter if responses were produced in the same way or in different ways in successive production cycles.

Is there a functional advantage to having a memory system that happens to fall prey to the parameter remapping effect? An advantage is that the only characteristics of a forthcoming response that need to be specified are the characteristics that distinguish the forthcoming response from its predecessor. For example, if one must say "a" with a different stress level than before, all that is necessary is to alter the stress level. This method of preparing forthcoming responses is likely to be more efficient than programming each response "from scratch" (Rosenbaum, 1980, 1983).

Motor Programs

I have allowed a word to enter this discussion which has become the subject of intense debate among students of human motor control. It is *motor program*; the related term is *motor programming*. In the late 1960s, the motor program was defined as "a set of muscle commands that are structured before a movement sequence begins, and that allows the sequence to be carried out uninfluenced by peripheral feedback" (Keele, 1968, p. 387). Keele wrote this definition when the major issue in motor-control research was the extent to which skilled movement depends on sensory feedback. He reasoned that if a movement sequence can be performed skillfully even when sensory feedback is unavailable, then one can conclude that the sequence can be controlled centrally. The word *program* denoted the set of commands within the central nervous system that allowed for such performance.

A number of complaints arose about the programming concept (Kelso, 1981; Meijer & Roth, 1988). One is that sensory feedback *has* an effect on movement. Much of the grace and subtlety of movement that is present when feedback is available deteriorates when feedback is withdrawn. This suggested that the concept of motor program as defined by Keele (1968) has limited utility.

The problem with this challenge is that a careful reading of Keele's (1968) definition shows that though a motor program may *allow* a movement sequence to be carried out uninfluenced by peripheral feedback, it does not *require* movement sequences to be uninfluenced by peripheral feedback.

Consider a conventional computer program. Such a program is designed to carry out procedures differently depending on what input values it receives or depending on the outputs it produces at earlier stages. Thus a conventional computer program is not immune to feedback and neither is a motor program.

Analogizing motor programs to computer programs is a second source of dissatisfaction with the motor program concept. The nervous system is quite different from a computer, the argument goes, so the term *program* is misleading. There clearly are differences between the nervous system and most modern computers. Computer systems today primarily rely on serial processing, whereas an important feature of the nervous system is that it relies extensively on parallel processing. Moreover, the individual processing elements of a computer are very fast, whereas neurons are comparatively slow. Nevertheless, computers are likely to change dramatically in the next few years. Indeed, there is a concerted effort to make them more "brainlike." When this happens, the complaint that human motor programs aren't like computer programs will no longer apply. The implication is that the complaint about computers is too narrowly related to current technology.

A third grievance about motor programs is related to the use of the term *muscle commands*. Use of this term led to the reproof that information guiding movement is more abstract than commands for muscle contractions (Tuller, Turvey, & Fitch, 1982). As was seen in the last chapter, only some efferent signals directly activate motor neurons; efferent signals also influence gains in feedback loops, for example. Moreover, as will be seen in later chapters, there is reason to doubt that information governing movement and stability is defined with respect to the activity of particular muscles or groups of muscles (Klapp, 1977b). Accepting these observations, the larger point is that difficulties with a particular term (*muscle commands*), used by one author (Keele, 1968) more than 20 years ago, need not rule out the underlying concept of a motor program. A motor program can now be viewed as a functional state that allows particular movements, or classes of movements, to occur.

The word *command*—whether viewed as a command for muscles or commands for perceptual states—has also raised criticism. Who decides what command to issue? And what defines the functional boundary between the sources of commands and their targets? Introducing the notion of motor program seems to require the notion of a motor *programmer*, which begs the question of how movements are generated. I agree with this concern, but I think that if the program is viewed in the broad terms given at the end of the last paragraph, the question of who or what does the programming becomes irrelevant.

Viewing the motor program as a functional state need be no more controversial than the concept of memory. To say that we have memories makes no particular claims about what form the memories take or how they are embodied physically. To say that the term *memory* is useless because it is not specific has the potential of endangering commitment to understanding the nature of information storage, and this, in my view, would be a grave mistake. Likewise, it would be most unfortuante if one were to deny the importance of detailed, testable hypotheses about the functional states underlying motor control, including the functional states allowing for the preparation of forthcoming movements and movement sequences. The term *motor program* is a convenient label for these states, and the term *motor programming* is a useful term for the processes by which the states evolve. Though neither term is specific (Kugler & Turvey, 1987), both terms invite inquiry into the detailed nature of motor preparation and control. Questions to be answered about motor programs are how information about the biomechanical properties of the skeletomuscular system are represented, how physical interactions with the external environment are taken into account or exploited, and so forth. As these questions show, research on motor programs need not devalue or ignore physical factors, as some critics have charged. Presumably we know a great deal about mechanics, even if only implicitly. Motor programs incorporate this knowledge so that movements can be prepared and carried out efficiently.

The Motor Output Buffer

Earlier, I touched on long-term and short-term memory for movement. Having said something about motor programs, I will end this chapter by considering the question of whether sensory buffers have analogs in the motor system. Is there a buffer for *outgoing* information—a motor output buffer, or what I have elsewhere called the MOB (Rosenbaum, 1990)?

Little research has been explicitly directed to this question, but several studies bear on it. In one of the first (Henry & Rogers, 1960), people were asked to carry out a series of manual movements as quickly as possible after hearing an auditory signal. The independent variable was the number of movements in the series. In one condition, subjects simply lifted the hand from a key after the signal came on. In another condition, they lifted the hand and then immediately reached out and grabbed a tennis ball. In a third condition, a still more complicated series of movements was required, but again the first movement was lifting the hand from the start key. Subjects were aware before the auditory signal of what tasks would have to be performed. Thus in principle they could fully prepare for the tasks ahead of time.

Suppose an index of full preparation is a fixed, minimal reaction time. If subjects could fully prepare all the tasks they would have to perform, then one would expect the first movement in the series always to have that fixed, minimal time. (The same outcome would be expected if subjects could only prepare the first movement, no matter how many movements had to be made.) Henry and Rogers (1960) found that reaction time increased with the number of movements to be performed. They proposed that commands for the forthcoming series had to be loaded into a buffer (what Henry and Rogers called a "memory drum") after the "go" signal sounded; as more commands were needed, the loading time increased. If this interpretation is correct, it implies that the motor output buffer has a limited storage capacity. It cannot hold instructions for an indefinitely large number of movements for an indefinitely long time before the movements are performed.

Alternative interpretations of Henry and Rogers' (1960) findings can be considered. One is that the kinematics of the first movement changed depending on the movements to follow. If this were the case, the observed reaction-time effect would be an artifact of the kinds of first movements that subjects chose to carry out in the three conditions of the experiment. Another possibility is that the components of the forthcoming sequence inhibited each other, much as in Estes' (1972) theory discussed earlier. With more inhibition, reaction time would increase. Still another possibility is that all the instructions were fully loaded into the motor output buffer before the go signal was presented (assuming for now that there is a motor output buffer), and the contents of the buffer had to be searched for the instruction associated with each movement. As more instructions occupied the buffer, the search time increased and reaction time grew (Sternberg, Monsell, Knoll, & Wright, 1978).

Based on Henry and Rogers' (1960) experiment alone, it is impossible to tell whether any of these explanations accurately accounts for the experiment's outcome. However, other studies following Henry and Rogers' have yielded systematic effects of task complexity on reaction time using other sorts of responses (Klapp, 1977a; Rosenbaum, 1987a; Sternberg *et al.*, 1978). This outcome casts doubt on the kinematic hypothesis raised above and strengthens the other, more centrally based hypotheses, all of which assume that there are limits on the number of movements that can be programmed in advance. This is what would be expected if there were a limited-capacity motor output buffer.

If the motor output buffer has limited capacity—that is, if it can only store a limited number of instructions for forthcoming movements at a given time—then one should be able to demonstrate that when one "spills the contents" of the buffer, its contents are indeed very small. A method that has been developed for this purpose is to require subjects to *stop* responding when a signal is presented (de Jong, Coles, Logan, & Gratton, 1990; Ladefoged, Silverstein, & Papçun, 1973; Osman, Kornblum, & Meyer, 1990; Slater-Hammel, 1960). In one study (Logan, 1982), it was found that skilled typists generally performed only a single keystroke after a stop tone sounded. If the contents of the motor output buffer contained instructions for more than one keystroke—say, instead, it contained instructions for an entire word—then the entire word would have been typed when the stop signal sounded. The fact that typists generally produced only one keystroke after a stop signal sounded (in those instances when any keystrokes occurred after the stop signal) suggests that the capacity of the motor output buffer is no greater than one "keystroke's worth" of motor instructions. This means, in turn, that the high speeds possible in typing and other motor tasks must be achieved through rapid access to memory structures located deeper in the memory system (Rosenbaum, 1990).

■ SUMMARY

1. A historically important theory of serial ordering is that the stimulus produced by a movement triggers the next movement in the sequence (*response chaining*). A difficulty with this theory is that successive movements often occur too quickly for one movement to be elicited by sensory feedback from the preceding movement. Another difficulty is that the same output can be followed by different outputs on different occasions. Still another problem is that interrupting sensory feedback does not always interrupt movement. Counterarguments to these challenges can be raised. Nonetheless, the theory is damned by the fact that behavior reflects sensitivity to rules.

2. Another theory of serial order (element-to-position associations) holds that associations are formed between the elements to be produced and markers or tags for their serial positions. If the markers are regarded as time tags, the theory potentially explains timing. The theory has several problems, however, including sensitivity to rules.

3. A third theory of serial order (interelement inhibition) assumes that elements of a sequence inhibit each other. The more inhibition an element receives, the later it occurs. Despite its apparent physiological plausibility, this theory encounters problems of implementation and storage and, like the two theories just summarized, neglects the capacity for rule-governed behavior.

4. Hierarchical theories of serial order are more successful. They provide a framework for understanding rule-governed behavior and accurately predict which sequences will be hard or easy to learn. They also provide a basis for understanding aspects of response timing.

5. Adams (1971) proposed a closed-loop theory of skill learning. According to the theory, learning reflects the development of perceptual reference conditions and means for satisfying them. The theory stimulated modern research on perceptual–motor skill development but was limited in scope and placed more emphasis on feedback than was ultimately justified.

6. An alternative theory of skill development is that the learner forms generalized motor programs. These are instructions for procedures which can be instantiated in various ways depending on the values taken on by their internal values or parameters. Evidence for parameter setting has been obtained in choice reaction-time experiments. The finding that variable practice can lead to better long-term retention than consistent practice also supports a prediction derived from the theory.

7. Another theory of skill learning is that low-level memory units promote the formation of higher-level memory units. Such a hierarchical theory can account for the Power Law of Learning, which relates speed of performance to amount of practice. The theory can also account for the observation that transfer from one task to another (such as speeded recitation of a sentence in one language followed by speeded recitation of a sentence in another language) is aided by the presence of high-level memory units common to both tasks (for example, a common meaning for the two sentences).

8. Hierarchical learning theory predicts that mental practice can aid learning through the strengthening of high-level memory units. Mental practice has been shown to aid learning of motor tasks, though not as much as physical practice. It is doubtful that the benefits of mental practice derive only from subtle muscle activity.

9. Fitts (1964) proposed a three-stage model of skill acquisition. First, there is a *cognitive* stage, during which basic procedures are learned and their execution is, in general, highly attention demanding. Then there is an *associative* stage, during which one tries out different task components and associates them to task success. Third, there is an *automatic* stage, during which the task can be performed with less deliberate attention, often with intermittent rather than continuous reliance on feedback.

10. No less important than increased speed and accuracy as skill develops is increased grace and efficiency. One way such improvements occur is that degrees of freedom, not permitted to vary early in practice, are allowed to vary at later stages.

11. The human information-processing system stores and represents information in different ways. Storage may last for varying amounts of time and may or may not be the subject of conscious attention. Information may also be subjectively coded in different forms, for example, visually or acoustically.

12. Procedural knowledge is distinct from declarative knowledge. Declarative knowledge can be expressed as propositions about persons, places, and things. Procedural knowledge often cannot be expressed propositionally. It underlies sequences of operations, including those used in perceptual–motor performance.

13. Long-term memory for skills is resistant to forgetting. Well-learned skills show little decrement following retention intervals of weeks, months, or even years.

14. Short-term or working memory is usually better for voluntarily selected movements than for passively induced movements. Location reproduction is generally superior to distance reproduction, suggesting that location information and distance information may be coded differently. Movement information may itself have a different representational format from spatial information.

15. When a series of responses is produced over and over again as quickly as possible, the speed of responding is higher when the responses are identical over repetitions than when they change. The result implies that traces of previously performed responses persist in working memory. Forthcoming responses may therefore be prepared by altering those parameters that distinguish the previous version of the response from the version needed next.

16. Motor programs are functional states that dispose the organism to carry out particular movements or classes of movements. The term has become controversial, but unnecessarily so in the author's opinion.

17. Just as there may be buffers for just-received sensory information, there may be motor output buffers for forthcoming movements. Two lines of evidence suggest that the human memory system is severely limited in its capacity to store instructions for immediately forthcoming motor responses (an indication of a buffer). The time to initiate movement sequences increases with sequence complexity. When people are instructed to interrupt ongoing sequences of rapid responses as quickly as possible, they can stop immediately without producing extended series of responses.

■ REFERENCES

Adams, J. A. (1971). A closed-loop theory of motor learning. *Journal of Motor Behavior*, **3**, 111–149.

Adams, J. A. (1976). Issues for a closed-loop theory of motor learning. In G. E. Stelmach (Ed.), *Motor control: Issues and trends* (pp. 87–107). New York: Academic Press.

Adams, J. A. (1984). Learning of movement sequences. *Psychological Bulletin*, **96**, 3–28.

Adnerson, J. R. (1985). *Cognitive psychology and its implications* (2d ed.). New York: W. H. Freeman.

Arutyunyan, G. H., Gurfinkel, V. S., & Mirskii, M. L. (1968). Investigation of aiming at a target. *Biophysics*, **13**, 536–538.

Baddeley, A. D., & Hitch, G. (1974). Working memory. In G. H. Bower (Ed.), *Psychology of learning and motivation* (Vol. 8, pp. 47–89). New York: Academic Press.

Baddeley, A. D., & Lieberman, K. (1980). Spatial working memory. In R. Nickerson (Ed.), *Attention and performance VIII* (pp. 521–539). Hillsdale, NJ: Erlbaum.

Bartlett, F. C. (1932). *Remembering*. London: Cambridge University Press.

Berko, J. (1958). The child's learning of English morphology. *Word*, **14**, 150–177.

Bernstein, N. (1967). *The coordination and regulation of movements*. London: Pergamon.

Best, J. B. (1986). *Cognitive psychology*. St. Paul, MN: West.

Bliss, J. C., Hewitt, D. V., Crane, P. K., Mansfield, P. K., & Townsend, J. T. (1966). Information available in brief tactile presentations. *Perception & Psychophysics*, **1**, 273–283.

Bower, G. H., Clark, M., Lesgold, A., & Winzenz, D. (1969). Hierarchical retrieval schemes in recall of categorized word lists. *Journal of Verbal Learning and Verbal Behavior*, **8**, 323–443.

Bryan, W. L., & Harter, N. (1897). Studies in the physiology and psychology of the telegraphic language. *Psychological Review*, **4**, 27–53.

Carson, L. M., & Wiegand, R. L. (1979). Motor schema formation and retention in young children: A test of Schmidt's schema theory. *Journal of Motor Behavior*, **11**, 247–251.

Chase, W. G., & Simon, H. A. (1972). The mind's eye in chess. In W. G. Chase (Ed.), *Visual information processing* (pp. 215–281). New York: Academic Press.

Conrad, R. (1965). Acoustic confusions in immediate memory. *British Journal of Psychology, 55,* 75–84.

Cowan, N. (1988). Evolving conceptions of memory storage, selective attention, and their mutual constraints within the human information-processing system. *Psychological Bulletin, 104,* 163–191.

Crossman, E. R. F. W. (1959). A theory of the acquisition of speed skill. *Ergonomics, 2,* 153–166.

Darwin, C. J., Turvey, M. T., & Crowder, R. G. (1972). An auditory analog of the Sperling partial report procedure: Evidence for brief auditory storage. *Cognitive Psychology, 6,* 41–60.

deGrott, A. D. (1965). *Thought and choice in chess.* The Hague: Mouton.

de Jong, R., Coles, M. G., Logan, G. D., & Gratton, G. (1990). In search of the point of no return: The control of response processes. *Journal of Experimental Psychology: Human Perception and Performance, 16,* 164–182.

Estes, W. K. (1972). An associative basis for coding and organization in memory. In A. W. Melton & E. Martin (Eds.), *Coding processes in human memory* (pp. 161–190). Washington, D.C.: V. H. Winston.

Feltz, D., & Landers, D. M. (1983). The effects of mental practice on motor skill learning and performance: A meta-analysis. *Journal of Sports Psychology, 5,* 25–57.

Fitts, P. M. (1964). Perceptual-motor skill learning. In A. W. Melton (Ed.), *Categories of human learning* (pp. 243–285). New York: Academic Press.

Fleishman, E. A., & Parker, R. F., Jr. (1962). Factors in the retention and relearning of perceptual motor skill. *Journal of Experimental Psychology, 64,* 215–226.

Fowler, C. A., & Turvey, M. T. (1978). Skill acquisition: An event approach for the optimum of a function of several variables. In G. E. Stelmach (Ed.), *Information processing in motor control and learning* (pp. 2–10). New York: Academic Press.

Fuchs, A. F., & Melton, A. W. (1974). Effects of frequency of presentation and stimulus length on retention in the Brown-Peterson paradigm. *Journal of Experimental Psychology, 103,* 629–637.

Glencross, D. J. (1980). Levels and strategies of response organization. In G. E. Stelmach & J. Requin (Eds.), *Tutorials in motor behavior* (pp. 551–566). Amsterdam: North-Holland.

Hale, B. D. (1982). The effects of internal and external imagery on muscular and ocular concomitants. *Journal of Sports Psychology, 4,* 379–387.

Henry, F. M., & Rogers, D. E. (1960). Increased response latency for complicated movements and a "memory drum" theory of neuromotor reaction. *Research Quarterly, 31,* 448–458.

Heuer, H. (1982). Binary choice reaction time as a criterion of motor equivalence. *Acta Psychologica, 50,* 35–47.

Ho, L., & Shea, J. G. (1978). Effects of relative frequency of knowledge of results on retention of a motor skill. *Perceptual and Motor Skills, 46,* 859–866.

Holding, D. H. (Ed.) (1989). *Human skills* (2d ed.). Chichester: John Wiley & Sons.

Hulse, S. H. (1978). Cognitive structure and serial pattern learning by animals. In S. H. Hulse, H. Fowler, & K. Honig (Eds.), *Cognitive processes in animal behavior* (pp. 311–340). Hillsdale, NJ: Erlbaum.

Hulse, S. H., Fowler, H., & Honig, K. (Eds.) (1978). *Cognitive processes in animal behavior.* Hillsdale, NJ: Erlbaum.

Jacobson, E. (1931). Electrical measurement of neuromuscular states during mental activities: VI. A note on mental activities concerning an amputated limb. *American Journal of Physiology, 43,* 122–125.

James, W. (1890). *Principles of psychology.* New York: Holt.

Johnson, P. (1984). The acquisition of skill. In M. M. Smyth & A. M. Wing (Eds.), *The psychology of human movement* (pp. 215–240). London: Academic Press.

Johnson, R., Wicks, G. G., & Ben-Sira, D. (1981). *Practice in the absence of knowledge of results: Motor skill retention.* Unpublished manuscript. University of Minnesota.

Jones, M. R. (1981). A tutorial on some issues and methods in serial pattern research. *Perception & Psychophysics, 30,* 492–504.

Kamon, E., & Gormley, J. (1968). Muscular activity pattern for skilled performance and during learning of a horizontal bar exercise. *Ergonomics,* **11,** 345–357.

Keele, S. W. (1968). Movement control in skilled motor performance. *Psychological Bulletin,* **70,** 387–403.

Kelso, J. A. S. (1981). Contrasting perspectives on order and regulation in movement. In J. Long & A. Baddeley (Eds.), *Attention and performance IX* (pp. 437–457). Hillsdale, NJ: Erlbaum.

Kelso, J. A. S., & Holt, K. G. (1980). Exploring a vibratory systems analysis of human movement production. *Journal of Neurophysiology,* **435,** 1183–1196.

Kelso, J. A. S., & Stelmach, G. E. (1976). Central and peripheral mechanisms in motor control. In G. E. Stelmach (Ed.), *Motor control: Issues and trends* (pp. 1–40). New York: Academic Press.

Klapp, S. T. (1977a). Reaction time analysis of programmed control. *Exercise and Sport Sciences Reviews,* **5,** 231–253.

Klapp, S. T. (1977b). Response programming, as assessed by reaction time, does not establish commands for particular muscles. *Journal of Motor Behavior,* **9,** 301–312.

Kroll, J. F., & Potter, M. C. (1984). Recognizing words, pictures, and concepts: A comparison of lexical, object, and reality decisions. *Journal of Verbal Learning and Verbal Behavior,* **23,** 39–66.

Kugler, P. N., & Turvey, M. T. (1987). *Information, natural law and self-assembly of rhythmic movements: A study in the similitude of natural law.* Hillsdale, NJ: Erlbaum.

Laabs, G. J. (1973). Retention characteristics of different reproduction cues in motor short-term memory. *Journal of Experimental Psychology,* **100,** 168–177.

Ladefoged, P., Silverstein, R., & Papçun, G. (1973). Interruptibility of speech. *Journal of the Acoustical Society of America,* **54,** 1105–1108.

Lashley, K. S. (1917). The accuracy of movement in the absence of excitation from the moving organ. *American Journal of Physiology,* **43,** 169–194.

Lashley, K. S. (1951). The problem of serial order in behavior. In L. A. Jeffress (Ed.), *Cerebral mechanisms in behavior* (pp. 112–131). New York: Wiley.

Leonard, J. A., & Newman, R. C. (1964). Formation of higher habits. *Nature,* **203,** 550–551.

Loftus, E. R., & Loftus, G. R. (1980). On the permanence of stored information in the human brain. *American Psychologist,* **35,** 409–420.

Logan, G. D. (1982). On the ability to inhibit complex movements: A stop-signal study of typewriting. *Journal of Experimental Psychology: Human Perception and Performance,* **8,** 778–792.

MacKay, D. G. (1981). The problem of rehearsal or mental practice. *Journal of Motor Behavior,* **13,** 274–285.

MacKay, D. G. (1982). The problem of flexibility, fluency, and speed-accuracy trade-off in skilled behavior. *Psychological Review,* **89,** 483–506.

MacKay, D. G. (1987). *The organization of perception and action: A theory for language and other cognitive skills.* New York: Springer-Verlag.

MacKay, D. G., & Bowman, R. W. (1969). On producing the meaning in sentences. *American Journal of Psychology,* **82,** 23–39.

MacNeilage, P. F. (1970). Motor control of serial ordering of speech. *Psychological Review,* **77,** 182–196.

Magill, R. A. (1989). *Motor learning* (3d ed.). Dubuque, Iowa: Wm. C. Brown.

McBride, E., & Rothstein, A. (1979). Mental and physical practice and the learning and retention of open and closed skills. *Perceptual and Motor Skills,* **49,** 359–365.

McDonald, P. V., van Emmerick, R. E., & Newell, K. M. (1989). The effects of practice on limb kinematics in a throwing task. *Journal of Motor Behavior,* **21,** 245–264.

Meijer, O. G., & Roth, K. (Eds.). (1988). *Complex motor behavior: The motor-action controversy.* Amsterdam: Elsevier Science.

Meyers, J. (1967). Retention of balance coordination learning as influenced by extended lay-offs. *Research Quarterly,* **38,** 72–78.

Miller, G. A. (1956). The magical number seven plus or minus two: Some limits on our capacity for processing information. *Psychological Review,* **63,** 81–97.

Minas, S. C. (1978). Mental practice of a complex perceptual motor skill. *Journal of Human*

Movement Studies, 4, 102–107.

Neisser, U. (1967). *Cognitive psychology.* New York: Appleton-Century-Crofts.

Newell, A. M., & Rosenbloom, P. S. (1981). Mechanisms of skill acquisition and the law of practice. In J. R. Anderson (Ed.), *Cognitive skills and their acquisition* (pp. 1–55). Hillsdale, NJ: Erlbaum.

Newell, K. M. (1985). Skill learning. In D. H. Holding (Ed.), *Human skills* (pp. 203–226). Chichester: John Wiley & Sons.

Osman, A., Kornblum, S., & Meyer, D. E. (1990). Does motor programming necessitate response execution? *Journal of Experimental Psychology: Human Perception and Performance, 16,* 183–198.

Paillard, J., & Brouchon, M. (1968). Active and passive movements in the calibration of position sense. In S. J. Freedman (Ed.), *The neuropsychology of spatially oriented behavior* (pp. 37–55). Homewood, IL: Dorsey.

Penfield, W., & Roberts, L. (1959). *Speech and brain mechanisms.* New York: Atheneum.

Pew, R. W. (1966). Acquisition of hierarchical control over the temporal organization of a skill. *Journal of Experimental Psychology, 71,* 764–771.

Polanyi, M. (1964). *Personal knowledge.* New York: Harper & Row.

Posner, M. I. (1967). Characteristics of visual and kinesthetic memory codes. *Journal of Experimental Psychology, 75,* 103–107.

Posner, M. I. (1978). *Chronometric explorations of mind.* Hillsdale, NJ: Erlbaum.

Povel, D-J., & Collard, R. (1982). Structural factors in patterned finger tapping. *Acta Psychologica, 52,* 107–124.

Pylyshyn, Z. W. (1981). The imagery debate: Analog media versus tacit knowledge. *Psychological Review, 88,* 16–45.

Restle, F. (1970). Theory of serial pattern learning: Structural trees. *Psychological Review, 77,* 481–495.

Richardson, A. (1967a). Mental practice: A review and discussion I. *Research Quarterly, 38,* 95–107.

Richardson, A. (1967b). Mental practice: A review and discussion II. *Research Quarterly, 38,* 262–273.

Roland, P. E., Larsen, B., Lassen, N. A., & Skinhoj, E. (1980). Supplementary motor area and other cortical areas in organization of voluntary movements in man. *Journal of Neurophysiology, 43,* 118–136.

Rosenbaum, D. A. (1980). Human movement initiation: Specification of arm, direction, and extent. *Journal of Experimental Psychology: General, 109,* 444–474.

Rosenbaum, D. A. (1983). The movement precuing technique: Assumptions, applications, and extensions. In R. A. Magill (Ed.), *Memory and control of action* (pp. 231–274). Amsterdam: North-Holland.

Rosenbaum, D. A. (1985). Motor programming: A review and scheduling theory. In H. Heuer, U. Kleinbeck, & K.-M. Schmidt (Eds.), *Motor behavior: Programming, control, and acquisition* (pp. 1–33). Berlin: Springer-Verlag.

Rosenbaum, D. A. (1987a). Hierarchical organization of motor programs. In S. Wise (Ed.), *Neural and behavioral approaches to higher brain functions* (pp. 45–66). New York: Wiley.

Rosenbaum, D. A. (1987b). Successive approximations to a model of human motor programming. In G. H. Bower (Ed.) *Psychology of learning and motivation* (Vol. 21, pp. 153–182). Orlando, FL: Academic Press.

Rosenbaum, D. A. (1990). On choosing between movement sequences: Comments on Rose (1988). *Journal of Experimental Psychology: Human Perception and Performance, 16,* 439–444.

Rosenbaum, D. A., Kenny, S., & Derr, M. A. (1983). Hierarchical control of rapid movement sequences. *Journal of Experimental Psychology: Human Perception and Performance, 9,* 86–102.

Rosenbaum, D. A., Inhoff, A. W., & Gordon, A. M. (1984). Choosing between movement sequences: A hierarchical editor model. *Journal of Experimental Psychology: General, 113,* 372–393.

Rosenbaum, D. A., Weber, R. J., Hazelett, W. M., & Hindorff, V. (1986). The parameter remapping effect in human performance: Evidence from tongue twisters and finger fumblers. *Journal of Memory and Language, 25,* 710–725.

Rumelhart, D. E., & Norman, D. A. (1982). Simulating a skilled typist: A study of skilled cognitive-motor performance. *Cognitive Science, 6,* 1–36.

Ryan, E. D. (1962). Retention of stabilometer and pursuit rotor skills. *Research Quarterly, 33,* 593–598.

Ryan, E. D. (1965). Retention of stabilometer performance over extended periods of time. *Research Quarterly, 36,* 46–51.

Schmidt, R. A. (1975). A schema theory of discrete motor skill learning. *Psychological Review, 82,* 225–260.

Schmidt, R. A. (1976). The schema as a solution to some persistent problems in motor learning theory. In G. E. Stelmach (Ed.), *Motor control: Issues and trends* (pp. 41–65). New York: Academic Press.

Schmidt, R. A. (1988). *Motor control and learning* (2d ed.). Champaign, IL: Human Kinetics Publishers.

Shaffer, L. H. (1975). Multiple attention in continuous verbal tasks. In P. M. Rabbitt & S. Dornic (Eds.), *Attention and performance V* (pp. 157–167). London: Academic Press.

Shea, J. B., & Morgan, R. L. (1979). Contextual interference effects on acquisition, retention, and transfer of a motor skill. *Journal of Experimental Psychology: Human Learning and Memory, 5,* 179–187.

Simon, H. A. (1972). Complexity and the representation of patterned sequences of symbols. *Psychological Review, 79,* 369–382.

Slamecka, N. J., & Graf, P. (1978). The generation effect: Delineation of a phenomenon. *Journal of Experimental Psychology: Human Learning and Memory, 4,* 592–604.

Slater-Hammel, A. T. (1960). Reliability, accuracy, and refractoriness of a transit reaction. *Research Quarterly, 31,* 217–228.

Smyth, M. M. (1984). Memory for movements. In M. M. Smyth & A. M. Wing (Eds.), *The psychology of human movement* (pp. 83–117). London: Academic Press.

Smyth, M. M., & Pendleton, L. R. (1989). Working memory for movements. *Quarterly Journal of Experimental Psychology, 41A,* 235–250.

Sparrow, W. A. (1983). The efficiency of skilled performance. *Journal of Motor Behavior, 15,* 237–261.

Sparrow, W. A., & Irizarry-Lopez, V. M. (1987). Mechanical efficiency and metabolic cost as measures of learning a novel gross motor task. *Journal of Motor Behavior, 19,* 240–264.

Spelke, E., Hirst, W., & Neisser, U. (1976). Skills of divided attention. *Cognition, 4,* 215–230.

Squire, L. R. (1987). *Memory and brain.* New York: Oxford University Press.

Sternberg, S., Monsell, S., Knoll, R. L., & Wright, C. E. (1978). The latency and duration of rapid movement sequences: Comparisons of speech and typewriting. In G. E. Stelmach (Ed.), *Information processing in motor control and learning* (pp. 117–152). New York: Academic Press.

Stillings, N. A., Feinstein, M. H., Garfield, J. L., Rissland, E. L., Rosenbaum, D. A., Weisler, S. E., & Baker-Ward, L. (1987). *Cognitive science: An introduction.* Cambridge, MA: Bradford/MIT Press.

Thorndike, E. L. (1927). The law of effect. *American Journal of Psychology, 39,* 212–222.

Tuller, B., Turvey, M. T., & Fitch, H. L. (1982). The Bernstein perspective: II. The concept of muscle linkage or coordinative structure. In J. A. S. Kelso (Ed.), *Human motor behavior* (pp. 253–281). Hillsdale, NJ: Erlbaum.

van Rossum, J. H. A. (1990). Schmidt's schema theory: The empirical base of the variability of practice hypothesis. *Human Movement Science, 9.*

Whiting, H. T. A. (1989). Toward a cognitive psychology of human movement. In P. C. W. van Wieringen & R. J. Bootsma (Eds.), *Catching up: Selected essays of H. T. A. Whiting* (pp. 195–230). Amsterdam: Free University Press.

Wickelgren, W. A. (1969). Context-sensitive coding, associative memory, and serial order in (speech) behavior. *Psychological Review, 76,* 1–15.

Winstein, C. J. (1987). *Relative frequency of information feedback in motor performance and learning.* Unpublished doctoral dissertation. University of California, Los Angeles.

Winstein, C. J., & Schmidt, R. A. (1989). Sensorimotor feedback. In D. H. Holding (Ed.), *Human skills* (2d ed., pp. 17–47). Chichester: John Wiley & Sons.

PART II
THE ACTIVITY SYSTEMS

4 WALKING

■ **INTRODUCTION**

There are several reasons for beginning our survey of motor activities with an analysis of walking. When human newborns are supported beneath their shoulders, they may exhibit a stepping pattern similar to that seen in walking adults (André-Thomas & Autgarden, 1966). Thus the capacity for walking is innate or "prewired" (Grillner, 1981). When walking occurs in functional contexts, the patterning of one's footsteps depends on the terrain over which one treads and the speed with which one wishes to reach one's destination. This raises the question of how ongoing feedback interacts with built-in programs for locomotion.

Locomotion takes many forms. Trotting, galloping, strutting, creeping, limping, swimming, and even flying all belong to the same broad performance class as walking. All these behaviors are characterized by rhythmic alternating activity of limbs on opposing sides of the body, usually carried out for purposes of propelling the body forward. Because walking is representative of all locomotory activities, I call this entire chapter *Walking*, though walking will not be the only form of locomotion to be described.

Walking and its related forms of locomotion are remarkably flexible. Based on incoming perceptual information, one can speed up or slow down, turn, step up, step down, or walk backward. The ease with which one can switch from one mode to another points to a sophisticated mechanism for selecting and initiating different locomotory patterns. Because the patterns are usually selected automatically on the basis of sensory input, it is reasonable to hypothesize direct links between perception and action.

The flexibility of walking is not entirely dictated by the external environment, however. Through internal decisions, people can readily adopt different gaits, including stylized, theatrical patterns such as limping, marching, and dancing. The fact that we can adopt different walking styles at will implies that walking can come under direct conscious control. Thus there are different levels at which walking can be controlled. How these levels are coordinated is another issue to be considered here.

■ DESCRIPTIONS OF WALKING

To understand how walking is controlled, it is important to describe it accurately. I have already mentioned some features of walking which can be observed without sophisticated equipment: Walking takes many forms, it is responsive to the structure of the external environment, it can be consciously controlled, and it is innately programmed. Another feature is that in unfortunate circumstances, as a result of trauma or disease, one's ability to walk may become severely impaired, leading to lack of coordination, weakness, or even paralysis.

With these preliminary observations in mind, let us begin the study of walking with a description of how the legs move when animals or people proceed over land at different speeds.

Gait Patterns at Different Speeds

In the late nineteenth century, the American photographer Eadweard Muybridge (1887/1957) set out to resolve a controversy of his day: When horses trot, do all their legs leave the ground at once? Muybridge set up the first time-lapse camera system to address this question (see Figure 4.1). His pictures revealed that all of a horse's feet do indeed leave the ground during trotting (Panels 4, 5, 9, and 10). More importantly for present purposes, his pictures also showed that a horse uses different gait patterns when it walks or trots. During walking, the horse adopts a three-legged stance (Panels C and D of Figure 4.1), but during trotting, the horse never has three legs on the ground at once.

Do people also change gait patterns when they change speed of locomotion? Figure 4.2 shows that they do. During walking, both feet are on the ground, but during running, only one foot is on the ground (Alexander, 1984).

Why does the gait pattern change with speed of locomotion? A simple answer (Alexander, 1984) can be arrived at by considering the simplified walker shown in Figure 4.3. This man's leg is assumed to be perfectly straight when his foot is on the ground. At this time his center of mass is also highest. When he steps forward, his center of mass descends in an arc, the radius of which equals l, the length of the man's leg. Suppose the man moves forward with velocity v. From physics, it is known that the acceleration of the center of mass is v^2/l. This quantity cannot exceed the acceleration due to gravity, g, unless the man deliberately pulls his body downward, which would counter the goal of moving forward. Thus v^2/l must always be less than or equal to g. Equivalently,

$$v \leq \sqrt{gl} \tag{4.1}$$

Figure 4.1 Engravings made from Muybridge's photographs of a horse engaged in walking (panels A–F) and trotting (panels 1–12). (Reprinted from *Scientific American*, October 19, 1878.)

Because g is about 10 m/sec^2 and the length of the leg of a typical adult is about 0.9 m, it is impossible to walk more quickly than about 2.5 m/sec. In fact, people usually switch from walking to running at about this speed (Alexander, 1984).

Why does running enable one to proceed more quickly than 2.5 m/sec? The reason is that walking is just a series of controlled *falls*, but running is a series of controlled *leaps*. Leaps are possible during running because the elastic recoil of the leg muscles and tendons enables the runner to "bounce" back after his (or her) foot strikes the ground.

If the shift from walking to running is due to physical factors, then the power requirements for walking should exceed those for running at or above the speeds where walking gives way to a run. The actual power requirements have been estimated from measures of oxygen consumption and carbon dioxide release (Margaria, 1976). As seen in Figure 4.4, the estimated power requirements do in fact become greater for walking than for running at around 2.5 m/sec. The power requirements for bicycling are the least at

Figure 4.2 Stages of walking (*top*) and running (*bottom*) in humans. (Reprinted from Alexander, 1984.)

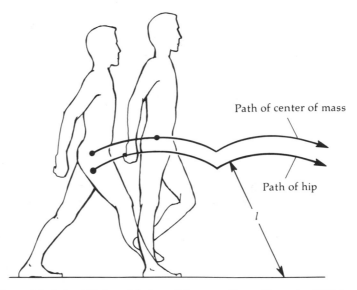

Figure 4.3 A simplified model of a walking man. (From Alexander, 1984.)

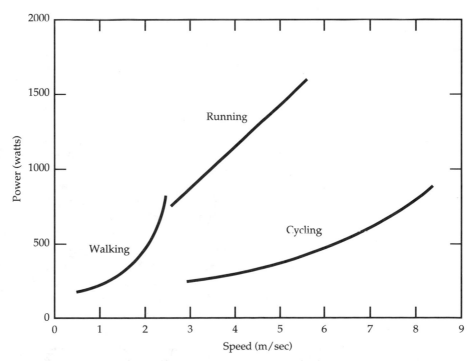

Figure 4.4 Power requirements of walking, running, and cycling at different speeds. (From Alexander, 1984.)

this speed because when one cycles, the center of mass of the body remains at a nearly constant height, so the mechanical energy of the body does not fluctuate between potential energy and kinetic energy in every stride, as in walking or running.

Regularities in Gait Patterns

Because changing locomotion speed is achieved by a dramatic change in gait patterns, one might suppose that there is little regularity in the patterns of locomotion that animals or people actually exhibit. In fact, considerable regularity is observed. One way the regularity is shown is through a perceptual demonstration devised by a Swedish psychologist, Gunnar Johansson (1973), following earlier work by Mayer (1895/1972). Johansson's method consists of filming a person who has a small number of luminious dots attached to his or her body. When the film is later viewed, only the lights can be seen; the actor's body and surroundings are invisible. Observers viewing the moving dot patterns have an unmistakable and immediate impression of a person in motion. Observers can see people walking, dancing, and running, and can even distinguish among their friends and between males and females (Cutting & Proffitt, 1981). The ability to see people in motion is not limited to adult observers. Infants between 4 and 6 months old are more likely to look at moving light patterns arising from someone running in place than to look at randomly moving patterns with the same number of lights (Fox & McDaniel, 1982).

It is a remarkable feature of visual perception that observers can see biological motion when presented with nothing more than a small number of moving dots. For such perception to be possible, there must be regularity in the gait patterns that people and animals display (Cutting, 1986). Some of those regularities can be identified here.

One is that the time that a leg swings through the air between successive footfalls (the *swing* phase) hardly changes with walking speed (see Figure 4.5). By contrast, the time that the foot remains on the ground (the *stance* phase) increases with the time spent in each step. This principle is remarkably widespread in the animal kingdom. It is seen in cockroaches (Pearson, 1976), lobsters (Macmillan, 1975), cats (Goslow, Reinking, & Stuart, 1973; Miller & Van der Meeche, 1975), dogs (Arshavsky, Kots, Orlovskii, Rodionov, & Shik, 1965), and humans (Herman, Wirta, Bampton, & Finley, 1976; Shapiro, Zernicke, Gregor, & Diestel, 1981). The swing phase has an approximately constant duration because the foot is flung forward in a ballistic fashion, with much of its trajectory being determined by gravity alone (McMahon, 1984).

Another kind of regularity that has been observed in analyses of gait concerns the time-varying angles of the knee and hip. During normal running, the angles of a runner's knee and thigh covary systematically. The relationship is shown in Figure 4.6A, in an *angle–angle* diagram (Enoka, 1988).

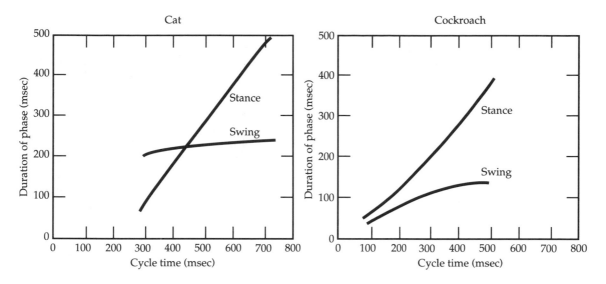

Figure 4.5 Duration of the stance phase and swing phase of the cat (*left*) and cockroach (*right*) as a function of cycle time. (From Pearson, 1976.)

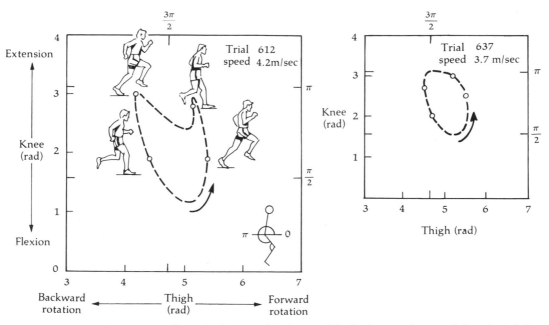

Figure 4.6 Angle–angle diagram of the knee and thigh of a normal runner (*left*) and of a below-knee amputee (*right*). There is less flexing of the knee joint in the amputee than in the normal individual. From Enoka, Miller, and Burgess (1982). Below-knee amputee running gait. *American Journal of Physical Medicine,* **61,** 66–84. Copyright © by Williams and Wilkins, 1982.

Such diagrams are useful for therapeutic purposes. They allow clinicians to determine the exact nature of a gait disorder and to chart progress made in therapy. The angle–angle diagram shown in Figure 4.6B, for example, comes from a person with a below-knee amputation who is wearing a foot prosthesis. The person's gait is still imperfect, as seen by comparing Figure 4.6B with 4.6A. Comparisons like this provide objective means of evaluating the effectiveness of different prosthetic designs.

A similar sort of analysis allows for the evaluation of gait in patients with cerebral palsy or other neurological damage. In one application (Teitelman, 1984), small lights are temporarily (and painlessly) attached to the lower extremities of patients with cerebral palsy. The positions of the lights are recorded as the patient walks. The time-varying angular changes of the knee, hip, or ankle are then analyzed to determine whether those changes differ from the patterns observed in normal individuals. By simultaneously recording the electromyographic activity of the leg muscles, it is sometimes possible to determine whether abnormalities in the pattern of joint angles are due to misordering of the activation of the leg muscles. Surgical rearrangement of the leg muscles is then undertaken to achieve occasionally more satisfactory timing patterns (Teitelman, 1984).

■ NEURAL CONTROL OF LOCOMOTION

As the last example illustrates, timing the activation and deactivation of leg muscles is a nontrivial task. How is the timing achieved?

Consider the activity of the muscles in one leg of a walking cat. Figure 4.7 shows that there are orderly patterns of muscle activity within the cat's leg during a step cycle. During the swing phase the flexors are active and the extensors are inactive, but during the stance phase the flexors are inactive and the extensors are active. This sequence of electromyographic activity accounts for the distinct types of motion observed in the swing phase

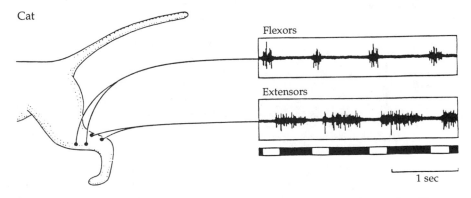

Figure 4.7 Extensor and flexor activity of the hind limb of the cat during locomotion. (From Pearson, 1976.)

and stance phase of locomotion. In the swing phase, when the flexors are active, the leg is retracted and pulled forward toward the next footfall. In the stance phase, when the extensors are active, the leg is pushed down so the body can be propelled forward.

Some of the earliest research on the neural regulation of leg-muscle activity was conducted by the British physiologist, Charles Sherrington (1906), who was knighted and received a Nobel prize for his research on this and related topics. Sherrington severed the cat's spinal cord and observed that rhythmic activity in the legs still occurred. His observation implied that the spinal cord can produce rhythmic movement without input from the brain. Sherrington believed that the spinal cord generates rhythmic movement through a *reflex chain*. According to this view, sensory feedback from one burst of muscle activity serves as the stimulus for the next burst.

The reflex-chain hypothesis came into question in 1911, when another British physiologist, T. Graham Brown, performed an experiment similar to Sherrington's. Brown severed the spinal cord of the cat to see what locomotory capacities would remain (as Sherrington had done). However, unlike Sherrington, Brown also eliminated sensory feedback to the spinal cord by cutting the dorsal roots (see Chapter 2). He observed that even after this procedure, rhythmic contractions of leg muscles continued. Because the rhythmic contractions occurred without input from the brain and without sensory input from the muscles, the spinal cord itself must have produced the efferent signals that allowed for the rhythmic leg contractions.

Brown's discovery had enormous theoretical significance, for it implied that sensory feedback contributes far less to movement than Sherrington had thought. Given the revolutionary impact of Brown's finding, it was therefore important to be sure that his procedure for eliminating sensory feedback was effective. Cause for concern was fueled by the discovery, made a number of years later, that some sensory feedback is transmitted through the ventral roots of the spinal cord as well as through the dorsal roots (see Grillner, 1981).

The later research vindicated Brown (Cohen, Rossignol, & Grillner, 1988; Grillner, 1981). In one procedure, called *fictive locomotion*, the spinal cord was functionally isolated by severing its connections to the brain and brain stem. In addition, the dorsal roots were cut below the level of the spinal transection, and the muscles were completely paralyzed to ensure that no feedback from the muscles would infiltrate the spinal cord via the ventral roots. (Paralyzing the muscles was achieved with curare, a neuromuscular blocking agent.) Recordings were then made of the activity of ventral roots of the isolated spinal cord to see what signals (if any) still emerged. The result was dramatic: Rhythmic bursts were recorded in the ventral roots. Furthermore, the distribution of bursts over different ventral roots was similar to that seen in behaving animals. Thus the fictive locomotion procedure confirmed that there are *central pattern generators* within the spinal cord and that these central pattern generators can provide the basis for locomotion in intact animals. Studies by other investigators confirmed that central pattern generators are widespread in the animal kingdom (Delcomyn, 1975).

Many questions are suggested by these findings. How are rhythm generators neurally organized? Are they situated within individual neurons (what some investigators call *pacemaker* cells) or do they exist by virtue of interconnections among several neurons? What is the role of sensory input? If efferent signals are generated autonomously, does sensory feedback have significance for rhythm generation? Finally, what is the brain's role in locomotion? I will consider each of these questions in turn.

Neural Circuits for Locomotion

Because the mammalian spinal cord is a highly complex structure, neurophysiologists interested in the control of locomotion have worked with animals that have somewhat simpler neural circuitry. One such animal is the cockroach. The gait patterns of the cockroach are similar to those of the cat in the respect that different sequences of footfalls occur as the cockroach modulates its speed of locomotion. Moreover, the duration of the cockroach's stance phase varies with the gait being performed, but the duration of its swing phase is essentially constant. Finally, when tiny electrodes are used to record muscular activity in the leg of the cockroach, flexor activity is observed during the swing phase and extensor activity is observed during the stance phase, as in mammals (Pearson, 1976). These similarities between locomotion in the cockroach and locomotion in other species are remarkable in and of themselves, for they suggest that locomotion may be controlled in common ways throughout the animal kingdom. The similarities also make the cockroach an appropriate model system in which to investigate the neural circuitry underlying locomotion in mammals.

Figure 4.8 shows a possible neural circuit for cockroach locomotion (Pearson, 1976). The circuit is known as a *flexor burst generator*. It is assumed to excite flexor motor neurons and to inhibit extensor motor neurons, both periodically. The periodicity of the flexor burst generator arises from mutual inhibitory influences among interneurons. The interneurons are excited by central command neurons which tonically (continually) activate the extensor motor neuron. When the common exit point for the flexor burst generator (interneuron 1) is turned on, it activates the flexor motor neuron as well as an interneuron which inhibits the extensor motor neuron. Thus the flexor motor neuron is normally off but is turned on by the flexor burst generator. Similarly, the extensor motor neuron, which is normally on, is turned off (indirectly) by the flexor burst generator. Because the flexor burst generator produces bursts of approximately constant duration, the activation time of the flexor motor neuron is approximately constant, which may explain why the duration of the swing phase is fixed. By contrast, the extensor motor neuron is always on, except when it is inhibited, and the length of time the extensor

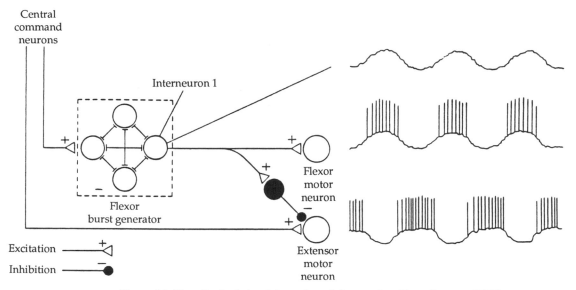

Figure 4.8 Hypothesized circuit for cockroach locomotion. (From Pearson, 1976.)

motor neuron has an outward effect depends on the duration of the step cycle. This aspect of the model may explain why the duration of the stance phase changes with the duration of the step cycle.

As satisfactory as this theoretical circuit may be for explaining the control of a single leg, it does not account for the coordination of multiple legs. The circuit must be elaborated to account for multileg coordination. Figure 4.9 shows an elaborated circuit. Two added features help account for interlimb coordination. One is inhibition between flexor burst generators for adjacent limbs; this feature can account for the fact that the cockroach never steps with adjacent legs simultaneously. The other feature is sensory inhibition, sent from a receptor on each leg to that leg's flexor burst generator.

The receptor suggested by Pearson (1976) was one that responds to mechanical loading of the leg. It is activated during the stance phase of the step cycle. As the animal pushes forward and the load on the leg is reduced, the receptor's activity diminishes and the flexor burst generator that it normally inhibits can produce flexor activity in the next period (giving rise to the next swing phase).

Although this model was proposed more than a decade ago it still remains to be proven physiologically (Cohen *et al.*, 1988). Nevertheless, some useful lessons can be learned from it. One is that one need not posit a single pacemaker cell to explain rhythmic activity. A group of cells can also give rise to rhythmic outputs. Having a group of cells generate rhythm may be preferable to having a single cell do so because the loss of that cell could be devastating for the behaving organism.

Second, the sequencing of leg movements may be modulated by sensory feedback. [Pearson's (1976) model required sensory feedback to trig-

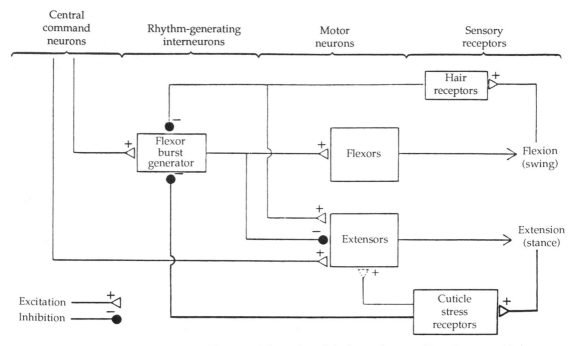

Figure 4.9 Possible network for cockroach limb coordination. (From Pearson, 1976.)

ger the swing phase.] If this idea is correct in general, it implies that the control of locomotion is achieved through an interplay of central pattern generators and sensory influences. This view has received wide support, as shown in subsequent sections.

The Role of Sensory Feedback

With the exception of Pearson's (1976) proposal about the role of feedback in the control of cockroach locomotion, none of the results I have presented force the conclusion that sensory feedback has an impact on walking. The other studies showed that even when the spinal cord receives no sensory input, it still generates highly organized patterns of efferent signals. Consider the following facts, however. Patients with *tabes dorsalis*, a disease of the dorsal roots of the spinal cord, have great difficulty walking (Kalat, 1980). When sensory feedback is eliminated from "spinal" animals (animals whose spinal cord has been separated from the brain), overall speed of locomotion is reduced, though the basic sequencing of steps is preserved (Carew, 1985). In fictive locomotion (described earlier), the time intervals between neural bursts recorded at the ventral roots for the extensor and flexor muscles are significantly longer than in chronic spinal cats whose muscles still work and provide feedback to the spinal cord

(Grillner, 1981). These results imply that sensory feedback does make some contribution to walking movements. How then can we account for the findings, reviewed earlier, which suggest a wholly central basis for locomotory control?

The contribution of sensory feedback can be appreciated by considering a study by Taub and Berman (1968). Prior to their work, it was widely believed that monkeys with deafferented limbs could not walk or manipulate objects, for when the limbs on one side of the body were deafferented, those limbs were not used. Then Taub and Berman (1968) severed the dorsal roots of *both* sides of the monkey's spinal cord. The result was that the monkeys could now use their limbs, though they did so more slowly and awkwardly than when feedback was available. Taub and Berman's (1968) finding implies that sensory feedback is not *necessary* for locomotion (or reaching) but it is useful for *tuning* movements. It is as if the nervous system has central *programs* for movement patterns, and the exact way those programs are carried out depends on information supplied from the sensory apparatus (Keele, 1968, 1981).

A prediction that can be made from this account is that the way sensory information affects locomotion (or any centrally programmed motor activity) should depend on the motor system's currently programmed state. This prediction has been supported both in theoretical and in experimental work. Theoretically, as seen earlier in Pearson's (1976) model of cockroach walking, feedback can affect the phase relations among the legs: If the flexor burst generator for a given leg receives inhibitory signals from that leg's load sensor, the burst generator does not fire and so does not inhibit neighboring burst generators, allowing the swing phase to be initiated.

Experimental work also confirms the prediction that sensory feedback has different effects depending on the animal's current motor state. When a cat is prevented from extending its hind leg, its leg immediately flexes, but this occurs only if the hind leg is prevented from extending at a critical point in the stance phase (Grillner, 1981). A related phenomenon is observed when the top of a cat's paw is touched with a rod during the swing phase or during the stance phase of the step cycle. (Forrsberg, Grillner, & Rossignol, 1975). Though the stimulus is assumed to be the same in these two cases, the cat's response is quite different. If the stimulus is applied during the swing phase, there is an enhanced flexion response, as if the animal were trying to raise its paw above an unexpected obstacle. However, if the stimulus is delivered during the stance phase there is an enhanced extension response, as if the animal were trying to ensure a foothold. Thus the same stimulus has opposite effects depending on when it is applied. The implication is that the nervous system provides for adaptive, context-dependent reactions through centrally programmed neural changes. The human nervous system does as well, for similar observations have been made in humans during the acts of walking or standing (Nashner, Woollacott, & Tuma, 1979).

Descending Effects

What is the brain's role in the control of walking? Figure 4.10 shows a laboratory setup that has proven useful for answering this question (Nashner, 1976; Nashner & McCollum, 1985). Subjects were asked to stand on a platform that could undergo a variety of sudden displacements. For example, it could slide back, which caused the subject to tilt forward, or it could tilt up (toward the subject's face) which caused the subject to sway back. The interesting feature of these platform maneuvers is that they both stretch the *gastrocnemius* muscle (the large muscle group on the back of the lower leg). In general, stretching the gastrocnemius gives rise to a reflex—contraction of that muscle. The fact that gastrocnemius contraction follows both types of platform movement creates a problem, however. When the platform slides back, the body tilts forward, so when the gastrocnemius contracts the effect is to oppose body sway, which helps stabilize the body. By contrast, when the platform tilts *up*, the body tilts *back*, and the resulting gastrocnemius contraction promotes backward tilt, which *destabilizes* the body. The question, then, is whether subjects can turn off the reflex when it has untoward consequences. The answer is that the reflex is attenuated when it has a destabilizing effect but continues to operate when it has a stabilizing effect (see Nashner & McCollum, 1985; Woollacott, in press).

The brain plays a role in the attenuation of the destabilizing reflex. This is shown by the fact that patients with damage to the cerebellum are less able than normal subjects to inhibit the reflex when its effect is destabilizing (see Woollacott, in press). Likewise, patients with vestibular damage exhibit abnormal responses when exposed to platform rotations (Allum & Pfaltz, 1985). Finally, in normal individuals, detailed studies of their muscle responses following experimentally induced postural perturbation indicate that the vestibular system coordinates the distribution of restoring forces over widely distributed sites in the body (Woollacott, in press). In general, entire configurations of muscles—muscle *synergies*—are activated in response to postural disturbances (Woollacott, in press). Muscle synergies can be elicited by electrical stimulation of the motor cortex (Humphrey, 1986; Massion, 1984).

The brain also affects the selection and control of gait patterns (Shik, Severin, & Orlovky, 1966). Shik *et al.* (1966) cut the spinal cord of the cat at different levels, and for each level determined what stepping patterns could be performed when the cat was placed on a treadmill. They found that when the spinal cord was cut below the brain stem (causing the spinal cord to be isolated from the brain stem and higher brain structures), coordinated gait could still occur. This outcome corroborates the results described by Brown (1911) and Grillner (1981). When the spinal cord was left connected to the brain stem but the brain stem was disconnected from higher brain centers, distinct patterns of gait could be elicited with electrical stimulation of the locomotor region (see Figure 4.11). As the strength of electrical stimulation increased and as the speed

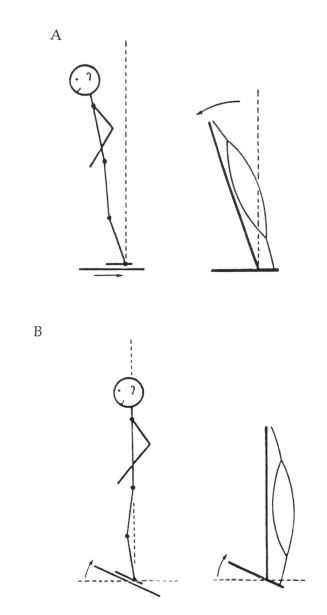

Figure 4.10 Experimental setup used by Nashner (1976). (A) Backward displacement of the platform induces a reflex response that *stabilizes* posture. (B) Upward displacement of the platform induces a reflex that *destabilizes* posture. Reprinted by permission of the publisher from Posture and locomotion by T. J. Carew, in *Principles of neural science* (2d ed.), pp. 478–486. Copyright © 1985 by Elsevier Science Publishing Co., Inc.

of the treadmill increased, the pattern of gait changed from walking to trotting to galloping. Similar effects have been obtained by injecting L-DOPA (a precursor of dopamine) into the same brainstem region (see Woollacott, in press).

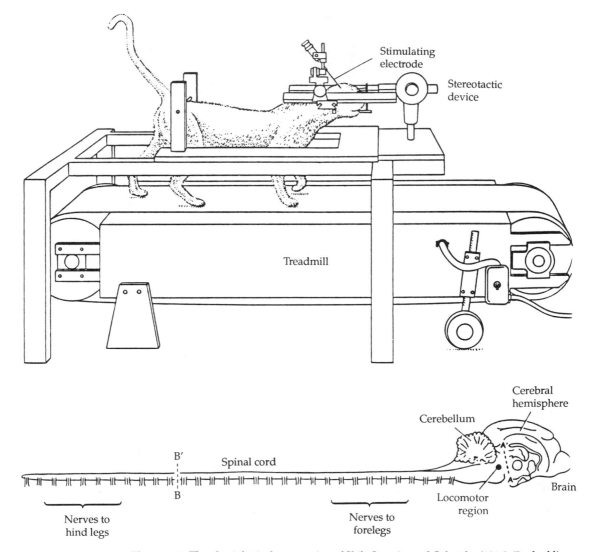

Figure 4.11 The physiological preparation of Shik, Severin, and Orlovsky (1966). Dashed lines between A and A' and between B and B' show transection locations. (From Pearson, 1976.)

Other studies have provided information about how the brain controls the speed and direction of walking or running (Freed & Yamamoto, 1985). Animals can be made to run clockwise or counterclockwise when dopaminergic cells in the substantia nigra are electrically stimulated. Whether the animal runs clockwise or counterclockwise depends on which hemisphere receives the stimulation. The substantia nigra is an area involved in the production of dopamine. When the substantia nigra produces lower-than-normal amounts of dopamine, Parkinson's symptoms can ensue.

Parkinson's patients have trouble initiating gait, often shuffling their feet while trying to walk forward or turn (Kalat, 1980). (See Chapter 2.)

Speed and direction of locomotion also appear to be controlled, at least in part, by a constellation of neurons called the *nucleus accumbens*. The amount of dopamine in this structure is related to the speed and direction of movement in treadmill-running rats. The *caudate nucleus*, a basal ganglia structure, plays a role in the regulation of posture. Depending on the degree of lateral or vertical curvature of a treadmill in which a rat is running, the amount of dopamine in the caudate nucleus (contralateral to the lateral direction of turning) increases or decreases (Freed & Yamomoto, 1985).

Another important role played by the brain in the control of walking is visual guidance. When cats are required to walk over a perfectly even surface, relatively little neural activity is observed in the corticospinal tract (see Georgopoulos & Grillner, 1989). However, when cats are required to walk over uneven terrain, the level of activity in the corticospinal tract increases markedly (Georgopoulos & Grillner, 1989). Transection of the corticospinal tract eliminates the capacity for climbing a ladder—another locomotory task requiring visually directed limb positioning. The corticospinal tract is also involved in manual aiming tasks, which suggests that the neural systems underlying the control of locomotion and the control of reaching and grasping (see Chapter 6) may overlap. Everyday observation suggests that they should, because many locomotory tasks, particularly among animals, require grasping as well as propulsion. Squirrels and monkeys must grab hold of the tree branches on which they run, for example. It is possible, in view of these observations, that the control of reaching and grasping may have evolved from the control of locomotion (Georgopoulos & Grillner, 1989).

How can we summarize the brain's role in the control of locomotion? In general terms, the brain serves as a supervisor. Some responses to sensory feedback during locomotion and balance occur too quickly to be mediated by the brain and instead must be mediated by the spinal cord alone. Yet the responsiveness of the spinal cord is altered by supraspinal influences. The brain may alter the reference conditions that the lower nerve centers try to satisfy. Without the brain's supervisory control, walking would be erratic and undisciplined. A chicken without a head provides a vivid example.

■ WALKING MACHINES

An effective way to test one's understanding of a biological system is to try to simulate it in an artificial device. In this regard, it is instructive to consider the efforts that have been made to build machines that walk. Walking machines are valuable for scaling uneven terrain (for example in military and exploratory missions) and for carrying passengers who cannot walk themselves. In deciding how to build such machines, it has been useful to identify essential conditions that any walking system must satisfy. Raibert and Sutherland (1983) listed five such conditions:

1. The machine must regulate its sequence of footfalls.
2. It must not tip over.
3. It must distribute load and lateral forces among all its legs.
4. It must ensure that the legs do not move beyond their travel limits or bump into each other.
5. It must ensure that chosen footholds provide adequate support.

Only a few successful walking machines have been built. In the nineteenth century, a patent was issued for a rudimentary walking machine, similar to modern walking toys (Raibert & Sutherland, 1983). Not until the 1960s was a machine built that was capable of true walking. This was a four-legged, electrically driven walking device built in 1966 at the University of Southern California. It was too small to be ridden by a human driver but too unsophisticated to be controlled without a person on board (McMahon, 1984). A much larger four-legged walking machine was built in 1968 at General Electric (McMahon, 1984). It was the size of an elephant and was extremely hard to control. A human driver sat atop the contraption and instructed the back legs how to move by moving his or her own legs and instructed the front legs how to move by moving his or her own arms. The task proved unmanageable for the driver, so this artificial walking elephant was left to stand in its stall.

A more successful device, designed in the early 1980s, had six rather than four legs (see Figure 4.12). Six is the smallest number of legs that provides a consistently stable base of support during locomotion because, with a six-legged walker, it is possible to alternate between one tripod (three-legged) stance and another. Three is the smallest number of legs needed for static balancing. A three-legged piano stool can stand on an even surface without an active control system. Thus the balance problem is significantly easier for a six-legged walking device than for a walking device with four or fewer legs, which is, perhaps, why insects have six legs.

Each leg of the device shown in Figure 4.12 had a pair of hydraulic actuators. Each actuator received input from a computer that responded to feedback from the machine's legs. The computer allowed for release of a fixed amount of oil to one or the other actuator for any given leg. Only one actuator for a leg received oil at a given time, so there was a kind of reciprocal inhibition between each leg's actuators, much as there is between the muscle antagonists of a biological limb. The decision about where the machine should tread and how quickly it should tread was left to the human operator, who sat on the machine. When the driver selected a path, the computer determined which legs were free to move and where the next step should be taken. The machine could turn, walk forward and back, and tilt up or down or to one side or the other. An important feature of the control system was that some of the adjustments were entirely passive. The actuators acted as passive hydraulic circuits, like the shock absorbers of a car, so compensations for elevations or depressions in the ground were

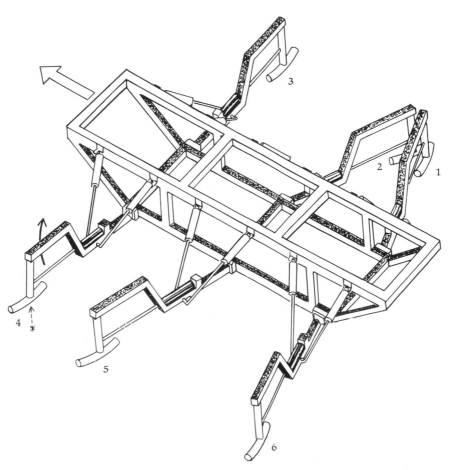

Figure 4.12 Six-legged walking machine. (From Raibert and Sutherland, 1983.)

achieved (within limits) without any involvement by the computer or human operator. Thus the computational burdens of guiding the machine were reduced by exploiting the machine's own physical structure. This design strategy appears to be used in biological walking systems as well (McMahon, 1984) and is recognized as a useful way of reducing the computational burdens of trajectory planning (Bizzi & Mussa-Ivaldi, 1989; Thelen, Kelso, & Fogel, 1987).

■ THE DEVELOPMENT OF WALKING

Machines that walk are developed through human craft. Human and animal walking develop through maturation and experience. As I mentioned earlier in this chapter, the capacity for walking is innate. Newborn colts or calves can stand up and walk within the first minutes of life. Human newborns exhibit stepping movements when held beneath the shoulders, provided their feet can touch the ground (André-Thomas & Autgarden, 1966). Some people have been so impressed with the newborn's capacity for stepping that they have encouraged newborns to swim. When held in water, newborns do indeed exhibit impressive, coordinated arm and leg movements (McGraw, 1943).

The development of walking follows a number of milestones (Shirley, 1931): The baby first lifts its head, then supports its body on its arms, next turns over, then sits up, then creeps, next walks with assistance, and finally walks alone. What accounts for this progression?

Neonatal Reflexes

One way to develop an account of the development of walking is to note that several reflexes come into play when walking occurs. In addition, some reflexes present in infancy disappear later in life (Easton, 1972). The disappearance of reflexes accompanies neurological changes which allow for mature walking behavior.

Consider some of the reflexes exhibited by infants (Figure 4.13). One, the *startle reflex*, is triggered by unexpected noise or changes in bodily position, particularly those that create sensations of falling. The baby's arms and legs move symmetrically, first outward, then upward, then inward. The hands open and clench, as do the legs.

Another infantile reflex, the *tonic neck reflex*, is an asymmetrical pose adopted by newborns up to about 16 weeks of age. The baby's head and arm extend to one side. On the opposite side, the arm and leg flex. The functional significance of the tonic neck reflex is unclear. One hypothesis is that it enables the infant to observe its own hand, thereby facilitating the development of hand–eye coordination. Although the tonic neck reflex normally disappears during development, it may remain available later in life (see Figure 4.14), providing a built-in pattern that can be called upon as necessary (Easton, 1972).

The *righting reflex* occurs when the infant is pulled up to a sitting position. When the righting reflex appears, the infant attempts to keep its head erect. The head may flop forward or back, however, due to poor coordination or weakness.

When pressure is applied to the palm of the baby's hand or foot, the fingers or toes curl up as if to grab the object. Because this *grasp reflex* is seen in the feet as well as the hands, it may be a throwback to a time when our prehuman ancestors lived in trees.

The *Babinski reflex* is another involuntary response to stimulation of the bottom of the feet. Named for the neurologist who first described it, the foot pulls up, the toes fan out, and the big toe is raised. The Babinski reflex disappears during normal development. Its presence in older children or adults signals neurological damage.

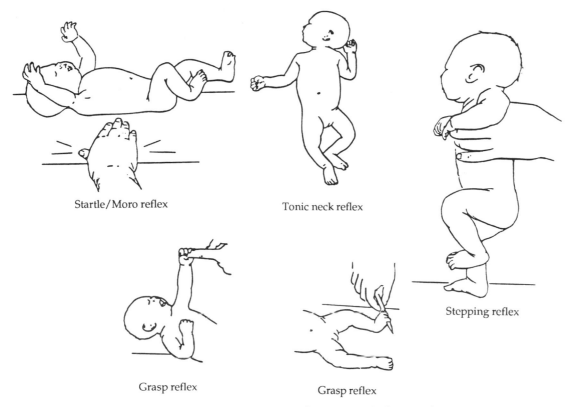

Startle/Moro reflex

Tonic neck reflex

Stepping reflex

Grasp reflex

Grasp reflex

Figure 4.13 Reflexes seen in the human infant.

The *crawling reflex* occurs in babies who have not yet learned to walk. As its name implies, this reflex is an alternating pattern of extensions and flexions of the arms and legs, performed with the belly on the ground.

The so-called *swimming reflex* is essentially the same as the crawling reflex, except that it occurs in water. An additional reflex is called upon when the baby is placed in water. If the baby's face happens to be submerged momentarily, the baby rarely chokes or aspirates water. Thus, the baby can inhibit its breathing. Other, more sophisticated means of coordinating breathing and movement have been documented (Bramble & Carrier, 1983).

I have already mentioned the *stepping reflex*, in which the baby alternately lifts and plants the two feet in succession when held so the feet come in contact with a solid surface. The stepping reflex is present in newborns but usually disappears by around 4 weeks of age, only to reappear at 8 months to 1 year. The reasons for the disappearance of stepping between 8 months and 1 year have been debated, and the arguments are worth reviewing.

Figure 4.14 Catching a fly ball can result in a pose strongly resembling the tonic neck reflex of infancy.

Disappearance and Reappearance of Stepping

Why does stepping disappear and then reappear in human infants? According to one view, the reasons are psychological (Zelazo, 1983). According to another view, they are physical (Thelen, 1983).

The departure point for the psychological hypothesis is that the reappearance of stepping coincides with the emergence of cognitive sequencing abilities. For example, at around 1 year of age, babies can recognize sequences of lights, as indicated by measures of smiling, vocalization, pointing, or changes in heart rate (Kagan, 1971). Zelazo (1983) suggested that because walking requires sequential control of motor units, the control of walking only becomes possible when cognitive sequencing has been achieved. At first, this idea may seem a bit far-fetched. One wonders why, for example, stepping was possible at an earlier age. On the other hand, judging from the fact that some parents boast about the early age at which their children start walking, some people obviously believe that early walking is a sign of precociousness (Zelazo, 1983).

In support of the psychological account of the reappearance of stepping, Zelazo (1983) noted that the development of walking and leg movements is facilitated by learning. For example, when babies are rewarded for kicking (for example, if kicking turns a mobile), more kicks occur (Rovee & Fagan, 1976; Thelen & Fisher, 1983). Moreover, when babies are encouraged to practice stepping, walking may develop somewhat earlier than when no practice is employed.

Thelen (1983) attributed the re-emergence of stepping to physical changes. She doubted the psychological view because walking is possible in animals that have very limited cognitive abilities (such as insects), because walking develops even in people who are profoundly retarded, and because decerebrate animals (animals with the cerebral cortex disconnected from lower nerve centers) can walk. Furthermore, reclining infants can kick throughout the first year of life, with the kinematic patterns of their kicks being virtually identical to the kinematic patterns of normal stepping movements (Thelen, Bradshaw, & Ward, 1981). Finally, 2- to 8-month-old infants can step proficiently when held upright in water (Thelen, 1983). These findings indicate that the capacity for stepping does not disappear between 2 and 8 months of age. The baby's nervous system can generate sequences of muscle commands required for stepping behavior all through the first year of life.

Why then does stepping usually not occur between 2 and 8 months of age? Thelen's (1983) answer is that the baby's legs are simply not strong enough to support its body. As seen in Figure 4.15, the baby's center of gravity is high above its legs, creating a mechanical disadvantage for the legs that is aggravated by the fact that the infant's legs are weak. As the baby's legs get stronger, and as the body's center of gravity descends, the mechanical demands of supporting the body are reduced and the possibility of walking returns. The simplicity of Thelen's (1983) explanation, together with the data she presented, suggests that her account of the disappearance and reappearance of stepping is correct.

From this controversy, a useful general lesson can be learned about the analysis of motor behavior: In attempting to explain behavioral phenomena, it is not always wise to look exclusively to the inner world of the mind, neglecting the observable physical world. Sometimes observable physical relations by themselves can explain important behavioral phenomena. (This issue will come up again in Chapter 11.)

Models of Motor Development

Although physical factors may account for the re-emergence of stepping around 1 year of age, not all developmental phenomena in motor control can be explained so easily. The reflexes discussed earlier, for example, disappear under normal conditions, presumably because of neurological changes.

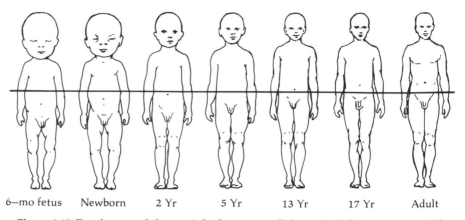

6–mo fetus   Newborn   2 Yr   5 Yr   13 Yr   17 Yr   Adult

Figure 4.15 Developmental changes in body structure (Palmer, 1944). (From Thelen, 1983.)

Researchers concerned with these changes have suggested that they are organized on the basis of three major principles, reviewed subsequently.

One is that during development, nerve fibers in the central nervous system undergo *myelination*, the process by which axons are coated with the fatty substance that allows for speeded neural transmission (see Chapter 2). Once this coating has formed, finer coordination becomes possible (Yakolev & Lecours, 1967).

Second, cortical centers come to take over functions that were previously performed by subcortical centers, or they inhibit those subcortical centers (McGraw, 1943). This explains why reflexes seen in young infants, such as the tonic neck reflex and the grasp reflex, are supplanted by other, more flexible behaviors. It also explains why primitive reflexes, such as the Babinski, are seen in patients with cortical damage. Similarly, tonic flexion of the extremities, seen in some patients with cerebral palsy, may result from abnormal cortical inhibition of lower motor centers. Finally, the postures adopted during sleep in normal adults are similar to those exhibited by babies, as if during sleep the inhibitory influences of the higher brain centers are temporarily suspended.

The third principle that helps account for the disappearance of infantile reflexes is that neural maturation proceeds in a distinct cephalo–caudal (head-to-tail) and proximal–distal direction (e.g., Woollacott, Debu, & Mowatt, 1987). This assumption helps account for the fact that refined movements occur early in the proximal musculature (such as the mouth) and only later in the distal extremities (such as the feet and fingers). Thus while stepping may wax and wane developmentally, rooting (the tendency of the head to turn toward a stimulus that affords sucking) and sucking are highly developed from birth onward. Functionally, the advantage of cephalo–caudal and proximal–distal maturation is readily apparent: It is more important for survival to be able to eat or drink than to play the piano or kick a soccer ball (no matter how much ardent musicians or athletes may argue to the contrary). Perhaps it is also for this reason that when dogs shake water from their bodies, they shake off the water from head to tail. (At least this is what I have observed at my neighborhood swimming hole.)

■ NAVIGATING

The final topic to be covered in this chapter is *navigation*, which I will define as the adaptive control of whole-body motion in predictable and unpredictable environments. Navigation depends on perception and memory as well as motor control. Perception is needed to determine the physical properties of the environment through which one moves. Memory is needed to recall where sites are located and what kinds of actions are afforded by the objects and terrain being met. Motor control, of course, is needed to carry out the physical actions that ultimately are selected. In this section, I first consider the role of perception in locomotion, focusing primarily on vision. Then I turn to the role of memory. (I will not discuss the role of *audition* in walking. For information on this topic, particularly in regard to the blind, consult Strelow, 1985.)

Visual Kinesthesis

As one moves through the environment, the pattern of light impinging on the retina (the light-sensitive portion of the back of the eye) varies with the layout of the visual world, with the conditions of illumination, and with the manner in which one moves. Given that we can normally respond to visual input remarkably well, it has been suggested that the visual system evolved so as to respond instantly to the geometric properties of optical input (Gibson, 1950, 1966, 1979). The central idea in this proposal is that the physical layout of the external environment is directly specified by the optical array emanating from it (that is, the light rays bouncing off it and coming to the eye). The visual system, according to this theory, need not decipher the structure of the external world by piecing together bits of visual evidence. Rather, the optic array itself contains adequate information to make the structure of the external environment immediately and unambiguously apparent. (This is not to say that computations need not be performed to perceive the external environment, as some critics of Gibson's theory have charged, but rather that the computations to be performed can be defined with respect to optical information alone.)

To appreciate this theoretical position, consider the following experiment (Lee & Aronson, 1974; Lee & Lishman, 1975). A person stands on a stable floor surrounded by a moveable chamber made of four walls and a ceiling (see Figure 4.16). The question of interest is how subjects will respond to this rather unusual arrangement. Will they stand still or will they sway in relation to the motion of the surrounding chamber, or perhaps even fall over?

The answer for normal adults is that they sway. Moreover, their swaying is related to the swaying of the room. When the wall in front of the subject approaches, the subject sways backward. When the wall recedes, the subject sways forward.

The reason subjects sway as they do is based on optics. When the wall of the swinging room approaches, the image of the wall on the subject's retina grows. Such an increase in retinal image size also occurs when one falls forward. Thus subjects may sway backward when the wall approaches, because the visual input received from an approaching wall specifies *forward* falling; backward swaying counteracts this illusory fall. By contrast, when the wall of the swinging room recedes from the subject, the image of the wall on the subject's retina shrinks, as occurs when one falls backward. Thus subjects sway forward because forward swaying counteracts this illusory fall.

As logical as this explanation is, it may not convey the immediacy and cogency of subjects' perceptual experiences in the swinging-room situation. To appreciate what the perceptual experience is like, recall your feelings while watching a movie filmed from a descending roller coaster or from an automobile speeding around a hairpin curve. If you ever saw such a movie, you know how compelling visually induced motion can be.

Lee and his colleagues argued that the swaying room creates just this sort of perceptual experience. Moreover, they argued that the body sway elicited in the swinging room illustrates several more subtle points. One is that kinesthesis (the perception of body movement) is not governed entirely within the body but can also be governed from outside, chiefly by vision. To capture this idea, Lee (like Gibson before him) used the term *visual kinesthesis*.

A second conclusion is that the effect of visual kinesthesis can be so powerful that it gives rise to overt physical responses. In the movie theater, you may have felt like you were being swung around in your seat while getting a participant's view of the chase scene or roller coaster ride. By recording body sway, Lee and his colleagues demonstrated that such bodily movements actually occur.

The third point to be drawn from the swinging-room experiment is that there is a regular relation between external input and the kinesthesis that accompanies it. One reliably sways backward or forward when the front of the room approaches or recedes because optic flow directly provides information about the actor's interaction with the external world (Cutting, 1986; Gibson, 1950, 1966, 1979; Lee & Thomson, 1982).

It is possible to characterize in precise mathematical terms the relations between optic flow and the actor's movement in the external environment. Lee (1976) identified one mathematical relation of considerable importance, which I will state here verbally: *The inverse of the rate of expansion*

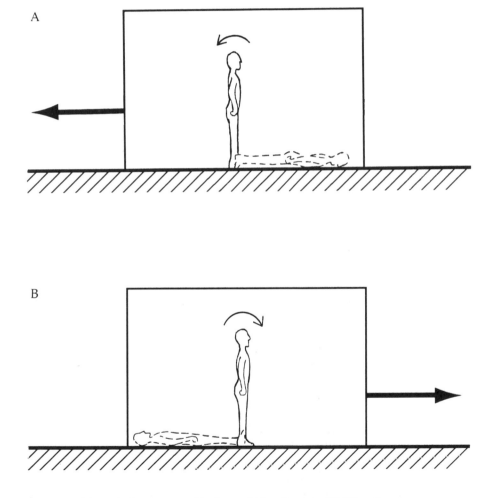

Figure 4.16 The swinging room used by Lee and his colleagues. (A) When the room approaches, the subject sways back to avoid falling forward. (B) When the room recedes, the subject sways forward to avoid falling back. (Adapted from Lee and Thomson, 1982.)

of the retinal image of an object equals the time remaining until contact is made with the object. Thus if an object is approaching the eye, its image on the retina expands, and the more quickly the object approaches the eye, the higher its retinal image expansion rate. At higher retinal-image expansion rates, less time remains until the object will be contacted, whereas at lower retinal-image expansion rates, more time remains until contact will occur. The beauty of this formula is that optical information alone specifies time-to-contact in the physical environment. Behavioral evidence from birds (Lee & Reddish, 1981) and people (Lee, Young, Reddish, Lough, & Clayton, 1983) suggests that the visuomotor system may in fact rely on this formula, or some analog of it, to regulate behaviors when time-to-contact matters.

Development of Visual Guidance

How does navigation develop? If visual input can directly specify how one is moving through the environment, one might expect very young children to rely on visual guidance during locomotion. Lee and his colleagues (Lee & Aronson, 1974; Lee & Lishman, 1975) tested this hypothesis by studying toddlers' responses to the swinging room. The result was dramatic. Unlike adults, whose body sway was amplified by the to and fro motion of the walls around them, toddlers sometimes were knocked off their feet when they tried to stand in the swinging room!

An implication of this outcome is that toddlers are sensitive to the same visual cues as adults. In fact, they may be even more sensitive, for they have less experience relying on their own proprioceptive input to control their standing behavior. Toddlers have a much harder time standing with their eyes closed than adults do, for example. Similarly, when adults try to stand on one foot or in an awkward posture, they sway more strongly in the swinging room than when both feet are planted firmly on the ground (Lee & Thomson, 1982).

Even if vision helps specify the nature of one's motion through the environment, the question remains of how the ability to coordinate visual and motor information changes developmentally. Some of the most influential research on this topic has been done with animals, in part because it is possible to influence animals' experience in ways that cannot be done ethically with children.

Figure 4.17 illustrates a classic experiment on the development of visuomotor coordination in kittens (Held, 1965). Two kittens were linked to one another in such a way that one kitten could walk freely while the other rode a small gondola that was transported through the same restricted visual environment by its partner. The important feature of the experimental environment was that both kittens received essentially the same visual input. The question was whether both kittens would develop the same level of visuomotor coordination.

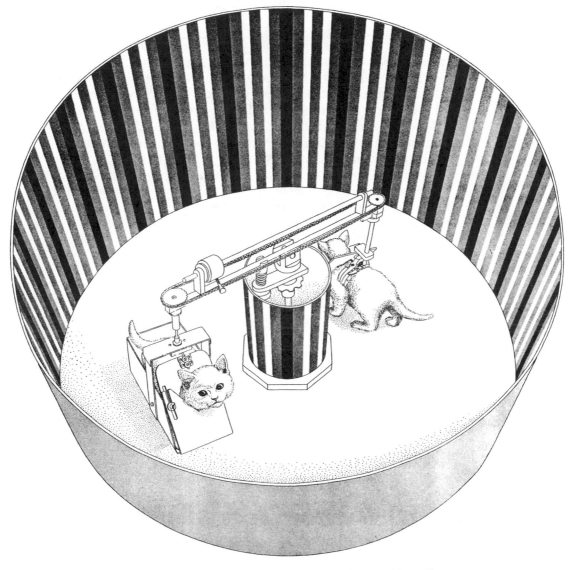

Figure 4.17 Held and Hein's experimental setup. (From Held, 1965.)

When the kittens were later tested, only the kitten that could move freely behaved normally. When the kittens were held in the air and slowly brought down to the edge of a table to see whether they would exhibit the normal visual "placing" reaction (extending the paw to contact the seen tabletop), only the freely moving kitten did so. The kitten that had been transported in the gondola appeared unable to recognize the approach of the table surface. In another test, when a large object was brought toward the kittens, only the kitten that had moved freely turned away from it.

How can these results be explained? Because the two kittens received the same visual input, the freely moving kitten did not simply have more visual experience than the passive kitten. Moreover, because the passive kitten could move inside the gondola when the room lights were on and could move outside the gondola when the room lights were off, it did not perform poorly because of muscle weakness or inadequate motor control. The best explanation is that the development of normal visuomotor coordination depended on the opportunity to correlate visual input with actively generated motor commands. When the passive cat moved its legs in the gondola, no consistent changes in visual input followed; that is, its movements and visual perceptions were uncorrelated. However, when the active cat moved its legs, the visual changes it received were directly linked to its movements, so its movements and visual perceptions could be correlated. The gondola study suggests, then, that growing kittens—and perhaps also growing children—need more than movement alone and perception alone to develop normal visuomotor coordination. They need to actively correlate the two kinds of experience to interrelate them adaptively.

To evaluate this claim further, it is worthwhile to consider an alternative interpretation of the gondola study. Perhaps the active kittens simply became more interested in their surroundings than the passive kittens. Thus the passive kittens paid less attention to their perceptual experience than the active kittens did. Several experiments reported by Hein (1974) discredit this hypothesis. In one, kittens were allowed to see with one eye while moving freely and to see with the other eye while being transported in the gondola. Only the eye that could see during active movement could later aid locomotion; the other eye was effectively blind. Apparently, each eye (or its corresponding brain region) learned on its own. If the kittens simply were more motivated when they could move freely, the sheer opportunity for free movement would have allowed both eyes to develop properly.

In another experiment, kittens wore a collar that eliminated sight of the feet and torso. These kittens could later avoid obstacles but could not reach for objects as well as normal cats do; a similar result was obtained with monkeys (Held & Bauer, 1967). These findings suggest that the mere opportunity to move actively in a lighted environment does not ensure normal visuomotor coordination. What is critical instead is the opportunity to correlate movements with the visual changes they engender.

■ MEMORY

Walking is rarely aimless. One usually walks to a remembered site. This implies that a complete understanding of walking requires a theory of spatial memory.

The history of research on spatial memory parallels the history of research on the control of walking. Early on, when walking was thought to be controlled by reflex chains, a number of investigators also thought there might be no spatial memory *per se*, only familiar sequences of locomotory responses. The idea was that when one walked to work, for example, the first step somehow triggered the second, the second step trigger the third, and so on. This is the Response Chaining theory, discussed in Chapter 3.

Such a theory possibly explains why it takes many of us so long to get to our desks in the morning, but it is not very satisfying from a logical standpoint. One can take a step from one's house and go to work or to any of a number of other places. Thus a given a footstep cannot uniquely specify what other steps will follow it (Lashley, 1951). If one supposes that the first step leading to work is slightly different from the first step leading to the beach, this merely begs the question of why those minute differences were present in the first place.

The reflex-chaining hypothesis predicts that an animal's ability to get to a location should be impaired if its normal actions for getting there cannot be employed. Thus if a rat has learned to run a maze and the maze is suddenly flooded, the rat should be unable to swim to the spot where it previously found food. Similarly, if a rat has learned to run a maze from a fixed starting point, it should have great difficulty getting through the maze when placed in a different starting position.

Experiments on maze running have disconfirmed these predictions (Tolman, 1948). Rats placed in an unfamiliar starting position of a maze can find their way to the usual reward location more quickly than if they are placed in a completely novel maze. Rats can also proceed effectively to the usual goal area of a familiar maze, even if they must suddenly swim through the maze or move in other unfamiliar ways (Olton, 1979; Tolman, 1948). These results argue against response chaining theory or any theory which suggests that animals learn paths to particular locations solely in terms of the movements they must make to reach those locations.

Route Maps and Survey Maps

The results just summarized also argue against the theory that animals (or people) only remember the *paths* they take to reach target destinations, regardless of the movements made along those paths. Such a representation can be called a *route* map. A route map embodies the procedures used to get from one part of an environment to another. A typical route map might be described by the instructions, "Drive down to the firehouse and make a right, then make a left at Smith's Drug Store, and then make a left where the old schoolhouse used to be."

Route maps can be contrasted with survey maps, which are like conventional cartographic representations. They embody spatial relations

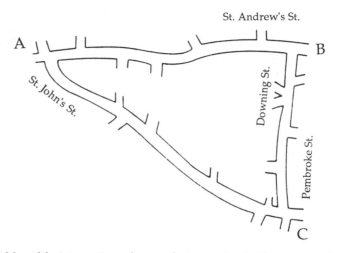

Figure 4.18 Map of the intersections whose angles were estimated from memory by the subjects in Moar and Bower's (1983) study. From I. Moar & G. H. Bower (1983). Inconsistencies in spatial knowledge. *Memory & Cognition,* **11,** 107–113. Reprinted by permission of the Psychonomic Society, Inc.

among points of interest, but not necessarily with information about the means of traveling from one of the points to another. Survey maps usually afford greater flexibility than route maps because they allow one to reach desired locations independently of the position from which one starts and independently of the means by which one travels.

What kinds of maps do people and animals use? Common experience suggests that as one first gets to know an area, one relies on a route map. Gradually, however, the route map changes to, or is supplanted by, a survey map.

That route maps are actually used was shown in some striking demonstrations of maze-running behavior in rats (Olton, 1979). After thousands of occasions in which rats ran from one point to another to get food in a maze, they passed right over the food if it was suddenly placed along the way to the familiar feeding site. If the maze had elevated arms rather than arms enclosed in walls, the rats actually ran over the ends of the arms if the normal arm extensions were suddenly removed. People are also subject to these sorts of errors. When one alters a habitual travel regimen (for example, driving home from work) to make an unusual detour (say, to pick up some lox at the delicatessen), the detour may not always materialize (Norman, 1981). These examples show that travel from one point to another can become so automatized that a route map rather than a survey map may be used. Thus a route map may be used not only when one is first learning the layout of an area but also when one is traversing a path that is highly familiar.

Perhaps because survey maps are abstract, they are subject to distortion. Moar and Bower (1983) asked people in Cambridge, England to estimate, from memory, angles of three street intersections (see Figure 4.18).

Although each intersection had an angle of less than 90°, when the Cambridgians were asked to estimate each angle individually, they exhibited a strong bias toward 90°. This result implies that all three intersections could not have been represented in a single survey map, for if they had been, they would have formed an impossible triangle. Evidently, subjects maintained separate maps of the intersections in their memories. The maps were connected through some overarching scheme that did not explicitly or accurately represent the intersections' spatial relationships.

Memory and Feedback

The subjects in Moar and Bower's (1983) study may have misrepresented street intersections in memory, but they clearly did not fall off the sidewalk when turning street corners. The perceptual input one receives while moving through the environment helps adjust the detailed characteristics of one's movement and probably also helps update one's spatial memory. There has been relatively little research on this important topic, though the studies that have been done do provide some useful information.

Lee, Lishman, and Thomson (1982) filmed long jumpers as the jumpers ran toward the spot from which the jump is executed (the jump board). The variability of step positions was small in the early part of the run, increased dramatically near the end, and then returned to a small value around the launch point (see Figure 4.19). A plausible interpretation of this result is that the jumpers first ran in a highly routinized fashion, impervious

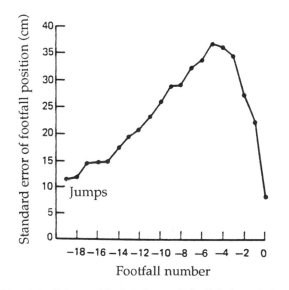

Figure 4.19 Variability of the distance of the long jumper's footfalls from the jumpboard as the long jumper approaches the jumpboard (footfall 0). From Lee, Lishman, and Thomson (1982). Regulation of gait in long jumping. *Journal of Experimental Psychology: Human Perception and Performance, 8,* 448–459. Copyright © 1982 by the American Psychological Association. Reprinted by permission.

to the detailed characteristics of the visual feedback they were receiving, then they relied on visual feedback to adjust the positions of their feet, and finally got their feet into the stereotypic position needed for effective jumps. According to this account, the jumpers did not rely exclusively on memory or on visual feedback. Instead, as they ran down the runway, they shifted from one mode of control to the other. This example illustrates how locomotion depends on a complex interplay of memory, perception, and motor commands.

■ SUMMARY

1. Several issues lie at the heart of research on the control of walking and other forms of locomotion: What neural mechanisms underlie locomotory patterns? How is locomotion influenced by sensory feedback? What is the role of high-level (brain) control?

2. To understand how walking is controlled, one must first understand its characteristic patterns. Distinct gait patterns characterize different speeds of locomotion; over wide ranges of speed, one does not simply speed up or slow down but switches from a walk to a run. The reason for the switch can be understood in terms of physics. With simplifying assumptions, it can be shown that it is impossible to walk faster than $\sqrt{gl}$, where g denotes acceleration due to gravity and l denotes the length of the leg. For speeds greater than $\sqrt{gl}$ (about 2.5 m/sec), it is necessary to switch to a run.

3. Gait patterns display so much regularity in normal circumstances that it is possible visually to recognize walking patterns as such when only a few lights, affixed to the walker's joints, can be seen. The step cycle of each leg consists of a stance phase, whose duration varies with gait, and a swing phase, whose duration is roughly constant. There are also characteristic time-varying changes in the angles of the knee and hip, easily seen in *angle–angle* diagrams, which may be useful for diagnosing gait disorders.

4. Rhythmic activity of the leg muscles can occur in cats whose spinal cords are disconnected from the brain. This implies that the spinal cord alone has central rhythm generators. When sensory feedback to the spinal cord is eliminated and the leg muscles are prevented from moving, the spinal cord still displays rhythmic activity of the sort underlying locomotion.

5. Although locomotion relies on central rhythm generators, it is also affected by sensory feedback. The timing of walking movements differs when sensory feedback is present or absent, and the same sensory input has different effects on behavior depending on when it occurs in the step cycle.

6. Reflex responses to postural disturbances are modulated by the brain. The stretch reflex of the gastrocnemius muscle can be attenuated when this reflex destabilizes the body. The ability to attenuate the reflex is impaired in patients with vestibular damage. Structures in the brain also help govern transitions from one gait pattern to another. Varying the intensity of stimulation in the brain stem helps produce different gait patterns.

7. The corticospinal tract is active during stepping movements requiring precise visuomotor coordination. Because many of the same brain sites are also active during visually guided manual reaching, locomotion and manual control may share common control mechanisms.

8. By drawing on information about the kinematics and physiology of locomotion, scientists have begun to develop machines that can walk. In devising such devices, it has been useful to list the conditions that all walking systems must satisfy. Among these are the need to maintain stability and to prevent collisions among the legs. An insight that has emerged from the design of artificial walking systems is that the complexity of locomotory control can be reduced by exploiting the physical properties of the system whose motions are being regulated.

9. A number of reflexes that are present in infancy normally disappear during development. Examples are the stepping reflex, the grasp reflex, and the Babinski reflex. The stepping reflex is present at birth, it disappears for several months, and then reappears. One explanation of this phenomenon is that the reappearance of stepping coincides with, and is directly dependent on, the emergence of cognitive sequencing skills. Another explanation is that stepping is temporarily absent for mechanical reasons alone. The explanation based on mechanics appears to be correct.

10. Three principles provide a useful way of conceptualizing motor development. One is that nerve fibers become myelinated. The second is that cortical centers inhibit subcortical centers. The third is that development proceeds in a cephalo–caudal (head-to-tail) and proximal–distal direction.

11. Locomotion in the natural environment benefits from adaptiveness to visual information. Responses to visual information may be based on properties of optic flow. In support of this hypothesis, body sway can be induced by having a subject stand in a room with a stable floor and moving walls. The body sway that is observed is closely related to the sway of the room. Young children can be knocked off their feet by visual input in the swaying room.

12. Optic flow information may also provide information about the time remaining until one contacts an object. Time-to-contact is given directly by the inverse of the rate of expansion of the retinal image of the object.

13. During development, the ability to respond adaptively to visual input depends on the opportunity to correlate perceptions with actions. Kittens that can move actively and can concurrently see the external environment later demonstrate effective visuomotor coordination.

14. In addition to perception, memory for the environment is also important for the control of navigation. It is unlikely that internal maps of the surroundings reduce to memorized sequences of muscle movements, for it is possible to get to a target location in a familiar area from a variety of starting positions and through unfamiliar means of locomotion (for example, swimming in a suddenly flooded maze). When possible, people develop abstract spatial maps (*survey* maps) of their surroundings. In learning about new places, however, or in covering the same path many times, people may rely on a less abstract map which embodies the procedures to be followed to get from one location to another (a *route* map).

15. Perception and memory are used together to govern navigation. For example, long jumpers begin their run toward the jump board in a stereotyped fashion, without responding to detailed aspects of visual input, but as they approach the board, they modify their steps based on visual feedback.

■ **REFERENCES**

Alexander, R. M. (1984). Walking and running. *American Scientist*, **72**, 348–354.

Allum, J. H., & Pfaltz, C. R. (1985). Visual and vestibular contribution to pitch sway stabilization in the ankle muscles of normals and patients with bilateral peripheral vestibular deficits. *Experimental Brain Research*, **58**, 82–94.

André-Thomas, A., & Autgarden, T. (1966). *Locomotion from pre- to postnatal life*. Lavenham, Suffolk: Spastics Society.

Arshavsky, Y. I., Kots, Y. M., Orlovskii, G. N., Rodionov, I. M., & Shik, M. L. (1965). Investigation of the biomechanics of running by the dog. *Biofizika*, **10**, 665–672.

Bizzi, E., & Mussa-Ivaldi, F. A. (1990). Geometrical and mechanical issues in movement planning and control. In M. I. Posner (Ed.), *Handbook of cognitive science* (pp. 769–792). Cambridge, MA: MIT Press.

Bramble, D. M., & Carrier, D. R. (1983). Running and breathing in mammals. *Science*, **219**, 251–256.

Brown, T. G. (1911). The intrinsic factors in the act of progression in the mammal. *Proceedings of the Royal Society of London*, **84**, 308–319.

Carew, T. J. (1985). Posture and locomotion. In E. R. Kandel & J. H. Schwartz (Eds.), *Principles of neural science* (2d ed., pp. 478–486). New York: Elsevier/North-Holland.

Cohen, A. H., Rossignol, S., & Grillner, S. (Eds.) (1988). *Neural control of rhythmic movements in vertebrates*. New York: Wiley.

Cutting, J. E. (1986). *Perception with an eye for motion*. Cambridge, MA: MIT Press/Bradford Books.

Cutting, J. E., & Proffitt, D. R. (1981). Gait perception as an example of how we may perceive events. In R. D. Walk & H. L. Pick, Jr. (Eds.), *Intersensory perception and sensory integration* (pp. 249–273). New York: Plenum.

Delcomyn, F. (1975). Neural basis of rhythmic behavior in animals. *Science*, **210**, 492–498.

Easton, T. A. (1972). On the normal use of reflexes. *American Scientist*, **60**, 591–599.

Enoka, R. M. (1988). *Neuromechanical basis of kinesiology*. Champaign, IL: Human Kinetics Books.

Enoka, R. M., Miller, D. I., & Burgess, E. M. (1982). Below-knee amputee running gait. *American Journal of Physical Medicine*, **61**, 66–84.

Forssberg, H., Grillner, S., & Rossignol, S. (1975). Phase dependent reflex reversal during walking in chronic spinal cats. *Brain Research*, **55**, 247–304.

Fox, R., & McDaniel, C. (1982). The perception of biological motion by human infants. *Science*, **218** (29), 486–487.

Freed, C. R., & Yamamoto, B. K. (1985). Regional brain dopamine metabolism: A marker for the speed, direction, and posture of moving animals. *Science*, **229**, 62–65.

Georgopoulos, A. P., & Grillner, S. (1989). Visuomotor coordination in reach and locomotion. *Science*, **245**, 1209–1210.

Gibson, J. J. (1950). *Perception of the visual world*. Boston: Houghton Mifflin.

Gibson, J. J. (1966). *The senses considered as peceptual systems*. Boston: Houghton Mifflin.

Gibson, J. J. (1979). *The ecological approach to visual perception.* Boston: Houghton Mifflin.

Glass, A. L., & Holyoke, K. J. (1986). *Cognition* (2d ed.). New York: Random House.

Goslow, G. E., Reinking, R. M., & Stuart, D. G. (1973). The cat step cycle: Hind limb joint angles and muscle lengths during unrestrained locomotion. *Journal of Morphology,* **141,** 1–42.

Grillner, S. (1981). Control of locomotion in bipeds, tetrapods, and fish. In V. B. Brooks (Ed.), *Handbook of physiology* (Sec. 1, Vol. II, Part 2, pp. 1179–1236). Bethesda, MD: American Physiological Society.

Hein, A. (1974). Prerequisite for development of visual guided reaching in the kitten. *Brain Research,* **71,** 259–263.

Held, R. (1965). Plasticity in sensory-motor systems. *Scientific American,* **213** (5), 84–94.

Held, R., & Bauer, J., Jr. (1967). Visually guided reaching in infant monkeys after restricted rearing. *Science,* **155,** 718–720.

Herman, R., Wirta, R., Bampton, S., & Finley,F. R. (1976). Human solutions for locomotion: I. Single limb analysis. In R. Herman, S. Grillner, P. Stein, & D. Stuart (Eds.), *Neural control of locomotion* (pp. 13–49). New York: Plenum.

Humphrey, D. R. (1986). Representation of movements and muscles within the primate precentral motor cortex: Historical and current perspectives. *Federation Proceedings,* **45,** 2687–2699.

Johansson, G. (1973). Visual perception of biological motion and a model for its analysis. *Perception & Psychophysics,* **14,** 201–211.

Kagan, J. (1971). *Change and continuity in infancy.* New York: Wiley.

Kalat, J. W. (1980). *Biological psychology.* Belmont, CA: Wadsworth.

Keele, S. W. (1968). Movement control in skilled motor performance. *Psychological Bulletin,* **70,** 387–403.

Keele, S. W. (1981). Behavioral analysis of movement. In V. B. Brooks (Ed.), *Handbook of physiology* (Sec. 1, Vol. II, Part 2, pp. 1391–1414). Baltimore, MD: American Physiological Society.

Lashley, K. S. (1951). The problem of serial order in behavior. In L. A. Jeffress (Ed.), *Cerebral mechanisms in behavior* (pp. 112–131). New York: Wiley.

Lee, D. N. (1976). A theory of visual control of braking based on information about time-to-collision. *Perception,* **5,** 437–459.

Lee, D. N., & Aronson, E. (1974). Visual proprioceptive control of standing in human infants. *Perception & Psychophysics,* **15,** 529–532.

Lee, D. N., & Lishman, J. R. (1975). Visual proprioceptive control of stance. *Journal of Human Movement Studies,* **1,** 87–95.

Lee, D. N., & Reddish, P. E. (1981). Plummeting gannets: A paradigm of ecological optics. *Nature (London),* **293,** 293–294.

Lee, D. N., & Thomson, J. A. (1982). Vision in action: The control of locomotion. In D. J. Ingle, M. A. Goodale, & R. J. W. Mansfield (Eds.), *Analysis of visual behavior* (pp. 411–433). Cambridge, MA: MIT Press.

Lee, D. N., Lishman, J. R., & Thomson, J. (1982). Regulation of gait in long jumping. *Journal of Experimental Psychology,* **8,** 448–459.

Lee, D. N., Young, D. S., Reddish, P. E., Lough, S., & Clayton, T. M. (1983). Visual timing in hitting an accelerating ball. *Quarterly Journal of Experimental Psychology,* **35A,** 333–346.

McGraw, M. B. (1943). *Neuro-muscular maturation of the infant.* New York: Columbia Univ. Press.

McMahon, T. A. (1984). *Muscles, reflexes, and locomotion.* Princeton, NJ: Princeton Univ. Press.

Macmillan, D. L. (1975). A physiological analysis of walking in the American lobster (Homarus americanus). *Philosophical Transactions of the Royal Society of London,* **270,** 1–59.

Margaria, R. (1976). *Biomechanics and energetics of muscular exercise.* Oxford: Clarendon Press.

Massion, J. (1984). Postural changes accompanying voluntary movements: Normal and pathological aspects. *Human Neurobiology,* **2,** 261–267.

Mayer, E. J. (1972). *Movement.* New York: Arno Press & New York Times. (Originally published, 1895)

Miller, S., & Van der Meeche, F. G. (1975). *Brain Research,* **91,** 255–269.

Moar, I., & Bower, G. H. (1983). Inconsistencies in spatial knowledge. *Memory & Cognition,* **11,** 107–113.

Muybridge, E. (1887/1957). *Animals in motion.* New York: Dover.

Nashner, L. M. (1976). Adapting reflexes controlling the human posture. *Experimental Brain Research,* **26,** 59–72.

Nashner, L. M., & McCollum, G. (1985). The organization of human postural movements: A formal basis and experimental synthesis. *Behavioral and Brain Sciences,* **8,** 135–172.

Nashner, L. M., Woollacott, M., & Tuma, G. (1979). Organization of rapid responses to postural and locomotor-like perturbations of standing man. *Experimental Brain Research,* **36,** 463–476.

Norman, D. A. (1981). Categorization of action slips. *Psychological Review,* **88,** 1–15.

Olton, D. S, (1979). Mazes, maps, and memory. *American Psychologist,* **34,** 583–596.

Palmer, C. E. (1944). Studies of the center of gravity in the human body. *Child Development,* **15,** 99–163.

Pearson, K. R. (1976). The control of walking. *Scientific American,* **235** (6), 72–86.

Raibert, M. H., & Sutherland, I. E. (1983). Machines that walk. *Scientific American,* **248** (1), 44–53.

Rovee, C. K., & Fagan, J. W. (1976). Extended conditioning and 24-hour retention in infants. *Journal of Experimental Child Psychology,* **21,** 1–11.

Shapiro, D. C., Zernicke, R. F., Gregor, R. J., & Diestel, J. D. (1981). Evidence for generalized motor programs using gait pattern analysis. *Journal of Motor Behavior,* **13,** 33–47.

Sherrington, C. S. (1906). *Integrative action of the nervous system.* New York: Scribner.

Shik, M. L., Severin, F. V., & Orlosky, G. N. (1966). Control of walking and running by means of electrical stimulation of the mid-brain. *Biophysics,* **11,** 756–765.

Shirley, M. M. (1931). *The first two years: A study of twenty-five babies* (Vol. 1. *Postural and locomotor development*). Minneapolis: Univ. of Minnesota Press.

Smyth, M. L., Morris, P. E., Levy, P., & Ellis, A. W. (1987). *Cognition in action.* London: Erlbaum.

Strelow, E. R. (1985). What is needed for a theory of mobility: Direct perception and cognitive maps—Lessons from the blind. *Psychological Review,* **92,** 226–248.

Taub, E., & Berman, A. J. (1968). Movement and learning in the absence of sensory feedback. In S. J. Freeman (Ed.), *The neuropsychology of spatially oriented behavior* (pp. 173–192). Homewood, IL: Dorsey.

Teitelman, R. (1984). Stepping out. *Forbes,* June 18, 154–157.

Thelen, E. (1983). Learning to walk is still an "old" problem: A reply to Zelazo (1983). *Journal of Motor Behavior,* **15** (2), 139–161.

Thelen, E., & Fisher, D. M. (1983). From spontaneous to instrumental behavior: Kinematic analysis of movement changes during very early learning. *Child Development,* **54,** 129–140.

Thelen, E., Bradshaw, G., & Ward, J. A. (1981). Spontaneous kicking in month-old infants: Manifestations of a human central locomotor program. *Behavioral and Neural Biology,* **32,** 45–53.

Thelen, E., Kelso, J. A. S., & Fogel, A. (1987). Self-organizing systems and infant motor development. *Developmental Review,* **7,** 39–65.

Tolman, C. E. (1948). Cognitive maps in rats and man. *Psychological Review,* **55,** 189–208.

Woollacott, M. H. (1990). Stance and locomotion. In H. Heuer & S. Keele (Eds.), *Handbook of motor skills.* San Diego: Academic Press.

Woollacott, M. H., Debu, B., & Mowatt, M. (1987). Neuromuscular control of posture in the infant and child: Is vision dominant? *Journal of Motor Behavior,* **19,** 167–186.

Yakolev, P., & Lecours, A. (1967). The myelogenetic cycles of regional maturation of the brain. In A. Minkowski (Ed.), *Regional development of the brain in early life* (pp. 3–70). Philadelphia: Davis.

Zelazo, P. R. (1983). The development of walking: New findings and old assumptions. *Journal of Motor Behavior,* **15,** 99–137.

5 LOOKING

■ INTRODUCTION

To see, we must be able to move our eyes. Eye-movement control is one of the most extensively studied topics in the area of human motor control. This is to be expected since vision is arguably the most important sense for humans. Moreover, because eye movements are relatively unaffected by external, mechanical disturbances, they faithfully reflect the motor signals that drive them, making them an ideal system for motor control research.

Looking involves several subsystems. Some rotate the eyeball; others do not. The oculomotor (eye-movement) activities in which the eyeball does not rotate are *blinking*, *accommodation* (changing the focal length of the lens), and *pupillary responses* (which regulate the size of the opening through which light enters the eye). The activities in which the eyeball does rotate include *saccades* (the eye "jumps" that occur in tasks such as reading), *pursuit* movements (which occur when one visually tracks a smoothly moving target), and *nystagmus* (which occurs when one's eyes alternate between pursuit movements and saccades—for example, while looking out the window of a moving train). These types of eye rotation are *conjugate*; they turn the eyes in the same direction. By contrast, *vergence* movements carry the eyes in opposite directions, as when one shifts one's gaze between near and far objects or when one visually tracks an object, such as one's finger tip, as it moves toward or away from one's face.

In this chapter I will review some of the important features of these oculomotor activities. I will consider how each activity is triggered and what its main characteristics are. I will also consider how the activities are coordinated with one another and with movements of the head. The relation between perception and eye movements is another central issue in the analysis of oculomotor control; it too will see its way into the discussion.

■ BLINKING

Let us begin with one of the oculomotor activities in which the eyeball does not rotate: *blinking*. Blinking moistens the front surface of the eye, the *cornea* (see Figure 5.1), and protects the eye against approaching objects. The protective function of blinking is also manifested in another way. Blinks often occur reflexively when people are exposed to loud, unexpected noises.

A great deal of research has been done on the classical conditioning of the eyeblink. In these experiments, the subject (human or animal) learns to associate an arbitrary stimulus, such as a tone (the *conditioned* stimulus), with a stimulus that automatically elicits a blink, such as a puff of air directed to the open eye (the *unconditioned* stimulus). After repeated pairing of the tone with the airpuff, the subject learns to blink as soon as the tone is pre-

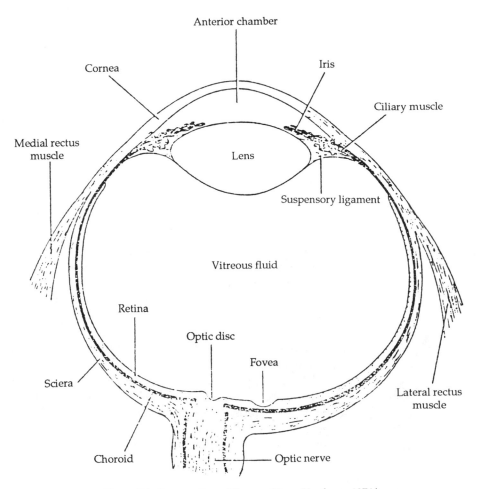

Figure 5.1 Cross section of the eye. (From Kaufman, 1974.)

sented. A small set of cells in the cerebellum appears to underlie conditioning of the eyeblink response, at least in rabbits (McCormick & Thompson, 1984). This finding suggests that memories may be neurologically localized.

Acquisition of eyeblink conditioning is not only a low-level process. It can also be learned vicariously. Subjects who watched a videotape of a person in an eyeblink conditioning experiment later acted as if they themselves had been conditioned (Bernal & Berger, 1976). This result suggests that responses can be learned without actually being performed—what is sometimes called *observational* learning (Bandura, 1986). Vicarious learning of the eyeblink response also demonstrates that though blinks can occur automatically or reflexively, they can also be consciously controlled. We can blink at will or blink with one eye (*winking*). The capacity to control movements automatically or deliberately is an important general feature of motor performance. To name just two other motor activities that can be controlled through either method, breathing can go on without attention or with considerable conscious control, as when one inhales for a doctor listening to one's lungs. Similarly, one can deliberately feign a limp.

Rates of blinking and the times at which blinks occur indicate one's cognitive state. Richard Nixon, in his first nationally televised news conference after the Watergate break-in, tried to indicate through his words and tone of voice that his administration had done nothing wrong. However, his eyeblinks revealed that he had cause for serious worry. Nixon blinked at a rate of 30 to 40 times a minute, whereas people at ease blink at rates of 10 to 20 times a minute (Vogel, 1989).

That blink rates increase with anxiety has been known since the 1920s, when two Scottish investigators secretly counted the blink rates of witnesses in a courtroom. Witnesses under stress blinked at higher rates than witnesses with no cause for worry (Vogel, 1989). More recently, electronic recording techniques have shown that people withhold blinks when taking in vital information (for example, when pilots fly aircrafts) but that they blink more often or for longer durations when they are highly stressed or fatigued. A practical consequence of these observations is that the automatic monitoring of eyeblinks could help provide information about the alertness of individuals involved in activities such as driving cars, flying planes, or monitoring nuclear power plants.

When blinks occur, the eyelids block the view of the external environment. Nevertheless, we do not see the world darken. The darkening is not too quick to be seen, for people can detect the dimming of a light that is shorter than the blink of an eye (about 200 msec). Volkmann, Riggs, and Moore (1980) hypothesized that when an eyeblink is initiated, activity within the central nervous system reduces sensitivity to visual change. To test this hypothesis, Volkmann *et al.* introduced an optic light fiber through the roof of the mouth and illuminated the fiber at different times relative to the subject's eyeblink. The rationale was that some light from the optic fiber would strike the back of the eye and so would be visible as a result of retinal stimulation. The question was whether the light would be less detectable around the time of the eyeblink.

As shown in Figure 5.2, sensitivity to the light decreased during the blink, as well as just before and after it. Since the light was not perceived through the eyelids, the change in sensitivity was not due to blockage of the light by the lids. Furthermore, since sensitivity declined *before* the eyeblink, the change was unlikely to have been caused by peripheral feedback from the lids or the areas around the eyes touched by the lids. Volkmann *et al.* (1980) suggested that the drop in visual sensitivity was related to the central generation of the eyeblink command. Their explanation is similar to one given in Chapter 1 for the perceived stability of the external environment during self-induced as opposed to externally induced visual motion: Corollary discharge from a motor center to a perceptual center indicates that a change in stimulation is about to occur; when the actual change takes place, it can be recognized as having stemmed from the bodily movement. In the case of blinking, the center responsible for triggering blinks can tell the perceptual center responsible for monitoring the brightness of the external environment to discount sudden darkening. When that darkening occurs, it need not be experienced.

As appealing as this idea may be, another possibility must also be taken seriously. Subjects in the study of Volkmann *et al.* (1980) sometimes made saccadic eye movements when they blinked, and these eye movements,

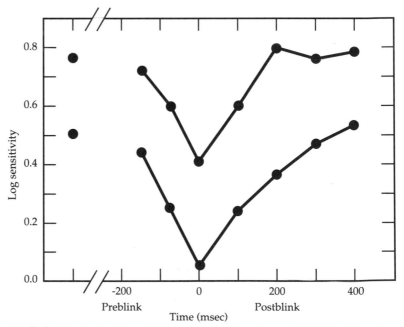

Figure 5.2 Reduction in visual sensitivity around the time of an eyeblink. Data from two subjects. (Data from Volkmann, Riggs, & Moore, 1980.)

or the central neural changes associated with them, could have reduced subjects' visual sensitivity. Saccades often occur during blinking (Collewijn, van der Steen, & Steinman, 1985), and it makes sense that they do, for it is hard to see during blinks and during saccades (as will be discussed subsequently). From the standpoint of adaptive visual functioning, therefore, it is better to shorten the time when vision is functionally impaired than to prolong it. Making saccades and blinks simultaneously achieves this purpose. Because blinks and saccades co-occur frequently, some investigators are not yet convinced that a central suppression mechanism, specifically associated with blinking, needs to be postulated (E. Kowler, personal communication).

■ ACCOMMODATION

Accommodation changes the curvature of the lens of the eye (see Figure 5.1), promoting visual focusing. It is triggered by blurriness, which is detected in the visual cortex. Following the detection of blurriness, neural signals are sent from the visual cortex to the third cranial nerve (the *oculomotor* nerve), which in turn sends commands to muscles within the eye. These muscles (called *ciliary* muscles) act on the lens via tiny fibers (*zonular* fibers). When the ciliary muscles contract, they tug on the zonular fibers, which in turn pull on the lens, stretching it and so reducing its curvature. The reduced curvature allows for focusing on distant objects. When the ciliary muscles relax, the lens becomes rounder, and it becomes easier to focus on nearby objects (Gouras, 1985b).

  The lens' ability to regain curvature when the ciliary muscles relax depends on the elastic property of the lens itself. The elasticity of the lens declines with age. This is why, as people get older, they are more likely to require spectacles. Detailed studies of the histology and biochemistry of the lens and zonular fibers have permitted identification of the complex set of factors that cause the age-related decline in lens elasticity (Koretz & Handelman, 1989).

■ PUPIL CONSTRICTION AND DILATION

When the eye is exposed to bright light the pupil reflexively constricts, limiting the amount of light that reaches the retina. When less light is presented, the pupil reflexively dilates, allowing more light to enter the eye. Pupillary responses are achieved by changing the contraction of the iris (see Figure 5.1). When bright light is directed to just one eye, pupil constriction occurs in the other eye as well. The absence of this consensual reaction in the other eye is a symptom of syphilis (Gouras, 1985b).

  Although pupil responses are reflexively controlled, pupil diameter also reflects voluntary states, especially the mental effort expended on a task (Beatty, 1982). Generally, the greater the mental effort, the greater the pupil diameter. For example, when people in a learning experiment memorize

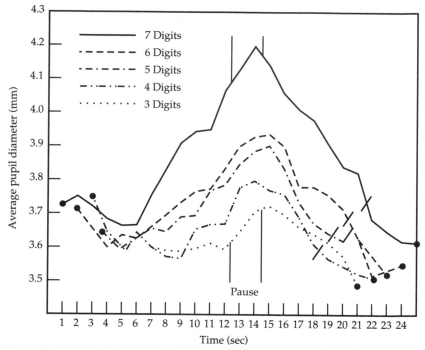

Figure 5.3 Changes in the diameter of the pupil during presentation and recall of digit lists containing 3–7 digits. Recall begins after the pause. (From Kahneman & Beatty, 1966.)

strings of aurally presented digits, their pupils enlarge with the presentation of each additional digit (see Figure 5.3). Later, when the subjects are asked to recall the digits, their pupils first enlarge and then decrease steadily as each digit is successfully recalled (Kahneman & Beatty, 1966).

The relation between pupil diameter and degree of cognitive activity may explain why candlelight is used in romantic settings. In the dim illumination of candlelight, one's pupils dilate, helping to convey the impression that one is interested in one's dining partner. People portrayed in photographs are perceived as being more friendly and interesting when their eyes are dilated than when their pupils are constricted (Hess, 1975).

■ GENERAL FEATURES OF EYE MOVEMENTS

Let us now turn to oculomotor activities that rotate the eyeball. It is useful first to understand why it is necessary to rotate the eyes at all and how, mechanically, eye rotations are achieved.

As seen in Figure 5.1, at the back of the eyeball is the light-sensitive area called the *retina*. Near the center of the retina is a small area called the *fovea*, which is specialized for color perception and fine pattern discrimination. The eye-movement activities to be discussed bring images of interest onto the fovea.

Why Moveable Eyes?

Why do the eyes move at all? Why not have a very large fovea or even compound eyes like insects (see Figure 5.4)? Considering this possibility is more than the stuff of fiction; it helps us understand the role of eye movements in perception.

If one traces the nerve projections from different parts of the retina to the visual processing areas of the brain, one finds that much more brain tissue is devoted to the processing of images cast on the fovea than to the processing of images cast on nonfoveal areas. If we had larger foveas, the visual processing areas of the brain would have to be massively enlarged.

Figure 5.4 Eye movements would be unnecessary if we had compound eyes, such as those of "Fly Man." (From Stan Lee presents: *Spidey Super Stories, Electric Company Magazine,* June 1986, No. 125, p. 26. Children's Television Workshop.)

Assuming that economizing on brain space is an important evolutionary principle, it follows that it is more economical to have minutely foveated, moveable eyes than to have massively foveated, immoveable eyes (provided that the neural machinery responsible for eye movements is itself reasonably compact).

Physical Dynamics

The eye rotates in three dimensions: horizontally, vertically, and torsionally (clockwise or counterclockwise with respect to the depth axis of the eyeball). Three pairs of *extraocular* muscles move the eyeball in these three dimensions (see Figure 5.5). One pair, the *lateral rectus* and *medial rectus*, is mainly responsible for horizontal movements. Another pair, the *superior rectus* and *inferior rectus*, is mainly responsible for vertical movements. A third pair, the *inferior oblique* and *superior oblique*, is mainly responsible for torsional movements. Usually, in any given eye movement, the extraocular muscles from more than one pair of muscles actively contract. This allows the eye to turn in more than one dimension at a time.

The extraocular muscles are directly innervated by three cranial nerves—the *oculomotor* nerve, the *trochlear* nerve, and the *abducens* nerve. These nerves emanate from oculomotor nuclei in the brain stem (Gouras, 1985a). The motor neurons innervating the extraocular muscles fire at higher frequencies and over a wider range of frequencies (100–600 impulses/sec) than spinal motor neurons (50–100 impulses/sec).

Because each oculomotor neuron has a distinct threshold for continuous firing, additional oculomotor neurons can be recruited by increasing the activation level of the neuronal pool in which they reside. As more of the neurons are turned on, the tension of the extraocular muscles increases, and

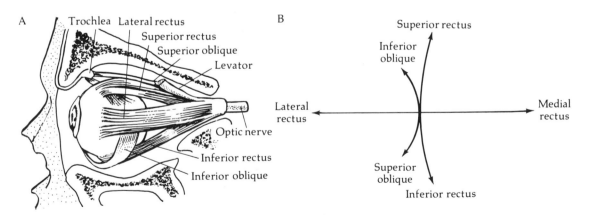

Figure 5.5 The extraocular muscles (A) and their principal directions of rotation (B). Reprinted by permission of the publisher from Oculomotor system by P. Gouras, in *Principles of neural science* (2d ed.), pp. 571–583. Copyright © 1985 by Elsevier Science Publishing Co., Inc.

the eye's angular deviation from the straight ahead (its *eccentricity*) increases. Gradually increasing the tension of the extraocular muscles appears to be the primary method for generating saccades less than 10–15° (Abrams, Meyer, & Kornblum, 1989; Robinson, 1981). For saccades greater than 10–15°, amplitudes are varied by regulating the time the agonists remain maximally active. Longer periods of activation are associated with larger saccadic excursions (Bahill & Stark, 1979).

These conclusions have been reached by recording the peak velocity of the eye as a function of the distance it covers. The velocity of the eye can be recorded through several techniques, one of which is to mount photodiodes on spectacle frames worn by the subject. The photodiodes point toward the eye and detect light reflected from the eye's surface. The amount of light depends on where the eye is pointing (because of the changing positions of the dark iris and lighter sclera). Through such recording techniques, it has been found that peak velocities of saccades generally increase with saccade amplitude, reaching a maximum at around 10–15° (see Figure 5.6).

This relation has been mathematically reproduced through a model of oculomotor control which assumes that amplitudes of saccades greater than 10–15° are varied by adjusting the durations of commands for maximally activated agonists, but that amplitudes of saccades less than or equal

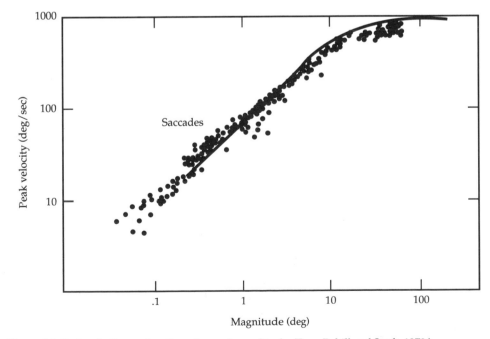

Figure 5.6 Peak velocity as a function of saccade amplitude. (From Bahill and Stark, 1979.)

to 10–15° are varied by adjusting durations as well as magnitudes of agonist activation levels (Bahill & Stark, 1979). Holding the eye at the target is achieved by setting the tensions of the agonists and antagonists so they balance out at the target position and by timing the onset of the antagonist activity so it promotes maintenance of the target position at the right instant.

An important feature of this model is that it has distinct components: timing control, force control, and mechanical elements such as damping associated with the viscosity of the eye in the socket. Each component can be affected by fatigue or pathology, giving rise to distinct forms of eye-movement disturbances. For example, when people are fatigued, they have an increased tendency to display a form of eye-movement pattern called *glissadic overshoot*. Here the eye overshoots the target and then drifts back toward it. Glissadic overshoot can be simulated by assuming that the holding position for the eye is set correctly but the signal that propels the eye toward the target is set incorrectly.

Even when people are not fatigued, they display variability in the characteristics of their eye movements. The nature of this variability supports the assumption that force and timing are distinct parameters for eye-movement control (Abrams *et al.*, 1989). It is interesting to note that independent force control and timing control have also been proposed for hand movements (Keele & Ivry, 1987).

■ MINIATURE EYE MOVEMENTS

Let us now consider the subsystems that physically rotate the eye. We will begin with miniature eye movements. These are only observable through special recording techniques, such as the photodiode recording system discussed earlier, or through careful perceptual experiments, such as the one illustrated in Figure 5.7.

There are three types of miniature eye movements, as shown in Figure 5.8. One is *tremor*, which can be thought of as random jitter. The amplitude of tremor is miniscule, less in fact than the diameter of a single visual cone. However, tremor *frequency* is quite high, around 90 Hz (cycles per second). The tremor of one eye is independent of the tremor of the other eye (Carpenter, 1977).

Another class of miniature eye movement is *drift*. Drifts are slow; their average velocity is only 1/60 degree of arc per second. They can cover as much as 5/60 degree of arc before being terminated (Ditchburn, 1973). (One degree of arc is approximately equal to the width of your thumbnail when viewed at arm's length.) Drifts bring the fovea toward fixation targets and therefore can be viewed as corrective (Steinman, Haddad, Skavenski, & Wyman, 1973).

A third class of miniature eye movements is *microsaccades*. As their name implies, these are just small saccades. Microsaccades are conjugate (parallel in the two eyes). They may serve a corrective function, bringing the

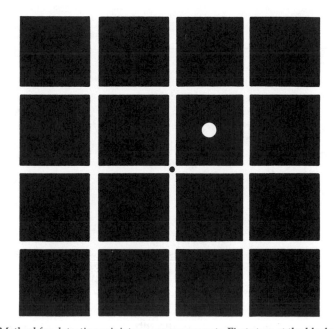

Figure 5.7 Method for detecting miniature eye movements. First stare at the black dot in the center of the array for at least 20 second. Then stare at the center of the white circle. The after-image of the array will move with your eye as it undergoes miniature movements. The interactions of the vertical and horizontal contours make the miniature movements apparent. Such interactions are the basis of many illusory effects in "op" art, popular in the 1960s. (From Carpenter, 1977. Reprinted by permission of Pion Ltd.)

fovea back toward a fixation target from which the eye has drifted, though on occasion they may also take the eye away from the target. Microsaccades differ from drifts and tremors in that they are influenced by volitional factors, such as the attentiveness of the subject.

The features just listed for microsaccades also characterize saccades. This has led to the proposal that microsaccades and saccades are actually members of a single functional category. It is possible to show that microsaccades and saccades are controlled the same way by plotting peak velocity of the eye against movement amplitude (see Figure 5.6). For microsaccades as well as saccades (that is, saccades covering small and large amplitudes) all the points lie on a straight line (Zuber & Stark, 1965). Because it is unlikely that this should be the case by chance alone, it appears that microsaccades and saccades rely on a common mechanism.

When one tries to maintain fixation on a stationary target, the eye often drifts away from the target and then returns to it via a rapid flick. This behavior serves a useful perceptual function: It ensures that a single set of photoreceptors is not continually stimulated. Recall from Chapter 1 that when a fixed set of photoreceptors receives a constant input (via retinal stabilization) the image fades away. When the eye drifts from a fixation target

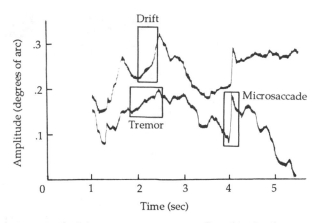

Figure 5.8 The three types of miniature eye movements, reflected in simultaneous recordings of the left and right eye. *Tremor* is a series of high-frequency, small-amplitude displacements. *Drift* is a relatively slow, larger-amplitude displacement. *Microsaccades* are rapid, relatively large displacements of the two eyes together. (From Carpenter, 1977. Reprinted by permission of Pion Ltd.)

and then returns to it, such fading does not occur, presumably because the photoreceptors of the retina are refreshed (Alpern, 1972; Ditchburn, 1973).

Another perceptual consequence of the instability of the eye during prolonged fixation is the *autokinetic* illusion. Stare at a fixed point of light in an otherwise dark chamber. A lit cigarette makes an ideal stimulus for this exercise (though perhaps for no other). You will see the point wander over a restricted spatial range. Careful studies of the eye movements that occur in this situation indicate that the autokinetic effect is due to oculomotor activity. The autokinetic illusion only occurs when the eye drifts (Barlow, 1952). Moreover, the stops, starts, and directions of motion that are visually experienced are directly linked to the movements of the eyes (Lehman, 1965). Some authors have proposed that the autokinetic illusion reflects the operation of a mechanism that compares retinal image displacements with oculomotor commands (or their prior intentions). According to this hypothesis, when retinal image displacements are detected without accompanying registration of oculomotor commands, the retinal image displacements are ascribed to the motion of the target rather than the motion of the eyes (Levy, 1972).

■ SACCADES

As I have already mentioned, saccades are rapid jumps that bring images of points of interest to the fovea. Generally, saccades are voluntary, though they usually do not require conscious intervention. The principal trigger for a saccade is retinal position error—having the desired target away from the fovea.

Figure 5.9 shows a typical saccadic scanpath of an observer looking at a picture. The scanpath is nonrandom. In general, observers repeatedly look at points that are most informative. The scanpath shown in Figure 5.9 was recorded with a special contact lens to which a lever was attached. The

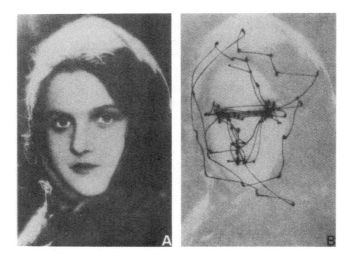

Figure 5.9 Scanpath of the eyes (*right*) in looking at a picture (*left*) for 1 minute. Reprinted by permission of the publisher from Oculomotor system by P. Gouras, in *Principles of neural science* (2d ed.), pp. 571–583. Copyright © 1985 by Elsevier Science Publishing Co., Inc.

movements of the lever were driven by movements of the eye, and by recording the lever movements it was possible to infer what eye movements were made (Yarbus, 1967). Other eye-tracking devices make it possible to record the position of the eye without fixing a sensor to the cornea. I have already mentioned one such method, which relies on corneal reflection. Reviews of these and other eye-movement recording techniques can be found in Ditchburn (1973) and Carpenter (1977).

Visual scanpaths and the timing of successive saccades have been studied to understand the rules governing visual perception and reading (Rayner, 1983). During reading, the eyes remain on words that occur with low frequency (such as "kiwi") longer than on words that occur with high frequency (such as "the"). When readers are presented with words that do not make sense in terms of what they have just read, their eyes dwell for a relatively long time on the odd word. Furthermore, there is a higher-than-normal likelihood of looking back to an earlier part of the passage (Rayner, 1983). Findings like these have provided a wealth of information about the visual processing of verbal information (Rayner, 1983; Rayner & Pollatsek, 1988).

Saccadic patterns have also been used to learn about altered states of consciousness. Rapid-eye-movement (REM) sleep is indicative of dreaming. If people are awakened when their eyes saccade beneath their closed eyelids (during REM), they are more likely to report dreaming than if they are awakened when their eyes are still (Webb, 1973).

Saccades are very fast. When a saccade is made, the eyeball can turn at rates of 600 to 700° per second, though peak velocities as high as 830° have been reported (Hyde, 1959). Peak velocity increases with the amplitude of the saccade (Bahill & Stark, 1979; Fuchs, 1967), as mentioned earlier.

The time to begin a saccade depends on a number of factors. When subjects simply direct their eyes to a suddenly illuminated point, their saccadic latencies depend on the kind of attentional set they have adopted. If the new target is unexpected, the time to start making a saccade to it can be 200 msec or longer. If the target is expected, the initiation time can be reduced (Vaughan, 1983). For example, a priming stimulus that reliably warns the subject of the whereabouts of a soon-to-be-presented target reduces the time to begin a saccade to it (Posner, 1978).

Saccadic latencies can also be reduced if the initial fixation target (the target being looked at initially) is extinguished before another saccadic target is presented (Saslow, 1967). The benefit of extinguishing the initial fixation target may come about because it takes time to disengage attention from the fixated target in order to make the saccade to the new target. If the initially fixated target is turned off, then according to this hypothesis, disengagement of attention can take place before the new target comes on (Fischer & Breitmeyer, 1987).

In the most extreme reduction of saccadic latencies, the latencies actually become negative with respect to stimulus onset—that is, the saccade begins *before* the target is presented. This occurs when observers fully anticipate targets, as, for example, in the task of looking back and forth at two targets that come on at predictable times and places. Under these circumstances, the eye can start saccading to the target even before it appears. This phenomenon reveals that saccades can come under voluntary, predictive control (Rashbass, 1961).

A related effect of predictive control is that the time to make the first saccade in a series of saccades increases with the number of saccades to be made, provided the subject knows that the entire series will be required (Inhoff, 1986; Zingale & Kowler, 1987). As will be seen later in this volume, similar results have been reported for manual and vocal responses (Sternberg, Monsell, Knoll, & Wright, 1978).

Once the process of initiating a saccade is far enough along, it is difficult or impossible to stop it. This property of highly prepared saccades was demonstrated in a study in which subjects stared at a fixation point which remained on for a while, then was turned off, and then was followed by a new target to which subjects could direct their eyes (Westheimer, 1954). On some trials, after the new target came on it was quickly extinguished and the original fixation point was reilluminated. The question was whether subjects could withhold their saccades to the new target. The result was that if the delay between illumination of the new target and reillumination of the fixation point was short enough (less than about 200 msec), subjects could usually refrain from making the saccade. However, if the delay exceeded 200 msec or so, subjects usually had no recourse but to move their eyes to the target, even though it had disappeared. Thus subjects encountered a "point of no return" for saccadic initiation. Once the initiation of the saccade went beyond a certain state of preparation, there was no way to stop it. [More recent investigations of the point of no return were reported by deJong, Coles, Logan, & Gratton (1990) and Osman, Kornblum, & Meyer (1990).]

Although it is impossible to stop a saccade once it has been initiated, it is possible to prepare a saccade while another is under way. This is most clearly demonstrated in the patterns of saccades that people make toward distant targets. For gaze shifts to a target 15° or farther from an initial fixation point, it is not uncommon for two saccades to be made toward the target. The first saccade covers most of the distance but tends to undershoot; the second saccade usually gets the image of the target onto the fovea. The important feature of the data from such double-saccade patterns is that the latency of the second saccade (70 msec) is usually much shorter than the latency of the first (200 msec) (Becker & Jürgens, 1979).

Is the second saccade programmed before the first saccade has ended? Evidence bearing on this question comes from studies in which visual targets are moved after an initial saccade is under way. The first saccade cannot be corrected, but subsequent corrective saccades can begin after the first saccade has been completed. Moreover, the corrective saccades have very short latencies (Becker & Fuchs, 1969). This suggests that visual perception is not prevented during saccades and that programming of the second saccade can occur during the first.

More information about the quality of visual perception during saccades comes from studies in which subjects look at a fixation point and then are presented a target to which they are supposed to redirect their gaze (Hallet & Lightstone, 1975). Sometimes, when the saccade to the target is under way, a second target, to which subjects are also supposed to direct their gaze, is presented. The important feature of the second target is that it remains on for only a brief time; in fact, it vanishes by the time the first saccade is completed. Nevertheless, under appropriate conditions subjects can still direct their eyes to the location of the now-invisible second target.

One implication of this result is that subjects can see the second target while making the first saccade. Another implication is that the visual system has information about the instantaneous location of the eye when the eye is making a saccade. This follows from the fact that, with the reduced form of stimuli used in the experiment (luminous dots in an otherwise dark environment), the image of the second target on the retina could not have indicated by itself where the second target was located in the visual field. Because subjects could direct their eyes to the second target, their visual systems must have registered where the target was located.

How was the location registered? Was the target coded with respect to *spatial* coordinates (where the target appeared in the outer world), or with respect to *retinal* coordinates (where the target was projected onto the retina)? The argument has been made (Mays & Sparks, 1980) that if the registration were retinal, subjects would have made saccades to locations that had the same distance and direction from the line of sight as the target had at its time of presentation. The fact that saccades went to the correct locations suggests that the registration was spatial instead.

Other studies have provided support for the spatial interpretation (Becker & Jürgens, 1979; Mays & Sparks, 1980). In one particularly dramatic experiment (Mays & Sparks, 1980), monkeys made saccades to briefly presented visual targets that were presented at unpredictable locations (see Figure 5.10). Just before the monkeys moved their eyes toward the stimulus, a small jolt of electricity was delivered to the superior colliculus. The effect of the electrical stimulation was to drive the eye to a new position. Nevertheless, after the eye arrived at this new position, it moved directly to the location where the visual target had appeared, even though the target was no longer visible. This outcome suggests that commands to move the eyes are not given in terms of directions or distances but rather in terms of target locations.

Was the command given in *spatial* coordinates, as Mays and Sparks (1980) contended, or was it given in *orbital* coordinates (with respect to the orientation of the eyeball within the head)? According to the latter interpretation (Steinman, 1986), when the target stimulus was presented, its *retinal* location was registered, but so too was its *orbital* location. The command to move the eye may have been represented therefore in terms of aligning the foveal axis of the eye with the orbital location of the stimulus. This representation differs from a *spatial* registration in that the coordinates of the external environment need not be invoked.

To the best of my knowledge, the question of whether saccades are defined with respect to spatial or orbital representations has not yet been resolved. *A priori*, the orbital view seems simpler. Programming an eye move-

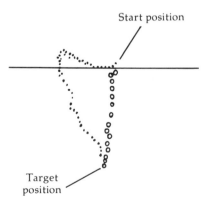

Figure 5.10 Position of the eye of a monkey before presentation of a stimulus, while being driven away from the target as a result of electrical stimulation of the superior colliculus, and then back toward the now-absent target (●), and position of the eye of the same monkey to the same stimulus location when no collicular stimulation is experimentally administered (○). (From Sparks & Mays, 1983.)

ment in orbital coordinates would entail setting relative tensions of extraocular muscle antagonists. This method allows a one-to-one mapping between relative tensions and orbital locations. Programming eye movements in spatial coordinates is more complicated, for the spatial coordinates must still be translated into appropriate muscle tensions. Perhaps it is not surprising, then, that brain cells have recently been found (in the supplementary eye fields, located rostral to the supplementary motor cortex) which fire predictably before achievement of particular *orbital* positions (see Wise & Desimone, 1988).

Saccadic Suppression

Some of the studies reviewed here suggest that visual perception is intact during saccades. It may therefore be surprising to learn that other studies have documented a dramatic *decline* in visual sensitivity when saccades are under way. This phenomenon is called *saccadic suppression*. Saccadic suppression was mentioned in Chapter 1 in connection with the fact that people cannot see their own saccades in the mirror. It is a phenomenon similar to (and, in the opinion of some investigators, identical to) the suppression of sensitivity during blinks, discussed earlier in this chapter. In general, when we make saccadic eye movements, we do not see the blurred image that presumably results on the retina. Laboratory tests have confirmed that the stimulus intensity needed to ensure visual detection during saccades is indeed higher than the stimulus intensity needed to ensure detection when the eyes are stationary (see Matin, 1974; Volkmann, 1976, for review). Our failure to see (or notice) visual events during saccades suggests that their conscious registration is suppressed.

What causes saccadic suppression? Several investigators have proposed that the phenomenon has peripheral origins. One hypothesis is that saccadic suppression arises from the smeariness of saccadically induced retinal images (MacKay, 1970). Another hypothesis is that saccadically induced stimuli are masked by the stimuli that appear just before and after saccades (Campbell & Wurtz, 1978). It has even been proposed that the physical layers at the back of the eyeball shear against one another when saccades are made and that this shearing motion reduces the visual resolution that the retina can provide (Richards, 1968).

An alternative class of hypotheses claims that saccadic suppression arises from central interactions between the oculomotor and visual systems. According to this view, the visual system is informed that commands for saccades have been (or are going to be) issued. The visual system then discounts or suppresses the retinal image displacements that result. A crucial piece of evidence for this position is that saccadic suppression *precedes* saccades by a short time, about 30–40 msec (Latour, 1962; Volkmann, Schick, & Riggs, 1969).

Regardless of the exact cause of saccadic suppression, a puzzle remains from the studies reviewed so far: If saccadic suppression is a real phenomenon, how can people respond accurately to visual stimuli that are presented when saccades are under way? One solution to the problem is to note that if sensitivity declines during saccades it does not follow that detection or localization is completely eliminated. After all, one may be able to determine where a stimulus is located even if it is dimmer than usual.

Another less obvious way of solving the puzzle is to note that saccadic suppression may be an artifact of the kinds of responses that are asked for in laboratory settings. If subjects are asked to report verbally about the location or presence of a stimulus that is presented during a saccade, their performance is poor (Matin, 1972). By contrast, if they are asked to make *automatic* responses to the stimulus, their performance is quite good.

A study by Skavenski and Hansen (1978) illustrates this curious point. They asked subjects to strike with a hammer in the dark at very briefly illuminated points presented during the subjects' saccades. The subjects protested that they could not see the targets, yet their hammer strikes were quite accurate. Moreover, the accuracy of hammer strikes was only slightly affected by the timing of the luminous points relative to the subjects' saccades (Hansen & Skavenski, 1985). The ability of subjects to strike a target shown during a saccade, in contrast to their inability to report verbally on the wherabouts of a stimulus presented while making a saccade (see also Bridgeman, Kirch, & Sperling, 1981), suggests that visual processing may be carried out in two distinct parts of the brain. One may communicate with conscious, verbal centers; the other may communicate with centers responsible for perceptual–motor coordination. People may be able to program saccades to targets that are presented while other saccades are under way because saccadic programming uses an automatic processing system. However, if people are asked to *say* where or whether a stimulus has occurred, this method of responding depends on a less automatic form of processing. Independent confirmation of the dissociation between these two forms of response has been reported by Weiskrantz, Warrington, Sanders, and Marshall (1974). They described patients with lesions in the visual cortex who could accurately reach for targets in space while claiming to be unable to see the targets. This phenomenon is called *blind sight*.

Saccades and Attention

Because saccades bring the eyes to points of interest, it is reasonable to suppose that they move the eyes to points that have attracted attention. Recent work on saccadic control has addressed the question of how attention and eye movements are interrelated. The concept of attention is one of the most alluring in psychology and neuroscience because attention seems to be intimately related to the still more mysterious concept of consciousness (Posner, 1978). If the positions of the eyes show where attention is directed, eye movements may indicate how attention shifts from one position to another.

Are spatial attention and eye position necessarily linked? A connection between them is suggested by the finding, mentioned earlier, that signals informing a subject of where a stimulus will appear reduces the reaction time to begin making a saccade to that location (Posner, 1978). The warning signal may be thought of as a prime for spatial attention, in which case the reduction of saccadic latencies following the warning signal can be taken to suggest that making a saccade normally depends on a prior shift of attention.

If shifts of spatial attention are necessary for saccades, it does not follow that saccades are necessary for shifts of spatial attention. There is evidence, in fact, that shifts of spatial attention can occur *without* eye movements. Posner and his colleagues (Posner, 1978) conducted studies in which subjects were asked to move their eyes either to primed or to nonprimed locations. In control conditions, subjects were asked to make a manual response (such as the release of a lever) as quickly as possible after the presentation of the primed or nonprimed stimulus, and not to make an associated eye movement. Priming was achieved by presenting a cue that indicated on which side of the fixation point the target stimulus would appear. Generally, the cue was followed by the stimulus it primed, but sometimes a different stimulus was presented. Reaction times were reduced when the presented stimulus was anticipated by the cue. Moreover, the degree of priming was essentially the same when subjects moved their hands without moving their eyes or moved their eyes without moving their hands. Thus spatial attention could shift without the eyes being involved. Shifting attention did not require saccades, though saccades may have required prior shifts of attention.

The experimental dissociation of saccades and spatial attention has allowed other investigators to determine where spatial attention and saccades are controlled within the brain. Wurtz, Goldberg, and Robinson (1982) trained monkeys to perform tasks like those used by Posner and his associates. While the monkeys performed the tasks, the electrical activity of cells in four brain areas was recorded: the *superior colliculus*, the *visual cortex*, the *frontal eye fields*, and the *posterior parietal lobe* (see Chapter 2). The results supported the hypothesis that there is a dissociation of eye movements and attention, for cells in these areas responded differently to the task demands (see Table 5.1).

Cells in the superior colliculus and frontal eye fields responded vigorously before saccades were made to primed targets, but did not respond above normal resting levels when manual responses were made without accompanying eye movements. Thus cells in the superior colliculus and frontal eye fields fired in relation to saccadic activity.

Cells in the visual cortex showed an increase in firing rates whenever visual stimuli were presented. The firing rates of cells in this area were only slightly higher when saccades were made to primed targets than when no saccades were made, and this was true regardless of whether manual

■ **Table 5.1** Brain Areas and Their Functions Related to Saccades and Visual Attention[a]

Brain area	Conditions yielding enhanced firing rates	Inferred function
Superior colliculus	Saccades but not manual responses to primed targets	Saccadic control
Frontal eye field	Saccades but not manual responses to primed targets	Saccadic control
Visual cortex	Target onsets irrespective of response or significance	Visual processing
Posterior parietal cortex	Saccades, or manual responses without eye movements to primed targets only	Attentional control

[a]Based on Wurtz, Goldberg, and Robinson (1982).

responses were performed. Thus the visual cortex responded to visual targets irrespective of their functional significance or accompanying motor response.

Firing rates of cells in the posterior parietal cortex were affected by the significance of the target, regardless of the type of response that was made. These cells responded vigorously when a stimulus called for a saccade or a manual detection response, but did not respond as vigorously when the same stimuli were presented and no response was required. Likewise, cells in this region responded only minimally when eye-movement or manual responses were made without an external visual stimulus. The observations suggest that the posterior parietal lobe is specialized for attention *per se* (Mountcastle, Lynch, Georgopoulos, Sakata, & Acuna, 1975). Consistent with this interpretation, people with damage to the posterior parietal cortex pay little or no attention to stimuli in the contralateral visual field, although they can *see* stimuli in that field. (This syndrome is known as *spatial neglect*.)

■ SMOOTH PURSUIT MOVEMENTS

The preceding section was concerned with saccadic eye movements. Now let us consider smooth pursuit movements. These movements keep the eyes fixated on a target that is either moving or stationary. As I said earlier, the saccadic system tries to match the position of the eye with the position of the target. The smooth pursuit system tries to match the *velocity* of the eye with the *velocity* of the target. Said differently, the main stimulus for smooth pursuit movements is retinal *velocity* error, whereas the main stimulus for saccades is retinal *position* error.

The maximum velocity of smooth pursuit movements is around 100°/sec, although the eye's tracking ability begins to deteriorate above velocities of 30°/sec. The accuracy of tracking with the smooth pursuit system improves if the target being tracked moves predictably. When a smoothly moving target is first selected for tracking, a saccade may be made to it before smooth pursuit begins (for example, if the target is far away from the current fixation point). Corrective saccades also occur if smooth pursuit tracking falters (Carpenter, 1977).

Unlike saccades, smooth pursuit movements usually cannot be initiated at will without an external target. For some time, it was thought that visible targets are necessary to elicit pursuit movements (Alpern, 1972; Robinson, 1968). However, it was later shown that people can make pursuit movements in the dark when tactile stimuli are drawn across their skin (Lackner & Evanoff, 1977). Similarly, people can smoothly pursue their own hands in the dark when their hands are moved actively or passively (Jordan, 1970; see Chapter 11). A few people are able to generate smooth pursuit movements in the absence of any external target (Westheimer & Conover, 1954), and it is not unusual for smooth eye movements to occur during REM sleep, at least in cats (Fuchs & Ron, 1968).

The muscles used for smooth movements and saccades are the same, but their mode of operation is different. In saccades, only muscle agonists are used to drive the eye to a new location (Robinson, 1964). In smooth pursuit movements, agonists and antagonists are activated simultaneously. This has been shown by recording the electrical activity of the eye muscles (Alpern, 1972). Such measurements indicate that smooth pursuit movements are produced by creating small differences in the tensions of the opposing extraocular muscles.

Smooth eye movements and saccades are also controlled through different neural systems. One source of evidence for this claim is that the two types of eye movement are affected differently by drugs and disease (Alpern, 1972). For example, the disease *multiple sclerosis* generally affects smooth pursuit movements but leaves saccades unscathed. Direct recording, stimulation, and ablation of various brain regions also suggest that smooth pursuit movements and saccades are controlled by different neural subsystems (Gouras, 1985a).

In spite of the differences between saccades and smooth eye movements, both eye-movement systems reflect the cognitive state of the subject. At one time it was thought that smooth eye movements are triggered exclusively by the detection of retinal velocity errors—a concept that, if correct, would have made it possible to model smooth eye movements entirely in terms of traditional servo models (Westheimer, 1954). However, nonvisual stimuli can elicit smooth eye movements, as has just been indicated. That smooth eye movements reflect people's *cognitive* states was demonstrated by recording subjects' eye movements when they looked at a stationary point which they knew would soon move in a particular direction (Kowler & Steinman, 1979). Prior to the motion of the stimulus, the subjects' eyes began to move smoothly, usually in the expected direction of stimulus motion (see Figure 5.11). Although the velocity of the anticipatory smooth eye movement was slight, from trial to trial its direction correlated closely with the direction in which the subject expected the stimulus to move. (The expected direction was manipulated by announcing to the subject before each trial where the

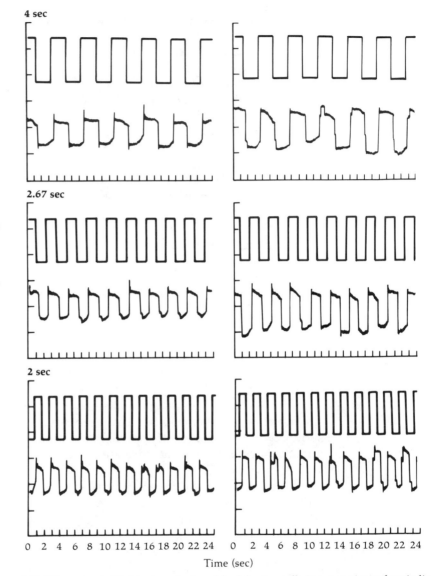

Figure 5.11 When a spot of light moves back and forth horizontally in a stepwise and periodic fashion (*upper trace*), the eyes not only track the light after it has moved, but also make anticipatory smooth movements in the direction of forthcoming stimulus motion (*lower trace*). The two columns show data from two observers. Each unit on the relative position scale corresponds to 1 degree, with upward points signifying rightward positions. The stimulus moved every 4 sec (*top*), 2.67 sec (*middle*), or 2 sec (*bottom*). (From Kowler & Steinman, 1979.)

stimulus would head.) Results like these indicate that smooth eye movements, like saccades, provide a "window to the mind." Though saccades and smooth eye movements may be controlled by different brain systems, both reflect the observer's mental state.

■ OPTOKINETIC NYSTAGMUS

Saccades and smooth pursuit movements can be effectively coordinated. This is seen in the phenomenon of *optokinetic nystagmus* (OKN), which can be observed by watching someone's eyes as he or she looks at one object after another outside a moving train or car. The eyes move in a sawtooth pattern (see Figure 5.12), alternating between smooth tracking movements (the *slow* phase) and saccadic jumps (the *fast* phase). Each smooth movement continues until the tracked object approaches the limit of the visual field, at which time the eye jumps back to the next object to be followed.

The OKN is often elicited, for clinical purposes, by surrounding a patient with a full-field rotating drum consisting of vertical stripes. The drum is used for diagnosing visual impairments, particularly in patients who are unable or unwilling to report on the clarity of their vision (for example, young children). Because the OKN can only occur if the patient can see the individual stripes of the rotating drum, the presence of the OKN indicates that the patient can see the stripes, even if he or she cannot say so. By varying characteristics of the stripes such as their width and contrast with the background, it is possible to evaluate the patient's visual capabilities quite accurately (Collewijn, 1981).

Is it the case that the slow and fast phases of the OKN use typical saccades and smooth pursuit movements? Several findings suggest that they do. One is that the slow phase of the OKN has the same velocity characteristics as smooth pursuit movements. In the slow phase of the OKN, as in single smooth pursuit movements, the eye tracks most effectively at velocities

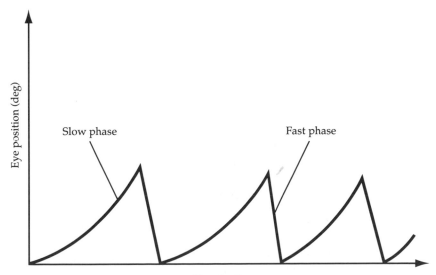

Figure 5.12 Optokinetic nystagmus pattern.

of 20 to 30°/sec, and the eye is no longer able to track when velocities approach 100°/sec (Carpenter, 1977). The saccades of the OKN (that is, the fast-phase movements of the OKN) have the same properties as isolated saccades (Carpenter, 1977). Thus the OKN can truly be regarded as a pattern of alternating saccades and pursuit movements. Because the OKN can be extremely accurate, it follows that precise coordination can be achieved between the saccadic and smooth pursuit systems.

■ THE VESTIBULO–OCULAR REFLEX

For all of the eye-movement systems discussed so far, I have conveniently ignored the fact that the head as well as the eyes can move. This is not merely because of possible narrow-mindedness on my part. It is also because all the studies I have reviewed so far were conducted with subjects holding their heads absolutely still, often keeping their teeth pressed onto a bite board. The studies were conducted in this way for technical reasons: Only recently has it become possible to accurately record the positions of the eyes while the head is free to move (Collewijn, Martins, & Steinman, 1983).

If the eyes are fully deviated toward one side or the other, it is pointless to try to move them to an even more eccentric position. A more adaptive behavior is to turn the head toward the target. However, when the head turns toward the target, keeping the eyes at a constant position with respect to the head would cause the direction of gaze to be even farther from the target than it was before. What is required is a method for coordinating the position of the head and the position of the eye. The method that Mother Nature has devised is the *vestibulo-ocular reflex* (VOR), which was introduced in Chapter 1.

The VOR comes into play when one tries to look at a stationary target as the head is rotating. When the VOR functions properly, the motion of the eyes compensates for the head motion. Head movements are sensed by the central component of the vestibular system—the *labyrinth* of the inner ear (see Figure 5.13). The labyrinth has three semicircular canals oriented at right angles to one another. If a canal undergoes angular acceleration, the fluid within it (the *endolymph*) changes its rate of flow, pushing against a membrane (the *cupula*) in one direction or the other depending on the sign of the acceleration (whether the fluid speeds up or slows down). As the cupula is deflected or experiences a pressure differential, tiny hair cells attached to it bend, causing neural signals to be sent to other brain centers, including the oculomotor nuclei. From there, efferent commands are delivered to the extraocular muscles, and the eye moves (Brown & Deffenbacher, 1979).

The role of the vestibular apparatus in controlling eye movements is apparent in a clinical procedure used to diagnose abnormal dizziness. Tepid water is introduced into the inner ear to stimulate the labyrinths. The result of this procedure is *vestibular–ocular nystagmus*, a pattern of alternating

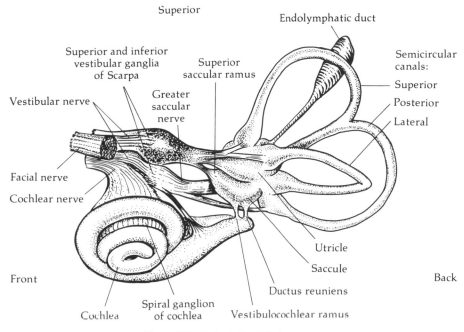

Figure 5.13 Labyrinth of the inner ear.

smooth and saccadic eye movements similar to that observed in OKN. Detailed characteristics of the nystagmus pattern allow for precise diagnoses about the state of the vestibular apparatus (Dell'Osso & Daroff, 1981).

What is the evidence for the claim that the vestibular system underlies normal eye–head coordination? Some of the most important evidence comes from experiments in which monkeys looked straight ahead and then turned the eyes and head toward visual targets presented to the side (Bizzi, 1974). Figure 5.14A shows position-versus-time curves for the eye and head of a monkey in this situation. The eyes and head begin moving at the same time, but because the eyes move more quickly, they reach the target before the head. To keep the eyes fixed on the target, the eyes counterrotate as the head continues to turn.

Figure 5.14B shows what happens when the monkey's vestibular system is surgically disrupted. When the head turns toward the target, the eyes do not counterrotate. Instead, they move along with the head and then are returned to the target more slowly than usual. This outcome shows that counterrotation of the eyes during head turning depends on the intact functioning of the vestibular system. Even 40 days after vestibular damage, counterrotation of the eye during head turning is severely impaired. After 120 days, some compensation occurs, however, as shown in Figure 5.14C.

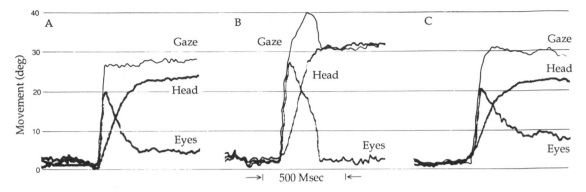

Figure 5.14 Coordination of the eye and head (A) in a normal monkey, (B) in a monkey 40 days after surgical disruption of the vestibule of the inner ear, and (C) in a monkey 120 days after surgery. (From Bizzi, 1974.)

Changes in the coordination of eye and head movements do not only occur as a result of long-term experiential changes. Changes in the coordination of the eye and head can come about quickly if a visual target comes to be expected at a particular location in the periphery. Under this condition, the head may actually lead the eye, with the initiation of the eye movement delayed long enough to allow the eye and head to arrive at the target simultaneously (Bizzi, 1974). This strategy eliminates the need for compensatory eye movements and therefore can be relied on when normal vestibular control is impossible.

■ VERGENCE MOVEMENTS

With the exception of some of the miniature eye movements discussed before, all the eye-movement activities I have considered so far keep the lines of sight of the two eyes parallel. Recall that these sorts of eye movements are called *conjugate*. Parallelism does not characterize all eye movements, however. During *vergence* movements the lines of sight of the two eyes cross. There are two kinds of vergence movements. *Convergence* brings the eyes inward toward the nose as the observer looks at a nearer or approaching target. *Divergence* brings the eyes outward toward the temples as the observer looks at a farther or receding target. When the visual target is very far away, the lines of sight again become parallel.

The primary stimulus for vergence movements is retinal disparity (Rashbass, 1981), a difference (often very slight) in the retinal projections of a stimulus on the retinas of the two eyes. Retinal disparity is not the only trigger for vergence movements, as shown in the following demonstration (Alpern, 1957). A target is slowly brought toward one eye while the other eye is blocked. Suddenly, a lens is placed in front of the seeing eye, so its image of the target is blurred. The response of the other, unseeing eye is immediate convergence toward the target. Since there is no retinal disparity in this situation, the trigger for the convergence is accommodation alone. Because targets at different distances usually require both vergence and accommodation, these two activities usually co-occur. Their joint action is called the *accommodation reflex* (Gouras, 1985a).

■ EYE MOVEMENTS AND SPACE CONSTANCY

When the eyes move, the image of the visual world moves across the retina. The same sort of retinal image displacement can also occur if the eyes are held still and objects move before them. How does one determine whether the visual world is stationary and the eyes are moving or the visual world is moving and the eyes are still? (This question was raised initially in Chapter 1.) There are at least two possible answers to this question (see Figure 5.15).

One is that the visual system receives signals from the oculomotor centers indicating how the eyes have been instructed to move. These instructions are then used to guide the interpretation of subsequent visual input.

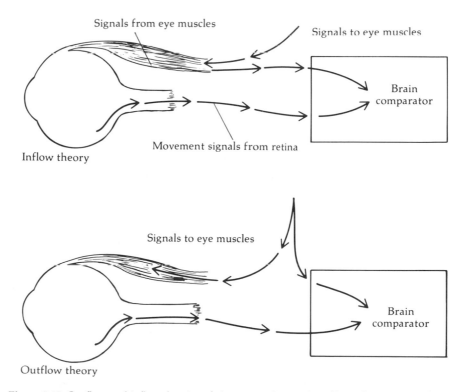

Figure 5.15 Outflow and inflow theories of visuomotor integration. (From Gregory, 1973.)

According to this *outflow* model, if an oculomotor signal is sent to move the eyes 4° to the right, a retinal displacement of 4° to the left is predicted. When the retinal displacement occurs, it is interpreted to mean that the visual world remained stationary. If no signal is sent to move the eyes and a 4° retinal displacement occurs, the displacement is interpreted to mean that the visual scene shifted.

An alternative to the outflow model is the *inflow* model. Here it is assumed that *feedback* from the eye muscles, rather than *commands* to the eye muscles, provides the signals used by the visual system to interpret retinal shifts. Reliance on feedback from the eye muscles has an advantage over reliance on oculomotor commands. Because oculomotor commands may not always be carried out perfectly, the comparison of retinal (visual) signals with oculomotor signals can cause inaccurate interpretations of visual changes. Such errors generally will not occur if retinal information is compared with feedback concerning actual eye movements.

Reliance on outflow has an advantage over reliance on inflow, however. Efferent information is likely to be available *before* muscle feedback returns. Thus a comparator that uses *efferent* information will be faster than one that uses *afferent* information. From the perspective of speed, the outflow model is therefore preferable to the inflow model.

The debate over inflow and outflow interested the great nineteenth century scientist, Hermann von Helmholtz ([1866]1962), who suggested that the debate could be resolved with the following simple demonstration. Close one eye and gently press against the lid of the other eye with your finger. As you repeatedly press your finger against your eye, you will probably see the visual world jump back and forth. This simple observation has a profound implication, though the path to understanding it must be followed carefully. When you move your eye with your finger, you cause the visual image to move across the retina. However, you do not generate the normal commands for eye movements. Because your eye moves, receptors in the extraocular muscles are activated. If feedback from the eye muscles were used to interpret retinal displacements, the visual system would not be "fooled into thinking" that the visual world had moved when your finger nudged your eyeball. The fact that you see the world move suggests that feedback from the eye muscles is not used in the everyday interpretation of retinal displacements. By this line of reasoning, the visual system relies on efferent commands or their copies to interpret movement-based retinal displacements (Sperry, 1950; von Holst & Mittelstaedt, 1950).

Now consider another demonstration that leads to the same conclusion. This one was reported by another giant of nineteenth century science, Ernst Mach. He claimed that when the eyes are immobilized by being bunged with putty, the person volunteering for this odd treatment sees the world move during attempted eye movements (Gregory, 1973). The interpretation of this phenomenon is like the interpretation of von Helmholtz's eye-nudging task. When the eyes are commanded to move but do not, normal feedback from the stretch receptors is presumably absent. The fact that one sees the world shift when the eyes are immobilized suggests that commands to move the eyes, rather than feedback from the eye muscles, allow for the interpretation of retinal displacements associated with eye movements.

To accept this argument, one must accept the assumption that feedback from the stretch receptors when the eye tries to move but cannot is comparable to the feedback that exists when the eyes are still because they have not been commanded to move. But suppose one doesn't accept this assumption. Suppose one allows for the possibility that feedback from the extraocular muscles is in fact somewhat different when the eyes are not commanded to move or when the eyes are commanded to move but cannot do so. Then the power of Mach's and Helmholtz's arguments is lost, and the debate between inflow and outflow theory remains unresolved. For example, if one assumes that some oculomotor commands are generated when the eye is pushed with the finger, or if one assumes that there is usable feedback from the eye muscles when the eyeball is pushed from the outside, then one needn't accept the outflow interpretation of Helmholtz's demonstration. In fact, because it is likely that people try to maintain visual fixation while carrying out Helmholtz's experiment, it may be incorrect to assume, as Helmholtz did, that there are no oculomotor commands or no feedback from the eye muscles when the eye is pressed manually.

A more decisive method for choosing between outflow and inflow is to physically disrupt the outflow–inflow loop. Pursuing this reasoning, Kornmuller (1930) reported that partial paralysis of the extraocular muscles results in the perception of illusory visual motion. Because the eyes presumably do not move (or barely move) in this situation, images of external visual stimuli remain fixed on the retina. Because there is little or no feedback from the eye muscles to indicate that the eyes have changed position, the visual centers must note that a central signal was issued to move the eyes. These centers presumably then "infer" that the world moved synchronously with the eyes.

As compelling as this argument may be, it needs to be qualified. Subsequent experiments in which volunteers allowed their eyes to be *totally* paralyzed did not report seeing illusory motion. However, these experiments were conducted in conditions of partial illumination, which may have affected the perceptual judgments that were given (see subsequent text). Another concern is that the eye muscles are richly endowed with stretch receptors (see Skavenski, 1972), so it seems odd that the eye muscles cannot provide information about the position or motion of the eye. For a time, it was believed that the receptors of the eye muscles provide no useful information, in part because it was reported that a person whose eye muscles were physically pulled with a forceps (and whose eyelids and eye were anesthetized) could not tell that his eye was being passively rotated (Brindley & Merton, 1960). However, this subject was probably under duress, so his report must be treated with caution.

A more careful study, reported by Skavenski (1972), indicates that proprioceptive information from the extraocular muscles may in fact be useful. Skavenski applied a contact lens to the cornea and attached a thread to a stalk projecting from the lens (see Figure 5.16). When the thread was pulled, it passively rotated the eyeball. Subjects in the experiment were responsible for indicating whether they thought their eyes were moved and, if so, in which direction. Though the experiment was conducted in complete darkness, subjects could detect passive motion of the eye and could accurately identify the direction of passive motion. Thus they had access to proprioceptive information from their eyes. In another experiment, subjects were able to counterrotate their eyes to adjust for an external load imposed on the eyeball. The fact that they could do so indicates that they detected proprioceptive input from their eye muscles (Skavenski, Haddad, & Steinman, 1972).

The latter results suggest that outflow may not be required to explain people's ability to distinguish self-generated visual motion and externally generated visual motion. A final argument for this conclusion is that in virtually all the studies that have supported outflow theory, subjects were exposed to highly restricted visual inputs (typically single points of light).

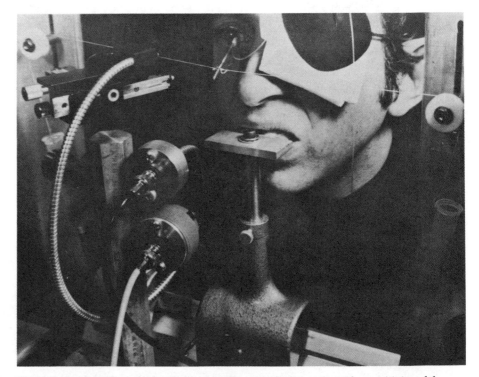

Figure 5.16 Apparatus used by Skavenski (1972, p. 224) to investigate the sensitivity of the eye to passive displacement. (From Steinman, 1975.)

When several light points can be seen, or when a natural visual scene is visible, most of the perceptual phenomena that support outflow theory are eliminated or significantly reduced (Bridgeman, 1983; Matin, Stevens, & Picoult, 1983). For example, a person whose eye muscles are paralyzed may see an isolated visual stimulus drift toward the floor (if the person is reclining), but the illusion vanishes if the room lights are turned on (Matin *et al.*, 1983). Similarly, one may see illusory motion of the illuminated digits of an electronic clock if one makes saccades when the room is dark (especially if the clock is off to the side), but there is no such illusion if the room is illuminated. Observations such as these suggest that retinal information alone may provide all the information necessary to distinguish externally and internally induced motion—a point that has been made by advocates of the ecological approach to perception (Gibson, 1979).

■ DEVELOPMENT AND PLASTICITY OF OCULOMOTOR CONTROL

One of the most remarkable features of the eye-movement system is its capacity for recalibration as a result of experience. I discussed recalibration in connection with the vestibulectomized monkeys of Bizzi (1974) and also in Chapter 1 (in connection with the VOR). Recall that in Bizzi's (1974) experiment, after the monkeys underwent surgical destruction of the vestibular apparatus, their eyes failed to counterrotate properly during head turns. With time, however, the amplitude of the initial saccade was adjusted so the eye reached the target and remained on it. Thus the monkeys could compensate for the altered relation between the movements of their eyes and the movements of their heads.

The plasticity of the oculomotor system can be observed without resorting to surgery. Consider what happens when one looks through a lens that shrinks an image (a *minifying* lens). If one wears such a lens in natural surroundings, one's eye movements will, on average, have smaller amplitudes than usual. Hoffman and Roffwarg (1983) asked six volunteers to wear minifying lenses for 12 days. When the minifying lenses were in place, the amplitudes of eye movements were significantly reduced. More surprisingly, eye-movement amplitudes also were affected during REM sleep (when the volunteers' eyes were, of course, closed). This outcome implies that the recalibration of eye movements was carried over to situations where there were no immediate visual errors.

A number of studies have shown that the gain of the vestibulo–ocular reflex changes rapidly when one wears magnifying or minifying lenses (Berthoz & Melvill Jones, 1985; Collewijn, Martins, & Steinman, 1981). Such plasticity is important because aspects of the visual system, such as the distance between the eyes or the strength of the extraocular muscles, change over the life span.

What of the normal course of development of eye-movement control? Most eye movements that humans can make can be made at birth. Ultrasound studies have shown that eye movements occur even prenatally (Birnholz, 1981). By around 16–23 gestational weeks, slow eye movements can be seen in ultrasound images, and by around 23 gestational weeks, rapid eye movements are observable. Opening of the eyelids can be detected by around 35 weeks. The fact that these activities develop at different times supports the idea that they are controlled by different neural subsystems.

Although eye movements occur prenatally, they also undergo progressive postnatal development, even past age 5. Kowler and Martins (1983) reported that normal 4- and 5-year-olds did less well at fixating a target and tracking it than adults did. There has been controversy about this report (Aslin *et al.*, 1983). Nevertheless, the study raises the interesting possibility that the development of visual acuity in children may be partly determined by factors related to oculomotor control. Insofar as this hypothesis is correct, it highlights the important interplay between visual perception and its motoric bases (see Coren, 1986, for further discussion of this issue).

■ SUMMARY

1. Looking relies on a number of oculomotor activities. Some rotate the eyeball whereas others do not. One nonrotational activity is blinking. Blinks can be classically conditioned. The learning that occurs appears to be registered in specific brain locations (at least in rabbits). Visual sensitivity is attenuated during blinks. Blink rates increase with anxiety and are suppressed during the assimilation of vital visual information.

2. Another oculomotor activity that does not result in rotation of the eyeball is accommodation. Accommodation helps focus blurry images. It is triggered by the detection of blurriness and is achieved by contracting and relaxing the ciliary muscles attached to the lens of the eye.

3. A third oculomotor activity that does not involve rotation of the eyeball is adjustment of pupil diameter. Like blinking, pupil responses have reflexive and voluntary components. The reflexive component is elicited, under normal conditions, by changes in illumination or by an approaching object. Pupil dilation allows more light into the eye, whereas pupil constriction reduces the amount of light that can enter. Pupil dilation indexes the mental load invested in a task and is often taken as a social cue about one's degree of interest in another person.

4. When considering activities that rotate the eye, it is natural to wonder why the eye rotates at all. The answer is probably that the foveal projection areas within the brain are massive compared to the nonfoveal projection areas. Moving the eye limits the necessary size of the fovea and the amount of cortex associated with it.

5. Eye rotation is achieved with muscles that work in combination to rotate the globe in the vertical, horizontal, and torsional dimensions.

6. The smallest eye movements, *miniature* eye movements, fall into three classes: drifts, tremors, and microsaccades. Although these movements are difficult to observe, the retinal jitter they cause appears to have important visual effects. If the retinal effect of the jitter is eliminated by stabilizing an image on the retina, the image quickly fades. Miniature eye movements also cause the *autokinetic illusion*—the tendency to see a single, stationary point of light wander about in a completely dark surround.

7. Saccades are the jumps of the eyes that occur when one reads or inspects a scene. During saccades, the eye can reach high velocities. The peak velocity of the eye increases with the amplitude of the saccade, up to a limit. The way in which peak velocities vary with saccade amplitudes has been used to model the physical dynamics of saccade generation.

8. Latencies to begin saccades are relatively long, though they may be reduced by attentional priming (which appears to be controlled primarily by the parietal lobe of the brain) and by the release of attention from an initially fixated stimulus. It is possible to program one saccade while another saccade is under way. The accuracy of the second saccade indicates that the visual system has access to extraretinal as well as retinal information.

9. In spite of the accuracy of visual perception during saccades, under some conditions visual sensitivity during saccades may be attenuated. This phenomenon is known as *saccadic suppression*. There has been debate about the sources of saccadic suppression. One possibility is that it has central origins. The other possibility is that its origins are peripheral.

10. Smooth pursuit movements occur when one tracks a continuously moving stimulus, although smooth pursuit movements can be generated at will in some individuals. Whereas saccades respond primarily to retinal position error, smooth pursuit movements respond primarily to retinal velocity error. Saccades and smooth pursuit movements are generated with different neural subsystems and are produced through different patterns of activity in the extraocular muscles. Muscle antagonists are activated simultaneously in smooth pursuit movements but are activated asynchronously during saccades.

11. Although saccades and pursuit movements are controlled by different means, they both reveal cognitive states. Expectancies about target motions give rise to anticipatory smooth eye movements.

12. There is effective coordination between saccades and smooth eye movements, as illustrated in *optokinetic nystagmus*, a pattern of eye movements characterized by rapid, regular alternations between quick and slow phases of ocular motility.

13. Coordination between the eye and head provides another example of the way in which different motor systems work together to promote effective vision. Eye and head movements are coordinated through the *vestibulo-ocular reflex* (VOR). Removal of the vestibular apparatus interferes with the eye's ability to counterrotate as the head turns toward a peripheral target. With experience, however, it is possible to find alternative strategies for coordinating the eye and head.

14. *Vergence* movements allow the eyes to focus on objects at varying distances from the viewer. In contrast to saccades and smooth eye movements, which are *conjugate* (keeping the lines of sight parallel), vergence movements are *disjunctive*; they cause the lines of sight of the two eyes to cross. The main stimuli for vergence movements are retinal disparity and the detection of blurriness.

15. The interaction between vision and eye movements has been pursued in great detail in connection with space constancy. The question is how we tell whether retinal displacements are due to motion of external stimuli or motion of the eyes. Outflow theory states that the brain compares visual input with copies of eye-movement commands. Inflow theory states that the brain compares visual input with feedback from the eye muscles. A third possibility is that visual information alone informs the viewer of the cause of retinal displacement. Evidence has been obtained for all three theories.

16. The final topic covered in this chapter was the development and plasticity of oculomotor control. There is evidence that eye movements occur even before birth. However, eye movements are readily modified by experience and may be controlled more and more precisely over the first five years of life.

■ REFERENCES

Abrams, R. A., Meyer, D. E., & Kornblum, S. (1989). Speed and accuracy of saccadic eye movements: Characteristics of impulse variability in the oculomotor system. *Journal of Experimental Psychology: Human Perception and Performance,* **15,** 529–543.

Alpern, M. (1957). The position of the eye during prism vergence. *American Journal of Ophthalmology,* **57,** 345–353.

Alpern, M. (1972). Eye movements. In D. Jameson & L. Hurvich (Eds.), *Handbook of sensory physiology* (Vol. 7, Part 4, pp. 303–330). Berlin: Springer.

Aslin, R. N., Ciuffreda, K. J., Dannemiller, J. L., Banks, M. S., Stephens, B. R., Hartmann, E. E., Kowler, E., & Martins, A. J. (1983). Eye movements of preschool children. *Science,* **222,** 74–77.

Bahill, A. T., & Stark, L. (1979). The trajectories of saccadic eye movements. *Scientific American,* No. 1, 108–117.

Bandura, A. (1986). *Social functions of thought and action: A social cognitive theory.* Englewood Cliffs, NJ: Prentice-Hall.

Barlow, H. (1952). Eye movements during fixation. *Journal of Physiology (London),* **116,** 290–306.

Beatty, J. (1982). Task-evoked pupillary responses, processing load, and the structure of processing resources. *Psychological Bulletin,* **91,** 276–292.

Becker, W., & Fuchs, A. F. (1969). Further properties of the human saccadic system: Eye movements and correction saccades with and without visual fixation points. *Vision Research, 9,* 1247–1258.

Becker, W., & Jürgens, R. (1979). An analysis of the saccadic system by means of double step stimuli. *Vision Research, 19,* 967–983.

Bernal, G., & Berger, S. M. (1976). Vicarious eyelid conditioning. *Journal of Personality and Social Psychology, 34,* 62–68.

Berthoz, A., & Melvill Jones, G. (Eds.) (1985). *Adaptive mechanisms in gaze control.* New York: Elsevier.

Birnholz, J. (1981). The development of human fetal eye movement patterns. *Science, 213,* 679–681.

Bizzi, E. (1974). The coordination of eye-head movements. *Scientific American,* No. 10, 100–106.

Bridgeman, B. (1983). Mechanisms of space constancy. In A. Hein & M. Jeannerod (Eds.), *Spatially oriented behavior* (pp. 263–279). New York: Springer-Verlag.

Bridgeman, B., Kirch, M., & Sperling, A. (1981). Segregation of cognitive and motor aspects of visual information using induced motion. *Perception & Psychophysics, 29,* 336–342.

Brindley, G. S., & Merton, P. A. (1960). The absence of position sense in the human eye. *Journal of Physiology (London), 153,* 127–130.

Brown, E. L., & Deffenbacher, K. (1979). *Perception and the senses.* New York: Oxford Univ. Press.

Campbell, F. W., & Wurtz, R. H. (1978). Saccadic omission: Why we do not see a grey-out during a saccadic eye movement. *Vision Research, 18,* 1297–1303.

Carpenter, R. H. S. (1979). *Movements of the eyes.* London: Pion.

Collewijn, H. (1981). The optokinetic system. In B. L. Zuber (Ed.), *Models of oculomotor behavior and control* (pp. 111–137). Boca Raton, FL: CRC Press.

Collewijn, H., Martins, A. J., & Steinman, R. M. (1981). In B. Cohen (Ed.), *Vestibular and oculomotor physiology* (Vol. 3, p. 312). New York: New York Academy of Sciences.

Collewijn, H., Martins, A. J., & Steinman, R. M. (1983). Compensatory eye movements during active and passive head movements: Fast adaptation to changes in visual magnification. *Journal of Physiology (London), 340,* 259–286.

Collewijn, H., van der Steen, J., & Steinman, R. (1985). Human eye movements associated with blinks and prolonged eye closure. *Journal of Neurophysiology, 54,* 11–27.

Coren, S. (1986). An efferent component in the visual perception of direction and extent. *Psychological Review, 93,* 391–410.

deJong, R., Coles, M. G., Logan, G. D., & Gratton, G. (1990). Searching for the point of no return: Response process control in speeded choice reaction performance. *Journal of Experimental Psychology: Human Perception and Performance, 16,* 164–182.

Dell'Osso, L. F., & Daroff, R. B. (1981). Clinical disorders of ocular movement. In B. L. Zuber (Ed.), *Models of oculomotor behavior and control* (pp. 233–256). Boca Raton, FL: CRC Press.

Ditchburn, R. W. (1973). *Eye movements and visual perception.* Oxford: Clarendon Press.

Dodwell, P. C. (1980). *Perceptual processing: Stimulus equivalence and pattern recognition.* New York: Appleton-Century-Crofts.

Fischer, B., & Breitmeyer, B. (1987). Mechanisms of visual attention revealed by saccadic eye movements. *Neuropsychologia, 25,* 73–83.

Fuchs, A. (1967). Saccadic and smooth pursuit eye movements in the monkey. *Journal of Physiology (London), 191,* 609–631.

Fuchs, A., & Ron, S. (1968). An analysis of rapid eye movements of sleep in the monkey. *Electroencephalography and Clinical Neurophysiology, 25,* 244–251.

Gibson, J. J. (1979). *The ecological approach to visual perception.* Boston: Houghton Mifflin.

Gouras, P. (1985a). Oculomotor system. In E. R. Kandel & J. H. Schwartz (Eds.), *Principles of neural science* (2d ed., pp. 571–583). New York: Elsevier.

Gouras, P. (1985b). Physiological optics, accommodation, and stereopsis. In E. R. Kandel & J. H. Schwartz (Eds.), *Principles of neural science* (2d ed., pp. 865–875). New York: Elsevier.

Gregory, R. L. (1966). *Eye and brain.* New York: McGraw-Hill.

Gregory, R. L. (1973). *Eye and brain* (2d ed.). New York: McGraw-Hill.

Hallet, P. E., & Lightstone, A. D. (1975). Saccadic eye movements to stimuli triggered by prior saccades. *Vision Research, 16,* 99–106.

Hansen, R. M., & Skavenski, A. A. (1985). Accuracy of spatial localization near the time of saccadic eye movements. *Vision Research, 25,* 1077–1082.

Hess, E. (1975). *The tell-tale eye: How your eyes reveal hidden thoughts.* New York: Van Nostrand-Reinhold.

Hoffman, J. H., & Roffwarg, H. P. (1983). Modifying oculomotor activity in awake subjects increases the amplitude of eye movements during REM sleep. *Science, 220,* 1074–1076.

Hyde, J. E. (1959). Some characteristics of voluntary human ocular movements in the horizontal plane. *American Journal of Ophthalmology, 48,* 85–94.

Inhoff, A. W. (1986). Preparing sequences of saccades under choice reaction conditions: Effects of sequence length and context. *Acta Psychologica, 61,* 211–228.

Jordan, S. (1970). Ocular pursuit as a function of visual and proprioceptive stimulation. *Vision Research, 10,* 775–780.

Kahneman, D., & Beatty, J. (1966). Pupil diameter and load on memory. *Science, 154,* 1583–1585.

Kaufman, L. (1974). *Sight and mind.* New York: Oxford Univ. Press.

Keele, S. W., & Ivry, R. I. (1987). Modular analysis of timing in motor skill. In G. H. Bower (Ed.), *The psychology of learning and motivation* (Vol. 21, pp. 183–228). San Diego, CA: Academic Press.

Koretz, J. F., & Handelman, G. H. (1989). How the human eye focuses. *Scientific American, 259* (1), 92–99.

Kornmuller, A. E. (1930). Eine experimentelle Anesthesie der äußeren Augenmuskeln am Menschen und ihre Auswirkungen. *Journal für Psychologie und Neurologie, 41,* 354–366.

Kowler, E., & Martins, A. J. (1983). Eye movements of preschool children. *Science, 215,* 997–999.

Kowler, E., & Steinman, R. M. (1979). The effect of expectations on slow oculomotor control. I. Periodic target steps. *Vision Research, 19,* 619–632.

Kowler, E., & Steinman, R. M. (1981). The effect of expectations on slow oculomotor control. III. Guessing unpredictable target displacements. *Vision Research, 21,* 191–203.

Lackner, J. R., & Evanoff, J. N. (1977). Smooth pursuit eye movements elicited by somatosensory stimulation. *Neuroscience Letters, 4,* 43–48.

Latour, P. L. (1962). Visual thresholds during eye movements. *Vision Research, 2,* 261–262.

Lehman, R. S. (1965). Eye-movements and the autokinetic illusion. *American Journal of Psychology, 78,* 490–492.

Levy, J. (1972). Autokinetic illusion: A systematic review of theories, measures, and independent variables. *Psychological Bulletin, 78,* 457–474.

MacKay, D. M. (1970). Elevation of visual threshold by displacement of retinal image. *Nature (London), 225,* 90–92.

Matin, L. (1972). Eye movements and perceived visual direction. In D. Jameson & L. Hurvich (Eds.), *Handbook of sensory physiology* (Vol. 7, pp. 331–380). Berlin: Springer.

Matin, L. (1974). Saccadic suppression. *Psychological Bulletin, 81,* 899–918.

Matin, L., Stevens, J. K., & Picoult, E. (1983). Perceptual consequences of experimental extraocular muscle paralysis. In A. Hein & M. Jeannerod (Eds.), *Spatially oriented behavior* (pp. 243–262). New York: Springer-Verlag.

Mays, L. E., & Sparks, D. L. (1980). Saccades are spatially, not retinocentrically, coded. *Science, 208,* 1163–1165.

McCormick, D. A., & Thompson, R. F. (1984). Cerebellum: Essential involvement in the classically conditioned eyelid response. *Science, 223,* 296–299.

Mountcastle, V. B., Lynch, J. C., Georgopoulos, A., Sakata, H., & Acuna, C. (1975). Posterior parietal association cortex of the monkey: Command functions for operations within extrapersonal space. *Journal of Neurophysiology, 38,* 871–908.

Osman, A., Kornblum, S., & Meyer, D. E. (1990). Does motor programming necessitate response execution? *Journal of Experimental Psychology: Human Perception and Performance, 16,* 183–198.

Posner, M. I. (1978). *Chronometric explorations of mind*. Hillsdale, NJ: Erlbaum.

Rashbass, C. (1961). The relationship between saccadic and smooth tracking eye movements. *Journal of Physiology (London)*, **159**, 326–338.

Rashbass, C. (1981). Reflexions on the control of vergence. In B. L. Zuber (Ed.), *Models of oculomotor behavior and control* (pp. 139–148). Boca Raton, FL: CRC Press.

Rayner, K. (Ed.) (1983). *Eye movements in reading*. New York: Academic Press.

Rayner, K., & Pollatsek, A. (1988). *Psychology of reading*. Englewood Cliffs, NJ: Prentice-Hall.

Richards, W. (1968). Visual suppression during passive eye movement. *Journal of the Optical Society of America*, **58**, 1559.

Robinson, D. A. (1964). The mechanics of human saccadic eye movement. *Journal of Physiology (London)*, **174**, 245–264.

Robinson, D. A. (1968). The oculomotor control system: A review. *Proceedings of the Institute of Electrical Engineers*, **56**, 1032–1047.

Robinson, D. A. (1981). Control of eye movements. In V. B. Brooks (Ed.), *Handbook of physiology* (Sec. I, Vol. II, pp. 1275–1320). Bethesda, MD: American Physiological Society.

Saslow, M. G. (1967). Effects of components of displacement-step stimuli upon latency of saccadic eye movement. *Journal of the Optical Society of America*, **57**, 1024–1029.

Skavenski, A. A. (1972). Inflow as a source of extraretinal eye position information. *Vision Research*, **12**, 221–229.

Skavenski, A. A., & Hansen, R. M. (1978). Role of eye position information in visual space perception. In J. Senders, D. Fisher, & R. Monty (Eds.), *Eye movements and the higher psychological functions* (pp. 15–34). Hillsdale, NJ: Erlbaum.

Skavenski, A. A., Haddad, G., & Steinman, R. M. (1972). The extraretinal signal for the visual perception of direction. *Perception & Psychophysics*, **11**, 287–290.

Sparks, D. L., & Mays, L. E. (1983). Role of the monkey superior colliculus in the spatial localization of saccade targets. In A. Hein & M. Jeannerod (Eds.), *Spatially oriented behavior* (pp. 63–85). New York: Springer-Verlag.

Sperry, R. W. (1950). Neural basis of the spontaneous optokinetic response produced by visual inversion. *Journal of Comparative and Physiological Psychology*, **43**, 482–489.

Steinman, R. M. (1975). Oculomotor effects on vision. In G. Lennerstrand & P. Bach-y-Rita (Eds.), *Basic mechanisms of ocular motility and their clinical implications* (pp. 395–415). Oxford: Pergamon.

Steinman, R. M. (1986). The need for an eclectic, rather than systems, approach to the study of the primate oculomotor system. *Vision Research*, **26**, 101–112.

Steinman, R. M., Haddad, G. M., Skavenski, A. A., & Wyman, D. (1973). Miniature eye movement. *Science*, **181**, 810–819.

Sternberg, S., Monsell, S., Knoll, R. L., & Wright, C. E. (1978). The latency and duration of rapid movement sequences: Comparisons of speech and typewriting. In G. E. Stelmach (Ed.), *Information processing in motor control and learning* (pp. 117–152). New York: Academic Press.

Vaughan, J. (1983). Saccadic reaction time in visual search. In K. Rayner (Ed.), *Eye movements in reading* (pp. 397–411). New York: Academic Press.

Vogel, S. (1989). In the blink of an eye. *Discover*, **2**, 62–64.

Volkmann, F. C. (1976). Saccadic suppression: A brief review. In R. A. Monty & J. W. Senders (Eds.), *Eye movements and psychological processes* (pp. 73–84). Hillsdale, NJ: Erlbaum.

Volkmann, F. C., Riggs, L. A., & Moore, R. K. (1980). Eyeblinks and visual suppression. *Science*, **207**, 900–902.

Volkmann, F. C., Schick, A. M., & Riggs, L. A. (1969). Time course of visual inhibition during voluntary saccades. *Journal of the Optical Society of America*, **58**, 562–569.

von Helmholtz, H. (1962). *Handbook of physiological optics*. New York: Dover. Originally published as *Handbuch der physiologischen optik* (Hamburg: Voss, 1866).

von Holst, E., & Mittelstaedt, H. (1950). Das Reafferenzprinzip. *Naturwissenschaften*, **37**, 464–474. (English translation in Dodwell, 1980)

Webb, W. B. (1973). Sleep and dreams. In B. B. Wolman (Ed.), *Handbook of general psychology* (pp. 734–748). Englewood Cliffs, NJ: Prentice-Hall.

Weiskrantz, L., Warrington, E. K., Sanders, M. D., & Marshall, J. (1974). Visual capacity in the hemianopic field following a restricted occipital ablation. *Brain,* **97,** 709–728.

Westheimer, G. H. (1954). Eye movement responses to horizontally moving visual stimulus. *Archives of Ophthalmology (Chicago),* **52,** 932–943.

Westheimer, G. H., & Conover, D. W. (1954). Smooth eye movements in the absence of a moving visual stimulus. *Journal of Experimental Psychology,* **47,** 283–284.

Wise, S. P., & Desimone, R. (1988). Behavioral neurophysiology: Insights into seeing and grasping. *Science,* **242,** 736–741.

Wurtz, R. H., Goldberg, M. E., & Robinson, D. L. (1982). Brain mechanisms of visual attention. *Scientific American,* **246** (6), 124–135.

Yarbus, A. L. (1967). *Eye movements and vision.* New York: Plenum.

Zingale, C. M., & Kowler, E. (1987). Planning sequences of saccades. *Vision Research,* **27,** 1327–1341.

Zuber, B. L., & Stark, L. (1965). Microsaccades and the velocity-amplitude relationship for saccadic eye movements. *Science,* **150,** 1459–1460.

6 REACHING AND GRASPING

■ INTRODUCTION

Much of human culture takes the form that it does because of what we do with our hands. We build houses, draw pictures, make bread, play musical instruments, and gesture—to name but a few manual activities—all because of the strength, flexibility, and precision of hand movements. Manual performance is so central to human experience that we often refer to our hands when discussing other topics. We say, "On the one hand or the other...," "...grab one's attention," "...these ideas go hand in hand," "...an offhand remark," and so on.

Because of the importance of manual control in human experience, several lines of research have been built around it. One is the control of drawing and writing, which I will cover in Chapter 7. Another is the control of keyboard performance, which I will present in Chapter 8. A third is the use of sign language, a topic that has been studied more from the perspective of linguistics than motor control (Poizner, Klima, & Bellugi, 1987). A fourth area is the control of reaching and grasping. These are the activities to be presented here.

Reaching and grasping depend on a balance of initial programming and subsequent correction. Initial programming is based in part on visual perception of the objects to be grasped. Based on visual information, we decide whether to pick up objects with one hand or two, whether to pick up objects with the hand oriented one way or the other (Rosenbaum, Vaughan, Barnes, Marchak, & Slotta, 1990), whether all the fingers or only some of them should be brought around the objects being grasped (Arbib, Iberall, & Lyons, 1985), and so on. Because the accuracy of initial programming depends on the accuracy of visual perception, some researchers have studied reaching and grasping as a means of learning about perceptual capabilities (Bower, 1974).

Reaches and grasps are programmed with respect to one's intentions. If an object is to be tossed, it is picked up differently than if it is to be gently placed in a container (Marteniuk, MacKenzie, Jeannerod, Athenes, & Dugas, 1987). Similarly, if an object is to be felt so its texture can be evaluated, the hand and finger movements that are made differ from those made when the object's temperature is to be assessed (Klatzky & Lederman, 1987).

Overview of the Chapter

This chapter is organized as follows. First, I consider the development of reaching and grasping. The main empirical question is when different aspects of reaching and grasping become evident.

Next I look at visual guidance. One issue concerns vision and movement: Given that we rely extensively on vision to help guide our hand movements, one might expect the mappings between vision and movement to be rigid by the time one reaches adulthood. The available evidence suggests otherwise. There is surprising flexibility in the mappings between the motor system and visual system. Similarly, there is considerable flexibility in the mappings between vision and touch. Why this is and how it is possible are considered in the first two parts of the section on visual guidance. This section ends with a discussion of how long it takes to alter one's reaches and grasps based on visual feedback. Arriving at an estimate of visual feedback time can be useful for other purposes, as seen later in the chapter.

The next section is concerned with manual aiming performance, primarily in adults. In manual aiming tasks, subjects typically try to touch a target as quickly as possible. The research question is how quickly the target can be reached depending on its distance from the start position, its size, and other factors. Detailed analyses of aiming movements indicate that the maximum speed of target attainment reflects a sophisticated balance of preprogramming and correction based on feedback.

The last part of the chapter concerns coordination. When we reach for and grasp objects, we use our fingers, hands, arms, and even our torsos and legs (to bring us near enough to the target to grasp it). Coordination of the limb segments turns out to have a number of adaptive regularities.

■ THE DEVELOPMENT OF REACHING AND GRASPING

By the time a human fetus is around $7^1/_2$ weeks of age it has fingers. By around 15 weeks of age it can open and close its hand (Hooker, 1938). By around 24 weeks of age, a prematurely born infant can use its hand in the same way as a full-term baby: It can automatically take hold of an object placed in its palm—a reaction known as the *grasp reflex* (Twitchell, 1971; see also Figure 4.13). The grasp reflex is powerful enough to support an infant's

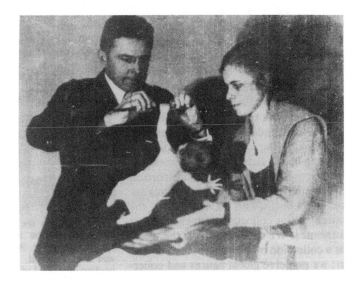

Figure 6.1 The grasp reflex. Still photograph from a film made by the psychologist John B. Watson in 1919. (Reprinted from Boakes, 1984.)

weight (see Figure 6.1). By around 6 months of age, the grasp reflex usually disappears (Touwen, 1971).

Direction

At an early age, infants preprogram their reaches in the correct general direction. Infants between the ages of 6 and 11 days can reach with rough accuracy for objects placed in different radial positions—0, 30, or 60° to the right or left (Bower, Broughton, & Moore, 1970). From this result, Bower *et al.* (1970) concluded that newborns not only have reasonably good control of their reaching movements, but that they also can obtain directional information through vision (Bower, 1974). Other studies have shown that the directions of infants' reaches become more and more precise during the first 4 or 5 months (Lockman & Ashmead, 1983; von Hofsten & Rönnqvist, 1988). By the end of this period, infants are so skilled at preprogramming the directions of their reaching and grasping movements that they can direct their hands to the future positions of moving objects, effectively "catching" the objects in midflight (von Hofsten, 1980).

Distance

Distance control also improves during the first 4 or 5 months. A method that has been used to arrive at this conclusion is to identify the distances over which infants are willing or not willing to reach. When an interesting object is out of reach, the infant should refrain from reaching for it, but when the same object is within reach, the infant should be willing to reach for it. If distances that elicit reaches are sharply demarcated from distances that do not elicit reaches, and if the boundary between the two kinds of distances approximates the length of the infant's arm, then one can conclude that the infant perceives distance veridically and has some awareness of his or her arm length.

Bower (1972) reported that infants as young as 7 to 15 days refrain from reaching for out-of-reach objects, although the distances that elicit reaches are not sharply divided from those that do not. Later, the boundary between reachable and unreachable distances becomes sharper, until by 5 months of age infants rarely reach for objects just beyond the maximum extent of the outstretched arm (Field, 1977; Gordon & Yonas, 1976).

Another indication of the quality of distance control is the slowing of the hand as the hand approaches an object to be grasped. By around 5 months of age, infants exhibit significant hand slowing just before contacting to-be-grabbed objects (von Hofsten, 1979; White, Castle, & Held, 1964). This suggests that 5-month-old infants are sensitive to the distance and direction of the object and to the position of the hand with respect to the object. Whether the slowing is preprogrammed or based on visual feedback (for example, seeing the hand get closer to the target) is still an open question. An experiment that could resolve the question would be to study the speed with which the hand approaches a target in the dark, given that the target was visible when the hand started reaching for it.

Orientation

As stated earlier, by around 5 months of age, babies exhibit accurate control of the directions and distances of manual reaches. The control of hand orientation appears to crystallize at a later age. Five-month-old babies orient their hands correctly around a vertically or horizontally oriented bar, but they do so only after physically contacting the bar. Nine-month-old babies, however, orient their hands in *anticipation* of bar contact based on vision alone (Lockman, Ashmead, & Bushnell, 1984).

Why do babies younger than 9 months not orient their hands correctly before contacting objects to be grabbed? One possibility is that they cannot visually discriminate vertical and horizontal lines. The fact is, however, that even 2-month-olds can make this visual discrimination (Essock & Siqueland, 1981). It is also not the case that 5-month-old babies are simply unable to turn their hands, for they can reorient their hands after physically contacting the objects they wish to handle. Apparently, babies younger than 9 months lack a fully developed *map* between visually perceived orientations and corresponding hand orientations.

Size

Another control parameter that appears to be mastered only by 9 months or later is related to the *size* of the object being grasped. When adults reach for objects of varying size, they vary the distance between the thumb and the other fingers (Jeannerod, 1981). Infants 9 months or older do so as well, but infants younger than 9 months do not (von Hofsten & Rönnqvist, 1988). It is doubtful that infants younger than 9 months are unable to visually distinguish large and small objects (von Hofsten & Rönnqvist, 1988). Furthermore, infants younger than 9 months are physically able to vary their grip size, for they can spread their fingers farther apart once they have felt a large object (von Hofsten & Rönnqvist, 1988). What is most likely is that infants younger than 9 months have not yet learned to preprogram grip size on the basis of visual information, just as infants younger than 9 months have not yet learned to preprogram hand *orientation* based on vision.

■ VISUAL GUIDANCE

Reaching for a seen object usually benefits from visual feedback. If you look at an object to be picked up but keep your eyes closed while reaching for it, your performance will suffer. (Try this demonstration for yourself.) This observation raises the question of how visual guidance is used in the control of reaches and grasps.

First, it is useful to recognize that visual feedback can be used more and more effectively over the course of development (see Figure 6.2). At around 5 months of age, babies perform about as well when reaching for objects that are seen only briefly as when reaching for objects that are continually visible (Wishart, Bower, & Dunkeld, 1978). After 5 months reaching benefits more and more from vision until, by around 9 months, the advantage of vision over lack of vision remains approximately constant.

Learning how to use visual feedback does not end in the first year. Adults can also learn to adjust their manual behavior based on exposure to new visual conditions. These conditions can be introduced by having people observe their hand movements through a mirror (which reverses right and left) or by having people observe their hand movements through lenses or prisms that invert, displace, rotate, magnify, or minify (shrink) the image.

One of the first studies of adaptation to such visual rearrangement was conducted in the late nineteenth century. The experimenter (George Stratton) wore an inverting lens for 8 days. He wished to learn how visual direction is appreciated. Stratton believed that we *learn* visual directions by associating visual experiences with other forms of sensory feedback, such as the proprioceptive input from hand movements. Thus if the hand is moved to the right, proprioceptive input indicates a rightward movement, and this input allows us to identify the associated visual input as coming from the

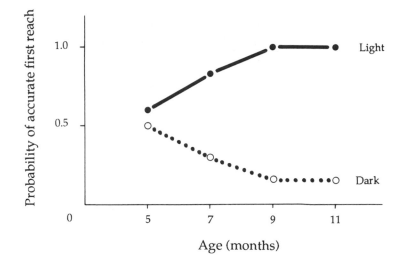

Figure 6.2 Accuracy of reaches made in the light (•) or dark (○) in babies 5–11 months of age. (Data from Wishart, Bower, and Dunkeld, 1978. Adapted from Hay, 1984.)

right rather than the left. Stratton reasoned that if people initially learn visual directions in this way, they should be able to learn new associations between visual and proprioceptive inputs.

Stratton's initial experiences were upsetting:

> If he saw an object off to the right, he would reach for it with his right hand and discover that he should have reached for it with his left hand. He could not feed himself very well, could not tie his shoelaces without considerable difficulty, and found himself to be severely disoriented in general. His image of his own body became severely distorted. At times he felt that his head had sunk down between his shoulders, and when he moved his eyes and head the world would slide dizzyingly around. [Kaufman, 1974, p. 417]

Gradually he adapted:

> As time went by, Stratton achieved more effective control over his body. He would reach with his left hand when he saw an object on the right. He could accomplish normal tasks like eating and dressing himself. His body image became almost normal, and objects did not appear to move about so much when he changed the positions of his eyes and head. He even began to feel as though his left hand was on the right and his right hand was on the left. As long as this new location of his body was vivid, the world appeared to be right side up. Frequently, however, he would experience his own body as upside down in a visually right-side-up world. The visual world became the standard with which he localized his body. [Kaufman, 1974, pp. 417–418]

When Stratton removed the inverting lens at the end of the eighth day of the experiment, he frequently made incorrect reaching movements.

However, he soon regained his normal perceptual–motor coordination. Because he could adapt to the inverting lens and then readapt to the normal environment, he showed that perceptual–motor coordination is highly malleable.

Did Stratton adapt to the inverted lenses by finding a new correlation between vision and *proprioception*, as he supposed, or did he adapt by finding a new correlation between vision and actively generated motor commands (or the intentions giving rise to those motor commands)? To test the latter hypothesis, Held (1965) showed subjects the reflected image of a square in a horizontal mirror. The subjects could move their hands beneath the mirror but could not see their hands. Their task was to mark the perceived corners of the square with a pencil, but because they could not see where the pencil marks were placed in relation to the square, the only way they could tell where the marks were placed was to compare the seen position of the square with the felt position of the hand. The question was how well observers could perform the task depending on the kind of training they received away from the marking task. One group actively moved their hands while watching their movements through a displacing prism. Another group simply looked at their hands through the displacing prism without making movements. A third group viewed their hands through the displacing prism as their hands were moved passively by the experimenter. After the training session, the three groups returned to the task of marking the corners of the square. Only the active-movement group exhibited significant adaptation to the prism; the stationary group and passive-movement group did not. Thus the group that could correlate the altered visual input created by the prisms with their own motor commands (or movement intentions) exhibited more adaptation than the groups that not could not achieve this correlation. Because the subjects in the passive-movement group received approximately the same proprioceptive feedback as those in the active-movement group, the results argue against Stratton's proposal that we learn to coordinate vision and touch by correlating visual and proprioceptive inputs. Rather, we learn to coordinate vision and touch by correlating visual information with motor commands or their underlying intentions (see also pp. 148–150).

The Relation between Vision and Touch

When one learns new correlations between the way things look and the way things feel, does vision change, does touch change, or both? In the early eighteenth century, the British philosopher, George Berkeley, argued that touch is more trustworthy than vision because touch puts one in direct contact with the external environment. If Berkeley had been asked to predict what would change in a prism adaptation experiment, he probably would have said that vision changes and that touch does not.

Subsequent experiments indicated that Berkeley would have been wrong. In one experiment, subjects looked through prisms that made a straight rod appear curved (Gibson, 1933). When the subjects were asked to describe how the rod looked and felt, they reported that the rod looked curved and also felt curved. Thus vision dominated over touch in this experiment. Similar results were obtained when subjects looked through a minifying lens at a cube lying on top of a cloth (Rock & Harris, 1967). The subjects in this study could reach under the cloth and feel the cube without seeing their hands. When they felt the cube, there was an objective mismatch between its felt and seen size. Yet subjects reported that the cube *felt* small—as small, in fact, as a physically smaller cube that was viewed normally. Thus for these subjects, as for the subjects in Gibson's (1933) experiment, vision dominated touch.

What accounts for visual dominance? One possibility is that vision captures attention less effectively than touch (Posner, Nissen, & Klein, 1976). Tapping someone on the shoulder is sure to get their attention, but raising one's hand—say, in a classroom—is less guaranteed. Vision may dominate over touch because touch has a greater alerting capacity than vision. An attentional bias favoring vision may help compensate for the stronger alerting capacity of touch (Posner *et al.*, 1976).

Regardless of the exact cause of visual dominance, the phenomenon may have some practical benefits. Consider the following curious observation (Tastevin, 1937, reported in Kaufman, 1984). A plaster replica of a person's finger was made to move in step with a subject's moving finger. When subjects saw the replica but not their own finger through a small window, they did not know that the finger being seen was not their own. In a similar demonstration (Rock & Harris, 1967), subjects were told that they would be able to watch their own hand through a window but, unknown to them, they actually saw the experimenter's hand through a mirror. Provided the experimenter's hand moved in synchrony with the subject's, the subject did not know that the hand being seen was someone else's.

These reports are curious and even a bit bizarre. Nevertheless, they suggest a possible strategy for physical rehabilitation and training. Someone regaining control of a limb might be helped by seeing an image of the limb with greater mobility than it actually has. Giving the patient the impression of limb mobility might provide him or her with the incentive to try moving the limb on his or her own. Over time, the amount of actual movement that the patient would have to produce to generate a fixed amount of apparent visual movement would increase. If the amount of actual movement increased during the treatment procedure, there would be reason to believe the visual illusion had helped.

Visual Feedback Time

How quickly can one respond to visual feedback in controlling hand movements? The question is important because if hand movements depend on visual feedback, the time needed to use visual feedback limits the rate at which hand movements, or sequences of hand movements, can be performed.

Suppose it takes t msec to process visual feedback. Movements that take longer than t msec should be impaired if visual feedback is suddenly withdrawn, but movements that take less than t msec should be carried out equally well regardless of whether visual feedback is present or not. This reasoning allowed Keele and Posner (1968) to estimate t. They trained subjects to move a stylus from a home position to a target position in different amounts of time (150, 250, 350, or 450 msec, ±10% for each target time). In a block of trials, the subject repeatedly tried to make the movement within the target time, but on some trials, the room lights were turned off unpredictably as soon as the movement began. Aiming accuracy was affected by the presence or absence of visual feedback only when movements took about 200 msec or more. From this outcome, Keele and Posner (1968) concluded that it takes about 200 msec to use vision to correct aiming movements. Subsequent research has suggested that visually based corrections may take less time than Keele and Posner (1968) proposed (Carlton, 1981; Zelaznik, Hawkins, & Kisselburgh, 1983). Nevertheless, the time for the visual feedback loop is most certainly greater than 100 msec.

■ AIMING

Much of the research on the control of hand movements has been concerned with the simple task of moving the hand from one position to another, generally as quickly and accurately as possible. This task was first studied in detail in the late nineteenth century by Robert Woodworth (1899), a psychologist at Columbia University. Woodworth was impressed by the speed and accuracy with which construction workers could hammer nails. How, he wondered, could these workers achieve the speed and accuracy they did?

To answer this question, Woodworth (1899) set up an experiment in which people moved a pencil back and forth through a slit, reversing the direction of movement at two visually marked locations. Woodworth recorded subjects' movements by allowing the pencil to draw a line on a paper roll that turned beneath the work surface. Subjects were asked to make the back-and-forth movements at different rates specified by a metronome. In one set of conditions, subjects made the movements with eyes open. In another set of conditions, they made the movements with eyes closed.

The results of Woodworth's (1899) study are shown in Figure 6.3. The dependent measure (on the vertical axis) is mean absolute error, defined as the mean absolute value of the distance between the point where the pencil reversed direction and where it should have reversed direction (the target). The independent measure (on the horizontal axis) is mean movement velocity. As shown in the figure, when subjects had their eyes *closed*, mean absolute error remained more or less constant as velocity increased. However, when subjects had their eyes *open*, mean absolute error decreased

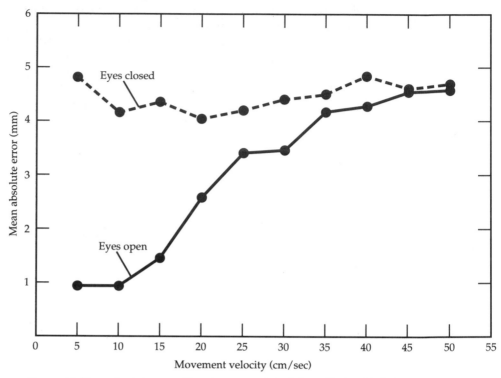

Figure 6.3 Mean absolute error of hand movement made by subjects with their eyes open or closed. (From Woodworth, 1899.)

as velocity decreased. Thus accuracy improved as movements slowed in the eyes-open condition but not in the eyes-closed condition.

Woodworth accounted for these results by assuming that in the eyes-closed condition subjects' movements were entirely preprogrammed; their movements were guided by what Woodworth called an *initial impulse*. However, in the eyes-open condition, the movements were both preprogrammed and corrected with visual feedback (what Woodworth called *current control*). Woodworth hypothesized that the first part of an aiming movement is achieved through initial impulse control and that later parts are achieved with current control. If a movement must be made in too short a time for current control work, it will be as error-prone as a movement that must be made when more time is available and feedback has been removed.

The idea that aiming movements have an initial ballistic phase followed by a feedback-based homing-in phase has been pursued by a number of investigators. One method they have used to test the idea is to have subjects move a stylus back and forth between two targets as quickly as possible, where the distance between the targets and the widths of the targets vary (Fitts, 1954). The time to bring the stylus from one target to another increases both with the distance between the targets and their narrowness. This relation was summarized by Fitts (1954) in the following equation:

$$MT = a + b \cdot \log_2\left(\frac{2A}{W}\right) \tag{6.1}$$

where MT denotes movement time, A denotes the amplitude (or distance) between the centers of the targets, W denotes the width of the target, and a and b are empirical constants. The term $\log_2 (2A/W)$ is called the index of difficulty. Equation 6.1 says that MT increases linearly with the index of difficulty. This prediction has been confirmed (see Figure 6.4). In fact, Equation 6.1 has been found to do an excellent job of predicting movement times for many other tasks as well: discrete ("one-shot") aiming movements (Fitts & Peterson, 1964), transferring pegs over a distance to be inserted into a hole (Annet, Golby, & Kay, 1958), moving a joystick or turning a handle to move a cursor on a screen (Jagacinski, Repperger, Moran, Ward, & Glass, 1980; Meyer, Smith, & Wright, 1982), throwing darts at a target (B. A. Kerr & Langolf, 1977), carrying out aiming movements under water (R. Kerr, 1973),

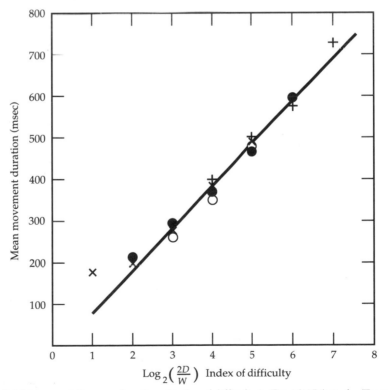

Figure 6.4 Movement time as a function of index of difficulty in Fitts' (1954) study. (From Meyer, Smith, Kornblum, Abrams, & Wright, 1990.)

and even manipulating objects under a microscope (Langolf, Chaffin, & Foulke, 1976). Because the equation is so powerful, it has come to be called *Fitts' Law* (Keele, 1968).

The Iterative Corrections Model

How can Fitts' Law be explained? One idea, embodied in the *iterative corrections* model (Crossman & Goodeve, 1963/1983; Keele, 1968), is that the law is attributable to current control. According to the model, an aiming movement consists of a series of discrete submovements, each of which is triggered by feedback indicating that the target has yet to be attained. By hypothesis, each submovement takes the hand (or the hand-held stylus) a fixed proportion of the distance to the target. If the hand is 20 cm from the center of the target and each submovement takes the hand 50% closer to the center of the target, then the first submovement brings the hand 10 cm from the target center, the second submovement brings the hand 5 cm from the target center, the third submovement brings the hand 2.5 cm from the target center, and so on. As the target narrows, the hand falls within the target later in the series of submovements. Similarly, as the distance of the target increases (for a given target width), the first submovement that brings the hand within the target is also delayed. Qualitatively, then, the model accounts for the relationships implied by Fitts' Law. Quantitatively, the model predicts a linear increase of total movement time with index of difficulty (Fitts' Law), provided one assumes that each correction takes a constant time (Keele, 1968).

The iterative corrections model has been supported by detailed analyses of movement trajectories. Discrete submovements of the sort assumed in the model have been recorded (Annet *et al.*, 1958; Carlton, 1981; Crossman & Goodeve, 1963/1983; Jagacinski *et al.*, 1980; Langolf *et al.*, 1976; Woodworth, 1899). An example is shown in Figure 6.5.

Further research has shown, however, that the iterative corrections model is somewhat off target. Contrary to the model, one does not always

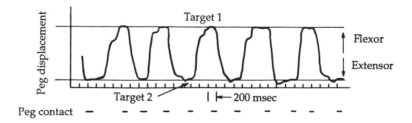

Figure 6.5 Peg displacement as a function of time in an aiming task performed under a microscope. The "plateaus" prior to the targets reflect momentary slowing of the hand. (Data from Langolf, Chaffin, & Foulke, 1976. Adapted from Smyth & Wing, 1984.)

see discrete submovements (Langolf *et al.*, 1976). (Discrete submovements appear as minima in the function relating absolute velocity to time.) Moreover, when distinct submovements are detectable, they do not have constant durations (Jagacinski *et al.*, 1980; Langolf *et al.*, 1976). Nor do they travel constant proportions of the distance remaining to the target (Jagacinski *et al.*, 1980). The latter results violate the assumptions of the model. These problems have led investigators to seek an alternative.

The Impulse Variability Model

One alternative assumes that Fitts' Law reflects the initial-impulse phase rather than the current-control phase (Schmidt, Zelaznik, Hawkins, Frank, & Quinn, 1979). The experiments that led to this model differed from the kinds of experiments that Fitts (1954) pioneered. Whereas Fitts' subjects were asked to get to a defined target area as quickly as possible but in a time of their own choosing, subjects in the experiments of Schmidt *et al.* were supposed to get to a target within a prescribed amount of time, trying to minimize the spatial variability of the endpoints of their movements. Specifically, subjects in the Schmidt *et al.* experiments were required to move within 200 msec (a time unlikely to permit much current control) to targets located between 10 and 30 cm from the home position. A single movement was made in each trial. The measure of primary interest was the spatial variability of the movement endpoints. Schmidt *et al.* observed that the standard deviation of the endpoints, W_e, increased with the distance (D) to be covered and decreased with the duration (T) of the movement:

$$W_e = k\left(\frac{D}{T}\right) \tag{6.2}$$

where k is a constant. Equation 6.2 can be rearranged as

$$T = k\left(\frac{D}{W_e}\right) \tag{6.3}$$

This relation between time, distance, and standard deviation of endpoints (what Schmidt *et al.* called "effective target width") is similar, though not identical, to Fitts' Law.

What property of the motor system could give rise to this relation? Schmidt *et al.* proposed that rapid arm movements are achieved by "flinging" the arm toward a target via a neuromotor impulse delivered to the arm muscles. The impulse causes the muscles to exert a burst of force for the first half of the total movement time. During the second half of the movement time, the limb "coasts" toward the target. A further assumption is that there is variability in the forces driving the arm toward the target as well as variability in the time during which the forces are produced. The standard deviation of the force is assumed to be proportional to the amount of force, and the standard deviation of the time during which impulses are delivered is assumed to be proportional to the amount of time during which the impulses are delivered. Thus if more *force* is used to cover a larger distance, more force variability results, and if more *time* is spent propelling the limb toward the target, more time variability results. Because time and force are assumed, in the model, to be independently controlled, the subject's job is to find the time and force that minimize the variability of both factors. According to Schmidt *et al.*, Fitts' Law represents the solution to this problem.

The impulse variability model has much to recommend it, at least as a model of very rapid movements. It recognizes the inherent variability of neuromotor processes, and it represents this variability in simple terms. Moreover, Schmidt *et al.* tested their assumptions about force variability and time variability in experiments where subjects were asked to make isometric movements, producing different magnitudes of force for varying amounts of time. As predicted by the model, the standard deviation of force was proportional to the amount of force produced, and the standard deviation of time was proportional to the amount of time in the movement.

As encouraging as these results are, the impulse variability model cannot account for all the effects observed in rapid aiming tasks. Submovements based on feedback are observed, yet the impulse variability model makes no provision for feedback-based correction. Furthermore, questions have been raised about the model's assumptions concerning force and time variability (Newell & Carlton, 1988), and flaws have been detected in the way Schmidt *et al.* derived Fitts' Law from their underlying assumptions, although Fitts' Law can be derived correctly if the assumptions are refined (Meyer *et al.*, 1982).

The Optimized Initial Impulse Model

So far, I have considered two radically different means of explaining Fitts' Law. One, the iterative corrections model, explains the law solely in terms of current control. The other, the impulse variability model, explains the law solely in terms of initial impulse. Neither model satisfactorily accounts for all the data on manual aiming, so a more successful model was sought. Such a model was introduced by Meyer, Abrams, Kornblum, Wright, and Smith (1988). Their *optimized initial impulse* model is a hybrid of the iterative corrections model and the impulse variability model.

The starting point for the optimized initial impulse model is shown in Figure 6.6. By hypothesis, the subject makes a first movement toward the target. If the movement lands within the target, the task is completed, but if the movement lands outside the target, another movement is necessary. The second movement can either land within the target or not. If the second movement does not reach the target, another movement must be made, and so forth. The subject's task is to reach the target as quickly as possible, so he

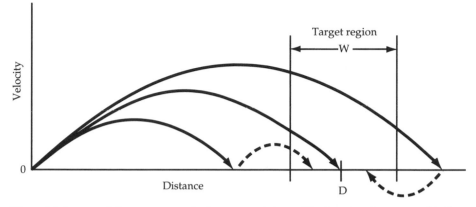

Figure 6.6 Representative sequences of submovements toward the target region assumed in the optimized initial impulse model of Meyer, Abrams, Kornblum, Wright, and Smith (1988). From Meyer *et al.* (1988). Optimality in human motor performance: Ideal control of rapid aimed movements. *Psychological Review*, **95**, 340–370. Copyright © 1988 by the American Psychological Society. Adapted with permission.

or she should ideally make just one high-velocity movement directly to the target. The problem is that, according to the model, the spatial accuracy of movements is imperfect. The standard deviation, S_i, of the endpoint of any movement i is assumed to increase with the distance, D_i, covered by that movement and decrease with its duration, T_i, that is,

$$S_i = k\left(\frac{D_i}{T_i}\right) \quad (6.4)$$

where k is a constant. The subject therefore faces a dilemma. To get to the target as quickly as possible, a movement with a long distance and short time could be performed, but this would result in a large standard deviation, and so a low probability of hitting the target. On the other hand, the subject could perform a series of movements with long durations and short distances and be sure of hitting the target, but in this case the total movement time would be very long. The best thing to do, then, is to find the balance of Ds and Ts that minimizes the total movement time. According to Meyer *et al.* (1988), Fitts' Law represents such an optimal balance.

I will not reproduce the mathematics through which Meyer *et al.* derived Fitts' Law, but it is interesting to note that through their derivation they showed that Fitts' Law is actually a special case of a more general relation:

$$T = a + b \bullet n\left(\frac{D}{W}\right)^{\frac{1}{n}} \quad (6.5)$$

where T is total movement time, D is the distance from the starting point to the center of the target, W is the width of the target, n is the number of submovements, and a and b are constants. (When a term is raised to a fractional power, such as $1/n$, it is taken to the nth root; for example, $16^{1/2} = \sqrt{16} = 4$.)

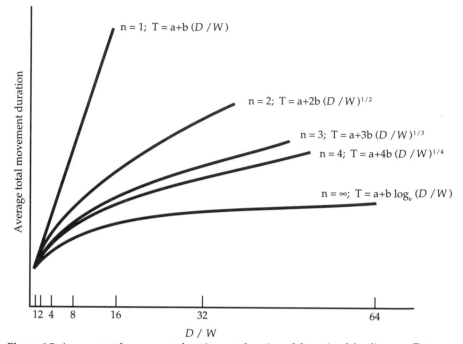

Figure 6.7 Average total movement duration as a function of the ratio of the distance, *D*, to a target and the width, *W*, of the target, according to the optimized initial impulse model of Meyer, Abrams, Kornblum, Wright, and Smith (1988). The parameter, *n*, is the maximum number of submovements. From Meyer *et al.* (1988). Optimality in human motor performance: Ideal control of rapid aimed movements. *Psychological Review* **95**, 340–370. Copyright © by the American Psychological Association. Reprinted with permission.

Figure 6.7 shows how *T* changes with *n* according to this equation. As *n* decreases, *T* increases more steeply with the ratio *D*/*W*. However, as *n* approaches infinity, the equation can be rewritten

$$T = a + b \bullet \log_e\left(\frac{D}{W}\right) \tag{6.6}$$

which of course is Fitts' Law. (Using logarithms to the base *e* rather than to the base 2 is inconsequential.) Thus Fitts' Law is a special case of Equation 6.5. It is the case in which subjects can make as many submovements as they wish. Although subjects do not make an infinite number of submovements, Fitts' Law, to the extent that it represents a limiting condition, provides a reasonably precise way of fitting movement-time data from a great many studies. Meyer *et al.* showed that total movement durations can in fact be shown to vary with number of observed submovements, in accordance with Equation 6.5. Furthermore, they showed that the number of submovements, when they have been measured, can be predicted by total movement time, distance, and width, as prescribed by the model. Thus Equation 6.5 does an excellent job of accounting for the results of aiming studies. In fact, it does such an excellent job that, out of respect for its first author, it might be called *Meyer's Law*. Equation 6.5 (Meyer's Law) is also interesting from a general psychological perspective, for it implies that, even when people engage in a task as mundane as bringing the hand to a target, they employ sophisticated strategies to optimize performance. This conclusion reinforces a point I made earlier in this volume, namely, that simple motor tasks may at first appear computationally trivial, but careful analysis reveals they are not.

The Mass-Spring Model

In the research just reviewed, subjects were instructed to move as quickly as possible to a target. Not all aiming movements are performed this way, however. It would be natural to expect that slower aiming movements are controlled through extensive reliance on feedback. However an experiment reported by Polit and Bizzi (1978) suggests that this is not always the case. This study deserves special attention because its results seem at first to be impossible.

Polit and Bizzi (1978) investigated monkeys' pointing responses to target lights (see Figure 6.8). On any given trial, one of the lights was turned on and the monkey was supposed to point to it, holding its arm there for 1 sec to receive a sip of juice. The monkey could not see its arm, so it received no visual feedback about the position of its arm relative to the light. The position of

Figure 6.8 Experimental arrangement used by Polit and Bizzi. From A. Polit & E. Bizzi (1979). Characteristics of motor programs underlying arm movements in monkeys. *Journal of Neurophysiology*, **42**, 183–194. Reprinted by permission of the American Physiological Society.

the arm was recorded with a splint attached to a vertical axle. The axle rotated when the monkey's arm moved, and the angular position of the axle was recorded. The axle could also be turned with a motor. When the motor came on, it caused the monkey's arm to be displaced. The motor was turned on unpredictably from trial to trial but usually came on after the target light was illuminated and before the monkey moved its arm.

The question Polit and Bizzi (1978) wished to answer was what would happen to the accuracy of pointing when the arm was displaced. For monkeys with normal proprioceptive feedback, pointing accuracy was high. Evidently, the monkeys felt their arms being displaced and introduced appropriate compensatory responses. An additional aspect of the experiment suggested that feedback was not the only source of information that monkeys relied on, however. After the initial phase of the experiment, the dorsal roots of the monkeys' spinal cords were severed. Cutting the dorsal roots prevented the monkeys from feeling anything below the neck (as was confirmed in behavioral and physiological tests). Consequently, the monkeys could not feel their arms being perturbed. Given this state of affairs, one would expect the monkeys to be unable to compensate for the perturbation. Yet they could. When the monkeys were again supposed to point to the target lights, they could do so accurately, even after the perturbation was applied.

How can this result be explained? Polit and Bizzi (1978) appealed to the notion that muscles act like springs (Asatryan & Fel'dman, 1965; Crossman & Goodeve, 1963/1983). To appreciate the analogy, consider the following experiment, which you can set up yourself. Take two identical rubber bands and attach one to one side of a hinged cylinder and the other to the other side, as shown in Figure 6.9A. Orient the cylinder perpendicular to the ground so the forces provided by the rubber bands are orthogonal to the force of gravity. Now pull the cylinder to one side and release it. It will swing back and forth for a while and then come to rest at approximately 90°. Next try releasing the cylinder from different starting positions. It will always return to the same final position. This property is known as *equifinality*. If the primate arm is controlled like the simple spring system of Figure 6.9A, it too should be able to arrive at the same final position regardless of the position from which it starts, even without feedback.

Unlike the cylinder in Figure 6.9A, a biological arm can get to *different* final positions. Can a simple spring system do the same? There are two ways that it can. One method can be demonstrated with a hinged cylinder and two rubber bands of different length but the same stiffness. (You can make two such rubber bands by cutting one rubber band into two pieces of unequal length). Attach the two rubber bands to either side of the cylinder and again try releasing it from different starting positions. Again it will always end up at the same final position, but this time the final position will not be at 90°; instead, it will be in the direction of the shorter rubber band (see Figure 6.9B). In general, the cylinder will end up at the position where the opposing forces of the two rubber bands balance out; this is known as the

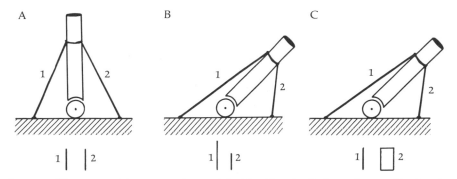

Figure 6.9 Illustration of the mass-spring model with a hinged cylinder and two rubber bands. (A) The resting lengths and stiffnesses of the rubber bands are equal. (B) The resting length of rubber band 1 is greater than the resting length of rubber band 2 but the stiffnesses are equal. (C) The resting lengths of the rubber bands are equal but the stiffness of rubber band 2 is greater than the stiffness of rubber band 1 (indicated by the thicknesses of the bands in the rest position).

equilibrium position. If the left rubber band has a shorter resting length than the right rubber band, the cylinder will end up pointing to the left. If the right rubber band has a shorter resting length than the left rubber band, the cylinder will end up pointing to the right. The greater the discrepancy between the resting lengths of the two rubber bands, the more extreme the cylinder's final position will be. (This follows from the fact that, for an ideal spring, the tension it exerts is proportional to the distance it is stretched from its resting position—a principle known as Hooke's Law). Because it is possible to obtain different equilibrium positions by changing the resting lengths of opposing springs, the biological motor system might achieve different limb positions by altering the resting lengths of the opposing muscles acting on the limb (Berkenblit, Fel'dman, & Fucson, 1986).

Another way to achieve different final positions with a simple spring system is to vary the stiffnesses of the springs (see Figure 6.9C). You can observe this effect by using two rubber bands of equal length but different stiffnesses. (You can use three identical rubber bands and place two on one side of the cylinder for this purpose.) Displace the cylinder and let it swing freely. It will end up in the direction of the stiffer rubber band. In general, the stiffer the rubber band on one side relative to the other, the farther away from 90° the final position will be. This outcome suggests that another way for a biological motor system to vary a limb's final position is to vary the stiffnesses of the limb's opposing muscles (Polit & Bizzi, 1978).

Why should it be advantageous for the motor system to treat muscles as springs? The main reason is that regulating muscle resting length or muscle stiffness is a simple way of moving a limb from one position to another. If the limb naturally behaves as a mass-spring system, it is sensible for the motor system to treat it as such. If the motor system could not exploit the springlike nature of muscle, it might be necessary to specify the entire trajectory of the limb, and this could turn out to be an onerous computational task. Treating the limb as a mass-spring system affords the possibility of significantly reducing the computational demands of trajectory planning.

Assuming that the study reported by Polit and Bizzi (1979) demonstrates reliance on a mass-spring strategy for *monkey* limb control, what evidence is there that the mass-spring model applies to *human* performance? One source of information is an experiment in which human patients lacking sensory feedback from their fingers moved a finger from one position to another without being able to see their finger movements (Kelso & Holt, 1980). After performing this task, the patients tried to reproduce the movement they had just performed, either passing the finger over the same *distance* or to the same *location* as in the first task. Location reproduction should be possible, according to the mass-spring model, even if the position of the finger cannot be sensed and even if the finger is passively displaced while moving toward the target. Distance reproduction, however, should be difficult, particularly if the finger is perturbed by an external force.

The results supported the mass-spring model. Although the patients could not feel their fingers, the fingers could be brought from one location to another, even when momentarily displaced by a torque motor. When the same patients were asked to cover the same *distance* as in the first task, their performance was significantly worse than when they were asked to reach the same location. The latter result suggests that subjects were not simply clever about finding ways of compensating for their handicaps.

One might worry that the mass-spring model can only be demonstrated with feedback-deprived subjects (human or nonhuman) who must compensate for unexpected limb displacements. The model's success is considerably more widespread, however. When a person with normal proprioception is asked to use the forearm to drag a load over a horizontal surface to a target, if the load is suddenly released and the subject does not attempt to compensate, the hand trajectories that result are as predicted by the model (Asatryan & Fel'dman, 1965). Furthermore, a computer simulation of the model (Cooke, 1980) predicts a characteristic of rapid aimed hand movements that has been obtained in many studies—a bell-shaped velocity profile, with the peak of the curve near the midpoint of the displacement (Abend, Bizzi, & Morasso, 1982; Cooke, 1980). Thus, the mass-spring model appears to be a viable model of limb-movement control. One of the most important features of the model is that it exploits the mechanical properties of muscle and in so doing reduces the computational demands of movement planning (Bizzi & Mussa-Ivaldi, 1989).

■ INTERSEGMENTAL COORDINATION

So far in this discussion of reaching and grasping, I have treated the hand as a single point. The only dependent measure in the research I have described has been the position of the hand (or a hand-held stylus) as a function of time. Reaching and grasping involve more than carrying the hand toward a target, however. The fingers, wrist, elbow, and shoulder must also move or be properly stabilized, and the torso must be supported so balance can be maintained (Bousset & Zattara, 1981; El'ner, 1973; Gelfand, Gurfinkel, Tsetlin, & Shik, 1966). If necessary, the actor must also walk, crouch, or jump to take hold of objects of interest. In the final section of this chapter I consider how such coordination occurs.

Transport and Grasp Phases

Reaching for and taking hold of an object appears to take place in two distinct phases—a *transport* phase and a *grasp* phase. During the transport phase, the hand is carried toward the object. During the grasp phase, the fingers wrap around the object. These two phases appear to be controlled by different areas of the brain. Damage to the pyramidal tract (fibers from the motor cortex that directly innervate skeletal-muscle motor neurons) results in impairments of fine finger control, including impairments in grasping objects. Damage to the extrapyramidal tract results in impairments of gross arm movements, including hand transports prior to object manipulation (Kuypers, 1973). Developmentally, the pyramidal tract also matures after the extrapyramidal tract (Lawrence & Hopkins, 1972), which may explain why fine finger control is possible only after gross arm movements are skillfully managed. Behavioral studies also support the hypothesis that the transport phase and grasp phase are governed separately. Changing the size of an object to be grasped does not affect the rate at which the arm is moved, but does affect the maximum separation between the thumb and index finger as the hand approaches the object (Jeannerod, 1981, 1984).

There is some dependence between the grasp and transport phases, however. The maximum separation between the thumb and index finger when the hand is brought toward an object depends on the speed with which the grasp must be completed. Thus when subjects try to reach for objects quickly, they spread their fingers farther apart than when they try to reach for the same objects at a leisurely pace (Wing, Turton, & Fraser, 1986). Greater finger widening increases the likelihood of capturing the object when the hand travels at high speed.

Another kind of dependence between transport and grasp concerns the timing of the opening and closing of the hand and the speed at which the hand is transported. As reported by Jeannerod (1981, 1984), the distance between the thumb and index finger is usually greatest when the hand begins the final, slow-approach phase of the movement (see Figure 6.10). Even individuals with prosthetic hands exhibit this relation (Fraser & Wing, 1981). The coincidence of maximal finger widening and the start of the slow-approach phase may reflect a tendency to time-lock related behavioral events. Having the events occur simultaneously may reduce the number of degrees of freedom that must be independently managed.

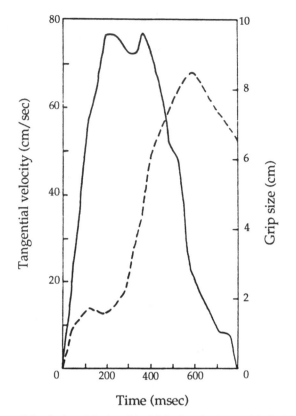

Figure 6.10 Tangential velocity of the hand (solid line) and grip size (dashed line) as a function of time. (Adapted from Jeannerod, 1984.)

Hand-Space versus Joint-Space Planning

As the hand moves to pick up an object, the angles of the shoulder and elbow joints usually change. Muscle torques are applied at these joints to cause the arm to move. The muscle torques are selected on the basis of a chosen path for the hand to follow through extrapersonal space.

Determining how the endpoint of a system of hinged levers will be displaced when certain torques are applied to the levers is called the *forward dynamics* problem. The *inverse dynamics* problem is the problem of determining the torques that should be applied to the levers given that the endpoint of the levers is supposed to traverse some path. The inverse dynamics problem is the one that usually must be solved in planning movements to spatial targets. One reason that it is interesting to ask how the joint angles of the arm change during aiming movements is to learn how the motor system solves the inverse dynamics problem.

Suppose the inverse dynamics problem is so hard for the motor system that it effectively sidesteps it. Suppose that instead of selecting a direct path for the hand to follow on its way to a target, the motor system actually selects a convenient set of muscle torques and then, perhaps after some trial and error in the planning process, allows the hand to get to the target through a path that may be straight or may just as well be circuitous. If this strategy were used, one would expect considerable simplicity in the patterns of joint angles seen during aimed hand movements but considerable complexity in the patterns of associated hand paths. By contrast, if the motor system had no difficulty with the inverse dynamics problem, and so could select direct hand paths and then find the muscle torques that produce them, one would expect simple hand paths but complex joint-angle patterns.

Another way of conceptualizing these alternatives is to say that the motor system either plans movements with respect to *joint space* using the intrinsic coordinates of the body, or with respect to *hand space* using the extrinsic coordinates of the external surroundings. (Recall that a similar distinction was considered in Chapter 5 for the control of eye movements; there the distinction was between spatial and orbital coordinates.) Figure 6.11 illustrates possible consequences of joint-space or hand-space planning. If planning is based on the extrinsic coordinates of hand space, the hand would be expected to move in a straight line. However, if planning used the intrinsic coordinates of joint space, then joint angles, or the function relating joint angles to time, would be expected to follow a straight line. Note that only one of these outcomes is possible. If the hand moves in a straight line, the joint angles cannot do so, and if the joint angles move in a straight line the hand cannot do so.

As mentioned in Chapter 1, Morasso (1981) recorded hand trajectories on a two-dimensional surface when people pointed to targets. He found that subjects' hands tended to move in straight lines. He also found that their joints went through complex angular changes. Even when subjects were explicitly instructed to draw curved lines, detailed analyses of their hand trajectories suggested that they actually generated series of straight-line segments (Abend, Bizzi, & Morasso, 1982). These results suggest that the nervous system can in fact plan hand movements in extrinsic coordinates.

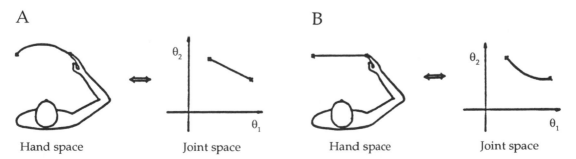

A   Hand space   Joint space θ_2 θ_1

B   Hand space   Joint space θ_2 θ_1

Figure 6.11 Trajectories expected if hand movements are planned in joint space (A) or in hand space (B). From Hollerbach & Atkeson, 1986. Adapted by permission of Springer-Verlag.

Once it has done so, it determines the muscle torques that should act on the joints.

Not all investigators are convinced that planning of hand movements is achieved in hand space. Hollerbach, Moore, and Atkeson (1987) proposed a way of directly controlling joints which also yields straight-line hand paths. The method is to vary the onset times for the motions of the joints, allowing all the joints to stop at the end of the movement. This method yields approximately straight hand paths, given appropriate onset delays (see Figure 6.12). Moreover, as predicted by the model, the motions of the joints of the arm appear to be timed so they reach their final positions at the same time (Kaminski & Gentile, 1986).

Another source of evidence that there may be joint-based planning is the observation that during the performance of simple pointing movements, invariant relations can be observed among the joints. Soechting and Lacquaniti (1981) studied how people perform the simple act of pointing to a target. Initially, the subjects stood with their arms hanging freely at their sides. When they felt ready to do so, they simply pointed to the target, located on a vertical surface directly in front of them. Soechting and Lacquaniti (1981) found that the peak angular velocities of the elbow and shoulder joints were reached at the same time. In addition, the ratio of the peak velocities of the two joints equaled the ratio of the radial distances that the joints covered. Such regularities would probably not be expected if the planning system did not take the joints into account.

A similar result was reported by Kots and Syrovegin (1966). They recorded the angular positions of the wrist and elbow during two tasks. In

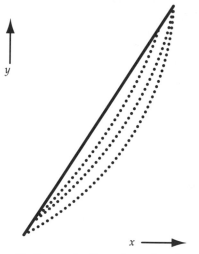

Figure 6.12 Motion of the hand in the x and y dimensions when the onsets of elbow and shoulder motion are staggered to varying degrees (corresponding to different curves). (From Hollerbach, Moore, & Atkeson, 1987.)

one (which can be called the *congruent-articulation* task), subjects attempted to flex the wrist while flexing the elbow or attempted to extend the wrist while extending the elbow. In the other task (which can be called the *incongruent-articulation* task), subjects attempted to flex the wrist while extending the elbow or tried to flex the elbow while extending the wrist. Kots and Syrovegin (1966) found that in the congruent-articulation task, the beginnings and ends of the joint motions occurred nearly simultaneously. However, in the incongruent-articulation task, the motions of the joints were not well synchronized. Apparently, the elbow and wrist joints were controlled by some *coordinative structure* (Turvey, 1977); they were not controlled independently. Having a coordinative structure could help reduce the number of degrees of freedom to be controlled (Bernstein, 1967).

Moving Two Hands at Once

Do coordinative structures only coordinate the joints of one arm? Consider the child's game of rubbing the stomach and patting the head. Because this ostensibly simple task is actually quite difficult, one might suppose that there are coordinative structures for the two arms as well.

A number of investigators have sought detailed descriptions of the interaction between the two arms. In the 1930s, the German physiologist Erich von Holst (see von Holst, 1973) recorded the activities of the two arms of human subjects as the arms were oscillated at different relative frequencies—1:1, 1:2, 2:3, and so forth. Only at relative frequencies of 1:1 and 1:2 could the two arms move in a stable fashion over repeated oscillations. (See also Chapter 1.)

Interactions between the two arms are also present when people point to two targets at once. Kelso, Putnam, and Goodman (1983) took advantage of the fact that the time to move the hand to a target depends on the target's index of difficulty, as discussed earlier in this chapter. Kelso *et al.* asked what would happen if each hand had to move to a target with a different index of difficulty. If each hand can be controlled independently, its movement time should depend only on the index of difficulty of the target to which it moves. The actual result was that the movement times of the two hands were approximately equal, even when the index of difficulty of the two targets differed; that is, the two hands departed for their respective targets and arrived there at about the same time. Because subjects were not instructed to synchronize the movements of their two hands, their tendency to do so presumably derived from the operation of a single mechanism governing two-handed movements.

What is the nature of this mechanism? One possibility is that each arm is controlled with one or more oscillators and that the oscillators are functionally coupled (Haken, Kelso, & Bunz, 1985). This hypothesis is attractive because coupled oscillators are likely to underlie locomotion and the arms were used for walking earlier in evolution (see Chapter 4). Evidence has been obtained for oscillator control of arm movements in studies where subjects first let one arm dangle freely, then press the arm against a rigid surface, and then dangle the arm freely again (Craske & Craske, 1986). When the arm hangs freely before being pressed against the wall, it displays some

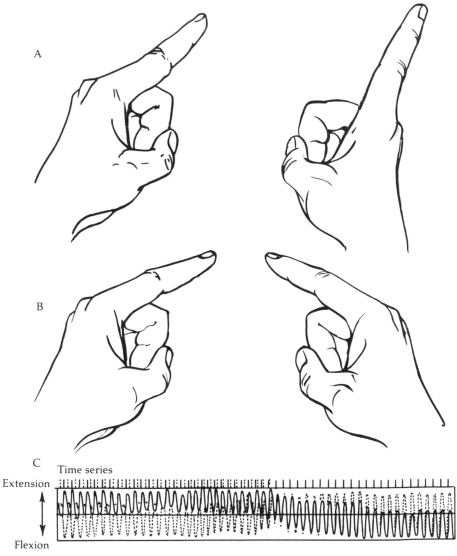

Figure 6.13 Coupling of the two index fingers. (A) At low frequency, the two fingers can stay in anti-phase (one finger extending while the other flexes). (B) At high frequency, only an in-phase relation can be maintained (both fingers flex or extend). (C) Time series showing the transition from anti-phase to in-phase relation as oscillation frequency increases. Position of right finger (——); position of left finger (- - -). (From Haken, Kelso, & Bunz, 1983.)

oscillation, as would be expected from the fact that the arm, when suspended from the shoulder, can be viewed as a pendulum (Fenn, 1938). More importantly, when the arm dangles freely after being pressed against the wall, it oscillates in the plane of the applied pressure. Craske and Craske (1986) suggested that oscillators responsible for the initial direction of motion become fatigued or adapted during the strenuous arm-pressing task. Later, when the oscillators are unable to contribute as much as they normally do, the observed direction of oscillation changes.

Another observation that accords with the oscillator hypothesis is one you can make yourself. Position your two index fingers as in Figure 6.13 so that the left index finger flexes and the right index finger extends. Now allow the fingers to reverse position, so the right index finger flexes and the left index finger extends. Alternate between these two positions, slowly at first, but then at higher and higher rates. Keep going faster and faster until your fingers move as quickly as possible. What you may notice is that your fingers switch from an anti-phase pattern (where one finger flexes as the other finger extends) to an in-phase pattern (where both fingers flex together or extend together). The switch only occurs in the anti-phase to in-phase direction. If you start at a slow rate with the fingers in phase, you probably will not switch to an anti-phase pattern as you speed up.

This phenomenon has been investigated in considerable detail by Haken *et al.* (1985), who modeled the switch in terms of nonlinear, coupled oscillators. Through mathematical derivations, Haken *et al.* (1985) showed that a nonlinear coupled-oscillator model can be used to account for this effect. I will give a more detailed account of the model in Chapter 11.

■ SUMMARY

1. There are two developmental milestones in the development of reaching and grasping. By around 5 months of age, infants can reliably preprogram the direction and distance of reaches and grasps. By around 9 months of age, they can reliably preprogram orientation and size.

2. The use of visual feedback is susceptible to experience. As shown in the late nineteenth century, people can adapt to inverting lenses. Originally it was thought that this adaptation is achieved by correlating changes of visual input with proprioceptive input. The modern view is that adaptation to visual distortion is made possible by the opportunity to correlate changes of visual input with motor commands or their underlying intentions.

3. Vision dominates touch. The way an object feels is generally affected by what it looks like, but not the reverse. Visual dominance may have practical benefits in physical therapy.

4. It takes between 100 and 200 msec to respond to visual feedback during manual aiming tasks.

5. A domain in which feedback processing has been studied in detail is the manual aiming task, where the subject moves the hand to a spatial target, usually as quickly as possible. Fitts (1954) introduced a formula for the time needed to reach a target depending on the distance of the target from the starting position and depending on the target's diameter. According to the formula, the time to reach the target increases with the distance of the target from the start position and decreases with the target's width. Because the formula does an excellent job of accounting for movement-time data from a wide range of tasks, it has been called Fitts' Law.

6. Several explanations have been offered for Fitts' Law. The *iterative corrections* model says it mainly reflects corrections of movement errors. The *impulse variability* model says it mainly reflects the initial impulse that drives the limb toward the target. The *optimized initial impulse* model, the most successful model to date, says that both factors are important.

7. A convenient way to move a limb from one position to another is to take advantage of the springlike properties of muscle. There are two ways to exploit these springlike properties. One is to change the resting lengths of the muscle; the other is to change the stiffness of one muscle relative to the other. Several studies suggest that either or both methods may be used. Treating muscles as springs is economical from a computational standpoint.

8. During reaching and grasping, two distinct phases of movement can be identified—the *transport* phase, during which the hand is brought toward the object, and the *grasp* phase, during which the fingers enclose the object. The transport and grasp phases may be controlled by different brain areas, and their underlying control mechanisms appear to develop at different rates. Some dependencies exist between the two phases, however.

9. Although it is convenient when studying reaching and grasping to view the hand as a single moving point, the hand is only one part of a complex set of joints. The hand often follows a straight path when people point to objects, an outcome that has been taken to suggest that movements are planned in the extrinsic coordinates of hand (or extrapersonal) space rather than the intrinsic coordinates of joint (or intrapersonal) space. The fact that the hand follows straight-line trajectories suggests that the motor system does not compromise spatial factors when solving the *inverse dynamics* problem—the problem of determining the muscle torques needed to bring an end-effector (such as the hand) through a desired spatial path. However, regularities in the relations of joint positions during aiming movements suggest that there may be some joint-based planning. Simultaneous flexion of the wrist and elbow is easier than flexion of the wrist and extension of the elbow or extension of the wrist and flexion of the elbow. The greater ease with which people can simultaneously flex (or extend) the wrist and elbow suggests that there are overarching *coordinative structures* for the two joints. Such coordinative structures may reduce the number of degrees of freedom to be managed during limb movements.

10. Coordinative structures also characterize interactions between the two arms and hands. There is a tendency for the two hands to begin and end aiming movements simultaneously. When the left and right index fingers flex and extend simultaneously, as the oscillation frequency increases there is a tendency for the fingers only to flex together or only to extend together. This phenomenon may reflect the operation of nonlinear coupled oscillators underlying control of the two hands.

■ REFERENCES

Abend, W., Bizzi, E., & Morasso, P. (1982). Human arm trajectory formation. *Brain*, **105**, 331–348.

Annet, J., Golby, C. W., & Kay, H. (1958). The measurement of elements in an assembly task: The information output of the human motor system. *Quarterly Journal of Experimental Psychology*, **10**, 1–11.

Arbib, M. A., Iberall, T., & Lyons, D. (1985). Coordinated control programs for movements of the hand. In A. W. Goodwin & I. Darian-Smith (Eds.), *Hand function and the neocortex* (pp. 111–129). Berlin: Springer-Verlag.

Asatryan, D. G., & Fel'dman, A. G. (1965). Functional tuning of the nervous system with control of movement or maintenance of a steady posture. I. *Biophysics*, **10**, 925–935.

Berkenblit, M. B., Fel'dman, A. G., & Fucson, O. I. (1986). Adaptability of innate motor patterns and motor control. *Behavioral and Brain Sciences*, **9**, 585–638.

Bernstein, N. (1967). *The coordination and regulation of movements*. London: Pergamon.

Bizzi, E., & Mussa-Ivaldi, F. A. (1989). Geometrical and mechanical issues in movement planning and control. In M. I. Posner (Ed.), *Handbook of cognitive science* (pp. 769–792). Cambridge, MA: MIT Press.

Boakes, R. (1984). *From Darwin to Behaviorism*. New York: Cambridge University Press.

Bousset, S., & Zattara, M. (1981). A sequence of postural movements precedes voluntary movement. *Neuroscience Letters*, **22**, 263–270.

Bower, T. G. R. (1972). Object perception in infants. *Perception*, **1**, 15–30.

Bower, T. G. R. (1974). *Development in infancy*. San Francisco: Freeman.

Bower, T. G. R., Broughton, J. M., & Moore, M. K. (1970). Demonstration of intention in the reaching behavior of neonate humans. *Nature (London)*, **228**, 679–681.

Carlton, L. G. (1981). Processing visual feedback information for movement control. *Journal of Experimental Psychology: Human Perception and Performance*, **7**, 1019–1030.

Cooke, J. D. (1980). The organization of simple, skilled movements. In G. E. Stelmach & J. Requin (Eds.), *Tutorials in motor behavior* (pp. 199–212). Amsterdam: North-Holland.

Craske, B., & Craske, J. D. (1986). Oscillator mechanisms in the human motor system: Investigating their properties using the aftercontraction effect. *Journal of Motor Behavior*, **18**, 117–145.

Crossman, E. R. F. W., & Goodeve, P. J. (1963/1983). Feedback control of hand-movement and Fitts' Law. *Quarterly Journal of Experimental Psychology*, **35A**, 251–278.

El'ner, A. N. (1973). Possibilities of correcting the urgent voluntary movements and the associated postural activity of human muscles. *Biophysics*, **18**, 966–971.

Essock, E. A., & Siqueland, E. R. (1981). Discrimination of orientation by human infants. *Perception*, **10**, 245–253.

Fenn, W. O. (1938). The mechanics of muscle contraction in man. *Journal of Applied Physics*, **9**, 165–177.

Field, J. (1977). Coordination of vision and prehension in young infants. *Child Development*, **48**, 97–103.

Fitts, P. M. (1954). The information capacity of the human motor system in controlling the amplitude of movement. *Journal of Experimental Psychology*, **47**, 381–391.

Fitts, P. M., & Peterson, J. R. (1964). Information capacity of discrete motor responses. *Journal of Experimental Psychology, 67,* 103–112.

Fraser, C., & Wing, A. M. (1981). A case study of reaching by a user of a manually-operated artificial hand. *Prosthetics and Orthotics International, 5,* 151–156.

Gelfand, I. M., Gurfinkel, V. S., Tsetlin, M. L., & Shik, M. L. (1966). Problems in analysis of movements. In I. M. Gelfand, V. S. Gurfinkel, S. V. Fomin, & M. L. Tsetlin (Eds.), *Models of the structural functional organization of certain biological systems* (pp. 330–345). Cambridge, MA: MIT Press. (American translation, 1971)

Gibson, J. J. (1933). Adaptation after-effect and contrast in perception of curved lines. *Journal of Experimental Psychology, 16,* 1–31.

Gordon, F. R., & Yonas, A. (1976). Sensitivity to binocular depth information in infants. *Journal of Experimental Child Psychology, 22,* 413–422.

Haken, H., Kelso, J. A. S., & Bunz, H. A. (1985). Theoretical model of phase transitions in human hand movements. *Biological Cybernetics, 51,* 347–356.

Hay, L. (1984). The development of movement control. In M. M. Smyth & A. M. Wing (Eds.), *The psychology of human movement* (pp. 241–267). London: Academic Press.

Held, R. (1965). Plasticity in sensory-motor systems. *Scientific American, 213*(5), 84–94.

Hollerbach, J. M., & Atkeson, C. G. (1986). Characterization of joint-interpolated arm movements. In H. Heuer & C. Fromm (Ed.), *Generation and modulation of action patterns* (pp. 41–54). Berlin: Springer-Verlag.

Hollerbach, J. M., Moore, S. P., & Atkeson, C. G. (1987). Workspace effect in arm movement kinematics derived by joint interpolation. In G. N. Gantchev, B. Dimitrov, & P. Gatev (Eds.), *Motor control* (pp. 197–208). New York: Plenum.

Hooker, D. (1938). The origin of the grasping movement in man. *Proceedings of the American Philosophical Society, 79,* 587–606.

Jagacinski, R. J., Repperger, D. W., Moran, M. S., Ward, S. L., & Glass, B. (1980). Fitts' Law and the microstructure of rapid discrete movements. *Journal of Experimental Psychology: Human Perception and Performance, 6,* 309–320.

Jeannerod, M. (1981). Intersegmental coordination during reaching at natural objects. In J. Long & A. Baddeley (Eds.), *Attention and performance IX* (pp. 153–169). Hillsdale, NJ: Erlbaum.

Jeannerod, M. (1984). The timing of natural prehension movement. *Journal of Motor Behavior, 26,* 3, 235–254.

Kaminski, T., & Gentile, A M. (1986). Joint control strategies and hand trajectories in multijoint pointing movements. *Journal of Motor Behavior, 189,* 261–278.

Kaufman, L. (1974). *Sight and mind.* New York: Oxford Univ. Press.

Keele, S. W. (1968). Movement control in skilled motor performance. *Psychological Bulletin, 70,* 387–403.

Keele, S. W., & Posner, M. I. (1968). Processing visual feedback in rapid movement. *Journal of Experimental Psychology, 77,* 155–158.

Kelso, J. A. S., & Holt, D. G. (1980). Exploring a vibratory system analysis of human movement production. *Journal of Neurophysiology, 43,* 1183–1196.

Kelso, J. A. S., Putnam, C. A., & Goodman, D. (1983). On the space-time structure of human interlimb co-ordination. *Quarterly Journal of Experimental Psychology, 35A,* 347–375.

Kerr, B. A., & Langolf, G. D. (1977). Speed of aiming movements. *Quarterly Journal of Experimental Psychology, 29,* 475–481.

Kerr, R. (1973). Movement time in an underwater environment. *Journal of Motor Behavior, 5,* 175–178.

Klatzky, R. L., & Lederman, S. J. (1985). *Hand movements: A window to haptic object recognition.* Paper presented at the Twenty-sixth annual meeting of the Psychonomoic Society. Boston.

Klatzky, R. L., & Lederman, S. J. (1987). The intelligent hand. In G. H. Bower (Ed.), *Psychology of learning and motivation* (Vol. 21) (pp. 121–151). San Diego: Academic Press.

Kornblum, S., & Requin, J. (Eds.), (1984). *Preparatory states and processes.* Hillsdale, NJ: Erlbaum.

Kots, Y. M., & Syrovegin, A. V. (1966). Fixed set of variants of interactions of the muscles of two joints in the execution of simple voluntary movements. *Biophysics, 11,* 1212–1219.

Kuypers, H. G. (1973). The anatomical organization of the descending pathways and their contributions to motor control especially in primates. In J. E. Desmedt (Ed.), *New developments in electromyography and clinical neurophysiology* (Vol. 3) (pp. 38–68). Basel: Karger.

Langolf, G. D., Chaffin, D. B., & Foulke, J. A. (1976). An investigation of Fitts' Law using a wide range of movement amplitudes. *Journal of Motor Behavior,* **8,** 113–128.

Lawrence, D. G., & Hopkins, D. A. (1972). Developmental aspects of pyramidal motor control in the rhesus monkey. *Brain Research,* **40,** 117–118.

Lockman, J. J., & Ashmead, D. H. (1983). Asynchronies in the development of manual behavior. In P. Lipsitt & C. K. Rovee-Collier (Eds.), *Advances in infancy research* (Vol. 2, pp. 114–136). Norwood, NJ: Ablex.

Lockman, J. J., Ashmead, D. H., & Bushnell, E. W. (1984). The development of anticipatory hand orientation during infancy. *Journal of Experimental Child Psychology,* **37,** 176–186.

Marteniuk, R. G., MacKenzie, C. L., Jeannerod, M., Athenes, S., & Dugas, C. (1987). Constraints on human arm movement trajectories. *Canadian Journal of Psychology,* **4,** 365–378.

Meyer, D. E., Abrams, R. A., Kornblum, S., Wright, C. E., & Smith, J. E. K. (1988). Optimality in human motor performance: Ideal control of rapid aimed movements. *Psychological Review,* **95,** 340–370.

Meyer, D. E., Smith, J. E. K., Kornblum, S., Abrams, R. A., & Wright, C. E. (1990). Speed-accuracy tradeoffs in aimed movements: Toward a theory of rapid voluntary action. In M. Jeannerod (Ed.), *Attention and performance XIII* (pp. 173–226). Hillsdale, NJ: Erlbaum.

Meyer, D. E., Smith, J. E. K., & Wright, C. E. (1982). Models for the speed and accuracy of aimed movements. *Psychological Review,* **89,** 449–482.

Morasso, P. (1981). Spatial control of arm movements. *Experimental Brain Research,* **42,** 223–227.

Newell, K. M., & Carlton, L. G. (1988). Force variability in isometric responses. *Journal of Experimental Psychology: Human Perception and Performance,* **14,** 37–44.

Poizner, H., Klima, E. S., & Bellugi, U. (1987). *What the hands reveal about the brain.* Cambridge, MA: MIT Press/Bradford Books.

Polit, A., & Bizzi, E. (1978). Processes controlling arm movements in monkeys. *Science,* **201,** 1235–1237.

Polit, A., & Bizzi, E. (1979). Characteristics of motor programs underlying arm movements in monkeys. *Journal of Neurophysiology,* **42,** 183–194.

Posner, M. I., Nissen, M. J., & Klein, R. (1976). Visual dominance: An information-processing account of its origins and significance. *Psychological Review,* **83,** 157–171.

Rock, I., & Harris, C. S. (1967). Vision and touch. *Scientific American,* **216**(5), 96–104.

Rosenbaum, D. A., Vaughan, J., Barnes, H. J., Marchak, F., & Slotta, J. (1990). Constraints on action selection: Overhand versus underhand grips. In M. Jeannerod (Ed.), *Attention and performance XIII* (pp. 321–342). Hillsdale, NJ: Erlbaum.

Schmidt, R. A., Zelaznik, H. N., Hawkins, B., Frank, J. S., & Quinn, J. T., Jr. (1979). Motor output variability: A theory for the accuracy of rapid motor acts. *Psychological Review,* **86,** 415–451.

Smyth, M. M., & Wing, A. M. (Eds.) (1984). *The psychology of human movement.* London: Academic Press.

Soechting, J. F., & Lacquaniti, F. (1981). Invariant characterisitcs of a pointing movement in man. *Journal of Neuroscience,* **1,** 710–720.

Tastevin, J. (1937). En partant de l'expérience d'Aristote. *Encephale,* **1,** 57–84.

Touwen, B. C. (1971). A study on the development of some motor phenomena in infancy. *Developmental Medicine and Child Neurology,* **13,** 435–446.

Turvey, M. T. (1977). Preliminaries to a theory of action with reference to vision. In R. Shaw & J. Bransford (Eds.), *Perceiving, acting, and knowing* (pp. 211–265). Hillsdale, NJ: Erlbaum.

Twitchell, T. E. (1971). Reflex mechanisms and the development of prehension. In K. J. Connolly (Ed.), *Mechanisms of motor skill development* (pp. 25–45). London: Academic Press.

von Hofsten, C. (1979). Development of visually guided reaching: The approach phase. *Journal of Human Movement Studies, 5,* 150–178.

von Hofsten, C. (1980). Predictive reaching for moving objects by human infants. *Journal of Experimental Child Psychology, 30,* 369–392.

von Hofsten, C., & Rönnqvist, L. (1988). Preparation for grasping an object: A developmental study. *Journal of Experimental Psychology: Human Perception and Performance, 14,* 610–621.

von Holst, E. (1973). *The behavioural physiology of animal and man: The collected papers of Erich von Holst* (Vol. 1). London: Methuen.

White, B. L., Castle, P., & Held, R. (1964). Observations on the development of visually directed reaching. *Child Development, 35,* 349–364.

Wing, A. M., Turton, A., & Fraser, C. (1986). Grasp size and accuracy of approach in reaching. *Journal of Motor Behavior, 18,* 245–260.

Wishart, J. G., Bower, T. G. R., & Dunkeld, J. (1978). Reaching in the dark. *Perception, 7,* 507–512.

Woodworth, R. S. (1899). The accuracy of voluntary movement. *Psychological Review Monograph Supplements, 3,* No. 3.

Zelaznik, H. N., Hawkins, B., & Kisselburgh, L. (1983). Rapid visual feedback processing in single-aiming movements. *Journal of Motor Behavior, 15,* 217–236.

7 DRAWING AND WRITING

■ INTRODUCTION

A primary function of the human motor system is to allow for communication with others. The activities I have considered so far—walking, looking, reaching, and grasping—only incidentally allow for communication. Drawing and writing, on the other hand, almost exclusively provide for the expression of thoughts to others. Based on this observation, a theoretical perspective can be suggested for analyzing drawing and writing. This perspective is based on the assumption that communicative acts represent the culmination of several internal translations. First, an abstract message is selected; the abstract message is an idea to be expressed. Then the abstract message is translated into appropriate linguistic or expressive segments. Finally, the segments are realized as series of efferent commands. If this model applies to all communicative acts, it should also apply to drawing and writing. This hypothesis has motivated much of the research on drawing and writing and has stood up well to experimental test.

I have already mentioned a finding that corroborates the stage model suggested above. Recall from Chapter 1 that people can write with a consistent style when using different effectors such as the hand or foot (see Figure 1.1). Likewise, writing style is preserved when one scrawls across a blackboard or on a small surface such as a check. These findings suggest that different production mechanisms provide alternative means of realizing the same high-level graphic representation (Wright, 1990). Said differently, the control of writing (and presumably drawing too) is at least partly hierarchical.

Perhaps the most intriguing question in the study of the control of drawing and writing is how the different output subsystems solve the problem of expressing the same high-level representations. One approach to this problem is to propose planning constraints that the output mechanisms obey. Such constraints help limit the range of behavioral options that must be considered in selecting appropriate responses. I have already discussed a planning constraint that happens to involve drawing (or drawinglike behavior). Recall from Chapters 1 and 6 that people tend to draw straight lines (or series of straight-line segments) between points on a plane (Morasso, 1981). It has been suggested that this tendency reflects a planning constraint for minimizing *jerk*, the third time derivative of position (Flash & Hogan, 1985; Hogan, 1984). As will be seen in this chapter, this constraint may also account for other aspects of people's drawing and writing behavior.

In addition to the question of how writing and drawing styles are preserved in widely differing output contexts, another question is why people's graphic outputs are so distinctive. The individuality of writing style is so reliable that signatures are used for identification purposes. It has been suggested that writing styles indicate personality traits. For example, writing analysts (*graphologists*) who subscribe to Freudian theory have suggested that the way one forms lower loops in letters such as "g" and "p" reflects the state of the unconscious *id* (the part of the psyche related to sexual urges, according to Freud). The overall slant and size of handwritten letters are also supposed to reflect one's extraversion or self-esteem (Hughes, 1966). Graphology is taken so seriously in some countries (notably Israel) that it is routinely used in hiring decisions. However, the validity of graphology is doubtful (Fischman, 1987).

Still another question about drawing and writing is why most individuals perform these activites more easily with one hand than the other. Relevant work will be summarized in the final part of the chapter.

■ DRAWING

Because the capacity to draw precedes the capacity to write, I begin with a discussion of drawing. First I consider the high-level control of drawing. Then I turn to the execution of drawing strokes.

The Planning of Strokes

Much of the research that has been done on drawing has been concerned with the *planning* of drawing behavior, especially in young children. Children's drawings become progressively more refined over the course of development (Goodnow, 1977), presumably because children become more and more sophisticated in their motor planning and control as well as their perceptual and attentional capabilities (Figure 7.1).

Because children can draw before they write, it has been suggested that early drawing behavior may provide clues about young children's cognitive abilities. It has been proposed, for example, that drawing may be governed by high-level rules of the sort underlying language processing

"*You moved.*"

Figure 7.1 Children are just as creative in defending their drawings as in producing them. Drawing by Lorenz; © 1987 *The New Yorker* Magazine, Inc.

(Goodnow & Levine, 1973; Van Sommers, 1984). Consequently, some investigators have proposed that the development of drawing may parallel the development of language.

Goodnow and Levine (1973) pursued this possibility in a seminal article entitled *The grammar of action: Sequence and syntax in children's copying.* Goodnow and Levine recorded the drawing paths that children followed when copying simple two-dimensional shapes such as squares and triangles. Based on their observations of the way these forms were copied, the authors proposed that people rely on several rules for sequencing drawing strokes. Two rules pertain to the starting point:

1. Start at the leftmost point.
2. Start at the top.

Two other rules pertain to the starting *strokes*:

3. Start with a vertical line.

4. Given a figure with an apex, such as a diamond or triangle, start at the top and descend the left oblique.

A final set of rules concern the general progression of copying:

5. Draw horizontal lines from left to right.
6. Draw vertical lines from top to bottom.
7. Keep the pencil on the paper at all times.

Goodnow and Levine (1973) proposed that if a child's overt copying behavior consistently follows any of these rules, the child can be assumed to use the rule, or some functionally analogous constraint, during the drawing process. They found, in fact, that as children grow older, their drawing performance conforms more and more closely to the seven rules listed here, suggesting that more of the rules (or the underlying constraints they represent) are deployed as children mature.

If the planning of drawing strokes does indeed rely on a set of rules, and if those rules are similar to the rules underlying linguistic performance, then children who have difficulty sequencing spoken words should also have trouble drawing lines in a rule-governed way. This prediction was confirmed in a study of children with profound sentence-formation difficulties (*agrammatic aphasia*). The children in the study (Cromer, 1983) were asked to copy figures such as the one in Figure 7.2. The order in which the lines were drawn deviated significantly from the order in which the lines were drawn by cognitively normal deaf or hearing children. The deaf and hearing children copied the figures in a way that took advantage of the figures' symmetric organization, tending to start at the top of the figure, drawing a left and right branch, proceeding down a level, and so forth. The agrammatic aphasic children, however, drew in a more haphazard fashion, often starting at the bottom of the figure and drawing all the way to the top before filling in the mirror-image line within that subsection. The failure of these children to capitalize on the hierarchical organization of the figure has been taken to suggest that the ability to sequence behavior, whether in the linguistic domain or in the domain of drawing, may depend on a central, amodal rule system (Keele, 1987).

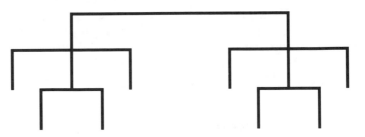

Figure 7.2 Stick figure to be copied by the children in Cromer's (1983) study.

Why should there be rules for drawing? One reason is that rules help simplify motor planning. For example, the availability of a simple left-to-right drawing rule (Goodnow and Levine's Rule 5) eliminates the need for complex decision making about which way to proceed when attempting to draw a horizontal line. Another reason to have rules is that they help reduce the number of distinct motor programs that must be maintained in memory. Suppose one had distinct programs for squares of different sizes. The storage requirements of this set of programs would be greater than if one had a single program that could be modified through a rule to allow for the production of large, small, or medium-sized squares. Rules therefore promote flexibility of performance while reducing memory storage costs.

If rules are useful for drawing, one would expect adults as well as children to rely on them. Investigations of adult copying and drawing behavior bear out this expectation. In an intensive study of the stroke paths used by adults while copying two-dimensional shapes, Van Sommers (1984) found that similar drawing paths were pursued by different individuals. The following statement captures some of the regularity Van Sommers observed:

> Take a pencil and quickly draw the sun the way it is typically illustrated in children's books—straight rays coming out of a simple circle.... If you are right-handed you very likely began at the top of the circle and drew in a counterclockwise direction. Then you probably put the first ray on at the top, starting at its upper end and drawing downwards toward the circle. The next ray was drawn to its right and as you progressed clockwise around the disk, you changed from drawing inwards to drawing outwards (usually after one or two strokes) and then reverted to inward stokes at about nine o'clock. [Van Sommers, 1986, p. 62]

What is the source of drawing rules? A reasonable first hypothesis is that they arise out of pressure to satisfy biomechanical constraints. People choose to draw so the writing surface can be held down while the pen is in motion, for example. They also try to avoid extreme joint angles, which perhaps explains why they change the direction of ray drawing as a function of ray orientation in the example just given.

Mechanical or biomechanical factors are not the only determinants of drawing strategies, however. Van Sommers (1984) found that people's drawing preferences are also sensitive to the verbal codes assigned to the shapes they copy. For example, when the pattern shown in Figure 7.3 was identified as a cocktail glass or as a man holding a telescope, it was drawn with different stroke patterns. When the shape was described as a cocktail glass, the glass was usually drawn first and the cherry was added later. When it was described as a man holding a telescope, the head was usually drawn first, the stem and feet were drawn second, and the arms were drawn third. Because the meanings attached to the patterns affected the way they were drawn, Van Sommers (1984) concluded that semantic or perceptual factors influence drawing plans. This outcome suggests that rules for copying are deployed *after* meanings or representational goals are defined. Drawing,

Figure 7.3 A figure that can be described as a man with a telescope or a cocktail glass with a cherry. The stroke patterns used to copy the figure depend on the description. (Adapted from Van Sommers, 1986.)

therefore, is a top-down process (see Chapter 3), which accords with the view that it is hierarchically controlled.

The Isogony Principle

No matter how sequences of drawing strokes are initially planned, if they are to be communicated to others, they must be physically realized. One way to study the execution of drawing strokes is to allow people to draw very simple patterns over and over again. In one such study (Lacquaniti, Terzuolo, & Viviani, 1983), subjects were asked to trace figure eights (see Figure 7.4A). The trajectory of the pen was recorded with a graphics tablet—a device that periodically records the x and y coordinates of the pen tip. Figure 7.4C depicts the most important result from the study. The ordinate represents the angle of pen movement relative to an arbitrary reference frame (see Figure 7.4B); the abscissa represents time. As seen in Figure 7.4 C, the absolute value of the average angular velocity in the top and bottom loops was nearly constant. (Average angular velocity corresponds to the *slope* of the angle-versus-time function.) Since the total angle of the top loop was 360° and the total angle of the bottom loop was also 360°, finding that each loop was drawn with a constant angular velocity implies that the total time to draw each loop was about the same. Lacquaniti *et al.* (1983) summarized this finding in the statement: *Equal angles are described in equal times.* They called this the *Isogony Principle*.

The success of the Isogony Principle for drawing figure eights is surprising in view of the fact that another control principle also could have operated. *A priori*, the time to draw each loop could have depended on its *length*, in which case the time to complete the top loop would have been shorter than the time to complete the bottom loop.

The Isogony Principle is an important constraint for drawing. It suggests two features of drawing control. One is that a complex, continuous curve such as a figure eight is segmented into components, each of which is

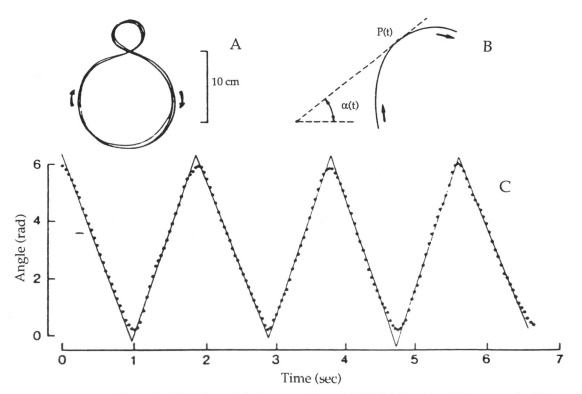

Figure 7.4 (A) A figure eight drawn continuously. (B) Method used to define the angle of the pen movement at each point in time (the angle was defined as the tangent to the trajectory formed with respect to a reference line). (C) Angle of pen movement as a function of time. (From Lacquaniti, Terzuolo, & Viviani, 1983.)

drawn as a distinct unit or stroke. (Research on handwriting, to be summarized later in this chapter, likewise suggests that letters are written by concatenating individual segments.) The second implication of the Isogony Principle is that timing appears to be a primary control feature in the execution of drawing. When people draw, or at least when they draw figure eights, they apparently try to complete each segment of the figure in a fixed amount of time.

Slowing on Tight Curves

Lacquaniti *et al.* (1983, 1984) observed another important regularity in drawing behavior. This regularity was observed in scribbling behavior, a sample of which is shown in Figure 7.5A. The angular velocity of the pen while drawing the scribble (see Figure 7.5B) varied irregularly as a function of time, but when the pen's angular velocity was plotted as a function of the curvature of the line being drawn, a regular data pattern was obtained (see

Figure 7.5C). The relation can be expressed by the equation

$$A(t) = kC(t)^{2/3} \qquad (7.1)$$

where $A(t)$ denotes angular velocity at time t, k is an empirical constant, and $C(t)$ is an index of curvature; note that $C(t)$ *increases* as the curve becomes *straighter*. Equation 7.1, or what Lacquaniti *et al.* (1983) called the *Two-Thirds Power Law*, implies that as a line segment becomes increasingly bent, the pen slows down more and more. A person drawing a curve therefore behaves like someone driving on a mountain road: To avoid falling off, he or she slows down at sharp turns.

An attractive feature of an equation like 7.1 is that one can ask whether a particular term of the equation changes with a particular change in task demands. Lacquaniti *et al.* (1983, 1984) pursued the possibility that the linear extent of the line being drawn might affect k, the estimate of the rate at which $A(t)$ increases with $C(t)^{2/3}$. If this term alone changes with variations in linear extent, the outcome would suggest that curves of varying length are drawn by globally scaling the gain of the manual control system.

To investigate this hypothesis, Lacquaniti *et al.* (1983, 1984) examined the production of spirals. The arms of a spiral have varying length. As the pen approaches the center of the spiral, the arms of the spiral become shorter (see Figure 7.6A). Figure 7.6B shows that during the drawing of spirals, the pen's angular velocity increases linearly with curvature raised to the 2/3 power, replicating what was observed for scribbles. In addition, distinct angular velocity lines can be seen for the distinct arcs of the spiral, with the slopes of the lines varying according to the length of the loop being drawn. Thus a single control parameter, corresponding to k, varied with the linear extent of the arc being drawn. The fact that such global scaling occurs for each *individual* line segment suggests that the drawing of spirals is achieved by segmenting the figure into a series of strokes.

What underlying mechanisms account for the Two-Thirds Power Law? Lacquaniti *et al.* (1984) suggested that the relation may result from the coupling of two independent oscillators. If the output of the oscillators is sinusoidal, the phase relations and relative amplitudes of the sinusoids can be modulated to produce curves of varying length and curvature. Detailed simulations have shown that coupled-oscillator systems can in fact generate a wide range of graphic outputs (Hollerbach, 1981), making this proposal attractive. Another appealing feature of the hypothesis is that oscillators are biologically realistic mechanisms (see Chapter 4).

Drawing Smoothly

Despite the apparent success of the Two-Thirds Power Law, some investigators have not been convinced by it. Wann, Nimmo-Smith, and Wing (1988) noted that significant departures from the 2/3 exponent have been observed in some studies of drawing and handwriting (Thomassen & Teulings, 1985). Wann *et al.* (1988) did not question the fact that angular velocity is generally a

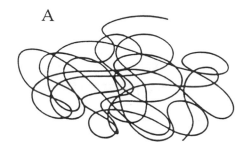

A

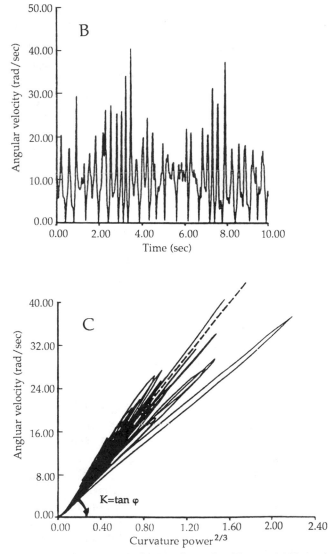

Figure 7.5 (A) A scribble produced by one subject in the study of Lacquaniti, Terzuolo, and Viviani (1984). (B) Angular velocity of the pen as a function of time. (C) Angular velocity as a function of curvature raised to the 2/3 power; each segment applies to a distinct segment of the trajectory. (From Lacquaniti, Terzuolo, & Viviani, 1984.)

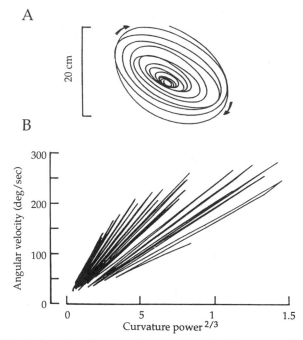

Figure 7.6 (A) A spiral produced by one subject in the study of Lacquaniti, Terzuolo, and Viviani (1984). (B) Angular velocity as a function of curvature raised to the 2/3 power; the slope of the angular velocity function depends on the linear extent of the arm of the spiral. (From Lacquaniti, Terzuolo, & Viviani, 1984.)

power function of curvature, but they took issue with the explanation of the power law in terms of sinusoidal oscillations. They said that while sinusoids are mathematically appealing, biological motor systems rarely behave in an ideal sinusoidal fashion (Saltzman & Kelso, 1987). Furthermore, while sinusoids are mathematically convenient, it is hard to see why they would have been favored in evolution.

A more biologically plausible explanation of the power law, according to Wann *et al.* (1988), is that people attempt to write as *smoothly* as possible. This goal is consistent with the minimum-jerk model of Hogan (1984) and Flash and Hogan (1985), discussed in Chapters 1 and 6. Recall that the minimum-jerk model specifies that movement trajectories are planned so as to minimize the mean-squared value of the third time derivative of position. Writing smoothly appears to be a goal in graphic production. Children, for example, write more smoothly as their writing improves (Wann, 1987). Wann *et al.* (1988) demonstrated that the minimum-jerk model could also give rise to the power law of Lacquaniti *et al.* (1983, 1984).

With the oscillator model and the minimum-jerk model as possible explanations of the Two-Thirds Power Law, how can we choose between them? At this stage, it is hard to do so, so I will reserve judgment. One possible reason to prefer the minimum-jerk model is that it may also account for people's tendency to draw straight lines when connecting two points (Flash & Hogan, 1985), as discussed earlier. The ability of the minimum-jerk model to account for both results could be taken to suggest that jerk minimization, or some constraint related to smoothness of performance, may be a determinant of drawing and writing behavior.

■ WRITING

Because writing and drawing are physically similar behaviors, it is reasonable to expect that they are controlled in similar ways. I have already suggested that both forms of graphic behavior may be controlled hierarchically. In this section I will review the evidence for the hierarchical control of handwriting.

Error Analyses

An influential source of support for the hierarchical control of handwriting comes from slips of the pen. Ellis (1979) compiled a list of such slips by recording his own writing errors over a period of 18 months (see Table 7.1). Sometimes he substituted one word for another (Example 1) or substituted one letter for another (Example 2). On other occasions, he repeated a letter too many times (Example 3) or replaced one letter with another, capitalizing the intruding letter if the replaced letter should have been capitalized (Example 4). On still other occasions, he made errors involving single writing strokes (Example 5).

To account for this pattern of results, Ellis proposed that writing is initiated in four stages, which he denoted (1) *word*, (2) *grapheme*, (3) *allograph*, and (4) *graph*. *Words* (Stage 1) are the entities selected in the first stage of the programming process. Errors in this stage lead to *lexical* errors (production of the wrong word). *Graphemes* (Stage 2) are the letters of the alphabet. Mistakes in grapheme selection account for errors of the sort shown in Examples 2 and 3. *Allographs* (Stage 3) are a grapheme's categorical variations, for example, the upper- and lowercase form of the letter "s." An allograph stage is suggested by errors like the one in Example 4. *Graphs,* or writing strokes, are

■ **Table 7.1** Examples of Writing Errors[a]

Example	Error	Description
1	*too* → *two*	Lexical error
2	*lapse from* → *lapse trom*	Letter substitution
3	*looks* → *loooks*	Letter repetition
4	*cognitive* → *Go...*	Letter substitution and case change
5	*Wednesday* → *Wednesduy*	Extra stroke

[a]Data from Ellis (1979).

selected at the lowest level of the hierarchy (Stage 4). Errors of graph selection lead to mistakes like the one in Example 5.

Agraphia

The slips of the pen just described were inadvertent errors made by a neurologically normal individual (as far as I know). Neurological patients produce errors which provide another source of support for the hierarchical control of handwriting. Some neurological patients have difficulty writing, though their motor control, perception, and spelling are otherwise intact. Their syndrome is known as *agraphia* (Roeltgin, 1985). Agraphia rarely occurs without other neurological impairments. However, the forms it takes comport with the hierarchical model because particular aspects of handwriting, corresponding to particular hierarchical levels, are selectively impaired.

A representative agraphic patient was described by Margolin and Wing (1983). This man suffered damage to the right frontal and parietal lobes (see Chapter 2). He could not write words on command, but he could copy words with a modicum of skill (see Figure 7.7). Based on a detailed analysis of this patient's writing and drawing, Margolin and Wing (1983) concluded that he had difficulty producing writing strokes. The patient's writing difficulties were not simply due to perceptual deficits, for he could copy reasonably well, and the errors he made were qualitatively different from those exhibited by normal individuals subjected to altered visual feedback (Smith, McCrary, & Smith, 1960). Because the patient did not have difficulty retrieving words, graphemes, or allographs (the first three stages in Ellis' model), his symptoms bear out the hypothesis that writing *strokes* are governed by a mechanism distinct from the mechanisms governing word, grapheme, or allograph selection.

Other agraphic patients exhibit writing deficits limited to words, graphemes, or allographs (Roeltgin, 1985). For example, Miceli, Silveri, and Caramazza (1985) described a patient who made frequent spelling errors while writing, though his writing strokes were essentially normal and the words he selected, although spelled incorrectly, were appropriate. Because this patient could accurately copy text, his deficit was apparently localized at the grapheme-selection stage (Margolin, 1984).

Reaction-Time Evidence for Grapheme Selection

Another way to test the hypothesis that there are distinct stages in the control of handwriting is to measure writing reaction times. Using this technique, Teulings, Thomassen, and van Galen (1983) obtained convergent evidence for the grapheme-selection stage. Teulings *et al.* (1983) displayed a single handwritten letter on a screen and then presented another letter, either to the left or right of it. The subject's task was to copy the complete letter pair as soon as possible after both letters appeared. The result was that the

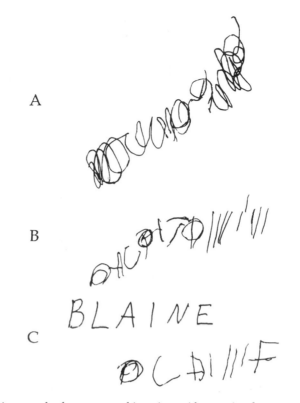

Figure 7.7 Writing samples from an agraphic patient with extensive damage to the right frontal and parietal lobes 1 month after stroke. (A) The man's signature. (B) His printed name. (C) A copied name, with the model above the copy. (From Margolin & Wing, 1983.)

time to start writing was shorter when the two letters matched than when they did not match. This outcome corroborates the hypothesis that subjects could access preformed letter-production programs (*graphemes*) before starting to write. Presumably, when a single letter-production program could be executed twice in a row, the time needed for programming writing behavior was less than when two distinct letter-production programs had to be executed.

There are other ways to account for the matching-letter advantage obtained by Teulings *et al*. One possibility is that matching letters could be seen (or visually coded) more easily than nonmatching letters. Teulings *et al*. argued against this view, however, based on data from studies of letter perception (see their paper for details). They also argued against another possible explanation of their result—namely, that subjects benefited from identical letter pairs because the letters in the pairs used common *strokes*. According to this hypothesis, subjects initiated matching letter pairs more quickly than nonmatching letter pairs because fewer strokes had to be specified in the matching-letter case. Other experimental manipulations led Teulings *et al.* to conclude that merely sharing strokes did not lower reaction times.

Reaction-Time Evidence for Allograph Selection

The reaction-time study I just summarized provided evidence for the grapheme-selection stage (Stage 2 in Ellis' model). Another reaction-time study provided evidence for the allograph-selection stage (Ellis' Stage 3). Stelmach and Teulings (1983) informed subjects that they would be required to write one of two letter strings but that one of the letter strings would be more likely than the other. The question was how the time to start writing the ultimately required string would depend on its relation to the other string possible. Making one of the letter strings highly likely encouraged subjects to prepare to write it. Writing the other string required a switch or redefinition of the initially readied program (Rosenbaum & Kornblum, 1982).

Stelmach and Teulings (1983) applied their priming paradigm to two choice contexts (see Figure 7.8). In one, the response alternatives were letter strings that required different letter *shapes*—the lower case strings *hye* and *ynl*. When the improbable member of this pair was performed (for example, *ynl* when *hye* was likely), the time to start writing was 128 msec longer than when the probable member was performed. In the other choice condition, the response alternatives differed with respect to *size*; the alternatives were a large and small rendition of the letter string *hye*. In this choice condition, when the improbable response was called for (for example, the small rendition of *hye* when the large rendition was primed), the reaction-time cost was only 63 msec, about half the cost in the shape-different condition. Stelmach and Teulings (1983) suggested that the reaction-time cost was

Figure 7.8 Letter pairs similar to those copied by subjects in the experiment of Stelmach and Teulings (1983). (*Left*) Two strings with different letter *shapes*. (*Right*) Two strings with different letter *sizes*.

smaller for the size-different condition than for the shape-different condition because letter size can be specified *after* letter shape, as assumed in Ellis' model.

Writing Size, Relative Timing, and Absolute Timing

Let us now consider in more detail how writing size is governed. Some authors have proposed that writing size may be controlled by modulating a single control parameter that allows one's writing to stretch or contract as if it were produced on a rubber sheet. This proposal was mentioned earlier in this chapter in connection with the production of spirals (Lacquaniti *et al.*, 1983, 1984). A possible mechanism for such uniform size scaling is an internal clock that paces graphic performance, where the clock's speed influences the size of the strokes produced. According to this hypothesis, writing size depends on writing *rate*. The principle is called *rate scaling*.

A test of the *rate-scaling* hypothesis was provided by Wing (1978). He measured writing times as subjects altered the overall size of their writing. As the letters grew larger, the time to produce the letters also increased, as predicted by the hypothesis.

Two other, more exotic studies also support the rate-scaling hypothesis. In one, subjects were asked to breathe nitrous oxide in oxygen while copying short prose passages (Legge, Steinberg, & Summerfield, 1964). As the concentration of nitrous oxide increased, the height of the produced letters increased. Nitrous oxide is a central nervous system depressant. When its concentration is increased, reaction time slows. Increasing concentrations of nitrous oxide may therefore lead to increases in writing size because the neural processes underlying writing performance become more sluggish.

The other exotic study involved hypnosis. Zimbardo, Marshall, and Maslach (1971) told hypnotized individuals "to allow the present to expand and the past and future to become distanced and insignificant." One of the behavioral changes they observed in individuals affected by these instructions was that their handwriting expanded.

If global rate scaling underlies variation in the overall size of written characters, does it also underlie the minute variations in letter size that occur when one writes within a given size window? For example, if one signs one's name repeatedly on a narrow strip of paper and particular letters happen to change size as the signature is repeated, are those size variations due to changes in writing rate?

Viviani and Terzuolo (1980) proposed that changes in writing rate do in fact cause spontaneous changes in writing size. They were led to this position by an observation which is reproduced in Figure 7.9. Each curve in this figure corresponds to the tangential velocity of a pen used by one person while writing the letter "a." Although the sizes of the strokes varied, when the tangential velocity profiles were arranged from top to bottom according to the total duration of the letter (shortest duration at the top,

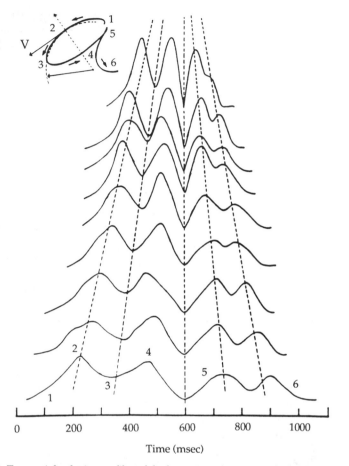

Figure 7.9 Tangential velocity profiles of the letter "a" when it was drawn quickly (*top*) and more slowly (*bottom*). (From Viviani & Terzuolo, 1980.)

longest duration at the bottom), Viviani and Terzuolo could fit straight lines through the reversal points (the points where the sign of the velocity changed from positive to negative, or vice versa). The fact that straight lines could be fit to the points means that the ratios of successive stroke durations within the letter were approximately constant, even though the absolute durations of the strokes varied. Apparently, changes in the *sizes* of the letter were associated with variations in the *absolute* times of the strokes, but the strokes' *relative* times were approximately constant.

The distinction between relative and absolute timing may help explain individual differences in writing style—an issue raised at the beginning of this chapter. Consider the curves in Figure 7.10. These curves, like the ones displayed in Figure 7.9, show a pen's tangential velocity profile as a

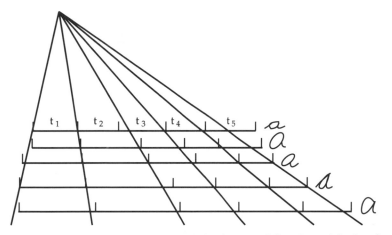

Figure 7.10 Times between pen direction reversals (in the vertical direction only) when five subjects wrote the letter "a." Each row is for a different subject. Each completed letter is shown on the right side. (From Vredenbregt & Koster, 1971.)

function of time during production of the letter "a." Each curve in Figure 7.10 comes from a different writer. The letter "a"s produced by the writers look different, of course, but the relative times of the strokes are approximately constant. This result suggests that the identity of a letter—what makes an "a" an "a," for example—may be defined by its relative timing pattern (not to mention its major spatial features). Differences in *absolute* timing from one writer to the next may explain why one person's writing looks different from another's.

The investigators who obtained the data shown in Figure 7.10 went on to build a writing machine that could produce letters with different forms (see Figure 7.11). The machine had two pairs of motors. One pair produced vertical movements; the other produced horizontal movements. To produce different letters and different forms of the same letter, the timing of the motors (when they came on and off) was varied, but no other control parameters were manipulated. (The mechanical inertia and viscosity of the system allowed smooth lines to be produced even though the motors were abruptly activated and deactivated.) Vredenbregt and Koster (1971) showed that this device could produce shape variations similar to those produced by different writers. Variations in the shapes of particular letters were produced by changing the absolute timing of individual strokes, but identities of letters were preserved by maintaining the relative timing of directional reversals of the moving pen. The writing machine was so successful that it inspired others to design artificial writing systems based on similar principles (Denier van der Gon & Thuring, 1965; Edelman & Flash, 1987; Hollerbach, 1981; Plamondon & Lamarche, 1986).

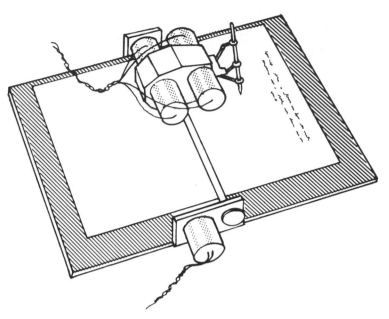

Figure 7.11 The writing device of Vredenbregt and Koster (1971).

Context Effects

One aspect of handwriting that is missing in Vredenbregt and Koster's (1971) model is sensitivity to context. The shape and timing of a letter depends on what letter precedes it (Greer & Green, 1983; Wing, Nimmo-Smith, & Eldridge, 1983) and on what letter follows it (Teulings *et al.*, 1983). For example, Greer and Green (1983) found that when people produce the same letter repeatedly (as in "ee" and "ll") they can write more quickly than when they alternate between different letters ("el" or "le"). Greer and Green (1983) proposed that when the same letter is produced over and over again, a single timing and force program can be used, but when different letters are produced in alternation, the program elements must be changed. Presumably, it takes time to make the needed programming changes, and this slows performance, as discussed in Chapter 3 in connection with the parameter remapping effect (Rosenbaum, Weber, Hazelett, & Hindorff, 1986). Greer and Green's (1983) work suggests that there are limits on the extent to which global rate scaling can be used in handwriting (Gentner, 1987). Nevertheless, their discovery of context effects is consistent with the hierarchical model advocated here because hierarchical models predict that the way a response is produced should depend on its relation to earlier and later responses (Jordan & Rosenbaum, 1989; Lashley, 1951).

■ WRITING AND HANDEDNESS

As mentioned at the start of this chapter, a striking feature of handwriting is that it is most often performed with the right hand. One way to develop an explanation for this fact is to note that the left hemisphere, which is primarily responsible for motor control of the right hand, is generally specialized for language. Since handwriting is a linguistic activity, the right hand might be specialized for writing because it is controlled by the "linguistic" hemisphere.

If this reasoning is correct, then for most people the same hemisphere should control language and handwriting. In fact, it appears that most individuals whose language is centered in the left hemisphere write with the right hand and that most individuals whose language is centered in the right hemisphere write with the left hand (Levy, 1982).

There are some individuals for whom this generalization may not apply, however. Levy and Reid (1976) proposed that people who write with the hand in an inverted position—that is, with the hand held above the line and the pen pointed down toward the bottom of the page (see Figure 7.12)—may have language and manual control centered in *different* hemispheres. These individuals are sometimes called "hookers," by reference to the hooked appearance of their hand. Their method of writing contrasts with the more usual method in which the hand is held below the line, with the pen pointing toward the top of the page. Hooking is rare in right-handed writers but occurs fairly frequently in left-handers; about 50% of left-handed American writers write with a hooked posture (Smith & Moscovitch, 1979).

To evaluate the hypothesis that hookers have language and writing in different cerebral hemispheres, Levy and Reid (1976) tested right- and left-handed writers who were either hookers or not in tasks designed to reveal whether the left or right hemisphere is specialized for language. In their experiment, a numeral and a nonsense syllable were flashed on a screen, with the horizontal positions of the stimuli randomized from trial to trial. The question was which stimulus would be reported. Levy and Reid (1976) assumed that the nonsense syllable would be reported with higher probability than the numeral if it was projected to the hemisphere specialized for language function. By appealing to the known anatomy of the visual system, they further assumed that if the nonsense syllable was reported with high probability when it appeared on the *right* side of the display the subject's *left* hemisphere was specialized for language, but if the nonsense syllable was reported with high probability when it appeared on the *left* side of the display the subject's *right* hemisphere was specialized for language.

The result was that for hookers the nonsense syllable was reported with higher probability when it appeared on the side of the screen *opposite* the writing hand, but for nonhookers the nonsense syllable was reported with higher probability when it appeared on the *same* side of the screen as

Left-handed
writers

Right-handed
writers

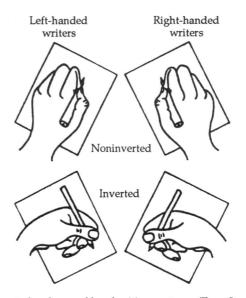

Noninverted

Inverted

Figure 7.12 Inverted and normal handwriting postures. (From Levy & Reid, 1976.)

the writing hand. This result suggests that for hooked writers, verbal function is localized in the hemisphere ipsilateral to (on the same side as) the preferred writing hand, whereas for nonhooked writers verbal function is localized in the hemisphere contralateral to (opposite) the preferred writing hand. The outcome confirms Levy and Reid's (1976) hypothesis that in hookers writing and language are controlled by different hemispheres, whereas in nonhookers writing and language are controlled by the same hemisphere.

As intriguing as this conclusion is, it appears to be wrong. A challenge to Levy and Reid's (1976) study came from Moscovitch and Smith (1979), who suggested that hookers may process *visual* information differently from nonhookers. In the Moscovitch and Smith (1979) study, hookers and nonhookers were asked to respond with either the left or the right hand to an auditory, visual, or tactile stimulus. In each block of trials, the identity of the stimulus and the identity of the response were known ahead of time, and the subject's task was simply to respond as quickly as possible after detecting the stimulus. Moscovitch and Smith (1979) found that hookers responded more quickly to visual stimuli presented opposite the responding hand than to visual stimuli presented on the same side as the responding hand. This result accords with Levy and Reid's (1976) hypothesis that for hookers, each hand is controlled by the *ipsilateral* rather than the *contralateral* hemisphere. Also consistent with Levy and Reid's (1976) hypothesis, *nonhookers* in Moscovitch and Smith's (1979) study were quicker to respond to visual stimuli presented in the visual field on the *same* side as the responding hand. (This result accords with Levy and Reid's proposal because it suggests that in nonhookers, each hand is controlled by the contralateral rather than the ipsilateral hemisphere.)

The problematic results for Levy and Reid (1976) concerned detection of auditory and tactile stimuli. For these stimuli, Moscovitch and Smith (1979) found that hookers *and* nonhookers responded most quickly when the stimuli were presented on the same side as the responding hand. This is what would be expected if each hand were primarily controlled by the contralateral hemisphere in *both* types of writers. The latter result flies in the face (and quite squarely between the eyes) of Levy and Reid's (1976) hypothesis.

How can Moscovitch and Smith's results be explained? Perhaps the simplest explanation is that hookers and nonhookers code visual stimuli in different ways. This hypothesis helps explain why laterality tests with a strong visual component are effective at distinguishing hooked and non-hooked left-handed writers (Smith & Moscovitch, 1979). It also fits with the result that electrophysiological measures reveal differences in the occipital lobe (a center for visual processing) but not in other brain areas (Herron, Galin, Johnstone, & Ornstein, 1979).

■ SUMMARY

1.   Writing and drawing may be controlled through a series of internal decisions or translation processes in which abstract representations of desired outputs are translated into specific, executable instructions. The translation operations can be viewed as steps to successively lower levels of a hierarchy. One source of support for this model is that writing style is preserved when people write with different effectors.

2.   To draw, one must determine the order in which drawing strokes are made. Research on drawing in children and adults suggests that distinct rules may be called upon during the planning of drawing behavior. The rules may ensure mechanical efficiency, but other factors—notably the semantic interpretation of the figure to be drawn—may also affect the order in which strokes are produced. Semantic biases in drawing provide added support for the view that drawing, and graphic behavior in general, is a top-down process.

3.   A way to study the execution of drawing strokes is to record the kinematics of the pen during simple, repetitive drawing tasks such as scribbling, drawing figure eights, or drawing spirals. Research on such elementary drawing tasks has suggested two principles for the control of drawing. One, the *Isogony Principle*, asserts that equal angles are covered in equal times. The Isogony Principle implies that figures are segmented into manageable pieces by the graphic production system and that segments, or sets of segments, are produced in equal amounts of time. The other control principle, the *Two-Thirds Power Law*, asserts that the pen slows down more and more the sharper the curve through which it moves. A possible explanation of this

principle is based on the coupling of oscillators. Another possible explanation is based on the assumption that it is desirable to move as smoothly as possible.

4.   Another way to study the control of handwriting is to classify the kinds of errors that writers make. Based on one such classification scheme, four principal stages in the initiation of handwriting have been proposed. The elements selected in these four stages are (1) the *word*, (2) the *grapheme* (or letter), (3) the *allograph* (or letter form, such as upper or lower case), and (4) the *graph* (or stroke).

5.   People with the neurological disorder *agraphia* display errors consistent with the hierarchical stage model. Some agraphic patients have difficulty producing well-formed writing strokes, although their spelling and word choices are appropriate. Others produce well-formed writing strokes but have difficulty spelling (in writing only), though their word choices are legitimate. The breakdown of specific aspects of handwriting in different individuals suggests that there are distinct mechanisms corresponding to those aspects, each susceptible to damage or deterioration.

6.   Reaction-time studies with normal individuals lend further support to the hierarchical model of writing. Facilitation of reaction times in various task conditions suggests that people can selectively ready grapheme-level programs or allograph-level programs.

7.   Writing size may be controlled by altering the speed of writing. Although *absolute* times of writing strokes may increase as writing size increases, *relative* times of strokes within letters or words remain remarkably invariant over size changes or writers. Writing machines have been designed on the basis of this observation. They produce recognizable letters that can simulate personal writing styles.

8.   A property of writing that must be captured in a complete theory of handwriting is the presence of context effects. The speed with which one letter is written depends on which other letters have just been written or are about to be written. Context effects suggest hierarchical control because they imply that information about forthcoming written responses is available when earlier written responses are produced.

9.   In most people, the hand used for handwriting is controlled by the brain hemisphere specialized for language. It has been proposed that this principle may not hold for people who write with a hooked hand posture ("hookers"). However, this proposal has been supplanted by the hypothesis that hookers and nonhookers may process visual or spatial information differently.

■ REFERENCES

Cromer, R. F. (1983). Hierarchical planning disability in the drawings and constructions of a special group of severely aphasic children. *Brain and Cognition, 2,* 144–164.

Denier van der Gon, J. J., & Thuring, J. P. (1965). The guiding of human writing movements. *Kybernetic*, **2**, 145–148.

Edelman, S., & Flash, T. (1987). A model of handwriting. *Biological Cybernetics*, **57**, 25–36.

Ellis, A. (1979). Slips of the pen. *Visible Language*, **13**, 265–282.

Fischman, J. (1987). Graphology: The write stuff? *Psychology Today*, No. 7, p. 11.

Flash, T., & Hogan, N. (1985). The coordination of arm movements: An experimentally confirmed mathematical model. *Journal of Neuroscience*, **5**, 1688–1703.

Gentner, D. R. (1987). Timing of skilled motor performance: Tests of the proportional duration model. *Psychological Review*, **94**, 255–276.

Goodnow, J. J., (1977). *Children drawing*. Cambridge, MA: Harvard Univ. Press.

Goodnow, J. J., & Levine, R. (1973). The grammar of action: Sequence and syntax in children's copying. *Cognitive Psychology*, **4**, 82–98.

Greer, K., L., & Green, D. W. (1983). Context and motor control in handwriting. *Acta Psychologica*, **54**, 205–215.

Herron, J., Galin, D., Johnstone, J., & Ornstein, R. E. (1979). Cerebral specialization, writing posture, and motor control of writing in left-handers. *Science*, **205**, 1285–1289.

Hogan, N. (1984). An organizing principle for a class of voluntary movements. *Journal of Neuroscience*, **4**, 2745–2754.

Hollerbach, J. M., (1981). An oscillation theory of handwriting. *Biological Cybernetics*, **39**, 139–156.

Hughes, A. E. (1966). *Self-analysis from your handwriting*. New York: Grosset & Dunlap.

Jordan, M. I., & Rosenbaum, D. A. (1989). Action. In M. I. Posner (Ed.), *Foundations of cognitive science* (pp. 727–767). Cambridge, MA: MIT Press.

Keele, S. W. (1987). Sequencing and timing in skilled perception and action: An overview. In A. Allport, D. MacKay, W. Prinz, & E. Scheerer (Eds.), *Language perception and production* (pp. 463–487). London: Academic Press.

Lacquaniti, F., Terzuolo, C., & Viviani, P. (1983). The law relating the kinematic and figural aspects of drawing movements. *Acta Psychologica*, **54**, 115–130.

Lacquaniti, F., Terzuolo, C., & Viviani, P. (1984). Global metric properties and preparatory processes in drawing movements. In S. Kornblum & J. Requin (Eds.), *Preparatory states and processes* (pp. 357–370). Hillsdale, NJ: Erlbaum.

Lashley, K. S. (1951). The problem of serial order in behavior. In L. A. Jeffress (Ed.), *Cerebral mechanisms in behavior* (pp. 112–131). New York: Wiley.

Legge, D., Steinberg, H., & Summerfield, A. (1964). Simple measures of handwriting as indices of drug effects. *Perceptual and Motor Skills*, **18**, 549–558.

Levy, J. (1982). Handwriting posture and cerebral organization: How are they related? *Psychological Bulletin*, **91**, 589–608.

Levy, J., & Reid, M. L. (1976). Variations in writing posture and cerebral organization. *Science*, **194**, 337–339.

Margolin, D. I. (1984). The neuropsychology of writing and spelling: Semantic, phonological, motor, and perceptual processes. *Quarterly Journal of Experimental Psychology*, **36A**, 459–489.

Margolin, D. I., & Wing, A. M. (1983). Agraphia and micrographia: Clinical manifestations of motor programming and performance disorders. *Acta Psychologica*, **54**, 263–283.

Miceli, G., Silveri, C., & Caramazza, A. (1985). Cognitive analysis of a case of pure dysgraphia. *Brain and Language*, **25**, 187–212.

Morasso, P. (1981). Spatial control of arm movements. *Experimental Brain Research*, **42**, 223–227.

Moscovitch, M., & Smith, L. C. (1979). Differences in neural organization between individuals with inverted and noninverted handwriting postures. *Science*, **205**, 710–713.

Plamondon, R., & Lamarche, F. (1986). Modelization of handwriting: A system approach. In H. S. Kao, G. P. van Galen, & R. Hoosain (Eds.), *Graphonomics: Contempoary research in handwriting* (pp. 169–183). Amsterdam: North-Holland.

Roeltgin, D. (1985). Agraphia. In K. M. Heilman & E. Valenstein (Eds.), *Clinical neuropsychology* (2d ed., pp. 75–96). New York: Oxford Univ. Press.

Rosenbaum, D. A., & Kornblum, S. (1982). A priming method for investigating the selection of motor responses. *Acta Psycholgica*, **51**, 223–243.

Rosenbaum, D. A., Weber, R. J., Hazelett, W. M., & Hindorff, V. (1986). The parameter remapping effect in human performance: Evidence from tongue twisters and finger fumblers. *Journal of Memory and Language, 25,* 710–725.

Saltzman, E., & Kelso, J. A. S. (1987). Skilled actions: A task dynamic approach. *Psychological Review, 94,* 84–106.

Smith, L. C., & Moscovitch, M. (1979). Writing posture, hemispheric control of movement and cerebral dominance in individuals with inverted and noninverted hand postures during writing. *Neuropsychologia, 17,* 637–644.

Smith, W. M., McCrary, J. M., & Smith, K. U. (1960). Delayed visual feedback and behavior. *Science, 132,* 1013–1014.

Stelmach, G. E., & Teulings, H.-L. (1983). Response characteristics of prepared and restructured handwriting. *Acta Psychologica, 54,* 51–67.

Teulings, H.-L., Thomassen, A. J., & van Galen, G. P. (1983). Preparation of partly precued handwriting movements: The size of movement units in handwriting. *Acta Psychologica, 54,* 165–177.

Thomassen, A. J., & Teulings, H.-L. (1985). Time, size, and shape in handwriting: Exploring spatio-temporal relationships at different levels. In J. A. Michon & J. B. Jackson (Eds.), *Time, mind, and behavior* (pp. 253–263). Berlin: Springer.

Van Sommers, P. (1984). *Drawing and cognition: Descriptive and experimental studies of graphic production processes.* Cambridge, England: Cambridge Univ. Press.

Van Somers, P. (1986). How the mind draws. *Psychology Today,* May, 62–66.

Viviani, P., & Terzuolo, C. (1980). Space-time invariance in learned motor skills. In G. E. Stelmach & J. Requin (Eds.), *Tutorials in motor behavior* (pp. 525–533). Amsterdam: North-Holland.

Vredenbregt, J., & Koster, W. G. (1971). Analysis and synthesis of handwriting. *Philips Technical Review, 32,* 73–78.

Wann, J. (1987). Trends in refinement and optimization of fine-motor trajectories: Observations from an analysis of the handwriting of primary school children. *Journal of Motor Behavior, 19,* 13–37.

Wann, J., Nimmo-Smith, I., & Wing, A. (1988). Relation between velocity and curvature in movement: Equivalence and divergence between a power law and minimum-jerk model. *Journal of Experimental Psychology: Human Perception and Performance, 14,* 622–637.

Wing, A. (1978). Response timing in handwriting. In G. E. Stelmach (Ed.), *Information processing in motor control and learning* (pp. 153–172). New York: Academic Press.

Wing, A. M., Nimmo-Smith, I., & Eldridge, M. A. (1983). The consistency of cursive letter formation as a function of position in the word. *Acta Psychologica, 54,* 197–204.

Wright, C. E. (1990). Generalized motor programs: Reexamining claims of effector independence in writing. In M. Jeannerod (Ed.), *Attention and performance XIII* (pp. 294–320). Hillsdale, NJ: Erlbaum.

Zimbardo, P. G., Marshall, G., & Maslach, C. (1971). Liberating behavior from time-bound control: Expanding the present through hypnosis. *Journal of Applied Social Psychology, 4,* 305–323.

8 KEYBOARDING

■ INTRODUCTION

In modern offices it is not uncommon to find typists who can produce 60 or even 90 words a minute. Assuming an average of 5 characters per word with 1 space between words, this amounts to 450 keystrokes a minute or 1 keystroke every 133 msec. Pianists can produce keystrokes at even higher rates because they play chords. If a pianist plays 3 notes with each hand at a rate exceeding 3 chords per second, then his or her keystroke rate is 18 keystrokes per second, or more than 1 keystroke every 56 msec on average. How are such high rates of performance achieved?

The rapidity of keyboard performance cannot be accomplished by responding to sensory feedback from each successive keystroke, for the time to respond to an external signal is usually greater than 200 msec. Since times between keystrokes are often shorter than 200 msec, there is likely to be an internal *plan* created before the keystrokes are performed (Lashley, 1951). Understanding the nature of this plan and the way it is executed is the central aim of Keyboarding research.

The organization of the chapter is as follows. First, I consider performance in reaction-time tasks. As mentioned above, the lengths of typical reaction times suggest that rapid keyboard sequences must be based on extended plans. This conclusion implies that reaction-time methodology is useful for resolving issues about the control of keyboard performance. As will be seen, it has also proved helpful in resolving other, more general questions about human information processing.

The second part of the chapter concerns performance in tasks requiring sequences of button presses. Such tasks have enabled researchers to develop detailed models of the memory representations underlying sequential behavior. One of these models assumes that manual response sequences are hierarchically controlled. Another assumes that there are internal timing mechanisms for motor production which may also subserve perception.

The next section of the chapter is concerned with typewriting. An important principle from typewriting research is that typists type quickly by moving their fingers and hands simultaneously. (This finding was mentioned in Chapter 1). Another insight from typing research is that features more primitive than the keystroke are explicitly specified when keystrokes are planned.

The coda of the chapter concerns piano playing. Much of the work in this area reinforces principles covered in the preceding sections. Two new ideas are presented, however. One is that variations in force can be used to communicate musical phrasing. The other is that the expressive speeding and slowing of a piece is far less spontaneous than might be expected. Because such expressive timing becomes highly routined over repeated performances, it may become an integral part of the memory representation for the piece.

■ REACTION TIME

The speed with which one reacts to a signal—one's reaction time (RT)—is a widely used measure of performance. When there is one possible signal and one response associated with it, the dependent measure is the *simple* RT. When there is more than one signal and each signal designates a unique response, the dependent measure is the *choice* RT. Choice RTs are usually longer than simple RTs.

Many factors affect simple and choice RT: the state of the subject, the nature of the stimulus, the nature of the response, the relations among these factors. The literature on RT is massive, so I will not attempt to review it all here. For reviews, see Keele (1986), Luce (1986), Meyer, Osman, Irwin, and Yantis (1990), Welford (1980), Woodworth (1938), and Woodworth & Schlosberg (1954). Some findings that are important for our immediate concerns are reviewed subsequently.

Simple Reaction Time

A number of factors influence simple RT. People who are younger or more alert generally have shorter simple RTs than people who are older or less alert (Woodworth & Schlosberg, 1954). People practiced at a reaction-time task generally produce shorter simple RTs than people who are unpracticed (Woodworth & Schlosberg, 1954). If a person is quite sure about when a signal will occur, his or her simple RT is usually shorter than if the time of the signal is uncertain (Klemmer, 1957). If the time of the signal is completely certain, responses can be made to coincide with or even precede the signal, yielding zero RTs in the former case and negative RTs in the latter. (Responses occurring after the signal have positive RTs.) Experimenters often admonish subjects not to produce negative RTs, and they sometimes introduce "catch trials" with no reaction signal to discourage subjects from anticipating. Because people are good at anticipating signal arrivals, it is reasonable to suppose that they have an internal timekeeping ability, perhaps made possible by one or more internal "clocks." I will return to this issue later in the chapter.

The strength of the reaction signal affects simple RT. People are generally faster to respond to bright lights than to dim lights, particularly when the intensity of the signal is uncertain (Teichner & Krebs, 1972). Similarly, people are generally faster to respond to loud sounds than to soft sounds.

The type of response to be made also influences simple RT. However, some of the response factors that one might expect to influence simple RT do not. There is hardly any difference between the simple RT of the dominant and nondominant hand, and there is hardly any difference between the simple RTs for different fingers (Woodworth, 1938; Woodworth & Schlosberg, 1954). Effectors of large mass generally have longer simple RTs than effectors of small mass. For example, the finger, forearm, and upper arm have simple RTs of 156, 166, and 173 msec, respectively (Anson, 1982). These RT differences are attributable to mechanical factors, for the simple RTs of electromyographic activity in these three effectors (the times when significantly electromyographic activity can be observed after the signal) are the same (Anson, 1982).

Choice Reaction Time

As mentioned before, choice RTs are generally longer than simple RTs. However, if the probability of a choice stimulus is high enough, the corresponding choice RT can approximate a simple RT. This outcome follows from the fact that simple and choice RTs occupy a probability continuum. In a simple RT task, the probability of a response reaches the maximum probability of 1.

Why do choice RTs decrease (get faster) for likely stimuli? Is the effect due to a change in stimulus processing, response processing, or both?

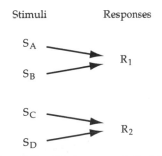

Figure 8.1 Mapping of stimuli to responses in Bertelson's (1965) study.

The question has been addressed by mapping more than one stimulus to a response, as shown in Figure 8.1 (Bertelson, 1965). If subjects respond more quickly to a stimulus because of their preparation to make a particular response, their choice RTs should be reduced by repeated testing of that response, regardless of which stimulus is assigned to it. By contrast if subjects respond more quickly to repeated presentation of a stimulus because of their perceptual set for that stimulus, their choice RTs should be reduced only by repeated presentation of the stimulus. Moreover, a switch to another stimulus should yield equally long choice RTs, regardless of whether the new stimulus summons the same response or a different one.

The results indicate that response preparation contributes to the speeding of responses associated with repeated tests of a stimulus–response pair. In Bertelson's (1965) experiment, two stimuli S_A and S_B were assigned to the same response. Stimulus S_A was presented repeatedly and choice RTs decreased accordingly. When stimulus S_A was replaced with stimulus S_B,

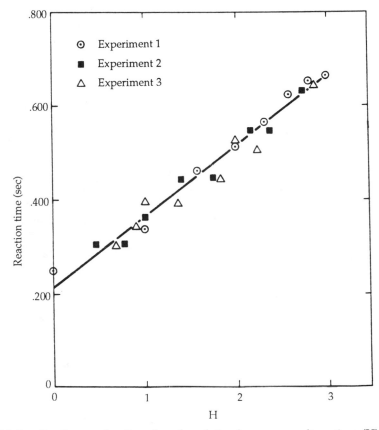

Figure 8.2 Reaction time as a function of number of stimulus–response alternatives (H). Data from three experiments and best fitting line ($\hat{Y} = 212 - 153X$), with correlation $r = .985$ between reaction time and H. (From Fitts & Posner, 1967.)

there was some elevation of choice RTs, but the elevation was much smaller than when stimulus S_A was replaced by a stimulus that called for a different response (S_C or S_D). Thus response preparation served to reduce choice RTs, but perceptual set also contributed to the repetition effect. [Other experiments have led to the same conclusion; for review, see Keele (1986).]

As the number of possible stimulus–response pairs in a choice RT experiment increases, the choice reaction time also increases. Figure 8.2 shows the results of such an experiment, where on each trial one of n lights was turned on and the subject's task was to press the key beneath it. Choice RT increased linearly with the logarithm (to the base 2) of the number of stimulus–response alternatives. This relation is known as the Hick–Hyman Law (Hick, 1952; Hyman, 1953). It is one of the most famous relations in RT research. In the Hick–Hyman Law, it is assumed that decision making can be characterized by the number of binary digits, or *bits*, that uniquely define a particular response. In effect, the subject is assumed to play "20 questions" to determine which response should be performed given that a stimulus has appeared. The number of bits (or "questions" for n equally likely stimulus–response alternatives is $\log_2 n$. According to the Hick–Hyman Law, bits are set (binary decisions are made) at a rate approximating the slope of the best-fitting straight-line function relating choice RT to $\log_2 n$. The rate is about 150 msec per bit of information (see Figure 8.2).

Stimulus–Response Compatibility

Characterizing decision making as a series of binary decisions accords with an influential theory of communication developed in the late 1940s, *information* theory (Shannon & Weaver, 1949). The theory's application to human information processing received a boost through the success of the Hick–Hyman Law, but then received a setback when it was shown that the amount of information that can be held in short-term memory depends not on how many "bits" the information has (roughly, the number of questions required to identify it), but rather on how many meaningful units or "chunks" it contains (Miller, 1956). It was not possible in 1956, nor has it since become possible, to measure meaningfulness in terms of information theory.

Another blow to information theory (or at least the Hick–Hyman Law) came from studies of *stimulus–response* (S–R) compatibility. In a representative (and classic) experiment (Leonard, 1959), subjects rested their fingers on small vibrators and whenever a vibrator came on, the finger resting on the vibrator was supposed to be pressed. As the number of possible vibrators increased, there was virtually no increase in choice RT. Thus choice RT did not consistently increase with the number of S–R alternatives.

What accounts for the virtual lack of an uncertainty effect in this situation? Leonard (1959) found that choice RTs *did* obey the usual uncertainty effect when subjects were asked not to respond with the stimulated finger but instead to respond with another finger, specifically assigned to the vibrator that came on.

Based on this pair of results—the virtual *absence* of an uncertainty effect when subjects pressed fingers that received vibration and the *presence* of an uncertainty effect when subjects pressed fingers that did not receive vibration—Leonard (1959) concluded that when the responding and stimulated finger were the same, there was a highly effective, or *compatible*, mapping between the stimulus and response. However, when the finger to be pressed did not directly contact the vibrator, the S–R mapping was less compatible, and subjects had to choose the required response through a more deliberate, time-consuming process, akin to the one implied by the Hick–Hyman Law.

Stimulus–response compatibility is an important factor in virtually all kinds of RT tasks, ranging from button pressing (Craft & Simon, 1970; Inhoff, Rosenbaum, Gordon, & Campbell, 1984) to handwriting (Greenwald, 1970) to speech production (Gordon & Meyer, 1987; Rosenbaum, Gordon, Stillings, & Feinstein, 1987). Stimulus–response compatibility has also been used to shed light on the codes used for movement initiation. Recall from Chapter 1 that Wallace (1971) studied how quickly subjects could respond to a visual signal on the left or right with the left or right hand when the hands were either crossed or uncrossed (Figure 1.8). He found that S–R compatibility was defined principally by the *spatial* relation between stimulus and response, not by the anatomical identity of the hand making the response. Thus subjects were faster to make a response on the same side of the body midline as the signal, regardless of whether the hand making the response was the left hand or right. This outcome suggests that S–R compatibility is defined primarily by the mappings between stimulus and response *locations* (see also Attneave & Benson, 1969; Wickens, 1938).

Response–Response Compatibility

Just as the relation between stimulus and response affects choice RT, so does the relation between or among possible responses. The interaction between responses is called *response–response*, or R–R, compatibility. Response–response compatibility can be defined as the tendency for a response to have different choice RTs depending on the other response or responses that can be tested.

One of the first reports of an R–R compatibility effect was presented by Kornblum (1965). Subjects in his experiment performed in two choice RT conditions. In one, they chose between button presses made with the index and middle fingers of the right hand. In the other, they chose between button presses of the index finger of the right hand and the index finger of the left hand. The signals were the same in these two conditions, but the choice RT for the right index finger (which was used in both conditions) turned out to be shorter when the alternative response was made with the left index finger than when it was made with the right middle finger. Thus the choice RT for the same response (or what was ostensibly the same response) following the same signal was affected by the identity of the other possible response.

What accounts for this result? Kornblum (1965) suggested that there is more competition or inhibition between fingers of the same hand than between fingers of different hands. The index and middle finger of one hand are linked mechanically, whereas the index finger of one hand and the middle finger of the other hand are essentially mechanically independent. You can demonstrate this difference for yourself by trying to hold one finger rigid while oscillating the other. It is nearly impossible to keep the index finger still while wiggling the middle finger of the same hand. By contrast, the stability of the index finger is hardly affected by oscillation of the index or middle finger of the *other* hand. Assuming that the greater independence between the fingers of the two hands makes it easier to prepare to respond with those fingers, it is possible to account for Kornblum's (1965) R–R compatibility effect in just the way he did. One simply needs to equate mechanical independence with preparatory independence. As will be seen later in this chapter, this explanation also finds support in typewriting research.

■ SEQUENCES OF FINGER PRESSES

In the studies I have reviewed so far, subjects pressed a button with one finger when a signal was presented. Because the aim of this chapter is to shed light on the control of extended sequences of keypresses, it is also important to consider tasks in which subjects perform more than one keypress per trial. Two laboratory tasks are relevant in this regard. In one, subjects press two or more keys simultaneously; that is, they produce *chords*. In the other, subjects produce *series* of keypresses, either in response to external signals indicating which key is to be pressed or on the basis of memory.

Simultaneous Keypresses

There has been remarkably little research on chord production, though it is indispensable in a number of practical domains. Pianists play chords, of course, as do courtroom stenographers when transcribing oral testimony. The most efficient way to type Japanese characters is also to press several keys at once (Yamada, 1983).

Rabbitt, Fearnley, and Vyas (1975) asked how quickly people could make chord responses on a keyboard, where the combination of keystrokes at any time was designated by combinations of lights above the keys. Rabbitt *et al.* (1975) found that the choice RT to produce a chord increased with the number of keystrokes within it. In addition, choice RTs were shorter for responses that used homologous fingers of the two hands (for example, the two index fingers or the two middle fingers) than for responses that used nonhomologous fingers of the two hands (for example, the left index finger and the right middle finger). Choice RTs also depended on the relation between the number of keystrokes in *successive* chords. As the number of keystrokes in a chord increased, the choice RT for the subsequent chord also increased. This result may have been due to the time demands of monitoring response accuracy, for Rabbitt *et al.* also found that the time to detect errors in a chord increased with the chord's complexity.

I know of only one other study of chord performance. Gopher, Karis, and Koenig (1985) studied performance on a chord keyboard where subjects tried to learn to produce different chords in response to different letters. There were three rules for assigning letters to chords (Figure 8.3). In one, the keys pressed with the two hands were *spatially* congruent, so if a letter was assigned to the two left keys for the left hand, the subject also had to depress the two left keys for the right hand. This meant that different fingers of the two hands had to be pressed simultaneously. In another arrangement, the keys pressed with the two hands were *manually* congruent, so all two-hand chords used homologous fingers. (Thus in this condition a given chord was produced with the two middle fingers, with the two index fingers, and so on.) A third arrangement combined spatial congruity and manual symmetry. This was achieved by vertically tilting the keyboards for the left and right hands (see Figure 8.3) so that homologous fingers pressed keys that were also spatially congruent. In all three conditions, subjects were shown letters and were asked to produce the corresponding chords as quickly and accurately as possible. The practical question was what arrangement of keys and

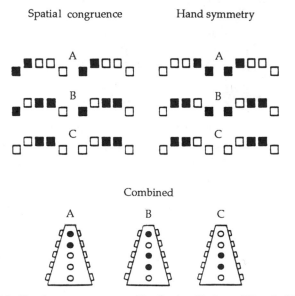

Figure 8.3 Chord arrangements used by Gopher, Karis, and Koenig (1985).

what assignment of letters to keys would be learned most easily. Gopher *et al.* found that performance was best in the combined arrangement, intermediate in the spatial-congruity arrangement, and worst in the hand-symmetry arrangement.

In considering what caused this outcome, one must first evaluate the possibility that the superiority of the combined arrangement was due to the vertical posture of the hands, which was unique for the combined-arrangement condition. When subjects from the combined-arrangement group were later asked to perform with their hands in the flat orientation, they still did very well. Moreover, when a new group of subjects was taught to adopt the same S–R mapping rule as the combined group but with their hands held flat, they also performed adroitly. Thus vertical hand postures alone did not ensure efficient chord typing. What is more likely is that the combined arrangement was especially effective because it allowed subjects to alternate between spatial and anatomical coding strategies. This interpretation implies that the way subjects mentally represent S–R mappings significantly affects their performance (Proctor & Reeve, 1989).

Sequences of Single Keypresses

Now consider the production of sequences of single keystrokes. We begin with studies in which successive keystrokes are evoked by series of distinct signals presented in rapid succession; the task is called serial choice RT.

Rabbitt and Vyas (1970) performed a serial choice RT experiment in which subjects were asked to press one key at a time with the index and middle fingers of the left and right hands following the appearance of one of four digits on a screen. Subjects were fastest when they pressed a finger of one hand after a response was made with the homologous finger of the other hand, they were somewhat slower when the finger to be pressed was on the same hand as the immediately preceding response but used a different finger (for example, left index finger after left middle finger), and they were slowest when the finger to be pressed used a different hand *and* was nonhomologous to the finger used in the immediately preceding response (for example, left index finger after right middle finger). One way to interpret this pattern of results is that when subjects used one hand after the other, they could prepare one response while the preceding response was being completed. When successive responses were made with one hand, the preparation of one response could not begin until the previous response was completed. This explanation is similar to the one given for Kornblum's (1965) finding. (It will prove useful again when we consider typewriting.)

What about the advantage of performing successive responses with homologous fingers, for example, right index finger after left index finger? The explanation just given does not account for this result. A way to explain the homologous-finger effect is to assume that the neural representations of homologous fingers are linked and that the activation of one neural representation primes the other. Recall that this hypothesis was supported in the chord study I just reviewed (Rabbitt, *et al.*, 1974), where people performed two-hand homologous finger combinations more quickly than two-hand nonhomologous finger combinations. As will be seen in the section on typewriting, aspects of typewriting behavior also support the hypothesis that there are functional links between homologous fingers.

In Rabbitt and Vyas' (1970) serial choice RT study, the sequence of signals from trial to trial was random. In other studies, investigators have examined performance when the train of response signals is structured. This work has shown that people are adept at taking advantage of structure when it is available. When signals follow a predictable pattern, people can respond to the signals more quickly and accurately than when the signals are unpredictable (Restle, 1970). For example, you probably would have a hard time learning to anticipate numbers in the sequence 416253415234, but you would have an easier time learning to anticipate numbers in the sequence 432154326543. The former sequence is random. The latter sequence has structure: It can be described as a series of four descending numbers, starting at 4, where the series ascends in steps of 1. Once this descriptive rule has been assimilated, the sequence can be performed rapidly and accurately. This implies that the internal representation for a sequence is more than just a linear sequence of event-to-event associations. Instead, rules defining relations among the events (as well as relations among the relations) also form part of the memory representation for the sequence. [This is not to say that linear associations are *never* used. They may be when rule-based descriptions have not been discovered or when the sequence is very short (Keele & Summers, 1976).]

When the memory representation for a sequence is rule based, it is hierarchical. This is so because rules defining relations among the basic elements of a sequence (for example, the keystrokes) presuppose superordinate relationships between or among the elements (Jones, 1981). For example, recognizing that the sequence 5432 is a one-step upward transposition of 4321, as implied in the preceding description, assumes that 4321 is recognized as a transposable unit.

Granted that sequences may be represented hierarchically, a question that remains is whether they are *executed* in a way that depends directly on that hierarchical organization. My colleagues and I tried to address this issue by asking subjects to perform short keyboard sequences entirely from memory (Rosenbaum, Kenny, & Derr, 1983). A representative sequence was IiIiMmMm, where I and i denote keypresses made with the right and left index fingers, respectively, and M and m denote keypresses made with the right and left middle fingers, respectively. Subjects were instructed to perform the sequence six times consecutively as quickly and accurately as possible. Try performing the task yourself.

Figure 8.4 shows the mean latency for each response in the sequence. The speed with which each response was performed depended on its serial position in the sequence. Responses 1 and 5 had the longest latencies, responses 3 and 7 had intermediate latencies, and responses 2, 4, 6, and 8 had the shortest latencies. The errors followed a similar pattern.

To account for these results, we elaborated a previously developed theory of memory retrieval (Johnson, 1972). According to our elaboration, motor programs are structured hierarchically and are "unpacked" during execution. The process can be likened to accessing files in a file cabinet. To access a file, the appropriate drawer must be opened, then the correct folder must be located, and then the correct file within that folder must be found. If the next file that is needed is in the same folder, it can be found relatively quickly, if it is in a different folder of the same drawer, more time is needed to find it, and if it is in a different folder and in a different drawer, the access time is longer still. The opportunity for making an error also increases with the number of compartments to be accessed.

Graphically, this process can be depicted as a tree-traversal process (see Figure 8.5). The picture allows one to count the number of nodes between successive responses. The question is whether the number of nodes predicts the delay between successive output events (retrieving one file after another or pressing successive keys). Happily, the model provides an excellent account of the latency data in our experiment. Latencies increased with the number of nodes to be traversed between successive keypresses. Furthermore, the number and types of errors also agreed with the model (see Rosenbaum *et al.*, 1983, for details).

The tree-traversal model of performance implies that the program for a sequence of keyboard responses is both structured and executed hierar-

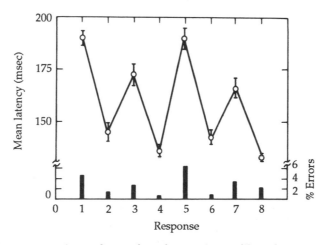

Figure 8.4 Interresponse time and errors from the experiment of Rosenbaum, Kenny, and Derr (1983). The times and errors associated with response 1 are restricted to productions of response 1 after response 8 in the second through sixth cycles of the sequence. From D. A. Rosenbaum, S. Kenny, & M. A. Derr (1983). Hierarchical control of rapid movement sequences. *Journal of Experimental Psychology: Human Perception and Performance,* **9,** 86–102. Copyright © 1983 by the American Psychological Association. Reprinted with permission.

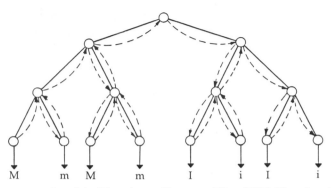

Figure 8.5 Tree-traversal model of Rosenbaum, Kenny, and Derr (1983). M, m, I, and i denote keypresses with the left and right middle fingers and left and right index fingers, respectively. From D. A. Rosenbaum, S. Kenny, & M. A. Derr (1983). Hierarchical control of rapid movement sequences. *Journal of Experimental Psychology: Human Perception and Performance, **9**,* 86–102. Copyright © 1983 by the American Psychological Association. Reprinted with permission.

chically (see also Collard & Povel, 1982). The success of the model implies that motor programs are not simply linear strings of instructions. If they were, the errors and latencies from our study would have been uniform across serial positions, which they were not. Another model that can be rejected assumes that motor programs are hierarchically organized but *executed* linearly. This model would have predicted a flat latency curve, which is not what was found. It appears then, that subjects relied on a full tree-traversal process to produce their responses. The fact that they did so suggests that the memory system responsible for storing low-level motor commands cannot hold a large number of commands at once. Accessing high-level memory codes (that is, traversing the higher branches of the tree) provides a way of generating responses whose motor commands cannot be maintained initially (along with commands for other preceding responses) in a low-level motor output buffer—what I have elsewhere called the MOB (Rosenbaum, 1990). (See Chapter 3 for further discussion of the motor output buffer.)

Control of Rhythm and Timing

So far I have considered how people control the serial order of responses that are to be produced as quickly as possible. It is now time to consider timing. The first question is how people vary delays between successive keypresses. In a typical experiment concerned with this question, people are asked to tap a key at a rate specified by a metronome. The metronome goes off soon after the person starts tapping and a computer records the times between the taps that the person produces. Among the results that have been obtained with this procedure, two are noteworthy for present purposes (Wing & Kristofferson, 1973). First, times between successive keypresses are negatively correlated. That is, if one interresponse interval is long, the next one tends to be short, and vice versa. The second important finding is that the variance of the interresponse intervals grows with the mean of the interval.

Wing and Kristofferson (1973) developed a model to account for these results. The model has two components (see Figure 8.6): A *motor delay* between the trigger of a response and its execution, and a *timekeeper delay* between the trigger for one response and the trigger for the next. According to the model, the observed interval between response i and response $i + 1$ is $C + d_{i+1} - d_i$, where C is the timekeeper delay between the trigger for response i and the trigger for response $i + 1$, d_{i+1} is the motor delay between the trigger for response $i + 1$ and its execution, and d_i is the motor delay between the trigger for response i and its execution.

Wing and Kristofferson's model predicts that successive response intervals should be negatively correlated. To see why, consider what happens if the motor delay for a response happens to be longer than normal. Because the response defines the end of one interval and the start of the next, the longer-than-usual motor delay results in a shorter-than-usual subsequent interval. Similarly, if the motor delay happens to be short, resulting in a short preceding interval, the interval after the response will be longer than usual. Thus variations in motor delays give rise to negatively correlated successive intervals. Such negative correlations have been observed in tapping studies, as mentioned earlier. In fact, they were reported as long ago as 1886 (see Wing, 1980) although they were then attributed to the operation of a feedback correction mechanism. The idea was that a central monitor compensated for timing errors in successive interresponse intervals in order to keep the mean interval close to the target. Such corrections have been shown to occur (see Wing, 1980), but they are not strictly required to account for the negative-correlation result.

Another implication of Wing and Kristofferson's model is that the variability of interresponse intervals should increase with the size of the interval produced. This prediction arises from the fact that a timekeeper (or clock) "pulsing" at a variable rate will give rise to more net variability as it pulses more. Figure 8.7 shows data consistent with this prediction. The data were obtained in an experiment in which subjects were supposed to tap a

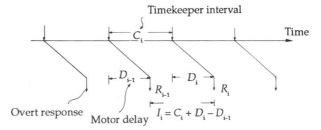

Figure 8.6 Wing's (1980) timing model. See text for explanation of notation.

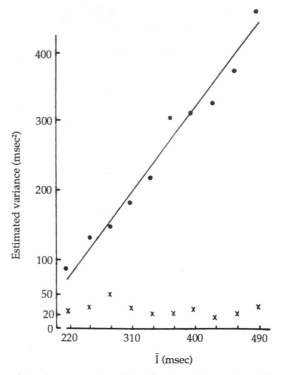

Figure 8.7 Estimated timekeeper variance (●) and motor-delay variance (x) as a function of mean interresponse interval ($\overline{I}$). (Adapted from Wing, 1980.)

finger repeatedly and as evenly as possible at a rate specified by a metronome. As the intertap interval increased (that is, as the tapping rate decreased) the variance of the intertap interval grew.

Perhaps the most intriguing aspect of Wing and Kristofferson's model is that it allows one to derive independent estimates of the variance of motor delays and the variance of clock delays. (The method for doing so relies on mathematical derivations which need not be reviewed here; see Pew & Rosenbaum, 1988, and Wing, 1980, for reviews.) Figure 8.7 shows that the estimates of clock variance and motor-delay variance behave as expected from Wing and Kristofferson's model. As the interresponse interval increases, the clock variance increases but the motor-delay variance remains approximately constant. This result confirms the hypothesis that motor delays and clock delays are independent.

Further support for the independence of motor delays and clock delays has been obtained in a patient with Parkinson's disease (Wing, Keele, & Margolin, 1984). In this patient, the disease was restricted to one brain hemisphere. The patient showed increased clock variance when using the hand contralateral to the *diseased* hemisphere but normal clock variance when using the hand contralateral to the *normal* hemisphere. Neither hand showed

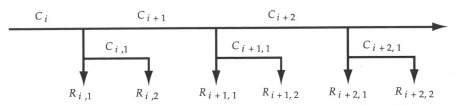

Figure 8.8 Hierarchical timing system of Vorberg and Hambuch (1978). C_i, C_{i+1}, and C_{i+2} denote clock delays for the ith, $i + 1$th, and $i + 2$th measure; $C_{i,1}$, $C_{i+1,1}$, and $C_{i+2,1}$ denote lower-order clock delays for the first interval within each measure; responses are denoted with subscripted Rs.

unusual motor-delay variance. Dissociating clock-delay variance and motor-delay variance in a neurological patient suggests that the two mechanisms have distinct physiological representations, a conclusion consistent with the assumption in the Wing and Kristofferson model that clock delays and motor delays are controlled independently.

Hierarchical Timekeepers

Wing and Kristofferson's (1973) timing model is linear. To increase the time between responses, one increases timekeeper delays, differences between motor delays, or both. An additive increase in either variable yields an additive increase in the interresponse interval. A possible drawback of this system is that in rhythmic performance it might be difficult to "keep the beat." That is, because there are no higher-level units controlling groups of responses, the delay between the first note in one measure and the first note in the next measure might be just as variable as the sum of the delays between the successive notes within a measure. From a musical standpoint, it would be desirable if the beat were steady even if the notes within measures happened to speed up or slow down. Listening to a drummer makes the point clear. The drummer's foot keeps pounding the bass drum at a relatively constant rate. Meanwhile, the drumsticks may strike the upper drums at rates that fluctuate depending on the difficulty of the sequence being performed or on subtle "bends" intentionally added to the rhythm.

Pounding a bass drum while other events are occurring exemplifies a model of timing and rhythm developed by Vorberg and Hambuch (1978, 1984; see Figure 8.8). The model assumes that high-level timers control delays between major downbeats and that lower-level timers control delays between other notes (or responses). The key feature of the model is that it is hierarchical.

How can the hierarchical-timekeeper model be tested? As mentioned above, if the downbeat of each measure is timed relative to the immediately preceding response, as in Wing and Kristofferson's (1973) model, the variance of the delay between successive downbeats should equal the sum of the variances of the delays between the notes lying between the downbeats.

However, if downbeats are timed only with respect to other downbeats, as in Vorberg and Hambuch's model, the variance of the delay between downbeats should be *smaller* than the sum of the variances of the notes between the downbeats.

This prediction was confirmed by Shaffer (1984) in a study of piano playing. Using a specially equipped piano that allowed for the electronic recording of individual keystrokes, Shaffer (1984) found, in performances of works by Bach, Beethoven, and Chopin, that the variance of delays from one downbeat to the next was less than the sum of the variances of the individual notes between the downbeats. Vorberg and Hambuch (1984) also tested their model and found support for it in sequences with unequal intervals. Sequences with equal intervals appeared to be timed linearly; for these sequences, downbeats did not confer any special reduction in timing variance. From this set of results, it appears that performers have available different methods of timing control depending on the complexity of the sequences being produced. Sequences with unequal intervals appear to be controlled hierarchically whereas sequences with equal intervals appear to be controlled linearly. For polyrhythms, still other methods appear to be called upon depending on the rhythmic relations of the notes played by the left and right hands (Jagacinski, Marshburn, Klapp, & Jones, 1988).

The Amodality of Timing

Because many responses must be timed with reference to external events—hitting an approaching baseball, playing a note in time with a conductor's downbeat, reaching out and shaking another person's hand—it is plausible that the mechanisms used for timing movements are also used for timing perceptual events. Several lines of evidence suggest that this is indeed the case.

One originates with Steven Keele and his colleagues at the University of Oregon (Keele, 1987; Keele & Ivry, 1987; Keele, Pokorny, Corcos, & Ivry, 1985). Keele *et al.* (1985) asked people to make regular tapping responses with the finger or foot. Over subjects, the variance of interresponse intervals correlated significantly between the finger and foot. Thus a person with low variability in finger tapping was also likely to have low variability in foot tapping. The individuals in this study also varied in their ability to judge brief intervals between auditory events. Most importantly, individuals who were good at perceptual timing were also good at motor timing. The correlation between tapping and perceptual judgment was about the same as the correlation between tapping with the finger and tapping with the foot. This result is what one would expect if one thought that timing is controlled with a mechanism that is amodal (not specifically tied to a particular modality).

In evaluating these data it is important to consider a possible artifact. It may be that some people are more conscientious than others or have less "neural noise" than others. If this were the case, one would expect people who are good at timing to be good at controlling muscle forces—another task that probably benefits from care or steadiness. Keele, Ivry, and Pokorny (1987) found, however, that accuracy of controlling muscle forces was *not* correlated with the precision of timing control, though the force control achieved with the finger was correlated with that achieved with the forearm or foot. From the fact that force accuracy was not correlated with timing accuracy, one can conclude that the significant correlations between motor timing and perceptual timing observed by Keele *et al.* (1985) were not artifactual. Moreover, timing and force may be governed independently, perhaps by different parts of the brain (Keele & Ivry, 1987). (Recall that independent control of force and timing was postulated for eye movements; see p. 168.)

A second line of evidence for the hypothesis that timing is amodal is that people have difficulty controlling rhythmic responses made with one hand while an opposing rhythm must be performed or perceptually monitored. Recall from Chapters 1 and 6 that people find it difficult to perform cyclical movements with one hand without influence from the other hand. For example, they find it difficult to tap rhythmic patterns with the two hands when the patterns are not integral multiples of one another. Tapping 3 against 4 is very difficult, for example (Peters, 1977). Likewise, it is difficult to tap one rhythm and orally produce another incompatible rhythm (Klapp, 1979). Finally, tapping one rhythmic sequence while listening to a sequence of tones with another rhythmic structure leads to disruptions in ongoing performance (Klapp *et al.*, 1985). The fact that rhythmic interference extends across output modalities (manual and oral) and between hearing and tapping suggests that the locus of the interference is not tied to a single input or output channel.

A third source of evidence for the amodality of timing is a study done in my laboratory (Rosenbaum & Patashnik, 1980) on preparation for timing production or judgment. In the production task, subjects pressed the left index finger and then the right index finger, with a prescribed delay between the two responses. The accuracy of the produced intervals relative to the target was indicated by feedback. Subjects were remarkably accurate in this task. The mean intervals they produced fell within a few milliseconds of the target, even for targets exceeding 1 sec (the maximum target interval was 1050 msec). To investigate preparation, we also required subjects to minimize the simple RT for the first tap after an imperative signal. Simple RT decreased with the length of the interval to be produced, and was longer when a second response was required than when no second response was required (see Figure 8.9A, B). (The latencies were *simple* reaction times because only one target interval was tested in each block of trials.)

We accounted for these results by assuming that subjects controlled the times between finger taps with an internal "alarm clock." The first response was triggered when the alarm-clock interval began, and the second response was triggered when the alarm-clock interval ended (when the alarm "went off"). We assumed that, to achieve maximum accuracy, the clock had to be set before being activated. Consequently, when the required precision of the interval was minimal the time spent setting the clock could be small, but when the required precision was high the clock had to be set more carefully and the required setting time increased.

In the time-*judgment* task, the second response was replaced with a mechanical pulse applied to the right finger. The subject was supposed to judge whether the interval between the finger tap and the mechanical pulse was greater or less than a target interval. The target intervals used in this task were the same as those used in the two-response task. As shown in Figure 8.9C,D, simple RTs to initiate the finger response in the judgment task were similar to the simple RTs in the production task (see Rosenbaum, 1983). Because the first finger response served to initiate a time delay in both conditions, the fact that similar results were obtained suggests that the timing mechanism was neither specifically motor nor specifically perceptual.

Integration of Serial Order and Timing

So far, I have discussed the timing and serial ordering of keystrokes as if they were two separate control problems. In practice they are not. If the timing of responses is specified, their serial order is necessarily determined (Rosenbaum, 1985). Said differently, once it is known that the time between event A and event B is +5 sec, then it follows that event A precedes event B (provided the + sign has been defined this way). Similarly, if it is known that the time between event A and event B is −5 sec, then it follows that event B precedes event A (again, provided the − sign has been appropriately defined). Thus once the timing of two events is specified, their serial order is also known. This observation suggests that serial order and timing may not require separate control mechanisms. The studies described next support this hypothesis.

Summers (1975) trained subjects to press nine keys in a specific order and with a specific timing pattern indicated by flashing lights. The durations

Figure 8.9 (A) Simple RT to press the left index finger when the right index finger would be pressed later or when the right index finger would not be pressed later (I = ∞). The target delays are enumerated on the abscissa. The relation between simple RT and mean interresponse interval was more pronounced when the interval had to be close to the target interval (stringent, ○) than when it did not have to be close to the target interval (relaxed, ●). (B) Variances of interresponse intervals were higher in the relaxed condition than in the stringent condition. (C) Simple RT to press the left index finger when mechanical vibration would be applied to the right index finger and the produced delay was to be judged against a standard or when no judgment was required (I = ∞). The accuracy requirement was stringent in this condition. (D) Estimated variance of the interval again increased with interval size. (Adapted from Rosenbaum & Patashnik, 1980.)

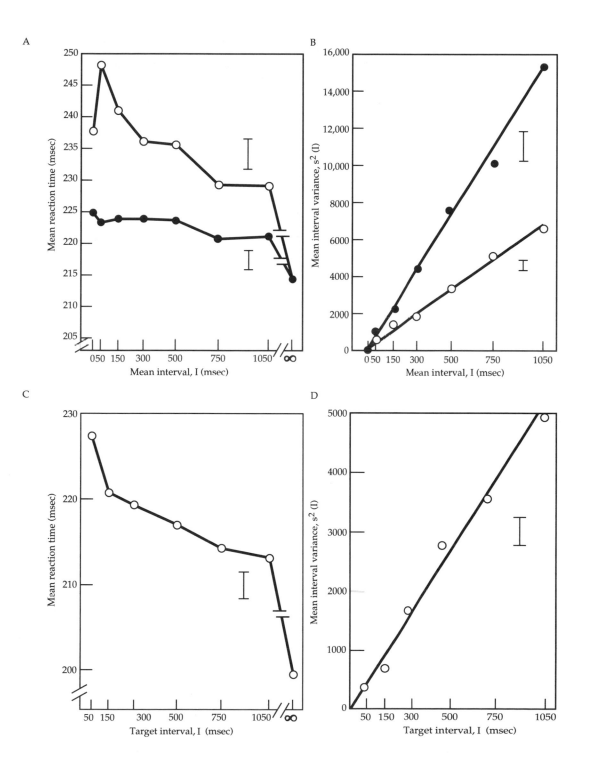

A

Mean reaction time (msec) vs Mean interval, I (msec)

B

Mean interval variance, s^2 (I) vs Mean interval, I (msec)

C

Mean reaction time (msec) vs Target interval, I (msec)

D

Mean interval variance, s^2 (I) vs Target interval, I (msec)

of the lights indicated the durations to be produced. For one group of subjects, the first light stayed on for 500 msec, the second light stayed on for 500 msec, the third light stayed on for 100 msec, and then this same "500-500-100" pattern was repeated two more times. For another group, the first light stayed on for 500 msec, the second light stayed on for 100 msec (rather than 500 msec), the third light stayed on for 100 msec, and then this "500-100-100" cycle was repeated twice more. The important feature of the experiment was that only the rhythms differed in the two conditions. The fingers making the responses and the locations where the responses were made were the same.

After performing the same sequence for nearly 500 trials over two sessions, all subjects were asked to perform the original sequence as quickly as possible but without regard to the original timing pattern. They succeeded at producing the sequences at a higher rate than before, but they could not escape the original rhythm (see Figure 8.10). This finding suggests that the timing of each finger sequence became an integral part of the memory representation for the sequence. With sufficient additional practice, the original timing pattern disappeared (Keele & Summers, 1976).

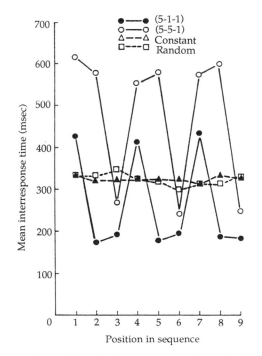

Figure 8.10 Interresponse intervals for a keyboard sequence learned with different prescribed intervals when it was produced at the originally practiced rate and then as quickly as possible. 5-1-1, ●—●; 5-5-1, ○—○; constant, ▲—▲; random, □—□. (From Keele & Summers, 1976.)

Adjusting the Rate of Production for Entire Sequences

If the timing of a sequence of keyboard responses becomes integrally related to the serial order of the sequence, then finding such an integral relationship suggests that the timing of the sequence was learned along with its serial order. Pursuing this line of reasoning, Terzuolo and Viviani (1980) provided one of the most intriguing and, as it turns out, controversial, findings in human motor control. Terzuolo and Viviani (1980) explored the possibility that adjustments in the overall rate of production for a response sequence can be achieved by modulating the rate at which a clock triggers all the responses within the sequence. Suppose you have learned to produce a sequence of four button presses so the delay between the first response and the second is 500 msec, the delay between the second response and the third is 250 msec, and the delay between the third response and the fourth is 100 msec. An efficient way to slow the entire sequence is to slow a clock that triggers all the responses. For example, to slow the sequence by 20%, you could increase the value of a "multiplicative rate parameter," r, from 1 to 1.2. Thus if the timing of the sequence were represented (symbolically) as $r(500,250,100)$, increasing r from 1 to 1.2 would cause the interresponse intervals to take on the values 600, 300, and 120 msec, respectively. Alternatively, if r increased from 1 to 1.5 to produce a 50% slow-down, the interresponse intervals would be 750, 375, and 150 msec, respectively. Plotting the interresponse intervals for $r = 1$, 1.2, and 1.5, the resultant pattern is a fan (see Figure 8.11A). Another way to plot the data is to turn them on their side, placing the successive responses of a sequence that are produced at a particular rate on a time line (see Figure 8.11B). When this is done, the result is a downward-spreading rather than an upward-spreading fan.

Terzuolo and Viviani (1980) presented timing data from typewriting which support the hypothesis that timing can be controlled with a multiplicative rate parameter (Figure 8.12). The data come from different renditions of the word *enclosed*, produced unintentionally at different speeds by one typist. As shown in Figure 8.12, the vertical fan effect was obtained, and straight lines could be fitted to the individual keystrokes, as predicted by the multiplicative rate model. Thus the data are consistent with the hypothesis that the overall speed of keyboard performance can be controlled by adjusting the rate at which a clock paces production of a scheduled sequence of keystrokes. Viviani and Terzuolo (1980) obtained similar results for handwriting (see Figure 7.9), which they took to suggest that this method of controlling response rates applies to different response systems.

Terzuolo and Viviani's (1980) model is compelling and their graph is striking. However, in a detailed review of the literature on the multiplicative rate hypothesis, Gentner (1987) concluded that the evidence favoring the hypothesis is tenuous. Gentner (1987) proposed a test of the multiplicative rate hypothesis that was more stringent than the one developed by Terzuolo and

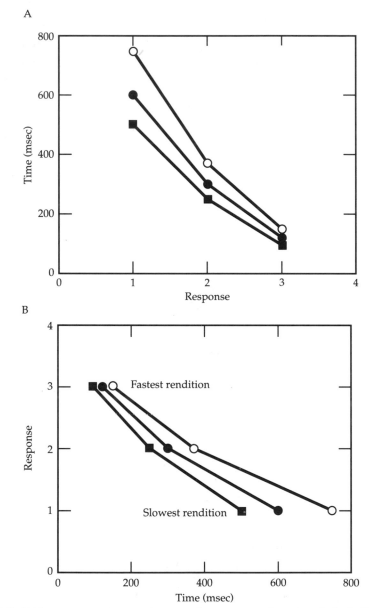

Figure 8.11 (A) Interresponse time as a function of response number when the basic time sequence has been scaled by a multiplicative rate parameter, r, with three different values. $r = 1.50$, ○; $r = 1.20$, ●; $r = 1.00$, ■. (B) Same data turned sideways.

Viviani (1980). He reasoned that if the hypothesis is correct, when a word is typed at different rates, the time to type any given letter in the word (after the immediately preceding letter) should be a constant proportion of the word's total duration. To understand this prediction, consider the hypothet-

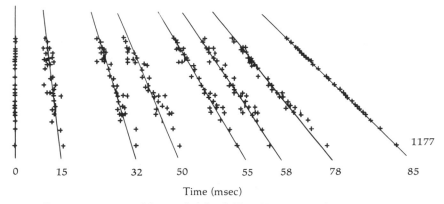

Figure 8.12 Fan representation of the word *enclosed*. (From Viviani, 1980.)

ical response sequence described earlier in this section. Recall that the sequence had interresponse times of 500, 250, and 100 msec at the fastest speed, interresponse times of 600, 300, and 120 msec at the intermediate speed, and interresponse times of 750, 375, and 150 msec at the slowest speed. The total durations for these renditions are therefore 850, 1020, and 1275 msec. Considering any of the responses in the sequence—say the last response—its latency is a constant proportion of the total sequence duration: $100/850 = 120/1020 = 150/1275 = .1176$. Constancy of this kind is therefore indicative of multiplicative rate modulation.

When Gentner (1987) tested this prediction, he did not find it to be generally supported, so he concluded that the multiplicative rate hypothesis is not generally correct. A question remaining from Gentner's (1987) analysis is whether his statistical test was too stringent. One difficulty with his test is that it is valid only if one assumes that all responses must have the same motor delay (Heuer, 1988). When this assumption is relaxed, the multiplicative rate hypothesis stands a better chance of survival.

■ TYPEWRITING

Let us now consider typewriting in more detail, having just mentioned one of the studies that used it. First, I will consider some historical issues surrounding typewriting research. Then I will discuss typing errors and what they reveal about the units of typing control. Next, I will focus on keystroke timing. The final part of this section will review an influential theory of typewriting control developed by Rumelhart and Norman (1982).

Historical Issues

Typewriter keyboards are so common today that it is hard to imagine that society ever functioned without them. In fact, the typewriter as we now know it did not come into wide use until the last century. The first practical typewriter was developed in Milwaukee in the mid-1800s and was manufactured by a company that then specialized in gun-making (E. Remington and Sons). Typewriters soon were used by professional authors. The first complete type-written manuscript was "Tom Sawyer" by Mark Twain (Cooper, 1983).

The most common arrangement of keys on the keyboard was developed by the entrepreneur who promoted the typewriter in the United States (Christopher Sholes). This is the *qwerty* keyboard, named after the positions of the top left keys (see Figure 8.13A). Rumor has it that Sholes chose the qwerty arrangement to make it hard to use. By placing common letter pairs far apart, Sholes supposedly attempted to discourage typists from jamming the keys by typing too quickly. The story is most likely false because large spaces between keys do not slow performance. Furthermore, the qwerty arrangement was introduced before typists typed quickly, owing to their ignorance of "touch-typing" (Gentner & Norman, 1984).

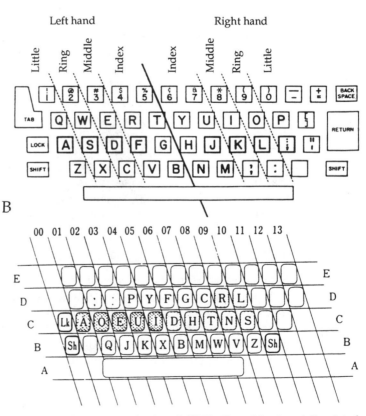

Figure 8.13 (A) The Qwerty keyboard. (B) The Dvorak keyboard. Reprinted from Cooper, 1983, by permission of Springer-Verlag.

Other keyboard designs have been developed since qwerty, and some of them permit slightly higher typing speeds than the qwerty arrangement. The best known example is the Dvorak keyboard (Figure 8.13B), designed at the University of Washington in the 1930s. The switch to Dvorak has been hampered by economic factors. It has been difficult to induce already skilled typists to relearn old typing habits, and it has been hard to pry typewriter companies from their established manufacturing designs, though in the long run their profit margins might improve if they did (David, 1985).

Whether typing is faster with 10 fingers or 2 (as in the "hunt-and-peck" method) was hotly debated in the early years of the typewriter. Resolution of the debate came in a highly publicized speed-typing contest held in Cincinnati in 1888 between two men claiming to be the world's fastest typist. The winner typed with 10 fingers and memorized the layout of the keyboard beforehand, enabling him to keep his eyes on the page as he typed. Because of his victory, touch typing came to be accepted as the preferred method for office personnel.

One of the first questions asked in the scientific study of typewriting was where the eyes are in relation to the hand. At what characters do typists look when typing? There has been remarkably little research on this topic, and most of it was done in the 1930s and 1940s (Butsch, 1932; Fuller, 1943). This work indicates that the eye typically leads the hand by about four to eight letters—a lag commonly referred to as the *eye–hand span*. The eye–hand span is considerably shorter than the *eye–voice* span—the lag between where one is looking and what one is reading aloud. (The eye–voice span is about 12 to 24 letters.) Delays between successive visual fixations are longer in typing than in reading, and locations of fixations appear less related to word boundaries when one types than when one reads (Cooper, 1983). Butsch (1932) summarized the role of eye movements in typing by saying that the typist "reads only rapidly enough to supply the copy to the hand as it is needed" (p. 113). As might be expected from this claim, typists often report that they have little or no comprehension of what they type (at least in copy-typing situations). Highly proficient typists can engage in conversations while typing and their typing speed and accuracy suffers little (Shaffer, 1975b).

What one transcribes has important effects on the speed with which one types. Transcribing words arranged in a haphazard order does not slow performance as compared to transcribing words that are ordered normally. Nonwords are typed significantly slower than words, however (Fendrick, 1937).

One way the importance of words over nonwords has been demonstrated is to vary the amount of preview that typists have of the material they are to copy. As shown in Figure 8.14, normal prose can be typed at a maximum rate when eight or more characters are visible in advance; the maximum rate for prose is approximately the same as the rate attained with fully previewed, random word streams. By contrast, random letter strings,

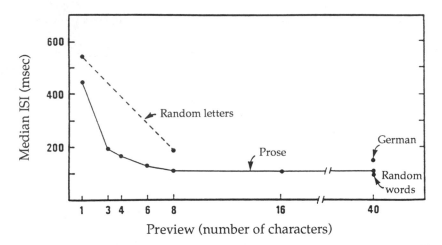

Figure 8.14 Median interstroke interval (ISI) when a variable number of characters could be previewed and where different kinds of material were to be typed. (From Shaffer, 1973.)

like random words, benefit from preview, but not as much. Even when eight characters of a nonword can be seen in advance, the mean typing rate is slower than when the eight characters form a word (Shaffer, 1973).

These effects of preview accord with Butsch's hypothesis that there is a "supply line" between the eye and the hand. In terms of information-processing models of performance, the results shown in Figure 8.14 suggest that perceptual information is held in a buffer until it can be accessed or decoded by a system that ultimately produces keystrokes (Cooper, 1983; Logan, 1983). Another implication of the preview results is that typists produce keystrokes in units no longer than a word. If the production unit were longer than a word, word order would have an effect on typing speed.

Units of Typing Control

Because words are typed more quickly than nonwords, words have special status as production units for typing. It does not follow, however, that words are the *smallest* units for typing. Because words are made of letter strings, it is possible that groups of letters, or even single letters, are production units for typing (that is, elements controlled directly by the motor system). One source of evidence that there are production elements smaller than the word is that typists can stop typing upon hearing a tone regardless of whether they are within or between words (Logan, 1982). If words were indivisible production units, it should be impossible to interrupt them.

Typists also stop within words when they spontaneously detect errors. Long (1976) asked typists to stop and correct errors as soon as any errors occurred. In the vast majority of cases, typing ceased as soon as an error was made. Similarly, Rabbitt (1978) asked typists simply to stop typing as soon as they noted an error. In 95% of the occasions when an error occurred, no subsequent keystrokes were made.

Some errors appear to be detected even *before* they are physically produced. Incorrect keystrokes are made less forcefully than correct keystrokes (Rabbitt, 1978), and incorrect keystrokes have longer latencies than correct keystrokes (Shaffer, 1975a). Because incorrect keystrokes are produced differently from correct keystrokes, information about the accuracy of the keystrokes must be available before the errors are manifested physically.

Are there regularities in the identities of errors that typists produce? Lessenberry (1928) compiled 60,000 typing errors and counted the number of times that a given letter was typed when that or another letter was (apparently) intended. Lessenberry (1928) found that the majority of errors consisted of hitting the key that was horizontally adjacent to the intended letter (for example, typing *miatake* instead of *mistake*), the next most frequent error was hitting the key vertically adjacent to the key that should have been struck (for example, typing *mixtake* instead of *mistake*), and the third most common mistake was substituting the finger of one hand for the like-named finger of the other hand—so-called *homologous* finger substitutions (for example, typing *d* instead of *k* with the middle finger).

Lessenberry (1928) suggested that hitting keys horizontally or vertically adjacent to the correct key was due to misaiming; the correct finger simply went too far to the left, too far to the right, too high, or too low. Subsequent film analyses revealed that this explanation was off target. Grudin (1983) found that when the wrong key was typed, it was almost always struck by the correct finger. Thus in an error such as *miatake*, the *a* was typed with the little finger, not the ring finger. Thus the error was not one of misdirecting the correctly chosen finger, as Lessenberry (1928) supposed, but instead entailed selecting the incorrect key and using the correct finger for that key. This observation suggests that keys and fingers are identified separately. Keys may be identified on the basis of their remembered spatial locations, but the fingers associated with those locations are selected separately, apparently in a distinct stage of processing, presumably *after* the spatial location has been picked.

Homologous finger substitutions, the third most common error recorded by Lessenberry (1928), add further weight to the hypothesis that fingers are explicitly identified during keystroke selection. The substitution of one finger for its twin suggests that decisions are made to use a particular *type* of finger but with an incorrect decision about the hand to which the finger belongs. For example, in substituting *k* for *d*, (both struck with the middle finger), the decision to use the middle finger is apparently dissociated from the decision to use the right or left hand (see pp. 89–90).

Error analyses suggest that there is yet another "low-level" keystroke feature that may play a role in typewriting control. Grudin (1983) and Munhall and Ostry (1983) observed that *b* and *n* are sometimes substituted for one another but *b* and *u* rarely are. The *b* and the *n* both have down and "inward" movement components (the hands are brought in from the home row of the keyboard), but *b* and *u* are achieved with movements of opposite direction (*b* goes in but *u* goes out). If movement *direction* were not specified explicitly, one would not expect *b-n* confusions to be more prevalent than *b-u* confusions.

Timing of Keystrokes in Typewriting

As stated at the beginning of this chapter, skilled typists can type at impressive speeds. Also, as mentioned in the last section, typing speeds are higher for words than for nonwords. In general, the higher the frequency of a word, the more quickly it can be typed (Fendrick, 1937; Gentner, Larochelle, & Grudin, 1988; Shaffer, 1973; West & Sabban, 1982). The frequency with which one letter follows another within a word (*digraph* frequency) also affects typing speed. The higher the digraph frequency, the shorter the time between the first letter and the second (Gentner *et al.*, 1988; Terzuolo & Viviani, 1980).

Times between keystrokes also depend on the relation between the finger and hand making the keystrokes. Transitions between keystrokes made by different hands are faster than transitions between keystrokes made by different fingers of the same hand, and transitions between different fingers of the same hand are faster than transitions between repeated keystrokes made by the same finger (Coover, 1923). The basis for this effect is entirely mechanical. Films of typists' hands reveal that the hands and fingers move continually, not waiting passively until previous keystrokes have been completed (see Figure 1.6). Each finger moves toward its target, subject only to mechanical interference by previous keystrokes (Gentner, Grudin, & Conway, 1980; Larochelle, 1983; Olsen & Murray, 1976).

Can other keystroke timing effects also be explained mechanically? For example, are word-frequency and digraph-frequency effects due to mechanical factors? The alternative hypothesis would be that word-frequency and digraph-frequency effects derive from *central* limitations, such as the speed with which typists can access lexical memory (the part of memory where word representations are stored).

One approach to this problem has been to study keystroke timing when subjects become highly prepared to produce brief bursts of keystrokes. According to one author, "... the inability to take advantage of a preparation interval seems to indicate that the programming of typing movements is intimately linked to their execution" (Ostry, 1983, p. 225). By this line of reasoning, if mechanical factors account for the fact that cross-hand transitions are faster than within-hand transitions, then even when typists can prepare keystrokes in advance, the cross-hand benefit should be evident.

A study by Sternberg, Monsell, Knoll, and Wright (1978) confirms this prediction. They asked skilled typists to produce letter strings from memory following the appearance of a reaction signal. On each trial, a letter

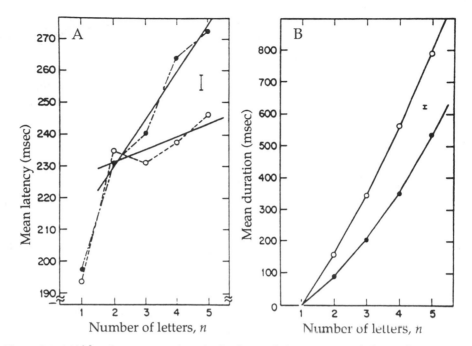

Figure 8.15 (A) Mean latency to produce the first keystroke in a sequence of n keystrokes following a reaction signal. Linear functions are fitted to the data for $n \geq 2$. (B) Mean durations are complete sequences. Alternating hands ●; one hand, ○. (From Sternberg et al., 1978.)

string appeared and then a series of warning tones sounded to enable subjects to become highly prepared to respond. On 85% of the trials, the reaction signal was presented at the end of the series of warning tones and the subject was then supposed to produce the sequence as quickly as possible. On the remaining 15% of the trials no reaction signal was presented and the subject was supposed to withhold his or her response. (These catch trials were included to discourage subjects from anticipating the signal.)

The data are shown in Figure 8.15. As shown in panel A, the time for the first keypress increased with the number of keystrokes to be typed. The rate of increase for the latency function was higher for keystroke sequences requiring strict hand alternation than for keystroke sequences requiring only one hand. The mean duration of the keystroke sequence (panel B) also increased with sequence length, and was longer for one-hand sequences than for two-hand sequences. A final result, not shown in Figure 8.15, is that keystroke times for words were indistinguishable from keystroke times for random letter strings.

Let us consider these data in light of the criterion given earlier for mechanical sources of performance effects. First, the difference between within-hand and between-hand timing was apparently due to motor execution, since this difference was obtained even under a state of high preparation. Second, the difference between words and nonwords found earlier by

Fendrick (1937) and Shaffer (1973) was apparently *not* due to execution, since this difference vanished when subjects could become highly prepared to type one string at a time.

Gentner *et al.* (1988) offered additional criteria for identifying peripheral and central sources of timing effects in typewriting. They focused on digraph- and word-frequency effects, seeking to determine why high-frequency words are typed more quickly than low-frequency words and why high-frequency digraphs are typed more quickly than low-frequency digraphs. (High-frequency words are not simply faster because they are made up of high-frequency digraphs, for the correlation between the frequencies of words and the frequencies of their constituent digraphs is modest; see Gentner *et al.*, 1988.) Gentner *et al.* (1988) reasoned that if the source of the digraph-frequency effect is central, then if a digraph is frequent in one language but infrequent in another, the speed of typing the digraph should be different in the two languages. On the other hand, if the digraph-frequency effect derives from peripheral factors, then, since the mechanics of the hands are the same for speakers of the two languages, the speed of typing the digraph should be the same for both groups. Using Dutch and American typists, Gentner *et al.* (1988) obtained evidence for a mechanical basis of the digraph-frequency effect. They found that the difficulty of producing digraphs did not depend on the frequency of the digraphs within the two languages. The difficulty of producing whole words, however, did depend on the words' frequency within the typist's language. (The typists studied by Gentner *et al.* were monolingual.) Based on these results, Gentner *et al.* concluded that word-frequency effects are centrally based but digraph-frequency effects are peripherally, or mechanically, based. Recall that I reached the same conclusion about word-frequency effects by considering the findings of Sternberg *et al.* (1978). These authors found that word-frequency effects disappeared under conditions of maximal single-word preparation.

Gentner *et al.* (1988) offered a further demonstration that word- and digraph-frequency effects have different origins. As shown in Figure 8.16, they found that words that were initially typed slowly were typed more and more quickly as they were repeated. By contrast, digraphs that were typed slowly at first continued to be typed slowly no matter how often they were repeated. The fact that digraphs did not improve with practice suggests that the factor limiting their performance was in the periphery, where practice presumably has little short-term effect on speed.

Rumelhart and Norman's (1982) Model of Typewriting

It would be gratifying if all the phenomena of typing performance could be accounted for with one unified theory. The most comprehensive theory that has been developed was proposed by Rumelhart and Norman (1982). It deserves careful scrutiny, not only because of its usefulness for the analysis of typewriting but also because of its historical importance for cognitive science

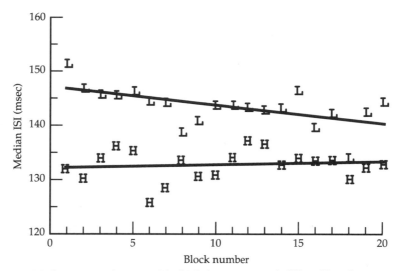

Figure 8.16 Median interstroke interval for high-frequency words (H) and low-frequency words (L) as a function of practice. (From Gentner, Larochelle, & Grudin, 1988.)

at large. Rumelhart and Norman's model was a precursor of "connectionist" models of memory and performance (Rumelhart, McClelland, & the PDP Research Group, 1986). A connectionist model consists of a collection of units, often represented as points or "nodes," joined by links. All the information stored in the network is embodied in its interconnections. In general, the only kind of activity in a connectionist network is activation or inhibition.

In Rumelhart and Norman's model of typewriting (see Figure 8.17) distinct nodes exist for each key of the keyboard. Nodes allow for associations between fingers and keys. The node for the letter "v" associates the left index finger with the "v" key, the node for the letter "e" associates the left middle finger with the "e" key, and so on. When a decision is made to type a word such as *very*, the *v*, *e*, *r*, and *y* nodes are activated, along with the connections among them. The connections define the serial order of the letters. The *v* node inhibits the nodes for *e*, *r*, and *y*, the *e* node inhibits the nodes for *r* and *y*, and the *r* node inhibits the node for *y*. Thus this is an interelement inhibition model (see pp. 83–85). When a node is activated, its keystroke is initiated, but once the keystroke has been initiated, its own node is inhibited. At first, the only node that is uninhibited is *v*, so the *v* keystroke is initiated. A short time later, the *v* node is inhibited and so it stops inhibiting the other nodes. As a result, one node is now uninhibited— the one for *e*—and so the *e* keystroke begins. Shortly thereafter, the *e* node is inhibited, so it stops inhibiting the nodes for *r* and *y*. The *r* node is then released from inhibition, so it is initiated, and finally its self-inhibition allows the *y* keystroke to begin.

In Rumelhart and Norman's model, nodes are self-inhibited as soon as their corresponding keystrokes are initiated, but they can also be self-inhibited before their corresponding keystrokes are completed. Because the

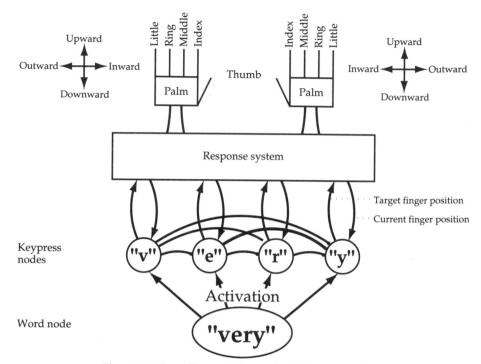

Figure 8.17 Rumelhart and Norman's (1982) typing model.

self-inhibition of a node can occur while its keystroke is still in progress, subsequent keystrokes can begin while preceding keystrokes are under way. This provides a way of explaining the simultaneous activity of hands and fingers during typewriting. Another important feature of the model is that many timing relations between keystrokes arise entirely from the mechanical coupling of the hands and fingers; they are not explicitly controlled by the network. If a keystroke is initiated while another keystroke is under way, its trajectory is influenced by the earlier stroke. Specifically, each keystroke proceeds more and more directly to its target the less it is mechanically coupled to the hand or finger still performing an earlier keystroke. If the keystroke being performed uses the identical finger to the keystroke before it, it undergoes a detour, if it uses a different finger of the same hand, it undergoes less of a detour, and if it uses the other hand, it undergoes even less of a detour. Thus Rumelhart and Norman's model relies on mechanical interactions to account for the within-hand and between-hand timing effects observed in typewriting.

Another important feature of Rumelhart and Norman's typing model is that it lacks a mechanism for timing, although it has a mechanism for serial ordering (inhibitory connections from "early" to "late" response nodes). At first, the absence of a timing mechanism is appealing, for generally one wants to have the most parsimonious model possible. Nevertheless, it may be that a timing mechanism is necessary. Grudin (cited in Gentner & Norman, 1984) observed that transposition errors preserve the timing of correct keystroke orders. When typists type *thme* instead of *them*, for example, the *m* is typed at the time that *e* usually occurs. *A priori*, one might expect *e* and *m* to be typed in the wrong order because the initiation of *m* happened to come a bit too early relative to the initiation of *e*. If this were the case, *m* and *e* would often by typed almost simultaneously, though by chance there would be a few instances in which *m* happened to come first. Grudin observed instead that the delays between *m* and *e* were usually as long as the delays between *e* and *m*. This surprising phenomenon suggests that timing may be independently represented in the plan for keystrokes, contrary to what Rumelhart and Norman assumed.

Another timing-related problem with Rumelhart and Norman's model is that it appears to make some wrong predictions about variations in overall typing rate. The only way to vary typing rates within Rumelhart and Norman's model is to change inhibition levels among letter nodes. When this is done, however, the simulated timing changes do not agree with those observed in real typing (Gentner, 1987, p. 272). Whether this problem can be fixed without an explicit timing mechanism remains to be seen.

One other assumption in Rumelhart and Norman's model that runs into problems is allowance for *type* nodes (for example, the *o* type) but not *token* nodes (for example, o_1 and o_2). Rumelhart and Norman assumed that there can be only one node per key. To account for the fact that some words use the same letter twice in a row, Rumelhart and Norman had to assume that there is a "doubling operator." Consistent with this assumption, they found that typists often double the wrong letter of a word with a repeated letter (for example, *llok* instead of *look*). The price paid for the exclusion of tokens is that sequences with repeating, displaced elements must be broken into two subsequences. For example, ABCA must be broken into two subsequences, one containing the first A and the other containing the second. A prediction arising from this state of affairs is that the typing of the first segment should be unaffected by characteristics of the second segment, and vice versa, since the two segments are assumed to be separate. Yet coarticulation effects are widespread in typing and extend across subsequences containing the same letter (Shaffer, 1975a). Hence this feature of Rumelhart and Norman's model needs to be revised. So too may the fact that, in its current form, the model does not acknowledge a lexical level of representation: It fails to predict that words should be typed more quickly than nonwords. The model also lacks a level of representation below the keystroke, and so does not predict homologous substitutions, homologous direction errors, and finger misidentification errors (reviewed earlier). Still, in spite of its shortcomings, Rumelhart and Norman's model is the most comprehensive and detailed model of typewriting currently available. It represents an important advance in the modeling of human motor control and should serve as a useful starting point for future research.

■ PIANO PLAYING

In typing, one's responsibility is to produce printed output as quickly and accurately as possible. The timing of keystrokes and the forces applied to the keys are usually not available for public scrutiny. In piano playing and other forms of musical performance, times and forces of keystrokes must be controlled to shape the rhythm, phrasing, and expressiveness of the piece being played. How are these aspects controlled?

A study by Sloboda (1983) provides useful information on this issue. He showed pianists two scores. The notes in the scores were the same but the positions of the notes with respect to the bar lines were different. Consequently, only the phrasing differed (see Figure 8.18). The pianists were asked to play the pieces for a listener. Because the notes were the same, any differences in phrasing had to be communicated through the timing or forces of the pianist's keystrokes. To study these features of performance, Sloboda used a piano—the same one used by Shaffer (1984a)—fitted with optical sensors. Two sensors were dedicated to each hammer. One detected movement of the hammer near its resting position, making it possible to record when the hammer left the home position and returned to it. The other sensor detected movement of the hammer near the string, making it possible to record when the hammer approached the string and returned from it. The travel time between the resting position and the string was used to estimate how hard the hammer struck the string, and therefore how loud the note was. Loudness was assumed to be inversely related to the hammer's travel time.

Figure 8.19 (top panel) shows the loudness profile for the 18 notes in the two sequences. Although the profiles were produced by the same pianist, they differed systematically. The peaks of the loudness functions were displaced by one note, as were the bars for the two scores. The times between the notes, however, were nearly identical (see Figure 8.19, bottom panel).

Several inferences can be drawn from these results. First, pianists can communicate musical meter by modulating keystroke force. Second, changes in the forces of keystrokes can be achieved without observable timing changes; pianists can independently vary keystroke times and forces, allowing for a wider range of expression than if force and time were depen-

Figure 8.18 Two musical scores by Sloboda (1983). The notes are the same, but their positions in the measures differ. (From Sloboda, 1983.)

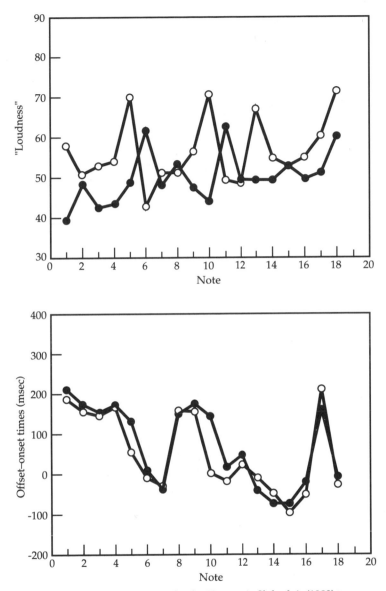

Figure 8.19 *Top panel:* "Loudness" values for the 18 notes in Sloboda's (1983) two sequences (sequence A, ○; sequence B, ●). Loudness was defined as the reciprocal of the time between when the hammer departed from its resting position and when it struck the string. *Bottom panel:* Times between release of one note and onset of the next for the same 18 notes. The data come from one pianist. (Data from Sloboda, 1983.)

dent. [This result is reminiscent of the finding, reviewed earlier in this chapter, that force control and timing control are only weakly correlated (Keele *et al.*, 1987).] The third implication is that when distinct timing profiles are observed for rapid series of keystrokes, they need not be attributed to force modulation alone. This makes it safe to attribute timing variations to internal control processes, as assumed by Rosenbaum *et al.* (1983) and Collard and Povel (1982).

The fourth implication of Sloboda's (1983) results stems from the fact that his data show a remarkable periodicity, stretching over an eight-note span (see Figure 8.19, bottom panel). Similar patterns have been observed by Shaffer (1984b), who found that the timing of keystrokes for a Chopin étude had a period of four bars, with peaks in the interstroke function at the start of each four-bar section corresponding to the major phrases of the piece. Patterns like these are similar to the ones reported by Collard and Povel (1982) and by my colleagues and me (Rosenbaum *et al.*, 1983), discussed earlier in this chapter (see Figure 8.4). As in the latter studies, the regular pattern of peaks and troughs in piano keystroke timing suggests hierarchical control of successive keystrokes and groups of keystrokes (Shaffer, 1984b).

One last comment about piano performance concerns the opportunity it affords for the study of free timing changes (*rubatos*). In Chopin's music, for example, the expressiveness of the piece depends on the pianist's judicious departure from a strict tempo. The rhythm must "bend" to reflect ebbs and flows of emotion. Little is known about the control of rubato, although it has been established that the rubato pattern for a piece becomes highly stereotyped with practice (Seashore, 1938; Shaffer, 1984a, 1984b).

Shaffer (1984a, 1984b) suggested that rubato is controlled at a lower level than musical meter (the "beat"). Controlling meter at a higher level allows it to remain fixed, free from local timing changes. (Recall my earlier comment about the drummer keeping the beat with his or her foot.)

There are many other interesting questions that could be addressed about piano playing (as well as the playing of other keyboard instruments). One is how pianists select fingering patterns when they sight read. Improvisation at the keyboard is another worthwhile, though difficult, topic for future investigation. Jazz pianists invent new keyboard patterns while playing. Recording the timing and intensity of their keystrokes might shed light on the process of musical invention.

■ SUMMARY

1. People can perform keyboard sequences at the typewriter or at the piano at high rates. Because times between keystrokes can be shorter than reaction times (RTs) to external signals (less than 150–200 msec), rapid sequences of keystrokes are probably based on central *plans*.

2. Studies of reaction time provide useful information about the preparation of motor responses as well as the organization of the information processing system. When subjects know in advance what signal will be presented and what response will have to be performed when it appears, the measure is the *simple* RT. Simple RTs depend on the subject's practice, alertness, and age, as well as the strength of the signal and, to a small extent, the type of response being performed. Mechanical inertia accounts for simple RT differences between large and small effectors.

3. When there are several possible stimuli and distinct responses associated with them, the time to respond is the *choice* RT. Choice RTs are usually longer than simple RTs. Choice RTs depend on response preparation as well as stimulus expectancy. They also increase with the number of possible stimulus–response (S–R) pairs, although the magnitude of this effect depends strongly on S–R compatibility. Choice RTs also depend on the relations between or among the responses that are possible. When there are two possible responses and they can be made with different hands, choice RTs are generally shorter than when the two possible responses are made with one hand.

4. Choice RTs for chord responses increase with the number of responses in the chord to be produced as well as the number of responses in the chord just performed. There is also a benefit in producing chords using homologous fingers of the two hands (for instance, using the left and right index fingers). Learning to produce chords associated with distinct stimuli is facilitated when the chords use homologous fingers and the constituent responses are spatially congruent.

5. Serial choice RTs (where each stimulus calling for a response immediately follows the preceding response) are fastest when successive responses are made with homologous fingers of the two hands. Thus the homologous-finger advantage is present in serial choice RT tasks as well as chord production tasks.

6. Sequences of finger patterns are facilitated when the sequences are hierarchically organized. Central programs for rapid finger sequences appear to be structured and executed in a way that depends on hierarchical organization.

7. When people intentionally vary delays between successive finger taps, they may rely on a mechanism that triggers responses at time intervals controlled by an internal timekeeper or clock. Variability of clock delays can be separated from variability of motor delays (that is, delays between central triggers and the ensuing responses).

8. When it is necessary to "keep the beat" while other, more rapid responses are occurring, it is desirable to rely on *hierarchical* timekeepers that control delays between beats independently of lower-level timekeepers that control delays within beats. As predicted by such a hierarchical-timekeeper model, variances of times between beats are sometimes *less* than sums of variances of times within beats.

9. Timekeepers subserve perception as well as motor control, and so can be said to be *amodal*. People adept at motor timing are also adept at perceptual timing. Rhythmic performance suffers when conflicting rhythms must be produced in disparate motor subsystems or when a rhythm must be produced while a conflicting rhythm is being perceptually monitored. The time to prepare for the production of a time interval is similar to the time to prepare for the perception of that same time interval.

10. The timing of a keyboard sequence can become integrally related to the memory for the serial order of that sequence. After a sequence has been performed repeatedly with a particular timing pattern, it is difficult to perform the sequence more quickly without a vestige of the original timing scheme.

11. Adjusting the overall rate of performance for a sequence of responses (keyboard or otherwise) may be achieved by altering the rate at which the individual responses are triggered. This may be done by adjusting a "multiplicative rate parameter" for the entire sequence, although the evidence for this strategy is controversial.

12. Typewriters became popular in the nineteenth century, as did the "qwerty" keyboard and the "touch-typing" method.

13. There is an eye–hand span of about four to eight letters in typing, implying that typists temporarily store in memory verbal material to be transcribed. Typists do better when typing words than nonwords, but randomly ordered words are typed as quickly as sentences. The latter outcome suggests that words are special production units for typewriting.

14. Although words may be special production units, they are not produced as indivisible units. Typists can stop typing within words upon hearing a stop tone or upon detecting an error. The fact that typing can cease at any point implies that individual keystrokes may also be important production units for typing.

15. Still lower-level units are implied by typing errors. Typists' mistakes suggest that key location, finger type (index, middle, ring, or little), hand, and the direction of motion of the keystroke are explicitly specified in typewriting control. Because all these features are needed to fully define a keystroke, the keystroke need not be viewed as the most fundamental unit of typing control.

16. Some aspects of the timing of keystrokes are attributable to mechanical interactions between the hands and fingers. Times between successive keystrokes made by the two hands are shorter than times between successive keystrokes made by different fingers of the same hand, and these in turn are shorter than times between successive keystrokes made by one finger. Film analyses indicate that these timing effects are due to differences in the opportunity for one finger to move toward its target as the previous

keystroke is being performed. Simultaneous movements are easiest when the preceding keystroke is made by the opposite hand, and is hardest (or impossible) when the preceding keystroke is made by the identical finger.

17. A model of typewriting control, developed by Rumelhart and Norman (1982), relies on mechanical interactions to account for observed timing effects. The model also assumes that there are nodes that allow for associations between fingers and keys. Inhibitory connections between nodes provide for the serial order of keystrokes. Rumelhart and Norman's model is a precursor of modern connectionist models of memory and performance.

18. Piano playing has rhythmic and expressive elements not found in typewriting. Pianists can convey different metrical organizations of the same notes by varying the times and forces of keystrokes.

19. The timing of piano sequences appears to be well remembered, for the subtle timing variations associated with rubato become routinized with practice. It is possible that, like the timing of finger-tapping sequences, rubato becomes an integral part of the memory representation for the sequence as a whole.

■ REFERENCES

Anson, J. G. (1982). Memory drum theory: Alternative tests and explanations for the complexity effects on simple reaction time. *Journal of Motor Behavior*, **14**, 228–246.

Attneave, F., & Benson, B. (1969). Spatial coding of tactual stimulation. *Journal of Experimental Psychology*, **81**, 216–222.

Bertelson, P. (1965). Serial choice reaction-time as a function of response versus signal-and-response repetition. *Nature (London)*, **205**, 217–218.

Butsch, R.L.C. (1932). Eye movements and the eye-hand span in typewriting. *Journal of Educational Psychology*, **23**, 104–121.

Collard, R., & Povel, D.-J. (1982). Theory of serial pattern production: Tree traversals. *Psychological Review*, **85**, 693–707.

Cooper, W. E. (1983). Introduction. In W. E. Cooper (Ed.), *Cognitive aspects of skilled typewriting* (pp. 1–38). New York: Springer-Verlag.

Coover, J. E. (1923). A method of teaching typewriting based upon a psychological analysis of expert typing. *National Educational Association*, **61**, 561–567.

Craft, J. L., & Simon, J. R. (1970). Processing symbolic information from a visual display: Interference from an irrelevant directional cue. *Journal of Experimental Psychology*, **83**, 415–420.

David, P. (1985). Clio and the economics of QWERTY. *American Economic Review*, May. (Cited in *The Stanford Observer*, April 1985, p.4)

Fendrick, P. (1937). Hierarchical skills in typewriting. *Journal of Educational Psychology*, **28**, 609–620.

Fitts, P. M., & Posner, M. I. (1967). *Human performance*. Belmont, CA: Brooks Cole.

Fuller (1943). *Reading factors in typewriting*. Unpublished doctoral dissertation. Graduate School of Education, Harvard University.

Gentner, D. R. (1987). Timing of skilled motor performance: Tests of the proportional duration model. *Psychological Review*, **94**, 255–276.

Gentner, D. R., Grudin, J., & Conway, E. (1980). *Finger movements in transcription typing*, La Jolla, CA: University of California, San Diego, Center for Human Information Processing (Technical Report 8001).

Gentner, D. R., & Norman, D. A. (1984). The typist's touch. *Psychology Today, 8,* 66–72.

Gentner, D. R., Larochelle, S., & Grudin, J. (1988). Lexical, sublexical, and peripheral effects in skilled typewriting. *Cognitive Psychology, 20,* 524–548.

Gopher, D., Karis, D., & Koenig, W. (1985). The representation of movement schemas in long-term memory: Lessons from the acquisition of a transcription skill. *Acta Psychologica, 60,* 105–1134.

Gordon, P. C., & Meyer, D. E. (1987). Hierarchical representation of spoken syllable order. In A. Allport, D. MacKay, W. Prinz, & E. Scheerer (Eds.), *Language perception and production* (pp. 445–462). London: Academic Press.

Greenwald, A. G. (1970). Sensory feedback mechanisms in performance control: With special reference to the ideo-motor mechanism. *Psychological Review, 77,* 73–99.

Grudin, J. G. (1983). Error patterns in novice and skilled typists. In W. E. Cooper (Ed.), *Cognitive aspects of skilled typewriting* (pp. 121–143). New York: Springer-Verlag.

Heuer, H. (1988). Testing the invariance of relative timing: Comment on Gentner (1987). *Psychological Review, 95,* 552–557.

Hick, W. E. (1952). On the rate of gain of information. *Quarterly Journal of Experimental Psychology, 4,* 11–26.

Hyman, R. (1953). Stimulus information as a determinant of reaction time. *Journal of Experimental Psychology, 45,* 188–196.

Inhoff, A. W., Rosenbaum, D. A., Gordon, A. M., & Campbell, J. A. (1984). Stimulus-response compatibility and motor programming of manual response sequences. *Journal of Experimental Psychology: Human Perception and Performance, 10,* 724–733.

Jagacinski, R. J., Marshburn, E., Klapp, S. T., & Jones, M. R. (1988). Tests of parallel versus integrated structures in polyrhythmic tapping. *Journal of Motor Behavior, 20,* 416–442.

Johnson, N. F. (1972). Organization and the concept of a memory code. In A. W. Melton & E. Martin (Eds.), *Coding processes in human memory* (pp. 125–159). Washington, D.C.: Winston.

Jones, M. R. (1981). A tutorial on some issues and methods in serial pattern research. *Perception & Psychophysics, 30,* 492–504.

Keele, S. W. (1986). Motor control. In J. K. Boff, L. Kaufman, & J. P. Thomas (Eds.), *Handbook of human perception and performance* (Vol. 2, pp. 30-1–30-60). New York: Wiley.

Keele, S. W. (1987). Sequencing and timing in skilled perception and action: An overview. In A. Allport, D. MacKay, W. Prinz, & E. Scheerer (Eds.), *Language perception and production* (pp. 463–487). London: Academic Press.

Keele, S. W., & Ivry, R. I. (1987). Modular analysis of timing in motor skill. In G. H. Bower (Ed.), *The psychology of learning and motivation* (Vol. 21 pp. 183–228). San Diego, CA: Academic Press.

Keele, S. W., & Summers, R. J. (1976). The structure of motor programs. In G. E. Stelmach (Ed.), *Motor control: Issues and trends* (pp. 109–142). New York: Academic Press.

Keele, S. W., Ivry, R. I., & Pokorny, R. A. (1987). Force control and its relation to timing. *Journal of Motor Behavior, 19,* 96–114.

Keele, S. W., Pokorny, R. A., Corcos, D. M., & Ivry, R. (1985). Do perception and motor production share common timing mechanisms: A correlation analysis. *Acta Psychologica, 60,* 173–191.

Klapp, S. T. (1979). Doing two things at once: The role of temporal compatibility. *Memory & Cognition, 7,* 375–381.

Klapp, S. T., Hill, M.D., Tyler, J. G., Martin, Z. E., Jagacinski, R. J., & Jones, M. R. (1985). On marching to two different drummers: Perceptual aspects of the difficulties. *Journal of Experimental Psychology: Human Perception and Performance, 11,* 814–827.

Klemmer, E. T. (1957). Simple reaction time as a function of time uncertainty. *Journal of Experimental Psychology, 54,* 195–200.

Kornblum, S. (1965). Response competition and/or inhibition in two choice reaction time. *Psychonomic Science, 2,* 55–56.

Larochelle, S. (1983). Some aspects of movements in skilled typewriting. In H. Bouma & D. G. Bouhuis (Eds.), *Attention and performance X* (pp. 43–54). Hillsdale, NJ: Erlbaum.

Lashley, K. S. (1951). The problem of serial order in behavior. In L. A. Jeffress (Ed.), *Cerebral mechanisms in behavior* (pp. 112–131). New York: Wiley.

Leonard, J. A. (1959). Tactual choice reactions. *Quarterly Journal of Experimental Psychology, 11,* 76–83.

Lessenberry, D. D. (1928). *Analysis of errors.* Syracuse, NY: L. C. Smith and Corona Typewriters, School Department. [Reprinted in A. Dvorak, N. Merrick, W. Dealey, & G. Ford (1936). *Typewriting behavior.* New York: American Book Company.]

Logan, G. D. (1982). On the ability to inhibit complex movements: A stop-signal study of typewriting. *Journal of Experimental Psychology: Human Perception and Performance, 8,* 778–792.

Logan, G. D. (1983). Time, information, and the various spans in typewriting. In W. E. Cooper (Ed.), *Cognitive aspects of skilled typewriting* (pp. 197–224). New York: Springer-Verlag.

Long, J. (1976). Visual feedback and skilled keying: Differential effects of masking the printed copy and the keyboard. *Ergonomics, 19,* 19–110.

Luce, R. D. (1986). *Response times: Their role in inferring elementary mental organization.* New York: Oxford University Press.

Meyer, D. E., Osman, A. M., Irwin, D. E., & Yantis, S. (1990). Modern mental chronometry. *Biological Psychology, 26,* 3–67.

Miller, G. A. (1956). The magical number seven plus or minus two: Some limits on our capacity for processing information. *Psychological Review, 63,* 81–97.

Munhall, K. G., & Ostry, D. J. (1983). Mirror-image movements in typing. In W. E. Cooper (Ed.), *Cognitive aspects of skilled typewriting* (pp. 247–257). New York: Springer-Verlag.

Olsen, R. A., & Murray, R. A., III (1976). Finger motion in typing texts of varying complexity. *Proceedings of the 6th congress of the International Ergonomic Association* (pp. 446–450).

Ostry, D. J. (1983). Determinants of interkey times in typing. In W. E. Cooper (Ed.), *Cognitive aspects of skilled typewriting* (pp. 225–246). New York: Springer-Verlag.

Peters, M. (1977). Simultaneous performance of two motor activities: The factor of timing. *Neuropsychologica, 15,* 461–465.

Pew, R. W., & Rosenbaum, D. A. (1988). Human motor performance: Computation, representation, and implementation. In R. C. Atkinson, R. J. Hernnstein, G. Lindzey, & R. D. Luce (Eds.), *Stevens' handbook of experimental psychology* (2d ed., pp. 473–509). New York: Wiley.

Proctor, R. W., & Reeve, T. G. (Eds.) (1989). *Stimulus-response compatibility: An integrated perspective.* Amsterdam: North-Holland.

Rabbitt, P. M. A. (1978). Detection of errors by skilled typists. *Ergonomics, 21,* 945–958.

Rabbitt, P. M. A., & Vyas, S. M. (1970). An elementary preliminary taxonomy for some errors in laboratory choice RT tasks. *Acta Psychologica, 33,* 56–76.

Rabbitt, P. M. A., Fearnley, S., & Vyas, S. M. (1975). Programming sequences of complex responses. In P. M. A. Rabbitt & S. Dornic (Eds.), *Attention and performance V* (pp. 295–317). London: Academic Press.

Restle, F. (1970). Theory of serial pattern learning: Structural trees. *Psychological Review, 77,* 481–495.

Rosenbaum, D. A. (1983). Central control of movement timing. *Bell System Technical Journal (Special Human Factors and Behavioral Sciences issue), 62,* 1647–1657.

Rosenbaum, D. A. (1985). Motor programming: A review and scheduling theory. In H. Heuer, U. Kleinbeck, & K.-M. Schmidt (Eds.), *Motor behavior: Programming, control, and acquisition* (pp. 1–33). Berlin: Springer-Verlag.

Rosenbaum, D. A. (1990). On choosing between movement sequences: Comments on Rose (1988). *Journal of Experimental Psychology: Human Perception and Performance, 16,* 439–444.

Rosenbaum, D. A., & Patashnik, O. (1980). A mental clock-setting process revealed by reaction times. In G. E. Stelmach & J. Requin (Eds.), *Tutorials in motor behavior* (pp. 487–499). Amsterdam: North-Holland.

Rosenbaum, D. A., Gordon, A. M., Stillings, N. A., & Feinstein, M. H. (1987). Stimulus-response compatibility in the programming of speech. *Memory & Cognition*, **15**, 217–224.

Rosenbaum, D. A., Kenny, S., & Derr, M. A. (1983). Hierarchical control of rapid movement sequences. *Journal of Experimental Psychology: Human Perception and Performance*, **9**, 86–102.

Rumelhart, D. E., & Norman, D. A. (1982). Simulating a skilled typist: A study of skilled cognitive-motor performance. *Cognitive Science*, **6**, 1–36.

Rumelhart, D. E., McClelland, J. L., & the PDP Research Group (1986). *Parallel distributed processing: Explorations in the microstructure of cognition* (Vol. 1, *Foundations*). Cambridge, MA: MIT Press.

Seashore, C. E. (1938). *Psychology of music*. New York: McGraw-Hill.

Shaffer, L. H. (1973). Latency mechanisms in transcription. In S. Kornblum (Ed.), *Attention and performance IV* (pp. 435–446). New York: Academic Press.

Shaffer, L. H. (1975a). Control processes in typing. *Quarterly Journal of Experimental Psychology*, **27**, 419–432.

Shaffer, L. H. (1975b). Multiple attention in continuous verbal tasks. In P. M. A. Rabbitt & S. Dornic (Eds.), *Attention and performance V* (pp. 157–167). London: Academic Press.

Shaffer, L. H. (1984). Timing in musical performance. In J. Gibbon & L. Allan (Eds.), *Timing and time perception* (pp. 420–428). New York: New York Academy of Sciences.

Shannon, C. E., & Weaver, W. (1949). *The mathematical theory of communication*. Urbana: Univ. of Illinois Press.

Sloboda, J. A. (1983). The communication of musical metre in piano performance. *Quarterly Journal of Experimental Psychology*, **35A**, 377–396.

Sternberg, S., Monsell, S., Knoll, R. L., & Wright, C. E. (1978). The latency and duration of rapid movement sequences: Comparisons of speech and typewriting. In G. E. Stelmach (Ed.), *Information processing in motor control and learning* (pp. 117–152). New York: Academic Press.

Summers, J. J. (1975). The role of timing in motor program representation. *Journal of Motor Behavior*, **7**, 229–241.

Teichner, W. H., & Krebs, M. J. (1972). Laws of simple visual reaction time. *Psychological Review*, **79**, 344–358.

Terzuolo, C. A., & Viviani, P. (1980). Determinants and characteristics of motor patterns used for typing. *Neuroscience*, **5**, 1085–1103.

Viviani, P., & Terzuolo, C. (1980). Space-time invariance in learned motor skills. In G. E. Stelmach & J. Requin (Eds.), *Tutorials in motor behavior* (pp. 525–533). Amsterdam: North-Holland.

Vorberg, D., & Hambuch, R. (1978). On the temporal control of rhythmic performance. In J. Requin (Ed.), *Attention and performance VII* (pp. 535–555). Hillsdale, NJ: Erlbaum.

Vorberg, D., & Hambuch, R. (1984). Timing of two-handed rhythmic performance. In J. Gibbon & L. Allan (Eds.), *Timing and time perception* (pp. 390–406). New York: New York Academy of Sciences.

Wallace, R. J. (1971). Stimulus-response compatibility and the idea of a response code. *Journal of Experimental Psychology*, **88**, 354–360.

Welford, A. T. (Ed.) (1980). *Reaction times*. London: Academic Press.

West, L. J., & Sabban, Y. (1982). Hierarchy of stroking habits at the typewriter. *Journal of Applied*

Wickens, D. (1938). The transference of conditioned excitation and conditioned inhibition from one muscle group to the antagonist group. *Journal of Experimental Psychology*, **22**, 101–123.

Wing, A. M. (1980). The long and short of timing in response sequences. In G. E. Stelmach & J. Requin (Eds.), *Tutorials in motor behavior* (pp. 469–486). Amsterdam: North-Holland.

Wing, A. M., & Kristofferson, A. B. (1973). Response delays and the timing of discrete motor responses. *Perception & Psychophysics*, **14,** 5–12.

Wing, A., Keele, S. W., & Margolin, D. I. (1984). Motor disorder and the timing of repetitive movements. In J. Gibbon & L. Allan (Eds.), *Timing and time perception* (pp. 183–192). New York: New York Academy of Sciences.

Woodworth, R. S. (1938). *Experimental Psychology*. New York: Holt.

Woodworth, R. S., & Schlosberg, H. (1954). *Experimental Psychology* (2d ed.). New York: Holt.

Yamada, H. (1983). Certain problems associated with the design of input keyboards for Japanese writing. In W. E. Cooper (Ed.), *Cognitive aspects of skilled typewriting* (pp. 305–407). New York: Springer-Verlag.

9 SPEAKING AND SINGING

■ INTRODUCTION

Like the other activities that have been discussed in this book, speaking and singing have a number of special properties. First, their most important output is auditory rather than visual or proprioceptive. Second, they are usually carried out for purposes of communication; most of the other activities I have considered are only occasionally performed with the direct aim of transmitting signals to others. Because of the centrality of communication in human affairs, and because of the uniqueness of human language, the control of speech has been studied in detail by investigators from a large number of disciplines—psychology, physiology, linguistics, engineering, and speech pathology (among others). The control of singing has received somewhat less attention than the control of speech because, at least for humans, singing is not the primary means of verbal communication. Here singing will also be covered in less detail than speech, not just because less research has been done on it, but also because most, but certainly not all, of the important principles of vocal control can be documented by considering speech alone.

The Issues

How should we approach the control of speech and singing? To begin with, it is useful to say what vocal outputs consist of. Some of the sounds we produce—coughing, burping, and sneezing—have vegetative or survival value. Because they are nonlinguistic, they will not be analyzed in this chapter. When we speak, we produce words. These in turn consist of *phonemes* (roughly, vowels and consonants) which allow for meaning distinctions in a language. "l" and "r" are phonemes in English, as shown by the fact that "lip" and "rip" have different meanings. In Mandarin Chinese, however, word meanings are never distinguished by "l" or "r". Thus, "l" and "r" are not phonemes in Mandarin Chinese. Speakers of Mandarin Chinese do, however, distinguish between "l" and "r"; they say "l" only at word beginnings and "r" only at word endings. "l" and "r" are therefore said to be two *phones* of Mandarin Chinese. Phones are sound categories that need not convey meaning. In English, "l" and "r" are distinct phones which also happen to be phonemes. In Mandarin Chinese, "l" and "r" are phones which happen not to be phonemes.

English, like Mandarin Chinese, has phones that are not phonemes. Place your hand in front of your mouth while saying "pit" or "spit." You should feel a burst of air following the "p" in "pit" but not in "spit." This indicates that the two "p" sounds are produced differently. The difference reflects a subtle rule of English that until now you probably knew only unconsciously: "p" in the initial position of a word is *aspirated* (it is accompanied by a breath of air), but "p" in a noninitial word position is unaspirated. (Actually the rule is not specific to "p"s, but this need not concern us here.) The fact that we distinguish between aspirated and unaspirated "p"s even though aspiration does not distinguish word meanings implies that aspirated and unaspirated "p"s are phones but not phonemes in English. Linguists refer to the elements making up and distinguishing phones as *phonetic features*. Aspiration is a phonetic feature of English. Distinct phones in a language that are not distinct phonemes are called *allophones*. The "p" in "spit" and the "p" in "pit" are English allophones. In Hindi (a language spoken in India), aspiration affects meaning, so aspirated and unaspirated "p"s are not allophones in this language.

If speech were only made up of phonetic features, it would sound unnatural, for when we speak, we also vary intonation and stress. In English, intonation and stress help convey meanings about entire phrases. Saying in a matter-of-fact way, "I'll pay you $90 to fix my car" means something different from exclaiming, "I'll pay you *$90* to fix my car!" The meanings of the individual words are the same, but the meanings of the sentences differ. Thus in English, intonation and stress provide cues to the listener about sentence- or phrase-level meaning. In other languages—so called *tone* languages—intonation affects word meaning as well as phrase and sentence meaning. Mandarin Chinese is a tone language. Some phonemes in this language are differentiated by pitch alone. In English, meanings of individual vowels and consonants are never distinguished by pitch alone.

Another aspect of speech that must be controlled by the speaker (and correspondingly used by the listener) is timing. We can speak at different rates, but we don't uniformly speed up or slow down our vocal output the way a record player does when it is run at 33, 45, or 78 rotations per minute. Instead, as we speak more quickly, we reduce the durations of vowels more than the durations of consonants. We also take various shortcuts, omitting all but the most critical elements needed to ensure intelligibility.

Finally, when we speak more quickly, we tend to flatten the intonation profiles of our speech (as you can confirm by reading this sentence as quickly as possible).

Maximum speech rates are about 200 words per minute. Because words in English have an average of 7 phonemes, this means that speakers of English can speak at rates of about 1400 phonemes per minute. It has been estimated, however, that it takes 1/10 of a second to produce a single phoneme. Using the latter figure, it follows that we should be able to produce no more than 10 phonemes a second, or 600 phonemes per minute. How do we manage to speak at more than twice that rate?

The answer is that phonemes are not produced one after the other, in a strictly serial fashion. Rather, the vocal apparatus makes use of parallel activity. (Recall that typists' fingers also move in parallel; see Chapters 1 and 8.) X-ray movies of the tongue, jaw, and other parts of the vocal tract (made by temporarily attaching tiny metal pellets to the speaker's articulators) have shown that the articulators move in several directions at once. You can observe the capacity for parallel articulation by looking into a mirror and watching your lips as you say (rather deliberately) the word *construe*. (Recall that in Chapter 1 you were asked to say "tulip" in front of a mirror.) Notice that your lips become rounded even before you say *str* (Kozhevnikov & Chistovich 1965; Daniloff & Moll, 1968). Anticipatory lip rounding illustrates the phenomenon of *coarticulation*—the tendency for different articulatory objectives to be met simultaneously, generally through parallel articulatory activity. Another example of coarticulation occurs in the word *boo*. When you say this word emphatically, your lips round before you produce the "b." Anticipatory lip rounding is not always necessary for saying "b," however, as you can see by saying "bed"; no anticipatory lip rounding occurs for this word. Thus anticipatory lip rounding only occurs in anticipation of vowels for which the lips need to be rounded.

As the preceding discussion indicates, there are many aspects of vocal output that must be controlled by the speaker (or singer). A theory of vocal control must be able to explain how these aspects are managed. In addition, it must explain why some sounds or sound combinations are part of our linguistic repertoire while other sounds or sound combinations are not. Some sounds are physically impossible to make—no one can shout as loud as a jet plane, for example—but other sounds are physically possible but rarely if ever uttered, at least in normal speech contexts. For instance, among the thousands of languages in the world, there appears to be none that uses, as part of everyday speech, brief "snoring" sounds (Ohala, 1983). Such sounds can of course be made, as bedmates can attest about their partners. The absence of snoring sounds in natural language cannot be attributed to a universal concern for etiquette, for the sounds made by speakers in some languages are considered rude by speakers of other languages. (Not all Americans are enamored of gutterals, for example.) A more likely reason is that the production of these sounds in ongoing speech would violate principles of biomechanical efficiency (Lindblom, 1983; Ohala, 1983) or deep-seated grammatical rules, perhaps common to all mankind (Chomsky, 1975). According to the latter view, computational factors rather than, or in addition to, biomechanical factors constrain the sound combinations of natural languages.

As we attempt to build a theory of speech production, we must also take account of the fact that speech can be produced in spite of physical changes to the vocal apparatus. A familiar example is talking with a pipe in one's mouth. The fact that professors can speak while holding pipes between their teeth suggests that their speech-production systems are tuned to the proprioceptive feedback they receive. Experiments with people who do not smoke pipes (or hold Ph.D.'s) show that this ability is widespread.

A final issue that must be dealt with in the analysis of speaking and singing concerns the interplay between vocal output and hearing. One important question is how we distinguish among heard speech sounds, given that cues for phonetic features are hard to identify in speech spectrograms (visual representations of speech signals); this topic will be discussed in some detail later in the chapter. A related question is how we regulate our ongoing vocal output as we hear ourselves speak and sing. A method that has been used to address this question is to delay the auditory feedback that a speaker or singer receives from his or her own voice. In the case of singing, delayed auditory feedback affects the frequency and amplitude of vibrato (the intentional wavering of the voice used by singers to produce rich-sounding notes). Changes in vibrato appear with feedback delays as short as 100 msec, suggesting that singers respond to auditory feedback as often as 10 times a second (Deutsch & Clarkson, 1959). A comparable result comes from delayed auditory feedback studies of speech. When auditory feedback from speech is postponed by 100 msec or more, speaking can be seriously disrupted, and the resulting speech pattern may resemble stuttering (Lee, 1950). Based on this finding, it has been suggested that one cause of stuttering may be a kind of perennial mismatch between expected and actual auditory feedback delays (Costello, 1985). Varying auditory feedback delays has therefore been explored as a treatment for stuttering (Harrington, 1987; Howell, Eli-Yaniv, & Powell, 1987).

Hearing is also essential for learning to speak normally (that is, as hearing people do). Efforts have been made to help the deaf learn to speak by encouraging them to match the visual representations of their speech sounds (obtained electronically) with those of hearing speakers (Nickerson, Kalikow, & Stevens, 1976).

If one has learned to speak with the benefit of hearing but hearing is lost subsequently, it is possible to continue to speak normally for weeks or even months. Beyond this time the quality of speech deteriorates. Manipulating the time that people can receive auditory feedback while learning to talk is not ethically possible, of course, so much of the research on this topic has been done with birds, a species that communicates through vocalization. I will review the work on bird song in the last part of the chapter. There it will be seen that a breakthrough in the understanding of the nervous system has come about by studying bird brains.

Overview of the Chapter

The chapter will be organized as follows. First, I will describe the vocal tract and articulatory dynamics. Here I will review the anatomy of the vocal tract and the mechanics of the air flow that creates sounds within it. Then I will turn to some of the problems that the articulatory system must solve to produce recognizable speech sounds. Key among these is the achievement of desired articulatory configurations. Because the articulators rarely occupy a single position before a given speech sound must be produced, the problem of achieving desired articulatory configurations is fundamental for speech control. It happens that the speech perception system is remarkably forgiving of variations in the speech signal. Listeners usually do not notice small, artificial deletions in the speech signal when the deletions are replaced by noise of approximately equal amplitude—a phenomenon known as *phonemic restoration* (Warren & Warren, 1970). Similarly, when people repeat what they hear as soon as they hear it—a task called *shadowing*—they instantly correct errors in the input (Marlsen-Wilson & Tyler, 1980). These findings indicate that people extract meaning from speech signals despite major variations in the signal itself. As a result, the speech-production system is relieved from having to "worry" too much about producing speech sounds that are perfectly accurate.

The next issue to be discussed is the relation between speech and hearing. Here I will review two influential theories. One claims that we recognize speech sounds by recruiting knowledge about how speech sounds are produced (Liberman, Cooper, Shankweiler, & Studdert-Kennedy, 1967). The other theory claims that the programming of speech uses perceptual representations of likely auditory consequences (Ladefoged, DeClerk, Lindau, & Papçun, 1972; MacNeilage, 1980). A variant of the latter theory, proposed recently, holds that invariant *relative* positions of the articulators define the target states toward which the articulators move. I will introduce a mechanism that can achieve relative positioning of the articulators.

The next section reviews a theory of coarticulation that makes use of a network of interconnected, neuronlike units (Jordan, 1986a,b). Network models are receiving an increasing amount of attention because of their apparent similarity to the brain.

Another model of this kind has also been found to account for phenomena related to the planning of sentences and their constituents (Dell, 1986). The phenomena being modeled are slips of the tongue. Traditionally, speech errors have been explained by assuming that information passes in a single direction from high to low levels in the language-production system (Garrett, 1982). The network model to be described (Dell, 1986) allows information to pass from high levels to low levels and vice versa.

The final topic to which I will turn is the brain's control of speaking and singing. Because much of our current knowledge of speech derives from analyses of speech disorders following brain trauma, it is useful to look for correspondences between the types of language disorders produced by damage to different parts of the brain and the types of speech errors that occur when the brain is intact. After briefly discussing this topic, I will consider the analysis of bird song.

There are two topics that will not be treated here in as much detail as might otherwise be desirable—the acquisition of speech and the diagnosis and treatment of speech disorders. The major points of basic research on the motor control of speaking and singing can be covered without delving into these topics, each of which requires considerable space and expertise to be dealt with adequately.

■ THE VOCAL TRACT AND ARTICULATORY DYNAMICS

In order to speak and sing, air must be pushed through the vocal tract. The resonance of the column of air in the tract gives rise to sound. To produce specific, desired sounds, the speech system must achieve relatively precise control of the shape of the vocal tract. It does so by modulating the behavior of three subsystems (see Figure 9.1)—the *respiratory* subsystem, the *laryngeal*

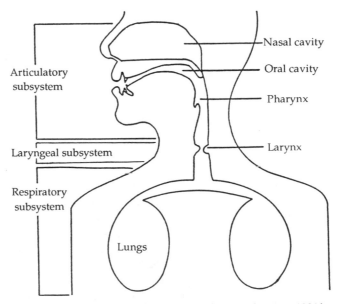

Figure 9.1 Cross section of the vocal tract. (From Lieberman, 1984.)

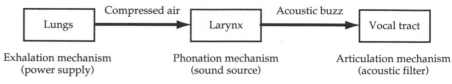

Figure 9.2 Schematic diagram of the vocal system. (From Harvey, 1985.)

subsystem, and the *articulatory* subsystem. Figure 9.2 presents a schematic diagram of these components.

The Respiratory System

The respiratory system includes the lungs and their associated muscle groups. Two major muscle groups promote inhalation. One, the *diaphragm*, lies at the base of the rib cage. Another, the *external intercostals*, lifts and expands the rib cage.

The major muscle group for *exhalation* is made up of the *internal intercostals*. These muscles pull down on the rib cage and thereby push air out of the lungs. The internal intercostals are the most important respiratory muscles for normal speech and singing, for they are the muscles that propel air out through the mouth and nose. In general, the greater the pressure of the escaping air, the louder one's voice.

Breathing when one vocalizes is very different from breathing when one is silent. During silence, inhalation and exhalation proceed at a more-or-less even rate, but during vocalization there is a short period of inhalation followed by a longer period of exhalation. In singing, it is sometimes necessary to take a deep breath in a short amount of time (during a short rest followed by a sustained period of uninterrupted singing). Detailed studies of the control of inhalation during singing indicate that singers (or at least professional singers) are skilled at regulating the amount of air they inhale and the speed with which they do so depending on the length and loudness of the phrase they are about to sing (Harvey, 1985).

The timing of respiratory muscle activity during the inhalation–exhalation cycle of speech has been carefully analyzed (MacNeilage & Ladefoged, 1976). After the lungs have filled with air, the rib cage recoils elastically from a state of complete or near-complete expansion. During this period, the external intercostals (which promote inhalation) remain active until receptors within them indicate that the lungs have been fully filled. After the elastic recoil process has continued for a while and the lung volume has decreased to a critical value (but one well above complete emptying of the lung), the external intercostals shut off, based on feedback from stretch receptors within them. This event signals the internal intercostals to contract, which allows for active exhalation and production of the next utterance. Because the internal intercostals do not contract until the lungs have begun to contract, they take advantage of the inertia of lung contraction.

As air is expelled from the lungs, the activity of the internal intercostals increases until, when the volume of the lungs reaches a critically low value, other muscles come into play to ensure that exhalation continues. Finally, when the lung volume reaches a base level, the next inhalation starts.

The above description illustrates sustained activity in the respiratory muscles. There is also transient activity. The internal intercostals produce clearly demarcated pulses. These pulses were once thought to occur at, and indeed define, syllable starts (Stetson, 1951), but subsequent work revealed that syllables need not be accompanied by transient activity of the internal intercostals (Ladefoged, 1967).

Laryngeal Mechanisms

As shown in Figure 9.1, the area above the trachea (the branching structure that feeds air to the lungs) contains the *larynx*. This structure serves four main functions: It regulates the characteristic pitch of the voice, it modulates aspiration (accompanying syllable-initial "p" sounds, for example), it allows for whispering, and it creates a subtle buzzing sound known as *voicing*. The role of voicing can be appreciated by placing your index finger and thumb on your Adam's apple while making two simple sounds: a prolonged "f" and a prolonged "v." When you say "v" you can feel your vocal cords vibrate, but when you say "f" you cannot. The "f" and "v" are distinguished by the presence or absence of vocal-cord vibration. The "v" is a voiced consonant, whereas the "f" is a voiceless consonant.

Voicing is controlled by adjusting the *distance* between the vocal cords, two folds that lie across the roof of the larynx. Figure 9.3 shows a picture of the vocal cords, taken with a special optic fiber camera system. During production of voiced consonants such as "v" and "b," the distance between the cords is small, but during production of unvoiced consonants such as "f" and "p," the

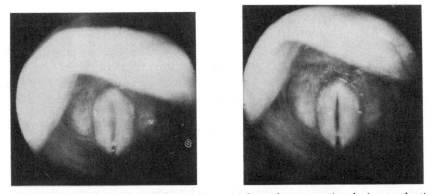

Figure 9.3 Photographs of the larynx in positions similar to those occurring during production of (*left*) voiced and (*right*) unvoiced consonants. (From Sawashima & Hirose, 1983).

distance increases to the point where air flowing between the cords does not cause vocal-cord vibration. The muscles involved in separating the vocal folds have been analyzed in some detail despite the formidable technical difficulties of doing so (MacNeilage, 1983; MacNeilage & Ladefoged, 1976).

The shape of the larynx accounts in part for the fact that some people have better singing voices than others (Sundberg, 1977). People with exceptionally fine singing voices can lower their larynxes significantly more than people with unexceptional singing voices. The enlarged cavity that accompanies larynx lowering allows for an extra formant (an extra concentration of energy in part of the auditory frequency range). This extra formant—or what is sometimes called the "singer's formant"—allows the voice to be projected more effectively than usual. As a result, a fine opera singer can be heard over an orchestra without a microphone. Someone unable to produce the extra formant would have to scream or rely on artificial amplification to be heard in comparable conditions.

It has been known at least since the time of Leonardo da Vinci that the vocal cords control pitch as well as voicing (Peschel & Peschel, 1987). da Vinci studied cadavers and concluded that the mass of the vocal cords affects vocal pitch. As the vocal cords enlarge, they vibrate at a lower frequency. During puberty in males, the release of male sex hormone causes enlargement of the vocal cords, causing the voice to drop. To prevent this from happening, boys at various times in history have been castrated (Peschel & Peschel, 1987; see Figure 9.4).

If changing the mass of the vocal cords were the only way to change pitch it would be impossible to change pitch rapidly. To bring about rapid pitch changes, the speech-production system regulates the frequency of vocal-cord vibration, principally by changing the stiffness of the vocal cords. To understand how this is achieved and why it has the desired effect, try the following simple experiment. Imitate the sound of a power lawn mower as it speeds up or slows down. To produce the sound of a slow-running lawn mower, let your lips flap back and forth passively while you force air through your mouth. Now gradually increase the stiffness of your lips to produce the higher-pitched sound of the mower "in high gear." Notice that your lips vibrate at a higher rate than they did before. As a result, a higher-pitched sound emerges. This is essentially what happens to your vocal cords when you produce sounds of varying pitch. The cords stiffen to vibrate at higher rates so higher-pitched sounds are produced, and they are relaxed to allow for vibration at lower rates so that lower-pitched sounds are produced. The vibration itself is entirely passive, driven by air pushed from the lungs and by counteracting physical forces (the Bernoulli effect).

Articulatory Mechanisms

So far, I have indicated how speakers and singers adjust the amplitude, frequency, voicing, and degree of aspiration of their vocal output. I have not yet

Figure 9.4 Two castrati. (From Peschel & Peschel, 1987.)

indicated how the many other distinctions in speech come about. How do speakers distinguish between "l"s and "m"s, for example, or between "g"s and "i"s? In general, how do speakers produce the range of consonants and vowels they do? The rich variation of speech sounds depends on the structures above the larynx. These include the pharynx (the cavity lying between the larynx and the mouth or oral cavity), mouth, jaws, lips, nasal tract, and velum (a movable flap connecting the nasal tract and oral cavity) (see Figure 9.1).

The Pharynx

The shape of the pharynx constrains the vowels that can be made. Because adult humans have long necks, low larynxes, and large, mobile throats (see Figure 9.5), their pharynxes have resonance properties suitable for production of certain vowels, such as [a], [i], and [u]. (The resonance of a body is the frequency at which it vibrates with the greatest amplitude for each unit of energy supplied.) The throats of human infants and of apes do not have

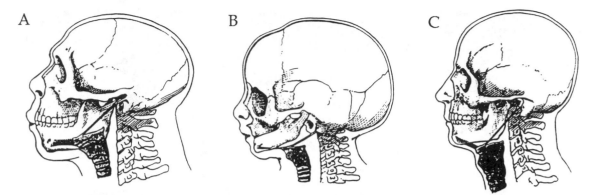

Figure 9.5 Skulls of the Neanderthal (A), human infant (B), and human adult (C). From *Language and Speech*, by George A. Miller. Copyright © 1981 by W. H. Freeman and Company. Reprinted with permission.

these characteristics. Human infants and apes have short necks, relatively high larynxes, and small immobile throats, making it impossible for them to say [a], [i], and [u]. Based on this observation, an intriguing hypothesis was proposed about the evolutionary origins of human language (Lieberman, 1984). According to the hypothesis, the Neanderthal ape, a prehuman species that lived about 35,000 years ago, was unable to say [a], [i], and [u] because its throat was apparently more like that of modern apes and human infants than like that of modern human adults. What is intriguing about this hypothesis is that, if it is correct, it would imply that the full range of human speech sounds developed recently in evolution (within the past 35,000 years) and therefore may have arisen through a genetic mutation (Chomsky, 1975).

Not all researchers are convinced that speech as we know it emerged this recently, however. Alternative interpretations of the fossil record as well as new archaeological samples have led other investigators to argue that our human forebears spoke much as we do as long as 2 million years ago (Bower, 1989).

Vowels

An effective way to understand how articulatory mechanisms allow for the production of different classes of speech sounds is to consider each class individually. This will be the approach in this section and the next. I will consider vowels first.

All vowels are voiced. Only consonants can be unvoiced. Vowels differ on several articulatory dimensions (see Figure 9.6). One is the position of the tongue body—either high or low in the mouth and toward the front or back of the mouth. To produce the vowel in "sin," for example, the tongue body is placed high in the mouth and toward the front; consequently this is a *high-front* vowel. To produce the vowel in "book," the tongue body is placed

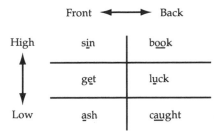

Figure 9.6 Locations of the tongue body in production of so-called *lax* vowels—vowels produced with the root of the tongue retracted. (*Tense* vowels, by contrast, have the tongue root advanced, as in "teen" or "boot.") (Based on Akmajian, Demers, & Harnish, 1979.)

high in the mouth and toward the back; this is a *high-back* vowel. The vowel in "get" requires placement of the tongue body low in the mouth and toward the front; hence this is a *low-front* vowel. The vowel in "luck" requires placement of the tongue body low in the mouth and toward the back; this is a *low-back* vowel. There is also a vowel that requires an extremely low front tongue placement (the "a" in "ash"), and there is a vowel that requires an extremely low back tongue placement (the "augh" in "caught").

Consonants

The production of consonants, like the production of vowels, depends on where the tongue is placed. Consonants are also affected by the positions and activities of the lips, jaw, and velum.

Linguists have categorized consonants according to their *manner* and *place* of articulation. Manner of articulation refers to the way the air stream is constricted by the articulators—for example, whether the air is momentarily stopped by closure of the lips. Place of articulation refers to the location where the constriction occurs. Tables 9.1 and 9.2 list several manners and places of articulation.

■ **Table 9.1** Manners of Articulation

Type	Example	Description
Stops	*pug*	Total interruption of air flow by lips, tongue, velum, or glottis
Constrictives	*forth*	Narrowing of air stream by lip or tongue
Nasals	*mine*	Nasal passage opened by lowering velum
Liquids	*reel*	Tongue tip near alveolar ridge
Glides	*wet*	Narrowing of air stream by lips with voicing and velum open
Affricates	*crutch*	Stop followed by constrictions

■ **Table 9.2** Places of Articulation

Type	Example	Description
Bilabials	*m, b*	Lips brought together
Labiodentals	*f, v*	Lower lip brought into contact with teeth
Dentals	*then*	Tongue tip brought into contact with teeth
Alveolars	*d, s*	Tongue tip brought into contact with alveolar ridge
Palatals	*rich*	Tongue body brought into contact with hard palate
Velars	*kid*	Tongue body brought close to soft palate
Glottals	*button*	Brief closure of the vocal cords

A number of points should be kept in mind as you study Tables 9.1 and 9.2. First, the tables do not list all the consonants of English (primarily to save space). It would be educational (and also entertaining) for you to "synthesize" other possible consonants by combining the features shown in Tables 9.1 and 9.2. (An example of such a "synthesized" consonant is the sound associated with the letters "ng," as in "song"; this is a velar/nasal.) Second, the entries in Tables 9.1 and 9.2 are for American English. Other languages use many of the same places and manners of articulation as in American English, but some other languages (or dialects) also use others. For example, French has *uvulars*, as in the "r" of "rouge," where the uvula (the little appendage hanging from the soft palate of the roof of the mouth) is touched or approached by the back of the tongue. Knowing that the examples in Tables 9.1 and 9.2 refer to American English should help you interpret the examples correctly. The "t"s in "button," for example, are reduced to glottal stops in American English, but in formal British English they are pronounced as hard "t"s. (Hard "t"s are produced by touching the tongue to the alveolar ridge, the protrusion behind the teeth, which you can feel with the tip of your tongue.) A final comment about Tables 9.1 and 9.2 is that, for ease of communication, I have not introduced the special symbols used in the field of phonetics to represent speech sounds precisely. These symbols can be found in a number of sources, such as Akmajian, Demers, and Harnish (1979) or Halle and Clements (1983).

Whereas Tables 9.1 and 9.2 introduce different types of articulatory features and consonants that possess them, it is also possible to construct tables that show, for any given consonant, the articulatory features it possesses. (Similarly organized tables can also be drawn up for vowels.) Representing consonants and vowels in this way was a major part of the approach taken by Chomsky and Halle (1968) in what has come to be called the "standard theory" of phonology. According to the standard theory, each phoneme is coded according to its distinctive features. Table 9.3 presents part of a distinctive-feature matrix for a few consonants in American English. Note that the entries in the table are pluses and minuses, reflecting

■ **Table 9.3** Binary Values of Selected Phonetic
Features for a Few English Consonants

Feature	Consonants							
	p	b	m	t	d	n	k	g
Nasal	–	–	+	–	–	+	–	–
Stop	+	+	+	+	+	+	+	+
Affricate	–	–	–	–	–	–	–	–
Sibilant	–	–	–	–	–	–	–	–
Glottal	–	–	–	–	–	–	–	–
Labial	+	+	+	–	–	–	–	–
Interdental	–	–	–	–	–	–	–	–

the fact that articulatory features are assumed in the theory simply to be present (+) or absent (–). For example, a consonant is assumed either to be or not be *nasal*—that is, produced with the velum closed or open. (When the velum is open, air can pass through the nasal cavity.) Similarly, a consonant either is or is not a *stop*—that is, it is produced with or without a complete constriction of the air stream. A consonant either is or is not an *affricate* (produced with a temporary stop of the airstream, released into a constrictive state). It is or is not a *sibilant* (a hissing sound). It is or is not a *labial* (made through lip closure). It is or is not *interdental* (made by pushing the tongue against the teeth, yielding a slight hissing sound). And it is or is not *glottal* (made by briefly stopping the air flow with the vocal cords).

Implicitly, standard theory suggests a way that distinct speech sounds might be produced: The articulators are brought to specific positions to ensure that particular articulatory features are present or not. In ongoing speech, a series of these articulatory positions must be achieved to ensure that the appropriate sequence of articulatory feature sets is produced.

As straightforward as this idea may seem, it runs into a major problem: Articulatory positions exhibit an enormous amount of variation, as seen in the next section.

■ VARIABILITY AND THE MOTOR THEORY OF SPEECH PERCEPTION

One source of evidence for the variability of speech comes from analyses of the acoustic properties of speech sounds. Such analyses have relied extensively on the sound spectrograph, a device that converts sound into a visible trace (see Figure 9.7). When sound spectrograms were first produced, they revealed something disconcerting. We hear distinct phonemes—for example, we recognize a "b" as a "b" regardless of whether it occurs in "bag"

H–U—M-AN M—O——TO-R CON—TR—O—L

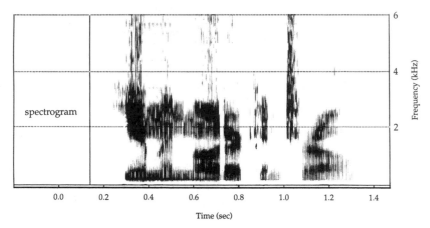

Figure 9.7 A sound spectrogram of the phrase "Human motor control" as spoken and kindly provided by Professor Neil Stillings, Hampshire College, Amherst, Massachusetts.

or in "big"—but sound spectrograms reveal little in common between the energy profiles of these two initial consonants. If we hear "b"s as "b"s but they are acoustically distinct, what is the source of the perceptual invariance?

In the 1960s a group of researchers at Haskins Laboratories in New York City (now in New Haven, Connecticut) suggested that we hear certain speech sounds as the same because, in effect, we invoke the commands needed to produce them. On this view, acoustic invariance arises from articulatory invariance. This is known as the *motor* theory of speech perception (Liberman *et al.*, 1967).

The motor theory has some precedents. Part of the legacy of behaviorism was the belief that the activity we call thinking is actually a subtle form of movement. To test this hypothesis, electromyographic recordings of the muscles of the mouth and throat were made while subjects engaged in various sorts of cognitive activity. The experiments showed that subtle movements do occur (Sokolov, 1972). However, other studies showed that subvocal activity is unnecessary for thought. One study relied on a heroic subject who allowed himself to undergo complete, temporary paralysis while being presented with new information that he was to recall later. After recovering from the paralysis, he could recall what was presented to him. Thus he could form new memories without overt motor involvement (Smith, Brown, Toman, & Goodman, 1947).

What does this outcome imply about the motor theory of speech perception? Plainly it rules out any form of the theory which holds that speech perception requires overt muscle activity. For the theory to be taken seriously, therefore, it must be taken to mean that when speech is heard, the listener accesses *knowledge* about speech production, though that knowledge need not be deployed overtly.

If the motor theory is interpreted this way, how could it ever be tested? Suppose, to begin with, that the commands *are* executed and that speech *is* produced. The motor theory predicts that the commands for any given consonant or vowel should be the same regardless of the context in which the consonant or vowel occurs. Since "b"s are always heard as "b"s, for example, the commands for "b" should be the same, or at least approximately the same, even if their spectrographic patterns differ.

One way to test this hypothesis is to measure the electrical activity of the speech musculature when particular phonemes are produced. If the motor theory is correct, the electrical activity associated with particular phonemes should always be the same. Initial studies, conducted in the late 1960s, provided somewhat encouraging support for this prediction, but as more data were collected, it became clear that the hoped-for invariances would not be found. For example, MacNeilage and DeClerk (1969) discovered that the electromyographic patterns of 36 consonant-vowel-consonant syllables differed considerably depending on the identity of preceding and following phonemes. This result (as well as others) implied that variability is more the rule than the exception in speech production (MacNeilage, 1970). Motor theory was therefore not supported by these studies.

If we do not produce invariant motor commands and our speech motor activity is highly variable, how do we reliably get out the speech sounds we do? One solution—if it can be called that—is simply to assume that the speech-production system is inherently noisy. One noted speech scientist proposed such a view at an early stage of research in this field:

> Imagine a row of Easter eggs carried along a moving belt; the eggs are of various sizes, and variously colored, but not boiled. At a certain point, the belt carries the row of eggs between the two rollers of a wringer, which quite effectively smash them and rub them more or less into each other. The flow of eggs before the wringer represents the series of impulses from the phoneme source. The mess that emerges from the wringer represents the output of the speech transmitter. [Hockett, 1955, p. 210]

This is not a very satisfying description. Speech may be difficult to analyze, but if it lacked underlying regularity, human communication would be even less reliable than the state of civilization indicates it is.

The Target Hypothesis

In 1970, Peter MacNeilage offered a theory to explain how the speech-production system might generate speech sounds reliably (MacNeilage, 1970). He proposed that feedback from the articulators is used, via the gamma system (see Chapter 2), to bring the articulators to specific target positions. Because the articulators can be in many different positions before a target position must be reached, the commands used to move the articulators need not be invariant.

Recall from Chapter 2 that the gamma system allows muscles to contract until they reach desired lengths. If an entire group of muscles must move to a target position, the gamma system can be used to bring each muscle to the position it must reach. Thus MacNeilage's (1970) target theory provides a plausible physiological mechanism for achieving target positions. A major advantage of the theory is that, in principle, it provides a way for the articulators to respond to physical disturbances or variations.

MacNeilage (1970) offered several kinds of evidence for his theory. One was that a patient with normal hearing and normal motor control but virtually no somesthetic feedback was unable to produce intelligible speech (MacNeilage, Rootes, & Chase, 1967). This outcome was consistent with the assumption that sensory feedback plays a role in speech production. (Sensory feedback is needed for the gamma system to work.) Similarly, experimental manipulations that temporarily disrupt oral feedback impair the quality of speech (Scott & Ringel, 1971).

Another result that fits with the theory is that people with normal feedback are adept at compensating for disturbances within the vocal apparatus. I have already mentioned that pipe smokers can speak intelligibly. MacNeilage (1970) noted that whenever one speaks with clenched teeth, the tongue and lip movements that must be made are dramatically altered relative to their normal pattern. The fact that speakers can speak intelligibly with clenched teeth suggests that they can make effective use of oral feedback and alter speech motor commands accordingly. If speech were produced with fixed commands, such compensation would be impossible.

A final result that MacNeilage adduced in support of his theory concerned the stability of articulatory targets despite variability in articulatory starting positions. MacNeilage, Krones, and Hanson (1969) found that with repetitions of an utterance, there was much less variation in final jaw positions than in initial jaw positions. Such consistency could reflect updating of jaw-position information with feedback. A related finding, reported by Kozhevnikov and Chistovich (1965), was that the maximum velocity of the lower lip as it approached the upper lip in producing /p/, /b/, or /m/ increased with the amount of lip opening for an immediately preceding vowel. Again, this result fits with the view that the speech-production system strives for final target positions.

As encouraging as the early results were for MacNeilage's (1970) target theory, further results found the theory to be wanting. One difficulty was that the muscle lengths required to produce intelligible speech when the teeth are clenched are in fact different from the muscle lengths that are normally required (Lindblom & Sundberg, 1971). Because the gamma system regulates muscle length, it alone cannot produce the effective compensations achieved by pipe smokers. A related result came from a study in which a block was placed between the lips of speakers who were asked to produce consonants that required lip closure (Smith & Lee, 1971). The target hypothesis predicted an increase in lip muscle activity with the block in place because the gamma loop would cause the muscles to work harder than usual to get to the target position. What was seen, however, was a *reduction* in lip muscle activity, not an *increase*. A final challenge to MacNeilage's theory was that quite different articulatory configurations can be used to produce vowels with similar acoustic characteristics (Nooteboom, 1970). If the gamma system were relied on to achieve desired articulatory targets, such wide variations would not be expected.

■ RELATIVE POSITIONS AND ACOUSTIC TARGETS

In the face of so much contradictory evidence for the spatial target theory, the theory could not be accepted. Faced with this somewhat discouraging state of affairs, some investigators stepped back and asked, "What is speech for?" Considering this basic question helped suggest a more accurate theory of how speech is controlled.

The reason we speak is to communicate with others, to transmit recognizable acoustic waveforms to listeners. Recognizing this point, several authors, including MacNeilage (1980), came to the view that commands for speech may be designed to achieve *acoustic* rather than *spatial* targets (Ladefoged *et al.*, 1972; Nooteboom, 1970). Recent developments have helped indicate how acoustically based targets might be achieved. The central insight is that proper acoustic results can be realized when the articulators achieve proper *relative* positions; the *absolute* positions of the articulators are less important (Abbs, 1986; Abbs, Gracco, & Cole, 1984).

A study that supported this point of view was concerned with the positions of the upper and lower lips when speakers repeatedly produced a simple utterance such as [apa]. As shown in Figure 9.8, the positions of the lips were inversely related: When the upper lip happened to be higher than usual the lower lip was lower, and when the upper lip happened to be lower than usual the lower lip was higher. From this observation, it appeared that the speech-production system controls the *relative* positions of the upper and lower lips, not their *absolute* positions. From an acoustic point of view this conclusion is sensible. When one wants to say /p/, for example, all that is needed is to bring the lips together; the exact location where they meet is relatively unimportant.

Several added points should be made in connection with Abbs' (1986) hypothesis. First, although I have mentioned the importance of relative spatial positions, other variables also seem to be represented as coordinated

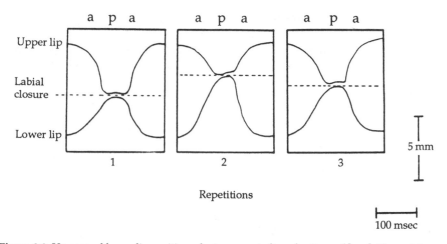

Figure 9.8 Upper and lower lip positions during repeated productions of [apa]. These data were obtained while the speaker clenched his teeth on a stationary bite bar which immobilized the jaw. (From Abbs, 1986.)

articulatory goals. For example, the relative *velocities* of the upper and lower lip may be regulated coordinatively. Relative lip velocities have been found to covary in the production of sounds for which proper relative velocities are important (Hasegawa, McCutcheon, Wolf, & Fletcher, 1976).

Second, the achievement of proper relative positions among articulators seems to be computed very rapidly, enabling the system to compensate almost immediately for perturbations within the speech apparatus (Lindblom & Sundberg, 1971). For example, Abbs, Gracco, and Cole (1984) found that within 20–30 msec of the sudden application of a downward load on the lower lip, there was a greater-than-usual descent of the upper lip, provided the utterance being produced demanded bilabial closure (see Figure 9.9). Compensations for unexpected disruptions are widespread in the vocal system. They occur in naive subjects, even if subjects are told not to compensate, even if the disruptions are introduced after movement has begun, and in remote articulatory sites if the compensation is adaptive for the current acoustic target (Kelso, Tuller, Vatikiotis-Bateson, & Fowler, 1984).

A third comment about Abbs' hypothesis is that it reflects a general tendency of the motor system to achieve *motor equivalence*—"the capacity of a motor system to achieve the same end product with considerable variation in the individual components that contribute to them" (Hughes & Abbs, 1976, p. 199). I discussed motor equivalence in Chapter 1, where I remarked that the capacity for motor equivalence reflects the motor system's ability to cope with unforeseen postural changes as well as externally introduced perturbations, damage, or disease. Speaking and singing demand this capacity as much as any other motor activity. Apart from speaking with a pipe in one's mouth, people can speak while eating, with extra weight on their

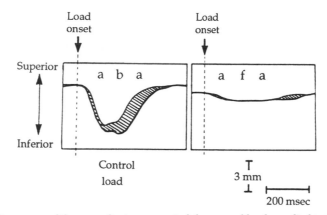

Figure 9.9 Responses of the upper lip to unexpected downward loads applied to the lower lip. The upper lip descends more than normally during production of [aba], which requires bilabial closure, but not during production of [afa], which does not. (From Abbs, 1986.)

chests, with lesions in areas of the spinal cord that cause paralysis in some respiratory muscles, and following the loss of teeth or the addition of orthodontic braces (Abbs, 1986)

It is interesting that one of the main sources of evidence for motor equivalence in speech production—the finding that the lips tend to reach correct relative positions when one lip is pulled down suddenly (as described earlier)—has been replicated for the fingers. In a pinching task, where one finger was unexpectedly pulled back as the other finger approached it, the response of the other finger was to cover a greater distance than usual, as required to achieve finger contact (Cole, Gracco, & Abbs, 1984). Here again, we see that the motor system achieves a functionally defined goal (bringing the fingers together) despite sudden impediments.

Another context in which this principle is seen to operate is in the arm. Reflex compensations at the elbow following perturbation of the whole arm are consistent with the goal of maintaining desired joint torques rather than maintaining any intrinsic muscle parameters such as muscle length or tension (Lacquaniti & Soechting, 1984).

A Mechanism for Relative Positioning

What mechanism might achieve this sort of motor equivalence? I will now introduce one possibility, and in so doing complete this part of the chapter. Figure 9.10A illustrates a simple pulley system which serves as a metaphor for the two lips. The weights on either end of the pulley represent the upper and lower lips. Because the weights are connected, when one of them is pulled in one direction, the other moves in the opposite direction. This has the effect of keeping an imaginary point $p = u + l$, at a fixed vertical position between the two weights, where u is the vertical position of the weight

A

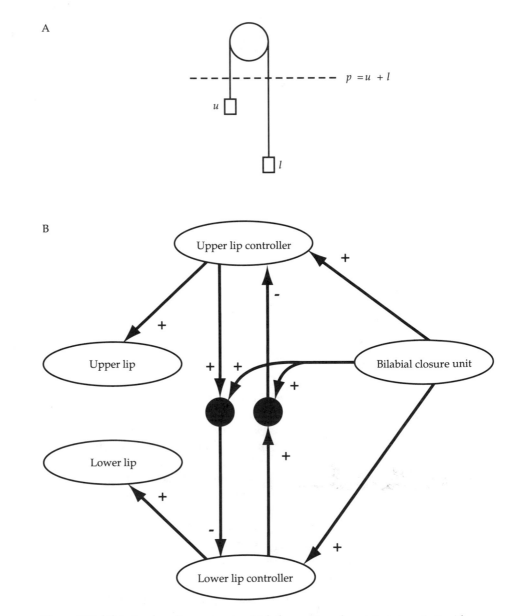

$p = u + l$

B

Figure 9.10 (A) A simple pulley system in which the position of a point p is invariant with respect to the positions of the upper weight u and lower weight l. (B) A circuit that can achieve similar invariance for the upper and lower lips. When the bilabial closure unit is turned on, it activates the upper and lower lip controllers as well as intermediate units (dark circles). Each intermediate unit is also activated by one of the lip controllers and has an inhibitory effect on the controller for the opposing lip. The inhibitory effect only occurs when the bilabial closure unit is on.

corresponding to the upper lip and *l* is the vertical position of the weight corresponding to the lower lip.

Neurophysiologically, to achieve such a relation between the upper and lower lips, one can use mutual inhibition between their respective motor neuron pools (Figure 9.10B). The inhibitory connection is only potentiated if the acoustic target requires achievement of a particular relative position (for example, if the speaker wants to produce a bilabial stop). A simple way for the inhibitory connection to work is that each lip inhibits the other by an amount related to its distance from a resting position (assumed for now to be where the lips are comfortably apart). Thus as the lower lip reaches a higher position, it exerts a greater inhibitory effect on the upper lip, and as the upper lip reaches a lower position, it exerts a greater inhibitory effect on the lower lip. If the lower lip cannot go as high as it usually does—for example, if the lower jaw is suddenly pulled downward—it inhibits the upper lip less than usual, and so the upper lip can descend toward the lower lip more quickly than it usually does.

I have implemented this scheme in a computer program where the lips (or representations of the lips) begin apart, and activation is provided to each lip in each time step until they meet. The lips then return to their original position, halving the distance back to the original position in each time step. Prior to meeting, each lip's position is simply the sum of the activation coming to it, plus its position in the previous time step, minus a proportion of the position of the other lip in the previous time step; the latter term corresponds to the inhibitory connection. If the lower lip gets stuck—that is, if it is not allowed to rise above some height before contacting the upper lip—the upper lip descends more rapidly than when the lower lip is allowed to cover its normal range (see Figure 9.11). Hence the upper lip appears to compensate for the perturbation applied to the lower lip, even though no active correction occurs. The lips meet at the same time regardless of whether they both move normally or if one lip cannot move beyond a set position.

The simplicity of this model leads me to believe that it comprises a reasonable approximation of the biological mechanism for relative positioning of the upper and lower lips. An important feature of the model is that it relies on a form of interaction that is seen at low levels of the motor system, for example, in reciprocal inhibition between muscle antagonists (see Chapter 2). Based on this observation, I suggest that even in achieving high-level goals like producing speech, the nervous system uses tried-and-true, simple mechanisms.

■ A PARALLEL DISTRIBUTED PROCESSING SYSTEM FOR COARTICULATION

The circuit shown in Figure 9.10B is one example of a class of models that is gaining considerable attention in cognitive and neural science. Because all

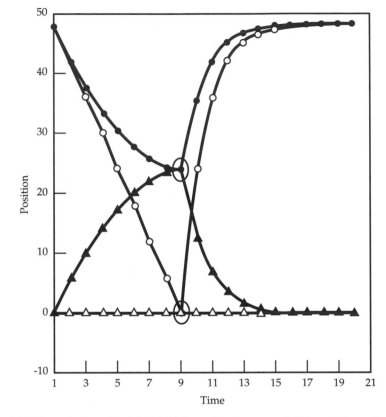

Figure 9.11 Theoretical results of the bilabial coordination network. When the lower lip (▲) can ascend normally, the upper lip (●) descends gradually. However, when the lower lip is prevented from ascending (△), the upper lip descends more rapidly (○). The lips meet at the same time in both instances (ovals).

behavior derives from the workings of the nervous system, behavioral scientists have become increasingly interested in the neural circuits that allow for the achievement of behavior (Brooks, 1986). Not all such work requires "wet" physiology, however. The formidable complexity of the brain also invites the design of *possible* circuits, where evaluation of the effectiveness of the circuit is done analytically or through computer simulation, as in the model I just described. In this section, I review another such model (Jordan, 1986a,b), designed to account for three of the most basic aspects of the production of speech: resistance to perturbations, parallel activity (exhibited in coarticulation), and serial ordering.

I mentioned an example of coarticulation earlier in this chapter—the tendency to round the lips one or more syllables before lip rounding is absolutely necessary. Another example, mentioned in Chapter 1, is *prenasalization* —opening the velum in anticipation of a nasal consonant (see Tables 9.1 and 9.3). An example of prenasalization is opening the velum before producing the nasal /n/ in *freon*; the velum opens even before the first syllable of this word (Moll & Daniloff, 1971). Anticipatory velar opening only occurs in languages for which nasalization carries no meaning. In English, opening the velum during pronunciation of *freo-* has no effect on the meaning of these phonemes, but in French it does, so in French, velar opening does not occur much in advance of the /n/. Coarticulation is therefore language dependent; it is not simply a result of the physical dynamics of the speech apparatus or low-level aspects of its control.

Jordan's system is made up of units connected in such a way that their pattern of activation allows units linked to muscles (*output* units) to bring about particular, desired actions. The starting point for Jordan's analysis is the assumption that any action can be described as an *n*-dimensional vector. The dimensions are simply independent characteristics of the action. In the case of speech, the dimensions can be phonetic features, such as nasalized, affricate, sibilant, and so forth (see Tables 9.1, 9.2, 9.3).

Suppose speech actions can be described in terms of three dimensions A, B, and C. Then a series of three successive speech actions can be represented as

$$
\begin{vmatrix} a_1 \\ b_1 \\ c_1 \end{vmatrix} \quad \begin{vmatrix} a_2 \\ b_2 \\ c_2 \end{vmatrix} \quad \begin{vmatrix} a_3 \\ b_3 \\ c_3 \end{vmatrix}
$$

where the left column refers to the first action, the middle column refers to the second action, and the right column refers to the third action. Suppose the vector $[a_1, b_1, c_1]$ defines the first target action and the language being spoken is insensitive to variations in dimension C when a_1 and b_1 take on the values desired in this case. The target vector for the first action can then be rewritten $[a_1, b_1, *]$, where * denotes an "indifferent" or "don't-care" value. (An example of a don't care value might be the degree of lip rounding when one says "t" in English; the acceptability of "t" is unaffected by lip rounding.) Similarly, if the value of b_2 does not have to be specified in the context of a_2 and c_2, the second target vector can be rewritten $[a_2, *, c_2]$. Finally, the third target vector can be rewritten $[a_3, b_3, *]$ if C need not be specified in the context of a_3 and b_3. Owing to the presence of don't-care values in the target vectors, the values they ultimately take on can be chosen to optimize the ease with which the other, constrained values can be successively produced.

Jordan's method for achieving optimization is to rely on a network whose units work in parallel and where the information coded in the network is represented through the strengths of the connections among the units. A network of this kind is called a *connectionist* system (Rumelhart & McClelland, 1986).

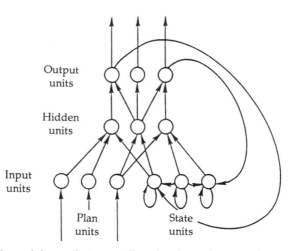

Figure 9.12 Network for producing serially ordered speech output. (From Jordan, 1986a.)

Jordan's connectionist system is shown in Figure 9.12. It has three types of units: *output* units, *hidden* units, and *input* units. Hidden units are like interneurons (see Chapter 2) in that they mediate input and output signals. They are used in Jordan's model, and in other comparable models, to ensure nonlinear relations between input-unit and output-unit signal strengths. Input units represent the plan to be carried out as well as the current state of the output units. In Jordan's model, disparities between desired outcomes (specified by the plan units) and actual outcomes (produced by output units) are reduced through a method called *back propagation*. When the first target action is $[a_1, b_1, *]$, because the produced value of dimension C does not matter (its value is *), no alterations are made for that dimension. However, on the next time step, when the target action is $[a_2, *, c_2]$, back propagation makes alterations on dimension C so the desired value, c_2, can be produced. The error reduction at this time generalizes to the previous time step, so the value c_2, needed at time 2, tends to be anticipated at time 1 (when the target value for dimension C is *). Similarly, the value b_3, needed at time 3, comes to be anticipated at time 2 (when the target value for dimension B is *).

What sets this model apart from previous models of coarticulation is that the selection of values is done automatically, without an intelligent overseer. The selection occurs entirely through partial activation of the units corresponding to the don't-care values. Partial activation allows for generalization across time, so the values that were initially unconstrained end up being influenced by values required later. The result of the interaction is coarticulation, and the coarticulations that have been generated with the network are similar to those actually observed. (The model predicts forward as well as backward coarticulation effects—that is, effects of preceding as well as forthcoming utterances, as observed in natural speech.)

Jordan's work represents an important advance in our understanding of speech production and motor control generally. It illustrates how a relatively simple network can achieve complex, planned behavior. The model also recasts phonetic features as *constraints* to be satisfied by the production system, rather than *a posteriori descriptions* of behavior, as in classical phonological theory (Chomsky & Halle, 1968).

■ HIGH-LEVEL CONTROL OF SPEECH

The discussion so far has been restricted to the problem of producing selected phonemes. Now let us turn to the question of how the various phonemes of succeeding words are selected and ordered. What control mechanisms regulate the serial ordering of words, phrases, and the sentences of which they are a part? Research on this question has relied extensively on speech errors, occurring either in spontaneous conversation or in specially designed word games.

Word Games

Pig Latin is a familiar example of a word game. Speakers of Pig Latin transfer the initial consonant or consonant cluster of a word to the end of the word and add an "ay" sound after that. Thus, "scram" becomes "amscray," "truck" becomes "ucktray," and so forth. Being able to carry out these transformations indicates that speakers are sensitive to the individual phonemes and phoneme clusters that make up words (Halle, 1962). Because it is ungrammatical in Pig Latin to say "cramsay" instead of "amscray" when the root word is "scram," the phoneme *cluster* is implicated as a distinct functional unit in the representation of speech.

Another example of a word game that reveals the psychological reality of phonemes and phoneme clusters is backward talking (Cowan, Braine, & Leavitt, 1985). People who can talk backward do not simply reverse the order of normal articulatory commands, as if they were running a tape recorder in reverse. Instead they reverse the sounds within individual syllables, proceeding from one syllable to the next in either the forward or backward direction (depending on the speaker). A backward speaker who produces syllables in the forward direction might transform the sentence "I can talk backward" into "I nac kawt cabdraw." One who produces syllables in the backward direction might say "Cabdraw kawt nac I." An important feature of the speech of backward talkers is that reversed phonemes rarely cross syllable boundaries. Thus "backward" becomes "draw-cab" rather than "drawk-ab" (for a backward speaker who produces syllables in the forward direction). This outcome provides evidence for the psychological reality of syllables (Treiman, 1983).

Backward speech also reveals that stress is represented independently of phonemes. Backward talkers usually maintain the temporal ordering of stress relations within words, even if this alters the original mappings of stresses to syllables. Thus the noun *con*trast is usually reversed as *tsart*noc rather than tsart*noc* (Cowan *et al.*, 1985). Maintaining the temporal ordering of stress suggests that stress patterns have the status of autonomous segments.

Laboratory Studies of Speaking Speed

Whereas Pig Latin and backward talking are word games that people play on their own, other word games (or gamelike tasks involving words) have been devised specifically for laboratory purposes. These tasks have yielded results complementary to those just described. For example, subjects in one study (Gordon & Meyer, 1987) learned to associate different four-syllable utterances with different signals. On each experimental trial, one signal was presented, and then, with a high probability, either that same signal was presented or, with a lower probability, one of the other signals was presented. Subjects were instructed to produce the utterance designated by the second signal as quickly as possible, which meant that it was adaptive for them to become highly prepared to say the utterance designated by the first signal.

The reaction time to say (or begin saying) the test utterance was shortest when it matched the initially prepared utterance, suggesting that subjects did indeed prepare to say the utterance associated with the first signal. More importantly, when the test utterance did not match the initially prepared utterance, reaction times were shorter when the two utterances had the same hierarchical syllable organization than when they did not (see Figure 9.13). For example, if the initially prepared sequence was "bee-bay-bah-boo," subjects were quicker to say "bah-boo-bee-bay" than to say "bah-bay-boo-bee." The first test sequence ("bah-boo-bee-bay") is hierarchically congruent with the initially prepared sequence; it simply reverses the order of the first and second syllable pairs. The second test sequence ("bah-bay-boo-bee") is not hierarchically congruent with the initially prepared sequence; it reverses the order of the middle and outer pairs of syllables. The fact that hierarchically congruent sequences are faster than hierarchically incongruent sequences suggests that syllables and syllable pairs are functional units for speech. This conclusion corroborates what we saw earlier in connection with backward speech, and fits with linguistic analyses of word morphology (word form) (Selkirk, 1982).

Why should syllables be organized hierarchically? One reason is that this form of organization makes it easy to modify words depending on their linguistic context. For example, adding or deleting prefixes and suffixes takes advantage of hierarchical organization, as does word contraction (Selkirk, 1982). Another advantage of hierarchical organization is that it allows properties of an entire speech sequence to be specified in a single step. This point was demonstrated in an experiment (Rosenbaum, Gordon, Stillings, & Feinstein, 1987) in which subjects were asked to say one of two

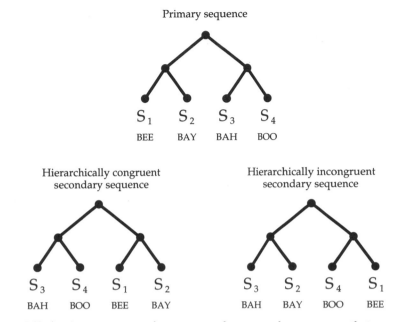

Figure 9.13 A primary sequence of utterances and two secondary sequences that are hierarchically congruent or incongruent with it. (From Gordon & Meyer, 1987.)

possible sequences depending on the identity of an auditory signal (see Figure 9.14). In one condition, each sequence consisted of one syllable starting with a hard "g" sound; the choice was "gee" versus "goo." In another condition, each sequence consisted of two syllables ("geebee" versus "gooboo"), and in another condition, each sequence consisted of three syllables ("geebeedee" versus "gooboodoo"). As shown in Figure 9.14, the time to start saying the designated sequence increased with the number of syllables. Moreover, the mean choice reaction time for a sequence was affected uniformly by its compatibility with the signal; that is, the choice reaction time for a sequence was shorter when the signal designating it was compatible with its distinguishing vowel (a high-pitched tone for the "ee" sequence and a low-pitched tone for the "oo" sequence) than when the signal was incompatible with the sequence's distinguishing vowel (a high-pitched tone for the "oo" sequence and a low-pitched tone for the "ee" sequence). The additive relation between sequence length and signal compatibility suggests that the vowel characterizing the entire sequence could be specified in a single processing stage (Sternberg, 1969). This is what one would expect if the sequence were represented hierarchically and a vowel assignment could be made for all the syllables at once (at the top of the hierarchy).

The other major result from this study—that reaction time increased with sequence length—also accords with the hierarchical model because it can be shown that initiating a long sequence requires the traversal of many

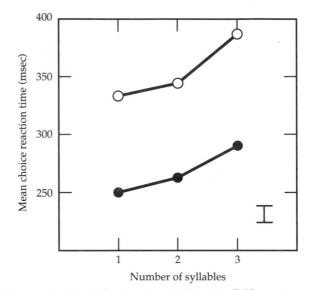

Figure 9.14 Mean reaction time to begin saying a 1-, 2-, or 3-syllable sequence when the signal designating each one was either compatible (●) or incompatible (○) with its distinguishing vowel. From D. A. Rosenbaum, A. M. Gordon, N. A. Stillings, & M. H. Feinstein (1987). Stimulus-response compatibility in the programming of speech. *Memory & Cognition,* **15,** 217–224. Reprinted by permission of the Psychonomic Society, Inc.

nodes from the root of the tree to the node corresponding to the first overt response (the leftmost terminal node) (Rosenbaum, 1985). Even when people are almost entirely sure that they will have to produce a previously identified vocal sequence, the time to begin producing the sequence increases with its length (Sternberg, Monsell, Knoll, & Wright, 1978). [Recall that Sternberg *et al.* (1978) obtained similar results for typewriting; see Chapter 8.]

Speech Errors

The physical production of speech is only one stage in the act of conversing. Before the articulators are set into motion, the speaker must formulate a message to be transmitted, the message must be put into words (if they are not already specified lexically), the words must be ordered, and a stress or intonation pattern must be selected. The question of how these functions are achieved before speech is produced has been addressed primarily through the analysis of speech errors. A speech error is an "unintended, nonhabitual deviation from a speech plan" (Dell, 1986, p. 284). Speaking backward is not a speech error because it is an intended departure from normal speech. Backward speakers do not appear to make the mistake of unintentionally speaking in reverse (Cowan *et al.*, 1985).

One of the first analyses of speech errors was provided by Sigmund Freud (1901/1966). He argued that mistakes in speaking express pent-up, unconscious thoughts, many of which are sexual in nature—hence the famous *Freudian slip*. An example of a Freudian slip would be the following. A person serving as a subject in a psychology experiment is supposed to read aloud nonsense syllables such as "Bine foddy." The subject happens to be tested by an experimenter who is provocatively attired. Under this condition, there is a fairly high chance that the subject will mistakenly say "Fine body" instead of "Bine foddy" (Motley, 1980). Errors of this kind demonstrate that Freud's theory is correct in some instances. However, because errors of this kind are not inevitable, it appears that people can also edit what they would otherwise say (as Freud assumed).

A source of evidence for editing is the observation that verbal slips contain fewer nonwords than words. Baars, Motley, and MacKay (1975) documented the prevalence of word errors by presenting subjects with lists of words, one at a time, to be read silently. The word *respond* was presented at some unpredictable point in the sequence, and at that point the subject was supposed to say aloud the last word pair presented before the *respond* prompt. A representative list follows. You should read it as subjects of Baars *et al.* (1975) did, covering all the words with a card and sliding the card down the column, word pair by word pair, reading each word pair silently until you come to the word *respond*. As soon as you encounter this word, say aloud the last word pair you read. Go ahead.

> ball doze
> bash door
> bean deck
> bell dark
> darn bore
> *respond*.

Did you say "barn door" rather than "darn bore"? This error occurred on 30% of the trials in the Baars *et al.* (1975) experiment. If you made this error (or were strongly tempted to do so), you fell prey to a phonological bias to begin the first word with a "b" and the second word with a "d."

Now repeat the procedure with the following list:

> big dutch
> bang doll
> bill deal
> bark dog
> dart board
> *respond*.

By the time you reached the final pair in this list, you again may have had a phonological bias to start the first word with a "b" and the second word with a "d." Had this bias been realized, you would have said "bart doard." But you probably did not make this error; in the experiment of Baars *et al.* (1975) it occurred in only 10% of the trials in which it was possible. Presumably "bart" and "doard" were not produced because they are nonwords; "barn" and "door" (the two error terms in the previous list) *are* words. The fact that people are more likely to err with words than with nonwords can be taken to suggest that they covertly edit their speech before producing it.

The latter statement implies that some of the factors contributing to speech errors and their prevention are not Freudian, in the sense of representing suppressed libidonal urges. Lexical status is unlikely to be something the superego cares much about. Because many (and perhaps most) speech errors do not pertain to sexual themes, influences of the sort that Freud cared about are not the only ones that cause slips of the tongue. The generally accepted position among psycholinguists today is that speech errors derive from mistakes in the otherwise normal workings of the speech planning and production process. Accepting this view, the study of speech errors can be embraced as a tool for investigating the normal organization of the planning and production of speech.

Table 9.4 presents the major types of speech errors that have been recorded in spontaneous conversations. The list is not exhaustive but illustrates the variety and regularity of errors that have been documented. There are several noteworthy features of the list. First, different kinds of linguistic units are involved: entire words, morphemes (the meaning-bearing parts of words, such as the final "s" that indicates a plural ending), phonemes, consonant clusters, and vowel–consonant combinations. Second, the errors reflect different sorts of disruptions, including misorderings (for example, anticipations, perseverations, shifts, and deletions) and "noncontextual errors" in which the exact source of error is hard to identify (for example, blends). A third feature of the errors is that for those involving interacting units, such as word exchanges (*Writing a letter to my mother → Writing a mother to my letter*) or phoneme exchanges (*York library → Lork yibrary*), the units participating in the interaction generally belong to the same linguistic category. For example, they are both words (*mother* and *letter*) or both phonemes (*L* and *y*).

Researchers who model speech production by studying speech errors have attempted to account for such regularities. An assumption common to virtually all the models (Dell, 1986; Garrett, 1975; Shattuck-Hufnagle, 1979) is that there are distinct tiers of linguistic representation for forthcoming sentences. These tiers have been referred to as the *semantic* level, the *syntactic* level, the *morphological* level, the *phonological* level, the *phonetic* level, and the *motor* level. The *semantic* level codes the linguistic meaning of the message the speaker intends to transmit (which may originate prelinguistically, in the mysterious "language of thought"). The *syntactic* level codes word order and factors affected by the grammatical relation between words. The *morphological* level codes the details of word formation, such as the presence of prefixes and suffixes. The *phonological* and *phonetic* levels break words and their affixes

Table 9.4 Types of Speech Errors[a]

Type	Examples	Unit involved
Sound errors		
Misordering		
Substitution		
Exchange	York library → lork yibrary	Phoneme
	Spill beer → speer bill	Rime constituent
	Snow flurries → flow snurries	Consonant cluster
	Clear blue → glear plue	Feature
Anticipation	Reading list → leading list	Phoneme
	Couch is comfortable → comf is . . .	Syllable or rime
Preservation	Beef noodle → beef needle	Phoneme
Addition		
Anticipatory addition	Eerie stamp → steerie stamp	Consonant cluster
Perseveratory addition	Blue bug → blue blug	Phoneme
Shift	Black boxes → back bloxes	Phoneme
Deletion	Same state → same sate	Phoneme
Noncontextual errors	Department → jepartment	Phoneme
(substitution, addition,	Winning → winnding	Phoneme
deletion)	Tremendously → tremenly	Syllable
Morpheme errors		
Misordering		
Substitution		
Exchange	Self-destruct instruction → self-instruct de . . .	Prefix
	Thinly sliced → slicely thinned	Stem
Anticipation	My car towed → my tow towed	Stem
Perseveration	Explain . . . rule insertion → . . . rule exsertion	Prefix
Shift	Gets it → get its	Inflectional suffix
Addition	Dollars deductible → dedollars deductible	Prefix
	Some weeks → somes weeks	Inflectional suffix
Noncontextual errors	Conclusion → concludement	Derivational suffix
(substitution, addition,	To strain it → to strained it	Inflectional suffix
deletion)	He relaxes → he relax	Inflectional suffix
Word errors		
Misordering		
Substitution		
Exchange	Writing a letter to my mother → writing a mother to my letter	Noun
Anticipation	Sun is in the sky → sky is in the sky	Noun
Perseveration	Class will be about discussing the test → . . . discussing the class	Noun
Addition	These flowers are purple → these purple flowers are purple	Adjective
Shift	Something to tell you all → something all to tell you	Quantifier
Noncontextual errors		
Substitution	Pass the pepper → pass the salt	Noun
	Liszt's second Hungarian rhapsody → second Hungarian restaurant	Noun
Blend	Athlete/player → athler	Noun
	Taxi/cab → tab	Noun
Addition	The only thing I can do → the only one thing	Quantifier
Deletion	I just wanted to ask that → I just wanted to that	Verb

[a]From Dell, 1986.

into phonemes and phones, respectively. The *motor* level permits the physical realization of the phonetic features that have been selected.

The models that have been proposed differ with respect to the way units are assumed to interact within and between these levels. At one end are models which assume that information passes only from high to low levels (Garrett, 1982). At the other end are models which assume that information passes from high to low levels and from low to high levels (Dell, 1986). Current models of speech production also vary with respect to the way choices are made about the units to be produced. Dell's (1986) model assumes spreading activation among units, with the choice of units (and so the likelihood of choosing the wrong unit) depending on its level of activation. An important property of Dell's model is that it does not require an editing operation to account for the prevalence of word errors over nonword errors. Words are more likely than nonwords because of the pattern of excitation and inhibition among units within and across levels of the network. More traditional models, such as those of Garrett (1982) and Shattuck-Hufnagle (1979), assume that choices among units are entirely rule governed, though they are subject to error. In Garrett's model, for example, if someone says "She's already trunked two packs" instead of "She's already packed two trunks," the error is assumed to result from an incorrect assignment of words to previously defined but as yet unfilled word slots. Rules establish that the slots should be filled with words and that both words should be nouns, but the insertion of words into the slots goes awry.

Note that in the above error, the affixes—the -s from *trunks* and the -ed from *packed*—attach properly to the switched words. This argues that a distinct morphological level is accessed after syntactic processing has begun.

Phonological processing also appears to occur after morphological processing has been completed. The reason is that phonemes accommodate to new morphological environments. For example, suppose one makes the mistake of substituting the word *outs* for the word *runs* (while describing a baseball game). This substitution requires a change in the "hardness" of the final "s." The "s" in "runs" is pronounced like a "z," whereas the "s" in "outs" is pronounced like a hard "s." Because the pronunciation that occurs is correct when "runs" switches to "outs," the hardness of the final "s" is accommodated to the new phonological environment. This outcome suggests that phonological processing follows morphological processing.

■ BRAIN MECHANISMS UNDERLYING SPEECH

As the preceding discussion has been meant to show, even when the speech-production system functions normally, it can falter occasionally and give rise to speech errors. Speech errors that occur when the nervous system is damaged provide another window into the control of speech. If particular characteristics of speech are affected by damage to particular brain sites, one can infer that those sites play some role in controlling the speech characteristics that have been impaired. Moreover, if the impaired aspects of speech correspond to particular, hypothesized stages in the speech-production process, one can go a step further and hypothesize that each of the stages is controlled by each of the damaged brain sites.

Over a century ago, a young French neurologist, Paul Broca, found that patients who had profound difficulty speaking also happened to have damage in the anterior left temporal lobe of the cortex. The area came to be called Broca's area, and the speech disorder that Broca identified is called

Broca's aphasia. The hallmark of Broca's aphasia is "telegraphic" speech. The patient speaks in short bursts, usually without function words (prepositions, conjunctions, and determiners). Broca's aphasia is not a disorder of motor control, for Broca's aphasics are able to produce the words that elude them in spontaneous conversation. For example, they can read aloud sentences such as "Two bee oar knot two bee," which are filled with words that sound identical to (and so are produced the same way as) function words (Gardner & Zurif, 1975). Another indication that the expressive difficulties of Broca's aphasics are not due to problems with motor implementation is that they cannot use function words in writing or in sign language. Thus it is not simply physical output that is damaged in Broca's aphasia, but the use of linguistic information.

Much recent work on aphasia has focused on the detailed properties of the grammatical capabilities that Broca's (and other) aphasics lack. A major issue is whether Broca's aphasics have lost syntactic knowledge or whether they have merely lost the ability to call up the necessary syntactic rules when generating speech. An important clue that they possess syntactic knowledge is that they can recognize ungrammatical sentences, even when the grammatical errors to which they are exposed deviate only subtly from correct usage (Linebarger, Schwartz, & Saffran, 1983).

Many workers concerned with the neurophysiological control of speech production have adopted a simple three-stage model consisting of *planning*, *programming*, and *execution* (Logemann, 1985). Disorders of planning (discussed previously) are referred to as *aphasias*. Disorders of programming are called speech *apraxias*. Patients with speech *apraxias* are unable to produce orderly sequences of phonemes, though they can physically produce individual phonemes or limited sequences of phonemes. Disorders of speech execution are called *dysarthrias*. Dysarthric speakers are unable to produce the articulatory gestures that ensure distinct pronunciation of individual phonemes (Logemann, 1985).

The existence of these distinct kinds of disorders supports the view that there are distinct stages in the production of speech. Moreover, distinct areas of the brain have been linked to each type of disorder. Patients with speech apraxia usually have lesions in the secondary motor area, whereas dysarthric patients usually have lesions in the primary motor cortex or the part of the brain stem from which the orofacial cranial nerves (the nerves innervating the mouth and face) emerge (Keller, 1987). Similarly, stimulation of the primary motor cortex produces uncontrollable vocalization and slurring of speech (Penfield & Roberts, 1959), whereas stimulation of the secondary motor cortex produces syllable repetitions and hesitations (Keller, 1987).

As neat as this picture is, it is important to keep in mind that the primary and secondary areas of motor cortex are not the only brain sites responsible for the programming and execution of speech. Brain stem nuclei are involved and there is evidence that the basal ganglia, cerebellum, and other cortical areas play a role (Gracco & Abbs, 1987). The complete picture of the brain's role in controlling speech production is therefore predictably complex.

One generalization about the brain's control of speech that has been known for at least a century is that the left cortical hemisphere is generally specialized for language. Broca recognized this fact when he saw that most aphasics had damage to the left hemisphere but not the right. His observation has been replicated many times, though it has also been recognized that left hemispheric control of language is more distinct for right-handed people (whose manual control is usually also centered in the left hemisphere) than for left-handed people.

One of the tantalizing questions raised by the discovery of brain lateralization for speech and manual control is whether it is unique to humans. Some dramatic evidence that it is *not* comes from studies of the control of bird song.

■ BIRD SONG

People rely on speaking more than on singing for everyday communication. For practical reasons therefore, more research has been done on speech than on song (but see Harvey, 1985; Sundberg, 1977). Much of the work that has been done on singing has concentrated on bird song. Bird song is an appealing topic for research, not just because of its aesthetic qualities, but also because one can determine how exposure to song at various points in the bird's life affects its ability to sing. (For ethical reasons, of course, comparable manipulations cannot be tried with people.)

A number of intriguing findings have been obtained through this approach (Hinde, 1971). Work with the chaffinch (a common bird in Europe) has shown that it has a species-characteristic song consisting of several short phrases (see Figure 9.15A). Under normal conditions, very young chaffinches produce a kind of rambling song of indefinite length—a kind of melodic "babble"—which gradually approximates the species-specific song of the adult. Chaffinches reared in isolation develop only a rudimentary form of the species song (see Figure 9.15B), but chaffinches reared in groups develop somewhat more elaborate versions that turn out to be peculiar to the group in which they are raised (see Figure 9.15C). Chaffinches who are kept in isolation after being exposed to the song of their species before they themselves can sing later sing a fairly good approximation to the normal species song, but not a perfect rendition of it. On the other hand, groups of chaffinches that are kept together after being exposed to the species song, but before they are able to sing, later sing the species song perfectly. Chaffinches reared in isolation who are not exposed to the species song until after the first breeding season usually cannot learn it, but chaffinches reared in isolation who are exposed to the species song *before* the first breeding season usually can learn it. Finally, when chaffinches isolated from birth are ex-

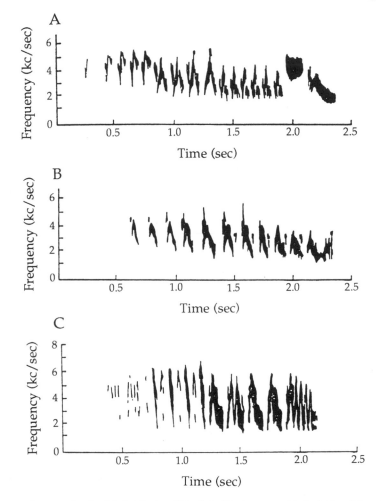

Figure 9.15 Song cycle of wild chaffinches (A), of chaffinches reared in isolation (B), and of chaffinches reared in small groups (C). (From Hinde, 1971.)

posed to taped songs that differ in various ways from the normal species song, their ability to learn the artificial song depends on its similarity to the species song; this is true even though all the notes in the artificial song are contained in the species song.

These results suggest that the acquisition of bird song depends on an interplay of innate tendencies, environmental conditions, and maturational factors. The role of innate tendencies is suggested by the fact that not all songs that chaffinches are physically able to sing are equally learnable. The role of environmental conditions is suggested by the importance of being exposed to the species song rather than some other song and of being around other birds after the first breeding season. The importance of maturational factors is suggested by the fact that after the first breeding season, a bird that has never been exposed to a song can never learn to sing it.

Significantly, these conclusions are qualitatively similar to conclusions of research on human language acquisition (Carroll, 1986). Children deprived of linguistic input are usually unable to recover from this deprivation if their first exposure to language comes only after puberty, though they have a chance of recovering from the deprivation if their first exposure comes before puberty. Additionally, children deprived of linguistic input who are in the company of other such children sometimes develop a language of their own which obeys many of the basic features of all human languages. Finally, the fact that all human languages may share a number of grammatical features suggests that there are genetic predispositions for the abstract form that human language takes (Chomsky, 1975). Given these similarities between the acquisition of human language and the acquisition of bird song, the brain mechanisms underlying bird song become especially interesting. If the study of the bird brain can reveal how heredity, experience, and maturation affect the way birds learn to sing, it may also suggest how those factors affect the way people learn to talk.

The most celebrated work on the brain mechanisms underlying bird song has been done by Fernando Nottebohm and his colleagues at Rockefeller University in New York City (Nottebohm, 1989). One of this group's noteworthy discoveries was that bird song is primarily controlled in the left hemisphere of the bird's brain. The discovery was made in studies of the canary. The studies involved cutting a nerve—the tracheosyringeal (TS) nerve—which innervates the muscles of the syrinx (the organ for song). Cutting the right TS nerve had little effect on the birds' singing ability, but cutting the left TS nerve had a deleterious effect. Further work showed that the left TS nerve is controlled by a center in the *left* hemisphere of the brain. Evidently for canaries, as for humans, the left hemisphere is specialized for the control of vocalization.

More recent work has yielded an even more startling result. After identifying the left-brain center for bird song, Nottebohm and his colleagues studied the properties of this center during song acquisition. Surprisingly, the volume of the brain center varied according to the intensity of song use. In the spring, when male canaries sing frequently, the center was found to be large, but in the fall, when they sing much less, the center was found to be much smaller.

That the center is involved in song *learning* became clear through several converging observations. Canaries with large song centers were better singers than canaries with small song centers. Female canaries given testerone (a male hormone) learned to sing (which they otherwise do not do), and their song centers also grew larger than normal. Finally, male canaries that were castrated, and so were unable to produce testerone, did not learn to sing, and their song centers also failed to grow.

These observations led Nottebohm to speculate that neurons in the song center might grow and die depending on the waxing and waning of testosterone. Proposing that new neurons grow in the brains of adult canaries represented a serious challenge to the prevailing view within neuro-science that new neurons cannot grow in adulthood. To challenge this view, Nottebohm had to prove that changes in the volume of the song center do not simply reflect changes in the size of already existing neurons. Through painstaking work, his group showed that neurons do indeed grow in the brains of adult birds. This raises the question of whether neurons also grow in adult human brains or can be made to do so. If they can, people with aphasia, speech apraxia, dysarthria, or other impairments might be helped in dramatically new ways.

■ SUMMARY

1. Language is made up of words, which in turn are made up of *phonemes* (sound categories that convey meaning) and *phones* (sound categories that do not necessarily convey meaning). The elements making up and distinguishing phones are *phonetic features*. Additional characteristics of speech are pitch, intonation, and rate.

2. We speak more quickly than would be possible if each phoneme were prepared only after the preceding phoneme was completed. The articulators move in parallel and anticipate forthcoming phoneme requirements. This phenomenon is called *coarticulation*.

3. Besides accounting for the production of phonemes and phones through coarticulation, a theory of speech production must explain why some speech sounds are universally absent. It must also explain how speakers and singers compensate for physical changes in the articulators (for example, while holding a pipe clenched between the teeth) and how speakers and singers coordinate vocal production and hearing, both during learning and during ongoing vocal output.

4. The vocal tract consists of three subsystems—the *respiratory* subsystem, the *laryngeal* subsystem, and the *articulatory* subsystem. Within the respiratory system, the *diaphragm* and *external intercostals* promote inhalation, and the *internal intercostals* promote exhalation. The timing of activity in these opposing muscle groups is partly based on muscle feedback about the volume and change of volume of the lungs.

5. The *larynx*, which lies at the base of the throat, serves four main functions: It regulates the characteristic pitch of the voice, it modulates aspiration (accompanying syllable-initial "p" sounds, for example), it is responsible for whispering, and it controls voicing.

6. The *pharynx*, which lies between the larynx and the mouth, has a shape that allows for the production of some vowels but not others. Fossil evidence has led some investigators to suggest that the vowels produced by human adults have only been produced within the last 35,000 years. Other investigators have argued that speech as we know it has been produced for at least 2 million years.

7. Different vowels are produced by varying the position of the tongue body in the mouth. The main dimensions along which the position of the tongue body vary are up–down and front–back.

8. Different consonants are produced by varying *manners* of articulation (ways of constricting the air stream in the oral cavity) and by varying *places* of articulation (locations where the air stream is constricted). It is possible to characterize consonants and vowels by assuming that each has a distinct manner and place of articulation. The "standard theory" of phonology assumed that each consonant and vowel can be characterized by the presence or absence of features defined by particular place–manner combinations.

9. There is enormous variability in the way speech sounds are produced. The variability is so great that visual inspection of speech spectrograms makes it unclear how people can recognize particular consonants or vowels when produced in different linguistic contexts. A proposed solution is that listeners recognize speech sounds by accessing knowledge about how they produce the sounds themselves (the *motor* theory of speech perception). The invariance in articulatory activity that would be expected if the motor theory were correct has been hard to find, however.

10. A theory of how speech sounds can be produced reliably assumes that the articulators aim for specific target positions. The movement of the articulators toward the target positions is mediated by the gamma system. Initial results were promising for the spatial target theory, but later results were less so.

11. A more recent theory is that the speech-production system attempts to bring the articulators to characteristic *relative* positions. As predicted in the theory, following external perturbations, there is rapid compensation that preserves relative positions needed for immediate articulatory goals. A possible mechanism for achieving invariant relative positioning relies on mutual inhibition between command centers for articulators whose relative positions must be coordinated.

12. A parallel distributed system has recently been proposed as a model of coarticulation. The system anticipates features of forthcoming actions because of generalization to states whose exact values at earlier (or later) times do not matter in the language being spoken.

13. Pig Latin and backward speech provide evidence for the psychological reality of syllables and the autonomous representation of stress. Laboratory studies of the reaction time to begin speaking when a switch must be made from an initially prepared utterance to another utterance suggest that the syllables of a word are represented hierarchically. Hierarchical organization provides a basis for specifying characteristics of an entire word in a single processing step.

14. Speech errors have been used to infer the major stages in the planning and production of words, phrases, and sentences. People are unlikely to produce nonwords when making speech errors—a result that has been interpreted to mean that speakers edit forthcoming utterances, as Freud once proposed. A more recent model shows that a parallel distributed processing system with distinct tiers corresponding to semantic, syntactic, morphological, phonological, phonetic, and motor levels can give rise to the prevalence of word errors without the need for an editing process.

15. Deficits in language production accompanying damage to the brain can be understood by assuming that distinct brain sites are related to distinct phases of language production. Three major types of language dysfunction accompany brain damage—*aphasia* (a language planning deficit), *apraxia* (a phoneme sequencing deficit), and *dysarthria* (a motor execution deficit).

16. Because it is impossible for ethical reasons to vary the amount of exposure that young children have to language, birds have been exposed to the songs of their species in a wide range of conditions so scientists can learn how species songs are acquired. The acquisition of bird song appears to depend on an interplay of hereditary, experiential, and maturational factors. Human language learning also appears to depend on these three factors.

17. Investigations of the acquisition and control of bird song by the bird's brain have revealed two remarkable principles. First the left hemisphere of the bird's brain is generally specialized for singing—reminiscent of the human brain's control of language. Second, new neurons appear to grow in the bird's brain when songs are learned—a result that upsets the dogma of neuroscience that during adulthood new neurons do not form in the central nervous system.

■ REFERENCES

Abbs, J. H. (1986). Invariance and variability in speech production: A distinction between linguistic intent and its neuromotor implementation. In J. S. Perkell & D. H. Klatt (Eds.), *Invariance and variability in speech processes* (pp. 202–219). Hillsdale, NJ: Erlbaum.

Abbs, J. H., Gracco, V. L., & Cole, K. J. (1984). Control of multimovement coordination: Sensorimotor mechanisms in speech motor programming. *Journal of Motor Behavior*, **16**, 195–231.

Akmajian, A., Demers, R. A., & Harnish, R. W. (1979). *Linguistics: An introduction*. Cambridge, MA: MIT Press.

Baars, B. J., Motley, M. T., & Mackay, D. G. (1975). Output editing for lexical status in artificially elicited slips of the tongue. *Journal of Verbal Learning and Verbal Behavior*, **14**, 382–391.

Bower, B. (1989). Talk of ages. *Science News*, **136**, (2) 24–26.

Brooks, V. B. (1986). *The neural basis of motor control*. New York: Oxford Press.

Carroll, D. W. (1986). *Psychology of language*. Monterey, CA: Brooks/Cole.

Carterette, E. C., & Friedman, M. P. (Eds.) (1976). *Handbook of perception* (Vol. 7, *Language and speech*). New York: Academic Press.

Chomsky, N. (1975). *Reflections on language*. New York: Pantheon.

Chomsky, N., & Halle, M. (1968). *The sound pattern of English*. New York: Harper & Row.

Cole, K. J., Gracco, V. L., & Abbs, J. H. (1984). Autogenic and nonautogenic sensorimotor actions in the control of multiarticulate hand movements. *Experimental Brain Research, 56,* 582–585.

Costello, J. M. (Ed.) (1985). *Speech disorders in adults*. San Diego, CA: College Hill Press.

Cowan, N., Braine, M. D. S., & Leavitt, L. A. (1985). The phonological and metaphonological representation of speech: Evidence from fluent backward talkers. *Journal of Memory and Language, 24,* 679–698.

Daniloff, R., & Moll, K. (1968). Coarticulation of lip rounding. *Journal of Speech and Hearing Research, 11,* 707–721.

Dell, G. S. (1986). A spreading activation theory of retrieval in sentence production. *Psychological Review, 93,* 283–321.

Deutsch, J. A., & Clarkson, J. K. (1959). Nature of the vibrato and the control loop in singing. *Nature (London), 183,* 167–168.

Freud, S. (1901/1966). *Psychopathology of everyday life* (A. Tyson, Trans.) London: Benn. (Original work published in 1901).

Gardner, H., & Zurif, E. (1975). Bee but not be: Oral reading of single words in aphasia and alexia. *Neuropsychologia, 13,* 181–190.

Garrett, M. F. (1982). Production of speech: Observations from normal and pathological language use. In A. W. Ellis (Ed.), *Normality and pathology in cognitive functions* (pp. 19–76). London: Academic Press.

Goldman-Eisler, F. (1968). *Psycholinguistics: Experiments in spontaneous speech*. New York: Academic Press.

Gordon, P. C., & Meyer, D. E. (1987). Control of serial order in rapidly spoken syllable sequences. *Journal of Memory and Language, 26,* 300–321.

Gracco, V. L., & Abbs, J. H. (1987). Programming and execution processes of speech movement control: Potential neural correlates. In E. Keller (Ed.), *Motor and sensory processes of language* (pp. 163–201). Hillsdale, NJ: Erbaum.

Halle, M. G. (1962). Phonology in generative grammar. *Word, 18,* 54–72.

Halle, M. G., & Clements, G. N. (1983). *Problem book in phonetics*. Cambridge, MA: MIT Press.

Harrington, J. (1987). A model of stuttering and the production of speech under delayed auditory feedback conditions. In H. F. M. Peters & W. Hulstijn (Eds.), *Speech motor dynamics in stuttering* (pp. 353–359). Vienna: Springer-Verlag.

Harvey, N. (1985). Vocal control in singing: A cognitive approach. In P. Howell, I. Cross, & R. West (Eds.), *Musical structure and cognition* (pp. 287–332). London: Academic Press.

Hasegawa, A., McCutcheon, M., Wolf, M., & Fletcher, S. (1976). Lip and jaw coordination during the production of /f, v/ in English. *Journal of the Acoustical Society of America,* **S84,** 59.

Hinde, R. A. (1971). The development of bird song. In K. J. Connolly (Ed.), *Mechanisms of motor skill development* (pp. 287–304). London: Academic Press.

Hockett, C. F. (1955). A manual of phonology. In *International Journal of American Linguistics (Memoir II)*. Baltimore, MD: Waverly Press.

Howell, P., Eli-Yaniv, N., & Powell, D. J. (1987). Factors affecting stutterers when speaking under altered auditory feedback. In H. F. M. Peters & W. Hulstijn (Eds.), *Speech motor dynamics in stuttering* (pp. 361–369). Vienna: Springer-Verlag.

Hughes, O., & Abbs, J. H. (1976). Labial-mandibular coordination in the production of speech: Implications for the operation of motor equivalence. *Phonetica, 44,* 199–221.

Jordan, M. I. (1986a). Attractor dynamics and parallelism in a connectionist sequential machine. In C. Clifton, Jr. (Ed.), *Proceedings of the 8th Annual Meeting of the Cognitive Science Society* (pp. 531–545). Hillsdale, NJ: Erlbaum.

Jordan, M. I. (1986b). *Serial order: A parallel, distributed processing approach* (Tech. Rep. No. 8604). La Jolla, CA: University of California, San Diego, Institute for Cognitive Science.

Keller, E. (1987). The cortical representation of motor processes of speech. In E. Keller & M. Gopnik (Eds.), *Motor and sensory processes of language* (pp. 125–162). Hillsdale, NJ: Erlbaum.

Kelso, J. A. S., Tuller, B., Vatikiotis-Bateson, E., & Fowler, C. A. (1984). Functionally specific articulatory cooperation following jaw perturbations during speech: Evidence for coordinative structures. *Journal of Experimental Psychology: Human Perception and Performance*, **10,** 812–832.

Kozhevnikov, V. A., & Chistovich, L. (1965). *Speech: Articulation and perception*. Moscow-Leningrad: Nauka. (Translation available from the Joint Publication Research Service, United States Department of Commerce, Washington, D.C.)

Lacquaniti, F., & Soechting, J. F. (1984). Behavior of the stretch reflex in a multi-jointed limb. *Brain Research*, **311,** 161–166.

Ladefoged, P. (1967). *Three areas of experimental phonetics*. New York: Oxford Univ. Press.

Ladefoged, P., DeClerk, J., Lindau, M., & Papçun, G. (1972). An auditory-motor theory of speech production. *UCLA Working Papers in Linguistics*, **22,** 48–75.

Lee, B. S. (1950). Effects of delayed speech feedback. *Journal of the Acoustical Society of America*, **22,** 824–826.

Liberman, A. M., Cooper, F. S., Shankweiler, D. P., & Studdert-Kennedy, M. G. (1967). Perception of the speech code. *Psychological Review*, **74,** 431–461.

Lieberman, P. (1984). *The biology and evolution of language*. Cambridge, MA: Harvard Univ. Press.

Lindblom, B. (1983). Economy of speech gestures. In P. F. MacNeilage (Ed.), *The production of speech* (pp. 217–245). New York: Springer-Verlag.

Lindblom, B., & Sundberg, J. (1971). Acoustical consequences of lip, tongue, jaw and larynx movements. *Journal of the Acoustical Society of America*, **50,** 1166–1179.

Linebarger, M. C., Schwartz, M. F., & Saffran, E. M. (1983). Sensitivity to grammatical structure in so-called agrammatic aphasics. *Cognition*, **13,** 361 392.

Logemann, J. A. (1985). Assessment and treatment of articulatory disorders in adults: State of the art. In J. M. Costello (Ed.), *Speech disorders in adults* (pp. 3–19). San Diego, CA: College-Hill Press.

MacNeilage, P. F. (1970). Motor control of serial ordering of speech. *Psychological Review*, **77,** 182–196.

MacNeilage, P. F. (1980). Distinctive features of speech control. In G. E. Stelmach & J. Requin (Eds.), *Tutorials in motor behavior* (pp. 607–621). Amsterdam: North-Holland.

MacNeilage, P. F. (Ed.) (1983). *The production of speech*. New York: Springer-Verlag.

MacNeilage, P. F., & DeClerk, J. L. (1969). On the motor control of coarticulation in CVC monosyllables. *Journal of the Acoustical Society of America*, **45,** 1217–1233.

MacNeilage, P. F., & Ladefoged, P. (1976). The production of speech and language. In E. C. Carterette & M. P. Friedman (Eds.), *Handbook of perception* (Vol. 7, pp. 75–120). New York: Academic Press.

MacNeilage, P. F., Krones, R., & Hanson, R. (1969). *Closed-loop control of the initiation of jaw movement for speech*. Paper presented at the meeting of the Acoustical Society of America, San Diego.

MacNeilage, P. F., Rootes, T. P., & Chase, R. A. (1967). Speech production and perception in a patient with severe impairment of somesthetic perception and motor control. *Journal of Speech and Hearing Research*, **10,** 449–467.

Marlsen-Wilson, W., & Tyler, L. K. (1980). The temporal structure of spoken language understanding. *Cognition*, **8,** 1–71.

Miller, G. A. (1981). *Language and speech*. New York: Freeman.

Moll, K. L., & Daniloff, R. G. (1971). Investigation of the timing of velar movements during speech. *Journal of the Acoustical Society of America*, **50,** 678–684.

Motley, M. T. (1980). Verification of "Freudian slips" and semantic prearticulatory editing via laboratory-induced spoonerisms. In V. A. Fromkin (Ed.), *Errors in linguistic performance* (pp. 133–147). New York: Academic Press.

Nickerson, R. S., Kalikow, D. N., & Stevens, K. N. (1976). Computer-aided speech training for the deaf. *Journal of Speech and Hearing Disorders, 41,* 120–132.

Nooteboom, S. G. (1970). The target theory of speech production. *IPO Annual Progress Report, 5,* 51–55.

Nottebohm, F. (1989). From bird song to neurogenesis. *Scientific American, 260* (2), 74–79.

Ohala, J. J. (1983). The origin of sound patterns in vocal tract constraints. In P. F. MacNeilage (Ed.), *The production of speech* (pp. 189–216). New York: Springer-Verlag.

Penfield, W., & Roberts, L. (1959). *Speech and brain mechanisms.* New York: Atheneum.

Perkell, J. S., & Klatt, D. H. (Eds.) (1986). *Invariance and variability in speech processes.* Hillsdale, NJ: Erlbaum.

Peschel, E. R., & Peschel, R. E. (1987). Medical insights into the castrati in opera. *American Scientist, 75,* 578–583.

Rosenbaum, D. A. (1985). Motor programming: A review and scheduling theory. In H. Heuer, U. Kleinbeck, & K.-M. Schmidt (Eds.), *Motor behavior: Programming, control, and acquisition* (pp. 1-33). Berlin: Springer-Verlag.

Rosenbaum, D. A., Gordon, A. M., Stillings, N. A., & Feinstein, M. H. (1987). Stimulus-response compatibility in the programming of speech. *Memory & Cognition, 15,* 217–224.

Rumelhart, D. E., & McClelland, J. L. (1986). *Parallel distributed processing: Explorations in the microstructure of cognition.* Cambridge, MA: MIT Press.

Sawashima, M., & Hirose, H. (1983). Laryngeal gestures in speech production. In P. F. MacNeilage (Ed.), *The production of speech* (pp. 11–38). New York: Springer-Verlag.

Scott, C. M., & Ringel, R. L. (1971). Articulation without oral sensory control. *Journal of Speech and Hearing Research, 14,* 804–814.

Selkirk, E. O. (1982). *The syntax of words.* Cambridge, MA: MIT Press.

Shattuck-Hufnagle, S. (1979). Speech errors as evidence for a serial order mechanism in sentence production. In W. E. Cooper & E. C. T. Walker (Eds.), *Sentence processing: Psycholinguistic studies presented to Merrill Garrett* (pp. 295–342). Hillsdale, NJ: Erlbaum.

Smith, S. M., Brown, H. O., Toman, J. E. P., & Goodman, L. S. (1947). Lack of cerebral effect of d-Tubercurarine. *Anesthesiology, 8,* 1–14.

Smith, T. S., & Lee, C. Y. (1971). *Peripheral feedback mechanisms in speech production models.* Paper presented at the VII International Congress of Phonetic Sciences, Montreal (August).

Sokolov, A. N. (1972). *Inner speech and thought.* New York: Plenum Press.

Sternberg. S., Monsell, S., Knoll, R. L., & Wright, C. E. (1978). The latency and duration of rapid movement sequences: Comparisons of speech and typewriting. In G. E. Stelmach (Ed.), *Information processing in motor control and learning* (pp. 117–152). New York: Academic Press.

Sternberg, S. (1969). The discovery of processing stages: Extensions of Donders' method. In W. G. Koster (Ed.), *Attention and performance II* (pp. 276–315). Amsterdam: North-Holland.

Stetson, R. H. (1951). *Motor phonetics.* Amsterdam: North-Holland.

Sundberg, J. (1977). The acoustics of the singing voice. *Scientific American, 237* (3), 82–91.

Treiman, R. (1983). The structure of spoken syllables: Evidence from novel word games. *Cognition, 15,* 49–74.

Warren, R. M., & Warren, R. P. (1970). Auditory illusions and confusions. *Scientific American, 23,* 30–36.

10 SMILING

■ INTRODUCTION

Perhaps no other stimulus is more significant to us as social creatures than the human face. Faces have been the subject of countless works of art, both literary and graphic. In everyday life, we look at faces to gather information about others' reactions. The capacity to pick up information from faces is present at a very early age. Newborns are more likely to look at faces than at other sorts of visual stimuli (Fantz, 1961; Kleiner & Banks, 1987) and they can discriminate facial expressions within the first 36 hours of life (Field, Woodson, Greenberg, & Cohen, 1982). Faces are also remembered remarkably well. People can recognize faces from high school yearbooks virtually perfectly even if they haven't seen the pictures, or the people depicted in them, for 50 years or more (Bahrick, Bahrick, & Wittlinger, 1975). No less remarkable is that, in face-to-face encounters, people can recognize others whom they haven't seen in years, despite dramatic facial changes accompanying the aging process. This capacity may be due in part to age-related changes that leave certain facial features invariant (Todd, Mark, Shaw, & Pittenger, 1980).

Facial *movement* attracts attention as much as, if not more than, facial *structure*. If faces were static, they would convey much less information than they normally do (as any poker player knows). The mobility of the face allows people to express a wide range of emotions. Efforts to count the emotions expressed by the face have yielded differing estimates (Averill, 1975; Storm & Storm, 1987). Yet there is little disagreement that there is a close link between facial expression and emotions. For this reason, analyzing facial expression as a means of reflecting emotion is a natural way to approach the subject of facial control.

To be consistent with the other chapter titles in Part II of this volume, I have selected the name of one motor activity (smiling) to refer to the entire class of activities of which it is an example. Smiling is not the only facial expression to be discussed, however, just as walking was not the only locomotory activity discussed in Chapter 4 and looking was not the only eye-movement activity discussed in Chapter 5.

Several questions about the control of facial expression will occupy our attention. First, how are expressions physically achieved? Second, how are they neurally controlled? Third, why are particular expressions associated with particular emotions? Fourth, what can be learned about the control of the face by studying imitation?

Ironically, though perception of the face has been one of the most widely studied topics in visual perception (Humphreys & Bruce, 1989), the *production* of facial expression has been one of the least studied topics in motor control. The reason, I believe, is that research on facial expression appears to have limited industrial (or military) utility. For example, in robotics, much work has been done on walking, looking, and reaching and grasping, for these are activities that robots are expected to perform. But robot *smiling* (to name one possible expression a robot might display) has not been pursued. Curiously, even in fiction dealing with robots, the physiognomy of the robot is always rigid. Perhaps the idea of an expressive machine is too close for comfort!

■ PHYSICAL CONTROL OF THE FACE

In approaching the analysis of facial expression, a first issue is how to describe expressions. One possibility is to use everyday terms like "happy," "sad," or "pensive," and to qualify these terms with intensity descriptors such as "extremely," "mildly," or "deeply." This approach has been used in some studies (Sackeim & Gur, 1978), but it is unreliable because of imperfect agreement about the meanings of the terms. Not everyone knows what is meant by a "pensive" expression, for example, or an "extremely sad" as opposed to a "moderately sad" look. Moreover, this coding scheme lacks a description of the face itself, so it is not useful for characterizing how the face physically conveys emotions.

Another approach is to seek a detailed physical description of the face and its poses. This method requires elaborate scoring techniques (Blurton-Jones, 1971; Ekman & Friesen, 1975). With it, as many as 44 expressions have been identified (Ekman & Friesen, 1978) and it has been found that some expressions last for minutes at a time while others are fleeting, lasting no more than 40 msec (Ekman & Friesen, 1975).

Because facial expressions depend on facial musculature, another method is to describe the activity of the musculature itself, relying primarily on electromyography. It has been assumed since Darwin ([1872]1965) that there is a close correspondence between facial expressions and the muscles that produce them. Electromyographic recordings have helped confirm this assumption. The recordings have shown that some expressions are produced by a number of muscles, whereas others are produced by just one. Raising the eyebrows is achieved with two branches of a single muscle—the medial and lateral aspects of the *frontalis* (Rinn, 1984); however, lowering the eyebrows is produced by the collective action of three muscles—the *corrugator*, the *procerus*, and the *depressor supercili* (part of the *orbicularis oculi*) (see Figure 10.1). In general, a given expression can be produced by one or more muscles, and a given muscle can be involved in several expressions.

The analysis of face-muscle activity also provides a way of determining what occurs when a facial expression appears to be a mixture of different expressions—for example, when one tries to conceal sadness with a "brave smile." The *zygomatic major* is responsible for smiling, whereas the *depresser anguli oris* is responsible for the downturning of the mouth which occurs during sadness. When clear smiling or pouting occurs, there is clear activity of only the *zygomatic major* or *depresser anguli oris*, respectively, but when a "brave smile" occurs, both muscles are active (Oster & Ekman, 1978; see also Ekman, Friesen, & O'Sullivan, 1988).

Electromyography is also useful for clinical purposes. It has been shown that the face muscles are selectively active when different emotions are induced, even when the face reveals little or nothing about the patient's emotional state. In one study, patients who were instructed to imagine a happy scene had increased EMG activity in the muscles normally associated with happy expressions—the *depressor angular oris, zygomatic*, and *mentalis* muscles. Instructions to imagine sad scenes resulted in increased activity of

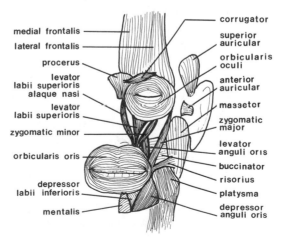

Figure 10.1 Muscles of the face. (From Rinn, 1984.)

muscles normally associated with sad expressions (the *corrugators*), and imagination of anger produced increased activity of the *angular oris*, a muscle that horizontally widens the lips (Schwartz, 1982).

■ NEURAL CONTROL OF THE FACE

The nerve fibers that innervate the facial muscles comprise the seventh cranial, or *facial*, nerve. This nerve subdivides into three main branches, supplying the upper, middle, and lower face, respectively. Within each of the three nerve divisions there are multiple subbranches.

The facial nerve innervating the left side of the face and the facial nerve innervating the right side of the face originate in opposite sides of the brainstem, in the left and right facial nerve nuclei. Within each facial-nerve nucleus, the cell bodies of the facial nerve fibers are organized topographically in a manner similar to the motor homunculus of the cerebral cortex (see Figure 2.12). Distinct regions of the nucleus map onto the upper face, middle face, and lower face. The facial-nerve nuclei receive inputs from higher brain centers, including the motor areas of the cerebral cortex and the extrapyramidal motor system.

Control of the Upper and Lower Face

The upper and lower face differ in their capacity for fine movement. The upper face, encompassing the eyes and forehead, can only move up or down, not from side to side, and in most people has restricted unilateral control. Many (but not all) people can elevate one eyebrow or the other, but few people can elevate one eyebrow and *then* the other (Rinn, 1984). Effectors in the lower face, by contrast, can move with greater autonomy. The mouth can move up, down, or sidewise and in virtually all people can move on just one side, as in pulling the corner of one's mouth down while leaving the other side fixed (Rinn, 1984).

These behavioral differences between the upper and lower face can be traced to the way the face muscles are centrally controlled. The parts of the facial nerve nucleus that project to the eyebrows and forehead receive direct cortical input from the contralateral motor cortex and from the ipsilateral motor cortex (DeMyer, 1980). By contrast, the parts of the facial-nerve nucleus that innervate the lower half of the face receive direct cortical input only from the contralateral motor cortex.

Because each side of the lower face is controlled only contralaterally, damage to one side of the brain can disrupt the motor capacities of the mouth and jaw (contralateral to the site of damage). However, because each side of the *upper* face is controlled by both sides of the brain, unilateral brain damage seldom disrupts the motor capacities of the eyebrows or forehead; the intact side of the brain continues to activate these parts of the face (DeMyer, 1980).

Volitional and Emotional Control

Figure 10.2 (left panel) shows an individual attempting to retract both corners of his mouth in response to a verbal command to smile. He could not follow this command successfully. The right panel shows the same man smiling spontaneously in response to an emotionally satisfying event. The man had a tumor in the face region of his right motor cortex. The fact that he could smile spontaneously but not deliberately suggests a fundamental neurologic distinction between volitionally triggered and emotionally triggered facial expression. The distinction cannot be attributed to different muscles, for the same muscles are involved in feigned and genuine smiles.

If the brain has two means of producing facial expressions—a deliberate and a nondeliberate (or "emotional") means—one might expect to find a disorder in which patients can make facial expressions in response to verbal instructions but not in response to their own emotional states. This would be complementary to the syndrome just described. The complementary syndrome does in fact exist. One symptom of Parkinson's disease is the so-called *masked face*. Patients with this disorder can move their faces in response to verbal instruction, but their faces do not move spontaneously in response to their own emotions. Recall that Parkinson's disease is associated with damage to the basal ganglia (see Chapter 2). Evidently, then, the basal ganglia are involved in emotional expression.

Other areas are also involved in emotional displays. Patients with *pseudobulbar palsy*, a disorder resulting from lesions of the pathways between the cerebral cortex and the brain stem, often exhibit dramatic emotional displays which are completely involuntary and at variance with the patients' emotional state. (Such lesions may result from multiple sclerosis, strokes, or amyotrophic lateral sclerosis, also known as motor-neuron disease.) Figure 10.3 depicts one such patient, a 61-year-old woman with amyotrophic lateral sclero-

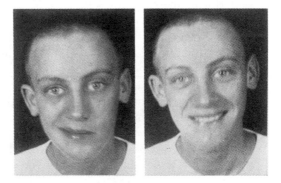

Figure 10.2 Verbally instructed smile (*left panel*) and spontaneous, emotional smile (*right panel*) in a patient with a tumor in the face region of the right motor cortex. Reprinted from DeJong, 1979, *The neurologic examination* (4th ed.). Copyright © 1979, Harper & Row, Publishers.

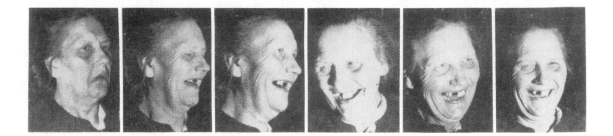

Figure 10.3 Uncontrollable laughter in a 61-year-old woman suffering from amyotrophic lateral sclerosis. The pictures show successive stages of laughing, which was completely involuntary and without the usual sense of mirth. (Reprinted from Poeck, 1969).

sis, who laughed uncontrollably. The emotions she reported while laughing were not mirthful. In fact, she reported being in pain during these episodes.

A final source of support for the distinction between deliberate and emotional facial expressions comes from the behavior of anencephalic babies. These babies have little or no cerebral cortex. Yet they are often observed to cry and show other emotional displays. In view of their age and lack of higher brain centers, their facial expressions may originate without conscious control, from more primitive "emotional" sources (Rinn, 1984).

Left–Right Differences

Having considered differences between the upper and lower face and differences between emotional and deliberate facial expressions, let us now consider one other distinction that has been drawn in the study of facial motor control—the distinction between the animacy of the left and right sides of the face. According to several authors, the left side of the face is more animated than the right (Bower, 1989; Moscovitch & Olds, 1982; Sackeim, Gur, & Saucy, 1978).

What causes this left–right difference? If one is willing to accept the premise, made famous in the popular press, that the left cerebral cortex is analytic and the right cerebral cortex is holistic and emotional, one can then accept the statement that the left side of the face is primarily controlled by the emotional hemisphere, whereas the right side of the face is primarily controlled by the nonemotional hemisphere.

There are difficulties with this hypothesis, however, which have been pointed out by Rinn (1984). Rinn observed that emotional expressiveness appears to be controlled by subcortical brain areas, yet only the cortex is thought to be functionally lateralized (Luria, 1973). He also noted that the difference between right-face and left-face expressiveness is only observed in face-to-face discussions with subjects and in situations where subjects are asked to pose. Left–right differences are not observed when subjects are unaware of being watched (Lynn & Lynn, 1938; Ekman, Hager, & Friesen, 1981). The latter result makes it difficult to accept the hypothesis that there is a fundamental neurological distinction between the emotional expressiveness of the left and right sides of the brain. If the left and right hemispheres truly differed in their capacity for producing emotional expressions, the differences in emotional expression would be likely to appear no matter how they were studied.

How then can one account for the fact that the left side of the face appears more expressive than the right side of the face in face-to-face discussions and in poses? Rinn's (1984) answer is that the left hemisphere may be more effective than the right at *inhibiting* emotions, so the right side of the face is more strongly inhibited than the left. At the heart of this proposal is the assumption that the cortex inhibits impulses from lower brain centers—an assumption well grounded in neurological evidence (Luria & Homskaya, 1970) and of course reminiscent of psychodynamic theory. An attraction of Rinn's hypothesis is that it accounts for the fact that left–right differences are more pronounced when people are aware of being observed than when they are not. When there is a cost in displaying emotions, the left cortex exerts its inhibitory influence, but when there is little or no cost in displaying emotions, the inhibition need not occur and the special inhibitory power of the left cortex goes unseen.

◼ ORIGINS OF EMOTIONAL EXPRESSION

Are facial expressions learned or innate? Because many behavioral functions mediated by subcortical centers are inborn (for example, breathing and sucking), and because facial control is largely subcortical, it would be reasonable if facial expressions were inborn as well. Added to this possibility is one that is even more tantalizing. If particular expressions are innate, so too may be their corresponding emotions.

Innateness and Universality

How can one tell whether facial behaviors are innate? One way is to determine whether they are universal. If people all over the world display a facial behavior, this suggests that they share a genetic program for that behavior. Moreover, if the *interpretations* of the behaviors are the same across all cultures—that is, if people everywhere see a given expression as representing the same emotion—this can be taken to suggest that the emotions are universal as well.

This reasoning was pursued by Paul Ekman and his colleagues (Ekman, 1975). In one study, university students from the United States, Japan, Brazil, Chile, and Argentina were shown photographs of people making facial expressions. The participants were asked to pick photographs from the set that depicted each of several emotions—anger, happiness, fear, surprise, disgust, or sadness. There was a high degree of agreement among the participants. No matter what country they came from, they recognized expressions of each emotion as the same.

The subjects in this experiment shared a literate Western tradition. Therefore, their agreement may have stemmed from common experience rather than common genes. To address this possibility, Ekman and his co-workers studied people from isolated, nonliterate cultures (in New Guinea and Borneo). The basic approach was the same, though it was modified somewhat to accommodate the fact that the people being studied could not read lists of emotions terms. Instead, they were read brief stories concerning fear, anger, and happiness and were then asked to point to the photograph that best depicted the emotion being described. The tribesmen showed virtually complete agreement about the best picture for each story (see Figure 10.4). Moreover, the pictures they selected for each emotion matched the pictures chosen by Western university students given the same task. Finally, when the tribesmen were asked to show what they would look like if they were protagonists in the stories, the expressions they adopted were later identified by American students as representing the emotions the tribesmen said they wanted to portray.

These results suggest that there is a universal basis for the expression of particular emotions. Nevertheless, one might still "raise one's eyebrows" about this interpretation, arguing that the universality of emotional expression may result from the universality of human experience. Consider a behavior that does not involve the face—breaking a stick with two hands. Assuming that people all over the world break sticks bimanually, it would be

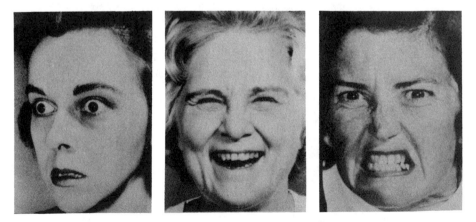

Figure 10.4 Photographs shown simultaneously to tribesmen in New Guinea during stories about fear ("She is afraid the pig will bite her"), happiness ("Her friends have come and she is happy"), and anger ("She is angry and is about to fight"). The pictures in the *left, middle,* and *right panels* were selected as the best for the surprise story, happiness story, and anger story, respectively. (From Ekman, 1975.)

unnecessary to conclude that there is a genetic program for bimanual stick breaking. What is more likely is that the physical properties of hands and sticks are such that this type of behavior is independently discovered by people everywhere. It is possible that all human cultures adopt the same expressions for the same emotions because of similar environmental or biological demands encountered by people throughout the world. One way to address this hypothesis is to study the facial expressions of babies. If it turns out that babies display the same facial expressions as adults, and the conditions that elicit their expressions are similar to those that elicit the comparable expressions in grown-ups, this outcome adds weight to the genetic argument.

As it turns out, babies smile when their needs are met, grimace when they are in pain, and in general make facial expressions like adults in similar circumstances. Even babies who are blind and deaf exhibit these patterns (Freedman, 1964; Goodenough, 1932). Thus it is unlikely that expressions and their meanings are based entirely on experience. This conclusion is further supported by the fact that human expressions are functionally related to animal expressions, as Darwin ([1872]1965) argued. Menacing looks in humans and animals are similar, as are submissive grins (Andrew, 1965). The human practice of raising the eyebrows may be based on the reflex seen in animals of perking up the ears in response to unexpected sounds. The same muscles are involved in both behaviors, as you can demonstrate for yourself by looking in the mirror while raising your eyebrows. When you raise your eyebrows, your ears will follow obligingly.

Causal Connections between Expressions and Emotions

In view of the fact that facial expressions are likely to have a genetic basis, the finding that there are distinct, primary expressions suggests that there may be genetically distinct, primary emotions. Ekman and Oster (1979) suggested that there are six such emotions: anger, happiness, disgust, sadness, fear, and surprise. To this list might be added interest and shame (Izard, 1977). Regardless of the exact number or identity of basic emotions, one's curiosity (another emotion?) prompts one to wonder about the direction of causation between the *expression* of emotions and their *experience*. Do we smile because we are happy or are we happy because we smile? William James, a founder of American psychology (see Chapter 3), suggested, along with a contemporary named Lange, that emotional experience results from physiological feedback from one's movements. According to the James–Lange theory of emotion, we do not smile because we are happy. Instead, we are happy because we smile. The emotions we experience come from the movements we perform. We may smile when we have learned that something is associated with pleasant events, but the happiness we *experience* comes from the feedback derived from the movements made at the time.

A report by Ekman, Levenson, and Friesen (1983) provides evidence for this counterintuitive proposal. Ekman *et al*. asked people familiar with facial posing (actors and scientists working on facial control) to make specifically defined facial expressions. In one condition, the subjects were asked to relive experiences in which particular emotions were strongly experienced. In another condition, the subjects were asked to move particular facial muscles without being told what emotions should be signaled by them; mirrors and coaching were used to elicit the appropriate movements. The question was whether specific patterns of autonomic activity would accompany the expressions. The reasoning was that if the production of particular facial expressions gives rise to specific emotions, and if those emotions are physiologically indexed by distinct autonomic changes, then specific patterns of autonomic function should be evident when particular poses occur.

The results confirmed the prediction. Measures of heart rate, electrical activity of muscles in the forearm, temperature of the right and left hand, and skin resistance showed distinct changes following different facial expressions. Heart rate was higher in anger and in fear than in happiness, and there was a larger decrease in skin resistance during sadness than during anger or disgust. Furthermore, many of these autonomic changes appeared when subjects made facial poses or relived emotional experiences. The magnitudes of the autonomic changes, and the differences among them, were more pronounced in the posing condition than in the relived-emotion condition.

These findings support the hypothesis that distinct patterns of autonomic activity are associated with distinct emotions and that these patterns of autonomic activity can be elicited by distinct patterns of facial activity. Notwithstanding the possibility that subjects identified the emotions they thought they should experience based on the expressions they made [a possibility Ekman *et al*. (1983) discounted on other grounds], the results support the James–Lange theory. They also provide a defense against the argument that autonomic responses are not differentiated enough to allow for the range of emotions we experience (Cannon, 1927).

Associations between Expressions and Emotions

Why are particular expressions and emotions associated as they are? Why do we smile when we are happy and frown when we are angry, for example? Why don't we smile when enraged or frown when ecstatic? The issue is complicated by the fact that some expressions made while experiencing one emotion are also made while experiencing other, incompatible emotions (Andrew, 1965; Konner, 1987). For example, we bare our teeth when we smile and also when we growl.

Darwin ([1872]1965) tried to answer the question of why particular facial configurations connote the emotions they do by appealing to his theory of natural selection. For Darwin, every emotional display serves (or once served) an adaptive function. Baring the teeth in response to a threatened attack, for instance, was an adaptive behavior insofar as potential attackers tended to be scared off by ominous displays. The adaptive value of bared teeth is straightforward, but the value of other displays, elicited in other situations, is less so. What is the benefit of pouting, for example? Because one can only guess what advantage pouting bestows, Darwin's theory as applied to this expression, may not be falsifiable. There are so many expressions with obscure adaptive functions that Darwin's theory, in general, becomes impossible to assess definitively.

The need for a theory with greater predictive power was recognized by an obscure French physician, Israel Waynbaum (1907), who proposed an entirely different view of the relation between emotions and facial activity. As reported by Zajonc (1985), Waynbaum proposed that different facial postures selectively affect the flow of blood to different parts of the brain. Furrowing the brows during intense concentration, for example, allows more blood to reach the cerebral cortex; this in turn may allow for more effective thinking. The relation between brow furrowing and blood flow is completely mechanical. During intense concentration, the brows furrow, the frontalis muscle contracts (see Figure 10.1), the eyeballs become swollen, and the jawbone protrudes. These changes in the position of the face effectively put a tourniquet on the external carotid artery as well as the facial veins (see Figure 10.5). When these vascular pathways are closed off, more blood is sent to the cerebral cortex. Perhaps for this reason, when people work hard on intellectual problems they engage in other seemingly unrelated behaviors such as rubbing the chin, chewing the fingernails, or scratching the head. These behaviors may divert more blood to the brain. Elevations of cerebral blood flow have in fact been observed during intense concentration (Ingvar & Risberg, 1967), although, as far as I know, no one has yet measured cerebral blood flow during chin rubbing, fingernail chewing, or head scratching.

Whereas frowning may increase the amount of blood to the brain, smiling may have the opposite effect. Smiling is achieved in part through contraction of the major zygomatic muscle, which causes the frontal vein to be gorged with blood. This causes blood to be diverted from the carotid artery. Contraction of the corrugator muscles, which also occurs during smiling, blocks the return of blood. During smiling, then, blood flow to the cerebrum may be temporarily blocked, but when this block is released, there can be "a surge of subjectively felt positive effect" (Zajonc, 1985, p. 17). A consequence of the discomfort associated with the rising cerebral blood pressure brought on by laughter (which can be viewed as a kind of intense smiling) is that tears may begin to flow; tears can act as an anesthetic (Frey, DeSota-Johnson, & Hoffman, 1981). Laughing may be healthy, (Cousins, 1984), according to this theory, because it provides a kind of "oxygen bath" for the brain. Sadness, on the other hand, reduces the amount of oxygen in the facial tissues. The cumulative effect may be a prematurely wrinkled, "care-worn" look (Zajonc, 1985).

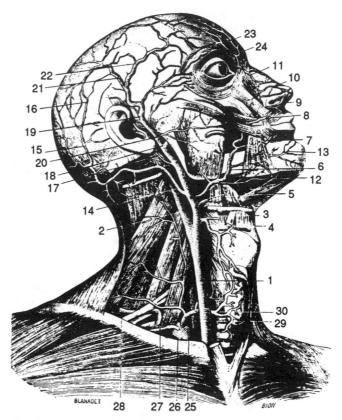

Figure 10.5 Circulatory system of the neck and head. The arteries relevant to the Zajonc–Waynbaum theory are the common carotid (1), the internal carotid (2), and the external carotid (3). (Reprinted from Sappey, 1888/89).

Waynbaum's theory of facial expression is clever in that it relies on principles of anatomy to explain psychological data. Moreover, it provides a way of accounting for seemingly disparate aspects of behavior. Nevertheless, the theory has come under attack. One charge is that it is no more disconfirmable than Darwin's theory (Fridlund & Gilbert, 1985). The mechanical effects of facial muscles on cerebral veins and arteries are intricate, so it is not always clear what effects particular facial expressions have on blood flow to various brain areas. In addition we do not have a complete understanding of the relation between brain activity and emotional experience. Even if one knows where blood flow in the brain is most intense, it is hard to say with certainty what emotion will follow. Finally, contrary to the Zajonc–Waynbaum theory, the absence of overt facial expression does not preclude emotional experience. Patients with facial paralysis report full-blown sadness, happiness, and other emotions, even though their overt expressions hardly change (Fridlund & Gilbert, 1985). (This outcome is also problematic for the James–Lange theory of emotion.)

■ SOCIAL INTERACTION

Because of the importance of facial expression in interpersonal communication, much of the work on the face has been conducted by social psychologists and students of nonverbal behavior. Some of the issues they have studied include rules for producing expressions in various social circumstances, differences between individuals in their expressiveness and ability to read others' emotional or cognitive states, and the ability to exaggerate or hide one's feelings (Feldman, 1982; Rosenthal, 1979; Siegman & Feldstein, 1987). Another issue that has been studied by social psychologists, which also happens to bear on motor control of the face, is *imitation*. This is the final topic to be reviewed in this chapter.

Imitation in Newborns

Field, Woodson, Greenberg, and Cohen (1982) demonstrated that newborns can imitate facial expressions in the first 36 hours of life. Each of 74 babies was held by a model who made distinct facial expressions of happiness, sadness, or surprise (see Figure 10.6). A video camera recorded the model's face, and another camera recorded the baby's face. Later, independent judges viewed the videotapes of the babies, trying to determine which expression the baby was responding to—that is, what face the model was making. The logic of the experiment was that if babies can perceptually discriminate facial expressions and can imitate those expressions, then it should be possible to say which face the model was making based on the baby's physiognomy. In fact, the judges could do this quite successfully. They guessed the model's expression with 76% accuracy; 33% was the level expected by chance alone.

The ability of the judges to tell what expressions the newborns were imitating implies that newborns can both discriminate facial expressions and produce them at will. Apparently, humans are equipped at birth with mechanisms for perceiving facial movements, generating complex facial movement patterns, and coordinating the two.

Imitation in Married Couples

With the capacity for imitation present at birth, it is perhaps not surprising that imitation persists throughout life. A recent study (Zajonc, Adelman, Murphy, & Niedenthal, 1987) suggests that lifelong imitation may affect what faces look like. The impetus for the study was the lore that the longer couples are married, the more similar they look. Zajonc *et al.* tested this belief by showing subjects photographs of men and women, side by side. Unknown to the subjects, all the couples were married and had been married for at least 25 years. The subjects' task was to rate the physical similarity of the couples and to guess whether they were married to each other. Only faces were shown in the photographs. Half the photographs came from the

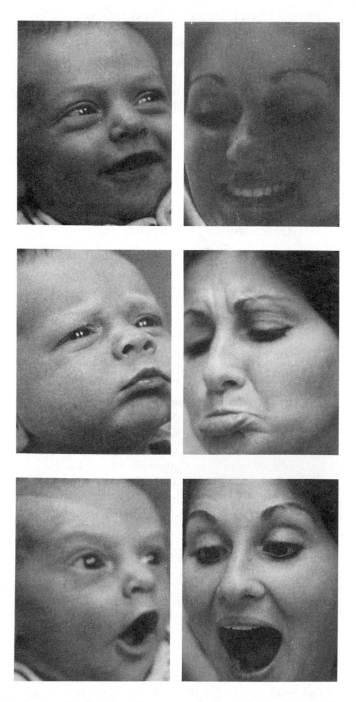

Figure 10.6 Imitation of an adult model's expressions of happiness, sadness, and surprise by an infant approximately 36 hours old. (From Field, Woodson, Greenberg, & Cohen, 1982.)

couples' first wedding anniversaries; half came from their twenty-fifth wedding anniversary. Ratings of the physical similarity of the two members of each couple, and ratings of the likelihood that the couple was married, were higher for the pictures taken after 25 years of marriage than for the pictures taken after 1 year of marriage.

Why did couples look more similar if they were married longer? Was it perhaps due to common eating habits over 25 years of living together? This seems unlikely, for when the photographed men and women were rank-ordered from heaviest to lightest, the correlation between men and women was higher for pictures taken from the 1-year photographs than for pictures taken from the 25-year photographs. Thus perceived weight for husbands and wives was more similar when the husbands and wives had been married for a brief time than for a long time. The tendency to see greater physical similarity between older couples was also not due to the couple's experiencing the same climate or living conditions, for all the couples had similar geographic and demographic backgrounds.

The key to understanding the effect was the degree of happiness the couples reported. Zajonc *et al.* (1987) asked the couples depicted in the photographs to answer questions about their marriages. When the happiness data were compared with the physical-similarity data, it was found that the higher the couple's reported happiness, the greater the perceived similarity of their faces. In addition, the more similar their attitudes, and the more often they shared worries and concerns, the more similar they appeared. Apart from the possibility that looking alike from the start may predispose couples to share each others' joys and sorrows for long periods of time, it may be, as Zajonc *et al.* suggested, that imitation promotes empathy, bringing couples closer together and—perhaps not just accidentally—making them look more alike.

■ SUMMARY

1. Faces and facial expressions are recognized from birth and can be remembered for many years.

2. Facial expressions have been described in terms of the emotions they convey, their detailed physical appearance, or their underlying electromyographic activity. With electromyography it has been shown that an emotional expression can be achieved with one or more muscles and that expressions can have very short or long durations. Mixed expressions, such as a "brave smile," are characterized by the simultaneous activity of muscles usually involved in different (often conflicting) expressions. Imagining emotional states can produce subtle activity in the associated facial muscles.

3. The left and right sides of the face are innervated, respectively, by the left and right facial nerves. The cell bodies of the facial nerves are located in the brain stem and are topographically organized, primarily with respect to the vertical dimension of the face.

4. The lower part of the face can be moved with greater precision than the upper part of the face. The likely reason is that the lower part of the face is controlled by one side of the brain whereas the upper part of the face is controlled by both sides of the brain.

5. Facial expressions can be instigated in a deliberate or nondeliberate ("emotional") fashion. The distinction is suggested by the inability of some patients with motor-cortex lesions to smile deliberately, by the inability of other patients with basal ganglia damage (Parkinson's patients) to smile emotionally, and by the inability of some patients with damage to the pathways between the cerebral cortex and the brain stem (pseudobulbar palsy) to suppress facial expressions at odds with their reported emotions.

6. The left side of the face is usually more animated than the right. The asymmetry may be due to the greater inhibitory effect of the left as compared to the right cerebral hemisphere.

7. Facial expressions appear to be genetically determined. They are displayed universally, almost always in the same emotional contexts, and in adults as well as infants (including newborns and infants who are both deaf and blind).

8. The James–Lange theory of emotion holds that we experience emotions based on sensory feedback from our movements. Thus we are happy because we smile and not the reverse. Some experimental evidence has supported this theory.

9. Why do we smile rather than frown when we are happy? In general, what explains the association of particular expressions with particular emotions? Two theories have been advanced. One is that the links can be traced to behavior patterns from earlier evolutionary times. The other is that different facial expressions selectively affect the flow of blood to different brain areas. Neither theory is wholly satisfactory.

10. Newborns can imitate facial expressions in the first 36 hours of life. This implies that they can perceive distinct expressions, produce distinct expressions, and accurately reproduce the expressions they perceive.

11. Couples who have been married for long periods tend to look more alike than they did after 1 year of marriage. The source of the greater similarity may be sustained imitation of one another's facial expressions.

■ REFERENCES

Andrew, R. J. (1965). The origins of facial expressions. *Scientific American*, **213** (4), 88–94.

Averill, J. (1975). A semantic atlas of emotional concepts. *Catalog of Selected Documents in Psychology*, **5**, 330.

Bahrick, H. P., Bahrick, P. O., & Wittlinger, R. P. (1975). Fifty years of memory for names and faces: A cross-sectional approach. *Journal of Experimental Psychology: General* **104**, 54–75.

Blurton-Jones, N. G. (1971). Criteria for describing facial expressions of children. *Human Biology,* **43,** 365–413.

Bower, B. (1989). Baby faces show the right side of emotion. *Science News,* **135,** 149.

Cannon, W. B. (1927). The James-Lange theory of emotions: A critical examination and an alternative theory. *American Journal of Psychology,* **39,** 106–124.

Cousins, N. (1984). *The healing heart.* New York: Avon.

Darwin, C. R. [1872](1965). *The expression of the emotions in man and animals.* Reprint. Chicago: University of Chicago Press.

DeJong, R. N. (1979). *The neurologic examination* (4th ed.). New York: Harper & Row.

deMyer, W. (1980). *Technique of the neurologic examination.* New York: McGraw-Hill.

Ekman, P. (1975). Face muscles talk every language. *Psychology Today* (September). 35–39.

Ekman, P., & Friesen, W. V. (1975). *Unmasking the face.* Englewood Cliffs, NJ: Prentice-Hall.

Ekman, P., Friesen, W. V., & O'Sullivan, M. (1988). Smiles when lying. *Journal of Personality and Social Psychology,* **54,** 414–420.

Ekman, P., Hager, J., & Friesen, W. V. (1981). The symmetry of emotional and deliberate facial actions. *Psychophysiology,* **18,** 101–106.

Ekman, P., Levenson, R. W., & Friesen, W. V. (1983). Autonomic nervous system activity distinguishes among emotions. *Science,* **221,** 1208–1210.

Ekman, P., & Oster, H. (1979). Facial expressions of emotion. *Annual Review of Psychology,* **30,** 527–554.

Fantz, R. (1961). The origin of form perception. *Scientific American,* **204** (5), 66–72.

Feldman, R. S. (Ed.) (1982). *Development of nonverbal behavior in children.* New York: Springer-Verlag.

Field, T., Woodson, R., Greenberg, R., & Cohen, D. (1982). Discrimination and imitation of facial expressions by neonates. *Science,* **218,** 179–181.

Frey, W. H., II., DeSota-Johnson, D., & Hoffman, C. (1981). *Journal of Ophthalmology,* **92,** 559–578.

Freedman, D. G. (1964). Smiling in blind infants and the issue of innate vs. acquired. *Journal of Child Psychology and Psychiatry,* **15,** 171–184.

Fridlund, A. J., & Gilbert, A. N. (1985). Emotions and facial expression. *Science,* **230,** 607–608.

Goodenough, F. L. (1932). Expression of the emotions in a blind-deaf child. *Journal of Abnormal and Social Psychology,* **27,** 328–333.

Humphreys, G. W., & Bruce, V. (1989). *Visual cognition.* Hillsdale, NJ: Erlbaum.

Ingvar, D. H., & Risberg, J. (1967). Increase of regional cerebral blood flow during mental effort in normals and in patients with focal brain disorders. *Experimental Brain Research,* **3,** 195–211.

Izard, C. E. (1977). *Human emotions.* New York: Plenum.

Kleiner, K. A., & Banks, M. (1987). Stimulus energy does not account for 2-month-olds' face preferences. *Journal of Experimental Psychology: Human Perception and Performance,* **13,** 594–600.

Konner, M. (1987). The enigmatic smile. *Psychology Today,* **21** (3), 42–44.

Luria, A. R. (1973). *The working brain.* New York: Basic Books.

Luria, A. R., & Homskaya, E. D. (1970). Frontal lobes and the regulation of arousal processes. In D. I. Mostofsky (Ed.), *Attention: Contemporary theory and analysis.* New York: Appleton-Century-Crofts.

Lynn, J. G., & Lynn, D. R. (1938). Face-hand laterality in relation to personality. *Journal of Abnormal and Social Psychology,* **33,** 291–322.

Moscovitch, M., & Olds, J. (1982). Asymmetries in spontaneous facial expressions and their possible relation to hemispheric specialization. *Neuropsychologia,* **20,** 71–81.

Oster, H., & Ekman, P. (1978). Facial behavior in child development. In W. A. Collins (Ed.), *Minnesota symposium on child psychology* (Vol. 11). Hillsdale, NJ: Erlbaum.

Poeck, K. (1969). Pathophysiology of emotional disorders associated with brain damage. In P. J. Vinken & G. W. Bruyn (Eds.), *Handbook of clinical neurology* (Vol. 3). New York: American Elsevier.

Rinn, W. E. (1984). The neuropsychology of facial expression: A review of the neurological and psychological mechanisms for producing facial expressions. *Psychological Bulletin,* **95,** 52–77.

Rosenthal, R. (Ed.) (1979). *Skill in nonverbal communication: Individual differences*. Cambridge, MA: Oelgeschlager, Gunn, & Hain, Publishers, Inc.

Sackeim, H. A., & Gur, R. C. (1978). Lateral asymmetry in intensity of emotional expression. *Neuropsychologia*, **16**, 473–481.

Sackeim, H. A., Gur, R. C., & Saucy, M. C. (1978). Emotions are expressed more intensely on the left side of the face. *Science*, **202**, 443–436.

Sappey, P. (1888/89). *Traité d' anatomie descriptive*. Paris: Delahaye Lecrosnier.

Schwartz, G. E. (1982). Psychophysiological patterning and emotion revisited: A systems perspective. In C. E. Izard (Ed.), *Measuring emotions in infants and children*. Cambridge: Cambridge University Press.

Siegman, A. W., & Feldstein, S. (Eds.) (1987). *Nonverbal behavior and communication* (2d ed.). Hillsdale, NJ: Erlbaum.

Storm, C., & Storm, T. (1987). A taxonomic study of the vocabulary of emotions. *Journal of Personality and Social Psychology*, **53**, 805–816.

Todd, J. T., Mark, L. S., Shaw, R. E., & Pittenger, J. B. (1980). The perception of human growth. *Scientific American*, **242** (2), 132–144.

Waynbaum, I. (1907). *La physionomie humaine: Son mécanisme et son rôle social*. Paris: Alcan.

Zajonc, R. B. (1985). Emotion and facial efference: A theory reclaimed. *Science*, **228**, 15–21.

Zajonc, R. B., Adelman, P. K., Murphy, S. T., & Niedenthal, P. M. (1987). Convergence in the physical appearance of spouses. *Motivation and Emotion*, **11**, 335–346.

PART III

PRINCIPLES AND PROSPECTS

11 CONCLUSIONS

■ INTRODUCTION

A lot of ground has been covered in this book. After a general introduction, I reviewed the physiological and psychological foundations of human motor control. Then I discussed seven activity systems: walking, looking, reaching and grasping, drawing and writing, keyboarding, speaking and singing, and smiling. More remains to be done, however. Several topics have not been covered, promising lines of inquiry have yet to be identified, and a summary of general principles still needs to be given.

One topic still to be covered is eye–hand coordination—an aspect of motor control that illustrates, perhaps more dramatically than any other, the intricate coupling that can exist between different activity systems. Another topic to be described is the catching and hitting of oncoming balls. This domain of performance combines several motor activities and demands precise integration of movement and perception. The third residual topic is individual differences. Why some people are more coordinated than others was broached in the opening paragraph of the first chapter, but so far little has been said about it.

■ EYE–HAND COORDINATION

In the preceding chapters, I treated the activity systems separately. This is didactically convenient, but it ignores the fact that, ultimately, for an organism to behave coherently, it must coordinate its motor subsystems. I have already indicated how some subsystems relevant to particular sorts of activities can be coordinated. The fingers and hand, for example, are well coordinated in normal reaching and grasping. Coordination of the eyes and hands requires orchestration of effectors that, unlike the fingers and hand, are anatomically remote.

A number of studies have shown that when people move the hand as quickly as possible from one location to another, the eyes generally move saccadically to the target location shortly before the hand; lags between eye and hand movements typically range from 60 to 100 msec (Angel, Alston, & Garland, 1970; Prablanc, Echallier, & Jeannerod, 1979). Nerve signals driving the eyes and hand may be delivered simultaneously, for arm-muscle EMGs begin at virtually the same instant as the first sign of eye movements (Biguer, Jeannerod, & Prablanc, 1982, 1985). These results suggest that the eyes and hand comprise a "pointing synergy" whose neural commands may be generated simultaneously (Jeannerod, 1988). Consistent with this hypothesis, eye-movement latencies and arm-movement latencies are usually positively correlated. Trial-by-trial correlations between times to start moving the eyes and times to start moving the hand can be as high as +.8 (Herman, Herman, & Malucci, 1981).

Because the eyes can generally travel to a target more quickly than the hand, the eye generally reaches the target before the hand and so dwells on the target before the hand arrives. What is the advantage, if any, of this method of control? The benefit may derive from the ability of the oculomotor system and manual-control system to share spatial information. The eye can "point" to the target, and the hand (or the system controlling the hand) can move to the target location, drawing on information about where the gaze is directed in space. The ability to move the eyes to a target aids hand movements, even when the target cannot be seen after the eyes have carried out the saccade (Abrams, Meyer, & Kornblum, 1990). This result indicates that the hand has access to spatial information about where the eye is pointing.

Equally dramatic evidence for the coupling of the eye and the hand comes from studies in which the eye tracks the hand during ongoing (slower) hand movements. The hand can be tracked by the eyes even when the hand cannot be seen (Gauthier, Vercher, Mussa-Ivaldi, & Marchetti, 1988). A moving image projected from one's own hand can be tracked more accurately than the projection of someone else's hand, even when the person whose eye movements are monitored does not know which hand is the source of the image displacement (Steinbach & Held, 1968). Perhaps most remarkably, the maximum velocity of smooth pursuit eye movements—about 40°/sec in the case of a conventional visual target (Westheimer, 1954)—is more than doubled (80 to 100°/sec) when the visual target is moved by the subject him or herself (Gauthier et al., 1988).

What allows for such tight coupling between the eyes and the hands in tracking one's own hand movements? Presumably, when one voluntarily moves one's hand, one can *predict* where the hand-driven stimulus will be. Prediction enables the oculomotor system to anticipate the position of the moving stimulus. (Tracking a conventionally driven external stimulus lends itself less well to reliance on anticipation.) So sophisticated is the anticipation that is possible when the eye tracks the hand that when the hand causes a target to reverse direction, the eye can track the target virtually perfectly (with no delay) at the reversal point (Gauthier et al. 1988). It is difficult to imagine how such near-perfect tracking could be based on a mode of control not involving some form of prediction. The model shown in Figure 11.1 presents a possible coordination scheme.

As tightly coupled as the eye and hand may be, they must also be free of one another in some circumstances. It would be maladaptive always to visually track one's hand movements. Driving a car with one's eyes on one's hands rather than on the road would be disastrous, for example. Young babies, and children with severe cerebral palsy, reportedly have difficulty dissociating their eyes and hands. If the hand happens to fall into view, visual attention is captured, and the eyes are "dragged along" by sight of hand (Gauthier *et al.*, 1988). In the course of normal development, such coupling breaks down so that, if necessary, the hands can perform one task and the eyes can be directed elsewhere. The importance of this observation is that eye–hand synergies are task dependent.

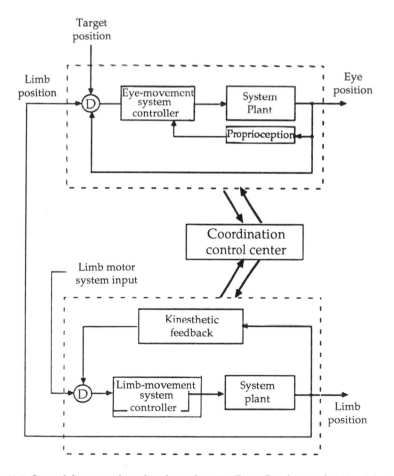

Figure 11.1 Control diagram of eye–hand coordination. From Gauthier *et al.*, 1988. Adapted by permission of Springer-Verlag.

■ HITTING APPROACHING BALLS

Not all forms of eye–hand coordination necessitate looking at one's hands. In batting an oncoming ball, batters are supposed to keep their eyes on the ball. Yet the action to be performed entails eye–hand coordination, for the hands (or the hands and arms) must be coordinated with the eyes (or with sight of the oncoming ball) to meet the ball at the right time and place with the appropriate force. The required coordination is abstract in the sense that the bat cannot simply be brought to the location to which the eye points (in contrast to the cases described earlier), because the oncoming ball often travels faster than the eyes (Bahill & LaRitz, 1984). In such cases, the batter must predict where the ball will be at a future time.

How do batters predict the trajectories of oncoming balls? One way to address this question is to consider the optical information that would allow an observer, in principle, to extrapolate a ball's trajectory. In Chapter 4 I mentioned a relation that might be used for this purpose. As shown by Lee (1976), the time to contact an object toward which one is moving at constant velocity—and equivalently, the time for the object to contact an observer if it is approaching him or her with constant velocity—is equal to the diameter of the closed optical contour of the object divided by the rate of expansion of the diameter; this rate is denoted τ (the Greek letter "tau"). Lee's τ principle implies that it is possible to tell when an object will be contacted by detecting the rate at which its image expands. When the image expands at a high rate, time to contact will be short, but when the image expands at a low rate, time to contact will be long. Birds diving into lakes (Lee & Reddish, 1981), flies landing on tables (Wagner, 1982), and people approaching walls behave as if they are sensitive to this principle (Lee & Thomson, 1982). Batters seem to be sensitive to it as well (Lee, Young, Reddish, Lough, & Clayton, 1983). Champion table-tennis players also appear to follow the τ principle, judging from the fact that they initiate their paddle swings at relatively consistent times during the approach of the ball; this is what would be expected if they began to swing when τ reached a critical value (Bootsma & Van Wieringen, 1988). Yet another indication that τ is used in hitting oncoming balls is that people do far better at hitting a ball coming right at them than at indicating when a ball will pass a point as it travels perpendicular to the line of sight (McLeod, McLaughlin, & Nimmo-Smith, 1986). In the perpendicular case τ cannot be used, but in the direct-line-of-sight case it can be.

Balls do not always travel in straight lines, nor do they always travel directly to the batter, and rarely do they move with constant velocity. All these conditions are required for unambiguous reliance on τ. Therefore, the τ principle, unadorned, cannot account for determination of time-to-contact in all situations where it might be useful. Mindful of this problem, some investigators have suggested other optical cues that might be used to establish time-to-contact as well as place of contact (Lee *et al.*, 1983; Todd, 1981).

Besides determining when a ball will be contacted and where it will be at that time, batters may also need to identify the direction in which the ball will be traveling at the moment of contact. To act on this information, the batter must move the bat so it gets to the right place at the right time, with adequate force, and directed so the ball is propelled toward the desired location. Clearly, there are many variables to control, which is perhaps why batting an oncoming ball is considered by some to be the most demanding of all perceptual–motor tasks. Regardless of whether this belief is correct, it is remarkable that batters can achieve the levels of performance they do. Expert cricket batters, for example, can contact 88% of the balls delivered to them within a time window of ±10 msec and 66% of the balls within a time window of ±5 msec (McLeod *et al.*, 1986). Comparable levels of accuracy have also been observed in table tennis (Bootsma & Van Wieringen, 1988).

How do batters and table-tennis players manage such high levels of performance? One view, traceable to Bernstein's (1967) emphasis on simplifying the degrees-of-freedom problem, is that they limit the number of variables to be controlled. Evidence consistent with this view has been obtained in studies of champion table-tennis players, whose forehand drives turn out to have nearly constant, extremely short durations (Tyldesley & Whiting, 1975). Thus a performance variable that potentially could be modulated (the duration of the arm swing) is kept approximately constant, possibly because the players move their arms as quickly as possible during the forehand strokes. What they modulate instead is the time they *initiate* the stroke (as well as the stroke direction).

Do champion table-tennis players fully preprogram their strokes? Full preprogramming eliminates another possible means of simplifying the motor control problem in this context—correcting the stroke during its execution on the basis of feedback. Constraining performance variables and relying on feedback are two of the most important means of solving the degees-of-freedom problem (Jordan & Rosenbaum, 1989).

Recent evidence suggests that batting oncoming balls may in fact rely on feedback. Batters almost always do better when they can see the ball throughout its trajectory than when part of the trajectory is obscured (Sharp, 1975; Whiting, Gill, & Stephenson, 1970). If bat strokes were fully preprogrammed, losing sight of the ball would not to be expected to impair performance.

Another source of support for the use of feedback during bat swings is the finding that batters can respond rapidly to unexpected perturbations of ball trajectories. When cricket batsmen swing at rapidly approaching balls that unexpectedly strike bumps on the playing surface, they can alter their ongoing swings in as little as 190 msec (McLeod, 1987). People also do better at hitting an oncoming ball when they can swing a bat continuously than when releasing a spring-loaded bat of the same size (Bootsma, 1989). Times to initiate the bat movement are more variable in the bat-swing condition than in the bat-release condition, suggesting that whatever variability there

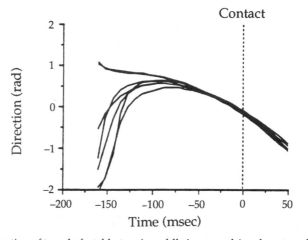

Figure 11.2 Direction of travel of a table-tennis paddle in seven drives by a top player. From R. J. Bootsma & P. C. van Wieringen (1990). Timing an attacking forehand drive in table tennis. *Journal of Experimental Psychology: Human Perception and Performance,* **16,** 21–22. Copyright © 1990 by the American Psychological Association. Reprinted with permission.

is in the time to initiate the bat swing is compensated for during the swing phase, perhaps because of corrections based on feedback (Bootsma, 1989).

A final source of evidence for ongoing correction during the act of striking an oncoming ball is that, among champion table-tennis players, the variability of the direction of movement of the paddle is greater at the *start* of the forehand stroke than at the moment the ball is *contacted* (Bootsma & Van Wieringen, 1990). Representative curves are shown in Figure 11.2. The convergence at the contact point could reflect preprogramming of the stroke, but detailed analysis of the trajectories suggests that, at least in some players, paddle movement is altered during the swing based on continued visual monitoring of the ball. This finding is all the more remarkable when it is noted that the paddle sometimes travels as quickly as 800°/second.

■ INDIVIDUAL DIFFERENCES

Considering champion table-tennis players leads one to wonder why some people are so much better at motor skills than others. Champion table-tennis players become champions through hours of practice. But for many people, it is quickly apparent that those hours would come to nought. Why then are some people coordinated and others clumsy? What is it, apart from hours of practice, that makes one person a champion and another a "klutz"?

Individual differences are inherently interesting insofar as most people (though not all!) are curious about how people differ. Understanding the basis of individual differences is also worthwhile for practical purposes because clumsy individuals have accidents, which one would like to prevent. Moreover, it has long been a dream of humankind that artistic gifts or athletic talents be imbued in others.

There is also a theoretical reason to inquire into individual differences. Differences among individuals provide a way of identifying dimensions of motor control. If the motor system is organized such that it "cares about" dimensions A, B, and C, then people good at controlling an aspect of movement corresponding to dimension A need not be good at controlling aspects of movement corresponding to dimensions B or C. Dimensions of motor control can therefore be identified by determining those aspects of performance that are independent within individuals.

This approach has borne fruit in the analysis of timing control (see Chapter 8). Using repetitive tapping, Keele and his colleagues (Keele & Ivry, 1987) found that maximum rates of tapping by different limbs are correlated within individuals: People who can tap quickly with the hand can also tap quickly with the foot, for example. Likewise, timing accuracy is correlated within people: Individuals who can tap accurately with the foot can tap accurately with the hand. That this ability is based on *timing* is suggested by the finding that people adept at producing time intervals are also adept at *perceiving* time intervals. Moreover, people skilled at timing are not necessarily good at varying force, and vice versa.

Clumsy children, whose timing abilities would be expected to be deficient, show significantly higher timing variability in rhythmic tapping tasks than do normal children (Williams, Woollacott, & Ivry, 1989). When asked to stand on a horizontal platform that can be suddenly displaced (see Chapter 4), clumsy children exhibit patterns of muscle timing that are less functionally suited to restoring balance than do normal children (Williams & Woollacott, 1988). In a similar vein, clumsy children take longer to respond to release of the arm (when it is initially held by a mechanical device) than do normal children, but clumsy children and normal children take about the same time to make the same response to visual stimuli (Smyth & Glencross, 1986). These results, taken as a whole, suggest that clumsiness may be a reflection of disturbed proprioception, timing, or both. This is not to say that clumsiness has no other underlying causes. Bumping into obstacles, as clumsy children do, presumably results from lapses of attention as well as lack of balance or timing.

Perhaps people who are good at timing or responding to proprioceptive inputs are just more able *generally* than people who are poor at these tasks. Perhaps they would do better no matter what task was given to them. I have already cited a finding that violates this prediction: Timing accuracy does not predict accuracy of force production. A more general prediction from the "general-ability" view is that there should high positive correlations across tasks requiring any arbitrarily selected motor skill. In fact, correlations between motor tasks are usually quite low. In a massive study by Parker and Fleishman (1960), over 200 people were tested on a battery of 50 tasks, and the scores on all pairs of tasks were correlated. The method was to obtain each subject's score on one task and each subject's score on another task, and then to calculate the correlation over subjects between the two sets of numbers. The process was repeated for every pair of tasks. Most correlations turned out to be below .4, which means that less than $.4^2 = 16\%$ of the variability in one task could be predicted by variability in the other. The few tasks that had higher correlations were so similar that it would have been worrisome if their correlations were any lower than they turned out to be. For instance, walking a balance beam 2 m long versus walking a balance beam 4 m long had a correlation of .85.

Low correlations have been observed in other studies as well. When people were supposed to climb up a gymnastics ladder in the middle of a floor and keep the ladder erect for as long as possible, their scores were almost completely uncorrelated with their scores in a task where they were supposed to balance on a seesaw (Bachman, 1961).

How can one reconcile the fact that, in general, correlations between motor tasks are low, but in some studies, such as those of Keele and his colleagues (Keele & Ivry, 1987), fairly high correlations have been obtained? One possibility is that every task demands a *set* of abilities, and only those tasks that happen to have many abilities in common (along with few differing abilities) are likely to yield substantial correlations. Simple tasks like tapping the finger or toe presumably use fewer abilities than complex tasks like climbing a ladder in the middle of a room. If two simple tasks happen to share their few underlying abilities, the correlation between the tasks will be high, but if the same number of abilities is shared by two complex tasks, the large number of other, differing abilities will reduce the intertask correlation.

Not all simple tasks are well correlated, however, even when their underlying requirements seem similar (Lotter, 1960). Thus the source of low correlations is still a bit mysterious. Perhaps abilities within individuals are as variable over time as are abilities among individuals. We all have our good days and bad days, which tends to blur differences among our ability levels.

These observations notwithstanding, investigators have found ways to extract from their data hints about what factors are likely to enable different individuals to perform better on some tasks than others. One method, called *factor analysis*, is a statistical technique designed to isolate factors that account for differences among correlations; the technique can be used even if the highest correlations are low. Based on factor analysis, a number of factors have been suggested, some of which, taken from a review by Schmidt (1988) of the work of Fleishman and his colleagues (Fleishman & Bartlett, 1969), are as follows:

1. *Control precision* Rapid precise movements must be made with relatively large body segments, as in driving a golf ball.
2. *Multilimb coordination* Several limbs must move concurrently and in a coordinated fashion, as in juggling.
3. *Reaction time* Response must be made as quickly as possible to an expected stimulus, as in starting to sprint in the 50-yard dash.
4. *Finger dexterity* Precise movements of the hands and fingers are required, as in performing microsurgery.
5. *Arm–hand steadiness* Unwanted movements of the upper extremity must be eliminated, as in riflery.

Motor control factors are not the only ones that predict task success, of course. Other factors that are likely to be important are an individual's physical characteristics, intelligence, and motivation. Being tall helps one play basketball, knowing what to do during microsurgery helps one to be an effective surgeon, and having the desire to succeed helps one capitalize on one's other abilities. These factors have historically been divorced from motor control research. A complete account of motor control must incorporate all the factors, however.

■ NEW APPROACHES

The individuals engaged in motor control research are nearly as differentiated in their styles of analysis as the individuals whose movement and stability they study. In this volume, I have reviewed a number of styles of analysis, ranging from jotting down and categorizing speech errors, to recording times of keypresses with a computer, to filming the kinematics of the legs or lips, to picking up neural action potentials with electrodes. In the next three sections, I describe three additional approaches that have gained prominence in recent years. All three have a number of appealing features and some possible drawbacks. It is unlikely that any one of them will completely replace the other approaches that have been pursued so far or completely dominate the other two. I have postponed presenting these new approaches because they are technically complex, theoretically sweeping, and, in at least two cases (the first two), somewhat nihilistic with respect to what has been achieved (or at least believed) about physical action. The three approaches are characterized by the terms *synergetics*, *ecology*, and *network modeling*.

■ SYNERGETICS

At the end of Chapter 6, I described a study (Haken, Kelso, & Bunz, 1985) in which subjects moved their two extended index fingers back and forth repeatedly (see Figure 6.13). In a typical version of the study, subjects held their hands as shown in Figure 6.13, starting with both index fingers pointing to the left. The task was to shift the index fingers so both fingers pointed to the right, then to move both index fingers so they pointed to the left again, then to return the fingers to the right, and so on. The movements were carried out in time with a metronome. Subjects could perform the task well provided the frequency did not get too high. If the frequency exceeded some value, an extraordinary event occurred: The coordination of the two fingers fell spontaneously into a new pattern. Whereas the two fingers pointed to the *left* at the same time or to the *right* at the same time at the lower frequency, at the higher frequency the two fingers either pointed *out* at the same time or *in* at the same time. Another way of describing this outcome is that when the frequency was low, subjects could extend one finger while flexing the other, but at higher frequencies, they could only extend both fingers at

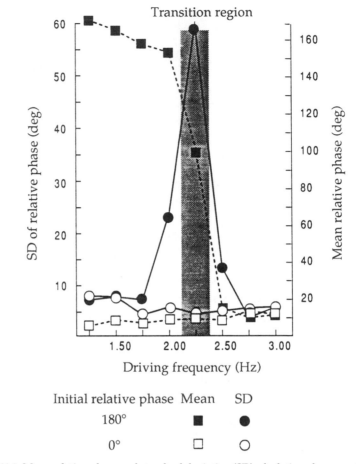

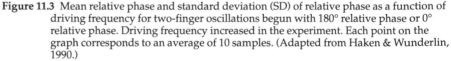

Figure 11.3 Mean relative phase and standard deviation (SD) of relative phase as a function of driving frequency for two-finger oscillations begun with 180° relative phase or 0° relative phase. Driving frequency increased in the experiment. Each point on the graph corresponds to an average of 10 samples. (Adapted from Haken & Wunderlin, 1990.)

the same time or flex both fingers at the same time. This switching effect is called a *phase transition*.

Relative Phase

Before expanding on synergetics, I need to introduce some other terms and findings. First, look at Figure 11.3, where the phase-transition effect is shown. The dependent measures are the mean *relative phase* and the standard deviation of the relative phase. The term "relative phase" needs to be understood to appreciate synergetics in this context. Relative phase refers to the angular deviation between two oscillating bodies. Consider two turntables, rotating at the same rate, with a point A on the rim of one turntable and a point a on the rim of the other turntable (see Figure 11.4). The position of A at any given time can be given by the angle $\angle ACB$, where C is the center of the left turntable and B is a fixed reference point. Likewise, the position of a at any given time can be given by the angle $\angle acb$, where c is the center of the right turntable and b is another reference point; note that b is colinear with c, B, and C. The difference $\angle ACB - \angle acb$ at any given time is the instantaneous relative phase of A and a. In Figure 11.4A, $\angle ACB - \angle acb = 0°$. In Figure 11.4B, $\angle ACB - \angle acb = 180°$. Other relative-phase values are also possible.

A key point about relative phase is that it remains constant if the rotation rates of the two turntables remain equal. The other key point is that relative phase can apply to two index fingers as well as to two points on a pair of turntables. Applying the concept to the two index fingers is complicated only by the fact that the left and right hands are mirror images of one another. Suppose, then, that b is placed on the left side of the right turntable (Figure 11.4C). Equating A with the tip of the left index finger, C with the left metacarpophalangeal joint (the joint where the index finger meets the hand), a with the tip of the right index finger, and c with the right metacarpophalangeal joint, when the two index fingers point directly toward one another, $\angle ACB = \angle acb = 0°$ and their angular difference, $\angle ACB - \angle acb$, is also $0°$. When the two fingers point straight ahead, $\angle ACB = \angle acb = 90°$ and their angular difference is again $\angle ACB - \angle acb = 0°$. As long as the two fingers move in and out in perfect synchrony (extending together and flexing together so their respective angles are the same), their relative phase always equals $0°$. When the two fingers move in alternation, one moving in by as many degrees as the other moves out and reversing direction at the same instant, their relative phase is always $180°$. (Just as for points on the turntables, other relative phases are also possible.)

Relative phase provides a convenient measure of coordination in the two-finger oscillation task. As seen in Figure 11.3, it provides a way of representing the change in coordination of the two fingers. Relative phase switches from $180°$ to $0°$ as the driving frequency (the frequency of the metronome) increases and reaches a critical frequency. Near the critical frequency, coordination also becomes highly unstable (see Figure 11.3). The standard deviation of the relative phase of the two fingers "explodes" at or near the critical frequency, provided the fingers start in the anti-phase mode ($180°$ relative phase) and the driving frequency approaches the critical frequency from a low (slow) value. The enhanced variability preceding the phase transition is called *critical fluctuation*.

It is worth emphasizing again that neither phase transitions nor critical fluctuations occur if the fingers first oscillate with $0°$ relative phase, and this is true regardless of whether the driving frequency exceeds the critical frequency or falls below it. The tendency of the fingers to switch from $180°$ relative phase to $0°$ relative phase as frequency increases but *not* to switch from $0°$ relative phase to $180°$ relative phase as frequency decreases is an ex-

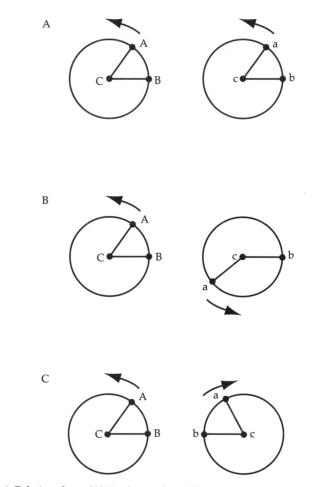

Figure 11.4 Relative phase: (A) 0° relative phase. (B) 180° relative phase. (C) Rearrangement for the two index fingers.

ample of a *hysteresis* effect—an effect whose magnitude or time of occurrence depends on the direction of change of some variable. (A heating system that turns on at a low temperature as temperature increases and shuts off at a high temperature as temperature decreases is a familiar example.) Hysteresis in the context of the two-finger oscillation task implies that 0° relative phase is an *attractor*. It constitutes a stable state for this system.

The Scope of Synergetics

Why have I chosen to discuss these findings in the context of significant new approaches to human motor control? The importance of the findings lies in their interpretation, based on the theory of *synergetics* (Haken, 1977, 1983). The problem to which synergetics is addressed is essentially the degrees-of-freedom problem, viewed in general terms: How does order arise at a macroscopic level from the microscopic elements making up a system? The thousands of muscle fibers in the heart, for example, act collectively to produce a heartbeat, and the millions of neurons in the brain give rise to organized thought and behavior. At a microscopic level, these systems (as well as others from the natural and physical world) have an enormous number of degrees of freedom; the number corresponds to the number of elements within them. But at a macroscopic level, this huge number is effectively reduced, corresponding to the fewer number of ways in which the system as a whole can behave. What mechanisms allow for this reduction from high dimensionality (many degrees of freedom) to lower dimensionality (fewer degrees of freedom)?

In approaching this question, there is a trap to be avoided—the trap of invoking hidden intelligence. One does not want to assume that there is a "homunculus" (a little man or woman in the brain) who somehow knows how to organize neural activity. Assuming such an agent would, of course, beg the question of how the brain allows for intelligence. A more satisfying solution is to assume (or at least hope) that the system has the capacity for *self-organization*. When a windblown drop of soapy liquid forms a bubble, or when a number of bubbles press against each other and form hexagonal shapes, these patterns emerge from properties of the liquid itself; no one (or no thing) tells the soap what to do. A central concept in synergetics is that a system consisting of many elements has the capacity for self-organization. In other words, the system as a whole permits its components to behave collectively in a lawful fashion. The motor system, for instance, may have properties that allow its elements (neurons, muscles, bones, and tendons) to organize into coherent collectives for action.

Supposing such self-organization exists, how is it to be described? The style of analysis adopted in synergetics is to provide mathematical descriptions of systems with nonlinear input–output properties. Nonlinearity is exemplified by phase transitions: Suddenly, as some parameter is altered and reaches a critical value, a dramatic shift occurs in the system's behavior. Nothing in the components of the system suggests in advance that the shift will occur, but the shift does occur, and it occurs predictably when the control parameter reaches the critical value.

In synergetics, the parameter whose variation can give rise to a nonlinear change in the behavior of the system is called a *control* parameter. The control parameter in two-finger oscillation is frequency; as frequency changes and reaches a critical value, the behavior of the system changes nonlinearly. The dimension or parameter that exhibits the nonlinear change is called the *order* parameter. In two-finger oscillation, the order parameter is relative phase.

Describing a system in terms of control parameters and order parameters allows one, in principle, to recognize similarities between apparently disparate systems. Particular kinds of nonlinearities observed in different systems give those systems synergetic "signatures." Being able to recognizing common signatures in different systems is one of the most intellectually satisfying features of synergetics.

Synergetics is not a theory of the *cause* of nonlinearity, however. Nor is it a theory that attempts to say in advance which systems will exhibit which kinds of nonlinearity or what their order parameters or control parameters will be. The theory's aims are purely descriptive, and in that sense modest. On the other hand, synergetics can and does make predictions about individual systems subjected to consistent control-parameter variations. Phase transitions and critical fluctuations in two-finger oscillation are highly replicable, for example (Schöner & Kelso, 1988).

Critical Slowing Down

Within synergetics, critical fluctuations are predicted to occur at phase transitions. As we have seen, this prediction is confirmed for two-finger oscillation. Another prediction is that as the control parameter for a system approximates the value where a phase transition occurs, another phenomenon, called *critical slowing down*, should also occur. Critical slowing down is the tendency of a system to take a long time to return to an unstable state after being pushed away from that state by some disturbance. The time to return to a *stable* state, in contrast, should be much shorter.

Consider again the case of two-finger oscillation. As discussed earlier, if the fingers oscillate at a low frequency with relative phase of 180°, then as the frequency increases and reaches a critical value, the fingers spontaneously fall into 0° relative phase; 0° relative phase is the attractor. Scholz, Kelso, and Schöner (1987) applied a brief torque at an unpredictable time to one finger while subjects performed the two-finger task. Subjects were instructed to return to the initial mode of oscillation once the torque was applied. When the initial relative phase was 0°, the time to return to the initial mode—what Sholz, Kelso, and Schöner (1987) called the *relaxation* time—was very brief. Likewise, when the initial relative phase was 180° and the driving frequency was low, the relaxation time was again very brief. However, when the initial relative phase was 180° and the driving frequency was near the critical frequency, relaxation time was long. The latter result confirms the prediction that critical slowing down should be seen in this condition.

Evaluation

How should synergetics be evaluated as a theory of human motor control? My evaluation is positive, although I also have reservations. On the positive side, the theory is elegant by virtue of its sophisticated mathematics. The underlying equations (not reviewed here) allow one to see that, at an abstract level of description, some aspects of motor performance are similar to other natural phenomena, such as the formation of laser light and the emergence of convection patterns in heated liquids (Haken & Wunderlin, 1990). Moreover, because the theory is mathematical, it is possible to derive, in a rigorous way, predictions that might not be obvious initially.

On the other hand, synergetics, like any theory, has limitations. One is related to its abstractness. Because synergetics applies to a wide range of systems—both biological and purely physical—the explanatory specificity it provides for any given system may be less than that afforded by a more special-purpose account. In the case of two-finger oscillation, some researchers may not be satisfied to learn that relative phase is the order parameter for the task, that frequency is the control parameter, that 0° relative phase is the attractor state, and so on. Though these individuals might accept the fact that terms like "order parameter," "control parameter," and "attractor state" have descriptive value, they might still want to know *why* the system has the properties it does, and why, by the same token, other motor subsystems do not have those properties. Why, for example, do we not hop when our running speed exceeds some value? Hopping, after all, is a case where the legs move together with 0° relative phase. The reason we don't hop, of course, is that hopping is less efficient than running (for humans). Still, nothing in synergetics *predicts* that humans will refrain from hopping as they run faster. Insofar as a theory of motor control should predict what behaviors will occur as a function of variables that ought to influence the behavior, synergetics' failure to predict that we run rather than hop might be counted as an embarrassing result.

Even within two-finger oscillation (the favorite example of motor synergeticists), it is not clear why frequency should be the control parameter or why critical frequency should have the value it does—around 2.25 Hz (see Figure 11.3). I am struck by the fact that 2.25 Hz corresponds to a period of .444 sec (that is, .444 = 1/2.25) and that .444 sec (the complete cycle time for the fingers) equals twice .222 sec. Thus the time for a half-cycle—when the fingers move from one spatial reversal point to another—is .222 sec, or about one reaction time (see Chapter 8). This observation suggests a possible way of accounting for the results of the two-finger oscillation task—namely, that it is easier to extend the two fingers simultaneously or to flex the two fingers simultaneously than to extend one finger while flexing the other. Simultaneous extensions use homologous muscles, as do simultaneous flexions, but extending one finger while flexing the other requires simultaneous activations of nonhomologous muscles (Kelso & Schöner, 1988). Flexion movements of the two index fingers have comparable durations, as do extension movements, but flexion movements have shorter durations than extension movements (as shown in an informal experiment in my laboratory). Therefore, a series of simultaneous extensions and simultaneous flexions will allow the two fingers to begin and end their movements together, but a series of simultaneous extension–flexion movements will result in the fingers' falling out of phase unless something is done to equate the durations of the movements (such as retarding the flexion response). As Kelso, Southard, and Goodman (1979) have shown, there is a tendency to begin and end two-hand movements together when the movements could begin and end asynchronously. When the biomechanics of the effector biases the movements not to begin and end together, as in the case of flexion of one finger paired with extension of the other, some modulating influence is needed to keep the fingers in step.

All these considerations suggest that controlling flexion–extension movements might be harder than controlling paired flexion movements or paired extension movements. If it takes time $t + h$ to initiate flexion–extension movements and time t to initiate paired flexion or paired extension movements, then whenever the movements must be initiated with a delay less than $t + h$, the system's only option may be to initiate the kinds of movements it can (that is, those movements that can be initiated in time t). The results one would expect from such a model are just the ones that have been observed.

A few caveats are in order about the explanation I have just advanced. One is that it may not be inconsistent with synergetics, only more concrete. The explanation may be viewed as addressing the operational principles underlying phase transitions, critical fluctuations, and critical slowing down in the context of the two-finger task. Synergetic descriptions are more abstract than descriptions based on programming ease or biomechanics (Pew & Rosenbaum, 1988). My suggestion about t and $t + h$, which is based on considerations of ease of motor programming, could be viewed in abstract terms as representing a threshold nonlinearity, from which phase transitions and related effects can arise (Kugler, 1986; Turvey, 1990). Alternatively, my explanation for *why* these phenomena are present may be viewed as a particular mechanistic (or computational) proposal, auxiliary to a more abstract description.

The second caveat is that coordination phenomena similar to those exhibited by the two index fingers of one person are also exhibited by two people watching each other swing their lower legs back and forth in time with a metronome (Schmidt, Carello, & Turvey, 1990). The two-person result might have a similar basis as the two-finger result, either expressed in the abstract terms of synergetics or, more prosaically, in terms of the greater difficulty of perceptually resolving the motions of two legs when they move in anti-phase as compared to in-phase mode (Turvey, 1990).

■ THE ECOLOGICAL APPROACH

Of the new approaches to motor control, perhaps the most challenging is one that has been championed by Michael Turvey and his colleagues (Kugler & Turvey, 1987; Turvey, 1990). This *ecological* approach shares features with synergetics but has distinguishing features as well. Like synergetics, it relies on mathematical analyses of dynamical systems. Unlike synergetics, it is committed to descriptions that acknowledge and are connected as closely as possible to the physical underpinnings of movement. While synergetics might inadvertently predict an outcome that is physically unlikely (such as hopping at high speeds), the ecological approach would take as its first responsibility the postulation of descriptions and predictions that are physically realistic. Beyond this, the ecological approach (at least in Turvey's hands), is meant to provide principled, "physicalized" restrictions on information and intention. The latter goal is still quite speculative and philosophical, so I will refrain from reviewing it here.

Direct Perception

For purposes of understanding this approach, begin by considering a framework for studying visual perception, advocated by James Gibson (1966, 1979). (Gibson's views were introduced briefly in Chapter 4.) Prior to Gibson, a prevailing view of how we perceive was embodied in the "constructionist" account, developed in the nineteenth-century by Hermann von Helmholtz. According to Helmholtz, the retinal image is ambiguous. Its ambiguity rests in the fact that the retina is (to a first approximation) a two-dimensional surface, but the world is three-dimensional. To recover the third dimension, Helmholtz argued, and to resolve other potential ambiguities, unconscious inferences must be drawn to help us "puzzle out" what's out there.

Gibson rejected this analysis. How could it be, he asked, that the visual system would have evolved without the ability to pick up *directly* the information specified by the optic array—that is, the array of light reflected from objects in the visual world? It ought to be, Gibson suggested, that there are regularities in the optic array which specify physical properties of the objects from which the optic array emanates (reflecting light). If this assumption is correct, then no inference is required, taking "inference" to mean a fallible, time-consuming, experience-based process. What vision scientists must do, Gibson asserted, is to investigate *ecological optics*—the ways in which information about events in the environment is specified by the structures of light fields, analyzed at the scale of animal–environment interactions. If these ways of specifying information turn out to be plentiful, then inference will be required rarely.

Direct perception may not be directly confirmable as a hypothesis about vision (Turvey, 1990), but it invites some methodological commitments and substantive concerns. One substantive concern is neonatal perception. The direct-perception view predicts that newborns should perceive the natural world virtually as well as adults. An impressive amount of evidence has confirmed that infants do indeed see at a much earlier age and far more accurately than was previously believed (Bower, 1982; E. J. Gibson, 1987).

The methodological dictate of Gibson's view is that one should look to the physical world to understand how we perceive within it. One should search for properties of optic arrays that provide unambiguous information relevant to behavior. A good example is Lee's τ principle, reviewed earlier in this chapter. Another example is a study I reported some time ago (Rosenbaum, 1975). I wondered whether people can directly perceive uniform acceleration. In the natural world, objects rarely move with constant velocity, so it is possible that the visual system is tuned in such a way that it can directly pick up acceleration information. When a body accelerates uniformly, its velocity steadily increases. This means that one could also perceive uniform acceleration by computing changes in velocity over time (given that acceleration is the first time derivative of velocity), or by computing changes of position over time more than once (given that acceleration is also the second time derivative of position).

The method I used to answer this question was to release a small sled on a frictionless linear track (see Figure 11.5). A thread extended from the sled to a bob suspended over a pulley on the opposite end of the track. When the bob was allowed to drop, the sled accelerated, traveling in the subject's field of view until it passed behind a screen with a marker placed a variable distance from the disappearance point (the edge of the screen). Subjects were supposed to press a button as soon as the sled passed behind the marker. The visible displacement of the sled was varied, as was the time of its visible motion. (The method of varying visible distance and visible time was to vary the mass of the bob.) Through statistical techniques (regression analysis), I showed that subjects' responses were best predicted by the

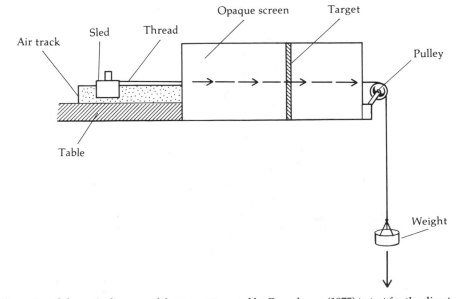

Figure 11.5 Schematic diagram of the apparatus used by Rosenbaum (1975) to test for the direct perception of acceleration.

acceleration of the sled rather than by the sled's average visible velocity, its visible distance or time, or its hidden distance or time. Thus in a rigorous statistical sense, it appeared that subjects directly perceived acceleration.

"Natural Physics"

Of what use is the concept of direct perception for the study of motor control, apart from the fact that movements are adaptive only if properly related to perceived events?

At an empirical level, the direct-perception framework suggests that the movement patterns of living organisms should have invariant physical properties which can be immediately and unambiguously perceived by other organisms. In Chapter 4 (Walking), I mentioned evidence commensurate with this prediction. There I reported that observers can readily identify actors walking and performing other familiar movement patterns when the actors had luminous dots attached to their joints but their bodies were otherwise invisible. When the same luminous dots were static (the actors remained perfectly still), the configurations were virtually impossible to recognize. A similar result applies to face perception. Observers can identify emotional expressions from dots attached to the moving face, even when the face itself cannot be seen (Bassili, 1979). When the face is static, emotional expressions are hard to discern.

These results suggest that movements have physical regularities to which the visual system is tuned. There is tight perception–action coupling in the perception of biological motion. From an evolutionary standpoint, the benefit of such coupling is easy to recognize. Lions preparing to attack a herd of gazelle pick out the individual whose gait pattern is abnormal; those are the animals that will be easy to catch. As for the more pleasant biological function of sex, the lithe motions of another person can be a potent attractor, whereas ungainly motions can have a repelling rather than attracting effect.

The claim that movements can be easily recognized does not imply, in any obvious way, how movements are *controlled*. Thus we are left with the question of what direct perception implies for theories of movement *generation*. Another line of study would seem to be required to address this question.

Strong proponents of direct perception argue that motor control (or action) cannot be studied separately from perception. Where, they ask, is the dividing line between the perceptual and motor systems? My answer is that none exists, and that this point has been made abundantly clear throughout this volume. For every subsystem I have discussed, connections between perception and action have proven tight and adaptive. On the other hand, as I said in Chapter 1, there is an advantage to studying motor control in its own right. The mechanisms for activating and deactivating muscles are plainly different from the mechanisms for seeing color, for example. *Applying* forces is a different kind of problem from *witnessing* forces being applied. The dividing line between perception and action may not be obvious, but for practical reasons focusing primarily on one system or another is a workable approach.

In practice, no one working in Gibson's tradition doubts this (as far as I know). The way many of them answer the challenge of finding a way to study action, given that perception and action are linked, is to suggest that physics, or "natural physics," should be applied to all natural systems. Their proposal is that common principles apply at many different scales and in many different guises. This being so (by hypothesis), the best place to start looking for common principles is in *physics*, where tools for describing underlying principles have been developed, perhaps more effectively than in any other discipline (Kugler & Turvey, 1987). If one adopts this perspective, it becomes possible to use conventional physical descriptions of movement and stability, with the expectation that the principles one discovers will represent deeper regularities.

The methodological implications of this perspective are clear and, in my view, healthy. First, one should be as clear as possible about what needs to be done *physically* in a motor control context. If one wishes to understand juggling, for example, the first thing to do is to describe the physical constraints that must be satisfied for juggling to occur (Beek, 1989). Without such a description, one may not know where to begin in the analysis. One may not even be able to distinguish juggling that is possible from juggling that is not (see Figure 11.6).

Describing the physical constraints of behavior can also help one avoid spinning unconstrained webs of psychological or neurological fancy. If babies between 2 and 8 months of age cannot walk because their upper bodies are too heavy (as discussed in Chapter 4), then that explanation is far simpler than one which assumes disappearing cognitive abilities during this same 6-month period. Looking for physical causes of behaviors is not to deny that there can be psychological or neurological causes, for many behavioral phenomena surely originate in the mind or nervous system. What the natural–physical perspective demands, however, is that, at the very least, physical causes should be carefully considered. From my perspective as a *cognitive* psychologist this methodological prescription should be heeded in all future studies of motor control.

Swinging Two Hand-Held Pendulums

Given what I have just said, it would be useful to know that physical accounts of behavior can account for interesting aspects of behavior. Using physics to show that infants cannot walk because their upper bodies are too massive relative to their legs is, arguably, not a profound insight (though it might be reassuring for worried parents or palliative for overzealous psychologists). I reviewed one example of a purely physical account of a nontrivial behavioral phenomenon in Chapter 4—the transition from walking to

Figure 11.6 A photograph of juggling that was probably faked. There is no blurr around the flying plates, it is unlikely that both jugglers would hold plates with both hands given the number of plates being juggled, and the four horizontal layers of plates should be more densely packed near the zeniths of flight. (From Beek, 1989.)

running. Now I will present another example, from the work of Kugler and Turvey (1987).

Consider the task of swinging two hand-held weighted rods back and forth at a comfortable frequency, with a relative phase of 180° (see Figure 11.7). The task is worth considering because, to a first approximation, many motor behaviors involve motions that are pendular; walking is an example. If a person swings just one weighted rod back and forth at a steady, comfortable tempo, the tempo he or she settles on should correspond to the natural period of the hand and weighted rod, viewed as a compound pendulum. A compound pendulum consists of a set of simple pendulums, and a simple pendulum consists of a single length and mass, turning about an axis of rotation (see Figure 11.8A). The natural period, T, of a compound pendulum consisting of the hand and a hand-held rod can be written

$$T = \left[\frac{4\pi^2 ML^2}{K + gML} \right]^{1/2} \tag{11.1}$$

where M denotes the mass of the hand and rod (with the mass assumed to be concentrated at a distance L from the axis of rotation), K denotes the stiffness of the hand musculature, and g denotes gravitational acceleration. The axis of rotation is assumed to pass through the wrist. (Recall that raising an expression to the 1/2 power is equivalent to taking its square root.)

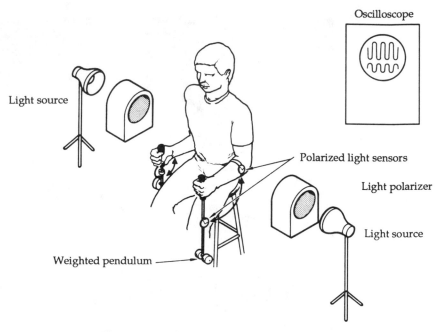

Figure 11.7 Task used by Kugler and Turvey (1987).

Now reconsider the task of swinging two rods at once, each with one hand. The Dutch physicist, Christiaan Huygens, showed in 1673 that it is possible to idealize a pair of pendulums as one (see Figure 11.8). His insight was that it is possible to determine what *simple* pendulum will have the same natural period as any given compound pendulum, including a compound pendulum consisting of two weighted rods whose masses, M_L and M_R, are concentrated at distances L_L and L_R from their respective axes of rotation. This pair of pendulums, thought of as one compound pendulum, has a sin-

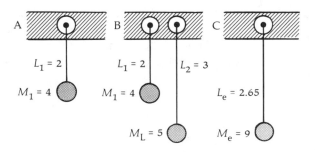

Figure 11.8 A simple pendulum (A), compound pendulum (B), and simple pendulum equivalent to the compound pendulum (C). Calculations of the equivalent mass, M_e, and equivalent length, L_e, are based on equations 11.2 and 11.3.

gle natural period which can be determined by finding out the natural period of an equivalent *simple* pendulum. The mass of the equivalent simple pendulum, M_e, is simply

$$M_e = M_R + M_L \tag{11.2}$$

The distance, L_e, of the mass of the equivalent simple pendulum from its axis of rotation is

$$L_e = \frac{M_R L_R{}^2 + M_L L_L{}^2}{M_R L_R + M_L L_L} \tag{11.3}$$

where the mass is assumed to be concentrated at distance L_e from the axis of rotation. Once one has determined M_e and L_e, these terms can be plugged into Equation 11.1, replacing M and L, respectively, and the natural period of the system can be found.

This analysis works well when applied to two weighted rods swinging from a beam. But does it apply to two weighted rods swung by a person? The answer is not obvious, for the coupling between the rods is far more complicated in the case of a person. In the case of a beam, there is only physical coupling between the rods. In the case of a person, there is neural as well as physical coupling.

When Kugler and Turvey (1987) asked subjects to swing two weighted rods back and forth with 180° relative phase at a single, comfortable tempo, the tempos that subjects spontaneously adopted for any given pair of rods conformed to the periods predicted by Equations 11.1–11.3. What is especially interesting about this outcome is that the common period adopted by the two hands often departed considerably from the period preferred by each hand on its own, given the length and mass of the rod it had to swing. Thus subjects treated the two pendulums as a single "virtual" pendulum. The strategy they adopted is physically efficient and may comprise an example of reducing degrees of freedom through natural physical means.

The two-hand pendulum experiment illustrates the kind of study that Turvey and his colleagues recommend. The experiment permits the injection of physical analysis into behavioral research so a class of behavior that otherwise might not have been understood can be illuminated.

Explaining the possible neural (or psychological) basis of the virtual-pendulum effect still remains. As I see it, two broad classes of explanation are possible. One, which can be called *physical and neural interaction*, assumes that distinct neural subsystems, dedicated to each hand, communicate with each other, and through their interaction settle on a solution to the coordination problem which corresponds to Huygens' solution. According to this explanation, the reason for settling on Huygens' solution inheres as much in properties of the nervous system as in conventional mechanics. [This seems to be the explanation preferred by Kugler and Turvey, (1987).]

Another possibility, which can be called *physical interaction*, is that the nervous system measures the effort expended by the subject when he or she tries out different periods. It settles on the period that demands least effort. The preferred period is the one predicted by Huygens because, when all is said and done, a person swinging two weighted rods is a physical system. This model assumes that the reason for choosing a given period inheres entirely in the mechanical demands of the task and that the nervous system merely serves as an "effort meter," possessing an associated mechanism for locking onto the command mode that yields the lowest effort reading.

■ NETWORK MODELING

The final approach to be discussed is one that I have already presented at several points in the book. In Chapter 4 I described a network model for locomotion (see Figures 4.8 and 4.9), in Chapter 8 I described a network model for typewriting (see Figure 8.11), and in Chapter 9 I described network models for two aspects of speech production (see Figures 9.10 and 9.12). Network modeling is not an entirely new approach, as these earlier examples indicate. In fact, it has been pursued since the 1940s, if not earlier (Hebb, 1949). Nevertheless, it is an approach that is gaining ground in leaps and bounds because of knowledge acquired about network behavior from years of working with networks and because modern computers allow for interactive testing of network properties. Such testing is often required because networks often give rise to nonlinearities that cannot be foreseen if one relies entirely on analytic techniques. Another impetus for the development of network models is their practical value. Tasks such as visual pattern recognition, which so far have been handled poorly through conventional computational methods (such as strict serial processing), may be handled better with networks that behave like the highly parallel neural networks of the brain.

A central concept in network modeling is that the elements of the networks being modeled are intrinsically unintelligent. The *interactions* of the elements bestow intelligence (or the appearance of intelligence) on the network as a whole. This property is one that synergeticists recognize in naturally occurring systems, as discussed earlier in this chapter. But where synergeticists *describe* emergent properties in already-existing natural systems, network modelers *create* systems whose emergent properties are meant to be adaptive for the tasks at hand.

Bullock and Grossberg's (1988) VITE Model

Because I have already presented several network models, I will not discuss this approach in as much detail as I discussed synergetics or the ecological approach. Instead, I will briefly review one model that exhibits a number of features that this sort of model can possess. It is the vector-integration-to-endpoint (VITE) model of Bullock and Grossberg (1988). VITE is just one example of the modeling work that has been pursued by Grossberg and his colleagues (Grossberg, 1987a,b; Grossberg & Kuperstein, 1989). It has recently been expanded by Bullock and Grossberg (1989; in press).

The essential components of the system are shown in Figure 11.9. These are: (1) the *target position command*, (2) the *present position command*, (3) the *difference vector*, (4) the *multiplier*, and (5) the *GO* signal. I will describe each of these components in turn.

When an animal wants to bring its limb to a new position, that position is assumed to be represented in terms of a target position command (TPC). The TPC can be created at any time and is represented in positional terms.

The present position command (PPC) carries information about where the limb is located at the moment. The PPC, like the TPC, is coded in positional terms. It is based on an efferent copy of outflow to the muscles rather than afferent feedback. The PPC is assumed to be updated at a rate that increases with its difference from the TPC: The greater the difference, the higher the rate at which the PPC is updated.

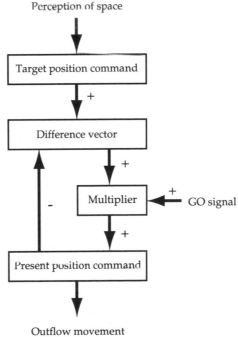

Figure 11.9 The VITE model of Bullock and Grossberg. From D. Bullock & S. Grossberg (1988). Neural dynamics of planned arm movements: Emergent invariants and speed-accuracy properties during trajectory formation. *Psychological Review*, **95**, 49–90. Copyright © 1988 by the American Psychological Association. Reprinted with permission.

The difference vector (DV) represents the difference between the TPC and the PPC. Specifically, DV = TPC − PPC. When the DV is large, a large discrepancy exists between the limb's present position and the target position. As the DV approaches zero, the present position converges onto the target position until equivalence between the two is attained (DV = 0).

The DV influences the PPC via a multiplier. When the value of the multiplier is large, the PPC rapidly shifts in the direction of the TPC, resulting in a high speed of movement. When the value of the multiplier is small, the PPC shifts more gradually toward the TPC and the speed of movement is lower. When the value of the multiplier is zero, the PPC stops shifting toward the TPC and movement stops. The multiplier and the DV are assumed to have independent effects on the rate of change of the PPC. The PPC changes more quickly the larger its associated DV and the larger its multiplier.

The multiplier is controlled by the GO signal, which is assumed to represent the will or arousal. As the GO signal activates the multiplier to a greater extent, the gain of the system increases, so the faster the discrepancy between the PPC and the TPC is reduced (hence the quicker the movement). The GO signal can be set to zero instantly, causing the multiplier instantly to go to zero.

The system is called vector-integration-to-endpoint because there is a TPC, PPC, and DV for each synergist; only the GO signal and the multiplier are assumed to be nonspecific. Each synergist can be viewed as a dimension of a vector, and the contributions of the synergists correspond to values on the dimensions. The position of the hand (when VITE is applied to arm movements) depends on the vector defined by the set of synergist values. The trajectory of the hand depends on the time-varying change in this vector.

VITE has the properties of a negative feedback loop for position control. It provides a means of reducing the discrepancy between the PPC and the TPC, although the information for reducing the discrepancy is communicated in the form of an efferent copy rather than peripheral feedback. The GO signal is the one feature not found in most rudimentary control systems.

VITE can account for a number of phenomena. Among these are the following:

1. *Freezing* Because the GO signal and the multiplier instantly can be set to zero, movements can stop in midcourse. Animals sometimes freeze, for example, as a defense against predators. [The ability to freeze may also constitute a problem for the mass-spring model, discussed in Chapter 6; see Bullock & Grossberg, 1988.]

2. *Straight-line hand paths* One of the most striking features of arm movements is that the hand tends to move in straight lines (Morasso, 1981; see pp. 218–221). Bullock and Grossberg (1988) observed that straight-line hand paths can arise if muscle synergists contributing to displacement of

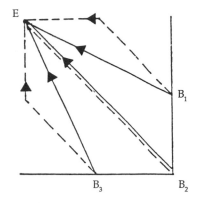

Figure 11.10 Consequences of two possible control strategies for moving from three beginning points, B_1, B_2, or B_3, to a common endpoint, E. In one strategy (dashed lines), the synergist producing vertical movement and the synergist producing horizontal movement contract at the same time and at equal rates; bent paths result. In the other strategy (solid lines), the two synergists contract at the same time but their contraction rates depend on how much vertical and horizontal movement is required; straight paths result. From D. Bullock & S. Grossberg (1988). Neural dynamics of planned arm movements: Emergent invariants and speed-accuracy properties during trajectory formation. *Psychological Review, 95*, 49–90. Copyright © 1988 by the American Psychological Association. Reprinted with permission.

the hand are activated and deactivated synchronously and their contraction rates depend on the magnitudes of their respective required displacements (see Figure 11.10). Suppose synergist A must cover a short distance and synergist B must cover a long distance in order for the hand to reach a target position. If the contraction rates of the two synergists are equal, synergist A will reach its terminal position before synergist B, and the limb as a whole will follow a bent path rather than a straight one. By making the contraction rates for the synergists proportional to their respective distances from the target position (that is, proportional to their respective DVs), the two synergists can begin and end their contractions together and the hand can travel in a straight line.

3. *Priming* Because the TPC can be set even if the GO signal is off, it is possible to prepare for a forthcoming movement. The DV is updated as the TPC takes on a new value regardless of whether the GO signal is on. As a result, when the GO signal is finally activated, there is a reaction-time saving because the TPC has already been computed. This capacity for preparation accords with neurophysiological data indicating that, prior to movement, populations of cells in the motor cortex gradually change their firing patterns, commensurate with forthcoming positioning requirements (Georgopoulos, Schwartz, & Kettner, 1986).

4. *Speed of changing direction* The model similarly accounts for the observation that the hand can change paths from one target to another without first coming to a halt (Georgopoulos, Kalaska, & Massey, 1981; see

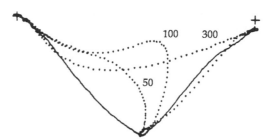

Figure 11.11 Movement of a monkey's paw continues when the movement is initiated toward a target at 2 o'clock and a second target is presented at 10 o'clock either 50, 100, or 300 msec after the first target is presented. From A. P. Georgopoulos, J. F. Kalaska, & J. T. Massey (1981). Spatial trajectories and reaction times of aimed movements: Effects of practice, uncertainty, and change in target location. *Journal of Neurophysiology, 46,* 725–743. Reprinted by permission of the American Physiological Society.

Figure 11.11). The continuity of movement arises from the continual updating of the PPC relative to the current TPC.

5. *Velocity profile invariance* As mentioned in Chapter 6, the hand usually exhibits a bell-shaped velocity profile during rapid aiming movements. Computer simulations based on the VITE model suggest that such bell-shaped velocity profiles can arise spontaneously from the relative contributions of agonist and antagonist synergists contributing to hand displacement. VITE also predicts departures from perfect bell-shaped velocity curves of the sort observed in the literature (Beggs & Howarth, 1972; Zelaznik, Schmidt, & Gielen, 1986).

VITE predicts other results as well, including speed-accuracy trade-offs and observed relations between movement duration and movement speed (see Bullock & Grossberg, 1988). Perhaps the most important aspect of the model, however, is related to item 5 above (velocity profile invariance). Other authors have proposed that bell-shaped velocity profiles may reflect an optimization criterion, such as minimizing mean squared jerk (Hogan, 1984), or rescalable force-time programs for muscle agonists and antagonists (Meyer, Smith, & Wright, 1982; Schmidt, Zelaznik, Hawkins, Frank, & Quinn, 1979). Bullock and Grossberg avoided explicit optimization criteria and explicit representations of movement trajectories or underlying force patterns. Rather, they sought regularities of movement arising from interactions of individual elements, none of which was cognizant of what the system as a whole was doing. Their apparent success in generating realistic velocity profiles suggests that global system properties can be rigorously derived from interactions of low-level elements. Looking for system properties through behavioral techniques is still valuable, however, insofar as those are the properties against which emergent network properties must be evaluated. Network modeling provides a way (now proven) of exploring how those emergent properties might arise.

■ GENERAL PRINCIPLES

What general principles can be culled from the information that has been summarized in this volume? In formulating an answer to this question, I am tempted, on the one hand, to suggest a global model for motor control. On the other hand, I feel it might be more prudent merely to suggest some properties that characterize the systems I have discussed. The second route is more attractive, for a global model, I fear, would be no more informative than a general analytic framework. Potentially, one could present a flow diagram with a stack of boxes, along with ascending and descending arrows connecting every pair of boxes. The picture might convey, in broad terms, what the organization of any given motor subsystem is like. But it would leave unanswered what the contents of the boxes are and how stacks corresponding to different subsystems communicate. I would rather not present such a picture, which is why I have only described it verbally (and with less than a thousand words).

Common properties of the motor subsystems can be articulated, however. One is the importance of *distinct parameters*. Throughout the volume, it has been seen that certain parts of the brain control different aspects of movement, that different receptors in the periphery respond to different sensory variables, and that movements involving particular activity systems seem to be controlled with respect to some movement features but not others. The result is so common that it is easy to miss its significance. *A priori*, the motor system could control movements holistically rather than parametrically (Goodman & Kelso, 1980). The extensive review I have provided suggests that a parametric conception is justified (Rosenbaum, 1980).

A second principle is that there are many *levels of control*. Particularly in the realms of writing, keyboarding, and speaking, distinct tiers of representation and control are apparent. These correspond to wide spans of behavior at high levels and narrow spans of behavior at low levels.

A third general principle is that *the motor system is tuned to perception*. As mentioned earlier in this chapter, the precision and adaptability of perceptual tuning is evident in every activity system that has been considered. We are able to react effectively to stimuli and to anticipate with great skill the perceptual consequences of our actions (Craik, 1943).

Another general property of the motor system is skillful *exploitation of mechanics*. To an increasing extent, researchers in the field are coming to recognize that using the physical properties of the body both enhances movement efficiency and facilitates movement control (Bizzi & Mussa-Ivaldi, 1989; Thelen, Kelso, & Fogel, 1987).

There are also *neurological or psychological limitations* that constrain the quality of performance. Speed–accuracy tradeoffs severely limit how well people can perform, even on simple tasks such as bringing the hand to a target. Neurological or psychological limitations appear in many other facets of motor performance.

The motor control system also monitors its own performance with respect to *physical and informational criteria*. At low levels, the system generally avoids extreme muscle stretch, for example. At higher levels, the system behaves as if it respects more global variables, such as those giving rise to bell-shaped velocity curves. For descriptive purposes, it has proven useful in many contexts to conceptualize movement selection and evaluation in terms of the minimization of well-defined costs (optimization).

Optimization criteria may not be represented as such within the motor system, in the sense that such criteria are explicitly considered when planning movements. Instead, they may merely be descriptions of the way the system behaves of its own accord, through the collective interactions of its individual elements. In this regard, the motor system may be *self-organizing*.

◼ PROSPECTS FOR THE FUTURE

Where do we go from here? I have already indicated some lines of study that I think will prove important in future work. Among these are network modeling, ecological and synergetic approaches, and approaches concerned with global functional properties of motor behavior. Two avenues that strike me as being particularly in need of further study are selection of macroscopic performance features and coordination of motor subsystems.

By "selection of macroscopic performance features" I mean the choice of large-scale properties of the way we do things. By what criteria do we choose to pick up objects with the left hand or right, for example? The choice is a big one, in the sense that when one arm or the other is deployed, major postural adjustments must be made, possibly with dramatic consequences for the kinds of movements that subsequently may be required. Similarly, how do people decide whether to pick up an object with the hand oriented one way or the other, as in the study summarized in Chapter 1 (Figure 1.4; see also Rosenbaum, Vaughan, Barnes, Marchak, & Slotta, 1990)? Surprisingly, there has been little research on decision making at this level of performance. Identifying the criteria that are relied on for large-scale movement decisions may reveal what criteria are important for the motor system at large. This level of analysis may also reduce the gap between cognitive psychological research on planning and traditionally studied topics of motor performance.

A second issue that needs more attention is how the motor subsystems are coordinated. Each of us possesses a walking system, a looking system, a speaking system, and so forth. By what means do we decide when to activate these systems and how to coordinate them? Very little is known about this topic. We do know that there can be tight coupling between the systems, as was seen (and hopefully grasped) in the brief review of eye–hand coordination given earlier in this chapter. More work of this kind, involving a broader range of subsystems, needs to be pursued. As Garfield the Cat reminds us (see Figure 11.12), if the motor subsystems do not functionally interrelate, the net behavioral outcome is of little use.

A final avenue for future work is the practical one. I mention this not as an afterthought but as a final thought. We who are scientists have, as an obligation to society, the betterment of the human condition. The fact that accidents occur because of misperformed movements, that machines are operated less efficiently than they might be, that skill training leaves much to be desired in some contexts, and that motor disabilities confound the lives of thousands of people all indicate that many practical improvements are still possible in domains where motor control plays a role. My fervent hope is that ongoing and future research in motor control and related disciplines will lead to significant improvements in all these domains.

Perhaps the area where research on human motor control may lead to the most unforeseen consequences is robotics. Nowadays, the capacities of robots are quite limited. Though robots can spot-weld, polish pianos, and engage in other tedious activities, they are notoriously ill-suited for tasks requiring rapid, intelligent adaptation to unpredictable environments. Consequently, one of the newest forms of robots is, in fact, not a robot at all because it does not manage its own input–output control. Rather it is an artificial extension of the human operator (see Figure 11.13). Such *teleoperated* robots (Goleman, 1989; Foley, 1987) have sensors that transmit signals to the human operator so that he or she may see, feel, or hear what the robot is exposed to. In turn, the operator carries out movements that are picked up by sensors on his or her body, and signals derived from the sensors are then sent to the robot so it can duplicate the movements the person has performed. This "proxying" of a human with a robot is an ingenious technique, but it reflects how little we know about perceptual–motor performance. Only when a robot can perform as skillfully as a person, without a person directly governing its behavior, will we be able to say that we know enough about motor control and perception to create a truly intelligent action device. Until then, the humbling reality is that we still have much to learn about perceiving and acting in the world around us.

Figure 11.12 Adaptive movement requires whole-body coordination.

Figure 11.13 Teleoperated robot. (From Goleman, 1989.)

■ SUMMARY

1. Though the eye and hand are physically removed from one another, they can be closely coordinated. The eye slightly leads the hand in discrete aimed hand movements and, by pointing toward the target before reaching the target, helps improve the accuracy of the hand movement. The eye can track movements of the hand virtually perfectly. The hand and eye appear to share common spatial information.

2. Striking an oncoming ball requires prediction of the ball's flight. Determining when the ball will arrive can, under certain conditions, be based on how quickly the image of the ball expands. Controlling the striking movement appears, in the case of forehand attacks by top table-tennis players, to be simplified by modulating the time when the stroke begins, as well as the stroke direction. Some correction of the stroke based on visual feedback may also occur when the stroke is in progress.

3. Individual differences have been demonstrated in response speed, timing accuracy, precision of force production, finger dexterity, arm–hand steadiness, and other factors. Clumsy children appear to be deficient in timing ability and proprioception. Within the normal population it has proven difficult to find strong predictors of grace or incoordination.

4. Synergetics is a new theoretical approach to motor control. It is concerned with nonlinear phenomena such as phase transitions in two-finger oscillation tasks, observed when the driving frequency for the oscillation exceeds a critical value. Other related phenomena are critical fluctuations and critical slowing down. Synergetics provides a mathematical description of such nonlinear phenomena without attempting to identify their causes. Some researchers prefer to identify (or hypothesize) causal mechanisms. A possible causal mechanism for the nonlinear effects observed in two-finger oscillation is the greater difficulty of controlling movements made with nonhomologous as compared with homologous muscles.

5. Another new approach to motor control—the ecological approach—begins with a commitment to physics and an acknowledgment that the perceptual and motor systems evolved in natural environments. The approach takes its cue from Gibson's theory of direct perception. As applied to action systems, the primary methodological prescription is to arrive at a coherent physical account of the task to be performed. Following this prescription, one may be able to account for behavioral phenomena with constructs already established in physics. An example is the mode of coordination adopted by people swinging two weighted rods with the two hands. The swinging frequency that people settle on is predicted by the theory of compound pendulums.

6. Network modeling is a technique that is likely to play an increasingly important role in motor control. The technique involves simulating the behavior of a configuration of dumb processing elements. Though the elements are ignorant of what the system as a whole is supposed to do, the patterns of interactions among the elements can give rise to emergent system properties that mimic what the nervous system (or a part of the nervous system) does. An example of such a network is the vector-integration-to-endpoint (VITE) model. VITE gives rise to a number of important motor control phenomena, including straight-line hand trajectories and bell-shaped velocity profiles.

7. General principles of motor control can be stated on the basis of the material reviewed here. These are the importance and ubiquity of distinct control parameters and levels of control, effective interaction with perceptual channels, exploitation of mechanics, neurological and psychological limitations, reliance on physical and informational criteria, and the capacity for self-organization.

8. Besides continuing the lines of investigation that have already shed light on human motor control, two additional areas seem especially important for the future. One is the selection of macroscopic features of movement, such as the determination of which hand should be used to pick up an object. The other is coordination of motor subsystems.

9. Robotics is a domain that may benefit from research in human motor control, and vice versa. To the extent that robots are now severely limited in their adaptability to unfamiliar environments, it is clear that much remains to be learned about motor control and related aspects of behavior.

■ REFERENCES

Abrams, R. A., Meyer, D. E., & Kornblum, S. (1990). Eye-hand coordination: Oculomotor control in rapid aimed limb movements. *Journal of Experimental Psychology: Human Perception and Performance, 16,* 248–267.

Angel, R. W., Alston, W., & Garland, H. (1970). Functional relations between the manual and oculomotor control systems. *Experimental Neurology, 27,* 248–257.

Bachman, J. C. (1961). Specificity vs. generality in learning and performing two large muscle motor tasks. *Research Quarterly, 32,* 3–11.

Bahill, A. T., & LaRitz, T. (1984). Why can't batters keep their eyes on the ball? *American Scientist, 72,* 249–253.

Bassili, J. N. (1979). Emotion recognition: The role of facial movement and the relative importance of upper and lower areas of the face. *Journal of Personality and Social Psychology, 37,* 2049–2058.

Beek, P. J. (1989). *Juggling dynamics.* Amsterdam: Free University Press.

Beggs, W. D., & Howarth, C. I. (1972). The movement of the hand towards a target. *Quarterly Journal of Experimental Psychology, 24,* 448–453.

Bernstein, N. (1967). *The coordination and regulation of movements.* London: Pergamon.

Biguer, B., Jeannerod, M., & Prablanc, C. (1982). The coordination of eye, head, and arm movements during reaching at a single visual target. *Experimental Brain Research, 46,* 301–304.

Biguer, B., Jeannerod, M., & Prablanc, C. (1985). The role of position of gaze in movement accuracy. In M. I. Posner & O. S. Marin (Eds.), *Attention and performance XI: Mechanisms of attention* (pp. 407–424). Hillsdale, NJ: Erlbaum.

Bizzi, E., & Mussa-Ivaldi, F. A., (1989). Geometrical and mechanical issues in movement planning and control. In M. I. Posner (Ed.), *Foundations of cognitive science* (pp. 769–792). Cambridge, MA: MIT Press.

Bootsma, R. J. (1989). Accuracy of perceptual processes subserving different perception-action systems. *Quarterly Journal of Experimental Psychology*, **41A**, 489–500.

Bootsma, R. J., & Van Wieringen, P. C. (1988). Visual control of an attacking forehand drive in table tennis. In O. G. Meijer & K. Roth (Eds.), *Complex motor behavior: The motor-action controversy* (pp. 189–199). Amsterdam: North-Holland.

Bootsma, R. J., & Van Wieringen, P. C. (1990). Timing an attacking forehand drive in table tennis. *Journal of Experimental Psychology: Human Perception and Performance*, **16**, 21–29.

Bower, T. G. R. (1982). *Development in infancy* (2d ed.). San Francisco: W. H. Freeman.

Bullock, D., & Grossberg, S. (1988). Neural dynamics of planned arm movements: Emergent invariants and speed-accuracy properties during trajectory formation. *Psychological Review*, **95**, 49–90.

Bullock, D., & Grossberg, S. (1989). VITE and FLETE: Neural modules for trajectory formation and postural control. In W. A. Hershberger (Ed.), *Volitional action* (pp. 253–297). Amsterdam: North-Holland/Elsevier.

Bullock, D., & Grossberg, S. (in press). Adaptive neural networks for control of movement trajectories invariant under speed and force rescaling. *Human Movement Science*.

Craik, K. J. W. (1943). *The nature of explanation*. London: Cambridge University Press.

Fleishman, E. A., & Bartlett, C. J. (1969). Human abilities. *Annual Review of Psychology*, **20**, 349–380.

Foley, J. D. (1987). Interfaces for advanced computing. *Scientific American*, **257** (4), 127–135.

Gauthier, G. M., Vercher, J-L., Mussa-Ivaldi, F., & Marchetti, E. (1988). Oculo-manual tracking of visual targets: Control learning, coordination control and coordination model. *Experimental Brain Research*, **73**, 127–137.

Georgopoulos, A. P., Kalaska, J. F., & Massey, J. T. (1981). Spatial trajectories and reaction times of aimed movements: Effects of practice, uncertainty, and change in target location. *Journal of Neurophysiology*, **46**, 725–743.

Georgopoulos, A. P., Schwartz, A. B., & Kettner, R. E. (1986). Neuronal population coding of movement direction. *Science*, **233**, 1416–1419.

Gibson, E. J. (1987). What does infant perception tell us about theories of perception? *Journal of Experimental Psychology: Human Perception and Performance*, **13**, 515–523.

Gibson, J. J. (1966). *The senses considered as perceptual systems*. Boston: Houghton-Mifflin.

Gibson, J. J. (1979). *The ecological approach to visual perception*. Boston: Houghton-Mifflin.

Goleman, D. (1989). New breed of robots have the human touch. *The New York Times*, August 1, C1.

Goodman, D., & Kelso, J. A. S. (1980). Are movements prepared in parts? Not under compatible (naturalized) conditions. *Journal of Experimental Psychology: General*, **109**, 475–495.

Grossberg, S. (Ed.) (1987a). *The adaptive brain. I. Cognition, learning, reinforcement, and rhythm*. Amsterdam: Elsevier/North-Holland.

Grossberg, S. (Ed.) (1987b). *The adaptive brain. II. Vision, speech, language, and motor control*. Amsterdam: Elsevier/North-Holland.

Grossberg, S., & Kuperstein, M. (1989). *Neural dynamics of sensory-motor control: Expanded edition*. New York: Pergamon Press.

Haken, H. (1977). *Synergetics: An introduction*. Berlin: Springer-Verlag.

Haken, H. (1983). *Advanced synergetics*. Berlin: Springer-Verlag.

Haken, H., & Wunderlin, A. (1990). Synergetics and its paradigm of self-organization in biological systems. In H. T. A. Whiting, O. G. Meijer, & P. C. van Wieringen (Eds.), *The natural-physical approach to movement control* (pp. 1–36). Amsterdam: VU University Press.

Haken, H., Kelso, J. A. S., & Bunz, H. (1985). A theoretical model of phase transitions in human hand movements. *Biological Cybernetics*, **51**, 347-356.

Hebb, D. O. (1949). *The organization of behavior: A neuropsychological theory*. New York: John Wiley.

Herman, R., Herman, R., & Malucci, R. (1981). Visually triggered eye-arm movements in man. *Experimental Brain Research*, **42**, 392-398.

Hogan, N. (1984). An organizing principle for a class of voluntary movements. *The Journal of Neuroscience*, **4**, 2745–2754.

Jeannerod, M. (1988). *The neural and behavioral organization of goal-directed movements*. Oxford: Oxford University Press.

Jordan, M. I., & Rosenbaum, D. A. (1989). Action. In M. I. Posner (Ed.), *Foundations of cognitive science* (pp. 727–767). Cambridge, MA: MIT Press.

Keele, S. W., & Ivry, R. I. (1987). Modular analysis of timing in motor skill. In G. H. Bower (Ed.), *The psychology of learning and motivation, Vol. 21* (pp. 183–228). San Diego: Academic Press.

Kelso, J. A. S., & Schöner, G. (1988). Self-organization of coordinative movement patterns. *Human Movement Science*, **7**, 27–46.

Kelso, J. A. S., Southard, D. L., & Goodman, D. L. (1979). On the co-ordination of two-handed movements. *Journal of Experimental Psychology: Human Perception and Performance*, **5**, 229–238.

Kugler, P. (1986). A morphological perspective on the origin and evolution of movement patterns. In M. G. Wade & H. T. A. Whiting (Eds.), *Motor skills acquisition in children: Aspects of coordination and control* (pp. 459–525). The Hague: Martinus Nijhoff.

Kugler, P., & Turvey, M. T. (1987). *Information, natural law and self-assembly of rhythmic movements: A study in the similitude of natural law*. Hillsdale, NJ: Erlbaum.

Lee, D. N. (1976). A theory of visual control of braking based on information about time-to-collision. *Perception*, **5**, 437–459.

Lee, D. N., & Reddish, P. E. (1981). Plummeting gannets: A paradigm of ecological optics. *Nature*, **293**, 293–294.

Lee, D. N., & Thomson, J. A. (1982). Vision in action: The control of locomotion. In D. J. Ingle, M. A. Goodale, & R. J. W. Mansfield (Eds.), *Analysis of visual behavior* (pp. 411–433). Cambridge, MA: MIT.

Lee, D. N., Young, D. S., Reddish, P. E., Lough, S., & Clayton, T. M. (1983). Visual timing in hitting an accelerating ball. *Quarterly Journal of Experimental Psychology*, **35A**, 333–346.

Lotter, W. S. (1960). Interrelationships among reaction times and speeds of movement in different limbs. *Research Quarterly*, **31**, 147–155.

McLeod, P. (1987). Visual reaction time and high-speed ball games. *Perception*, **16**, 49–59.

McLeod, P., McLaughlin, C., & Nimmo-Smith, I. (1986). Information encapsulation and automaticity: Evidence from the visual control of finely-timed actions. In M. Posner & O. Marin (Eds.), *Attention and performance XI* (pp. 391–406). Hillsdale, NJ: Erlbaum.

Meyer, D. E., Smith, J. E. K., & Wright, C. E. (1982). Models for the speed and accuracy of aimed movements. *Psychological Review*, **89**, 449–482.

Morasso, P. (1981). Spatial control of arm movements. *Experimental Brain Research*, **42**, 223–227.

Parker, J. F., & Fleishman, E. A. (1960). Ability factors and component performance measures as predictors of complex tracking behavior. *Psychological Monographs*, **74** (No. 503).

Pew, R. W., & Rosenbaum, D. A. (1988). Human motor performance: Computation, representation, and implementation. In R. C. Atkinson, R. J. Herrnstein, G. Lindzey, & R. D. Luce (Eds.), *Stevens' handbook of experimental psychology* (2d ed., pp. 473–509). New York: Wiley.

Prablanc, C., Echallier, J. F., & Jeannerod, M. (1979). Optimal response of eye and hand motor systems in pointing at a visual target. I. Spatio-temporal characteristics of arm and hand movements and their relationships when varying the amount of information. *Biological Cybernetics*, **35**, 113–124.

Rosenbaum, D. A. (1975). Perception and extrapolation of velocity and acceleration. *Journal of Experimental Psychology: Human Perception and Performance*, **1**, 395–403.

Rosenbaum, D. A. (1980). Human movement initiation: Specification of arm, direction, and extent. *Journal of Experimental Psychology: General*, **109**, 444-474.

Rosenbaum, D. A., Vaughan, J., Barnes, H. J., Marchak, F., & Slotta, J. (1990). Constraints on action selection: Overhand versus underhand grips. In M. Jeannerod (Ed.), *Attention and performance XIII* (pp. 321–342). Hillsdale, NJ: Erlbaum.

Schmidt, R. A. (1988). *Motor control and learning* (2d ed.). Champaign, IL: Human Kinetics Publishers.

Schmidt, R. A., Zelaznik, H. N., Hawkins, B., Frank, J. S., & Quinn, J. T., Jr. (1979). Motor output variability: A theory for the accuracy of rapid motor acts. *Psychological Review*, **86**, 415–451.

Schmidt, R. C., Carello, C., & Turvey, M. T. (1990). Phase transitions and critical fluctuations in the visual coordination of rhythmic movements between people. *Journal of Experimental Psychology: Human Perception and Performance*, **16**, 227–247.

Scholz, J. P., Kelso, J. A. S., & Schöner, G. (1987). Nonequilibrium phase transitions in coordinated biological motion: Critical slowing down and switching time. *Physics Letters*, **123**, 390–394.

Schöner, G., & Kelso, J. A. S. (1988). Dynamic pattern generation in behavioral and neural systems. *Science*, **239**, 1513–1520.

Sharp, R. H. (1975). *Skill in fast ball games: Some input considerations*. Unpublished doctoral dissertation. University of Leeds, Yorkshire, England.

Smyth, T. R., & Glencross, D. J. (1986). Information processing deficits in clumsy children. *Australian Journal of Psychology*, **38**, 13–22.

Steinbach, M. J., & Held, R. (1968). Eye tracking of observer-generated target movements. *Science*, **161**, 187–188.

Thelen, E., Kelso, J. A. S., & Fogel, A. (1987). Self-organizing systems and infant motor development. *Developmental Review*, **7**, 39–65.

Todd, J. T. (1981). Visual information about moving objects. *Journal of Experimental Psychology: Human Perception and Performance*, **7**, 795–810.

Turvey, M. T. (1990). The challenge of a physical account of action: A personal view. In H. T. A. Whiting, O. G. Meijer, & P. C. van Wieringen (Eds.), *The natural-physical approach to movement control* (pp. 57–93). Amsterdam: VU University Press.

Tyldesley, D. A., & Whiting, H. T. A. (1975). Operational timing. *Journal of Human Movement Studies*, **1**, 172–177.

Wagner, H. (1982). Flow-field variables trigger landing in flies. *Nature (London)*, **297**, 147–148.

Westheimer, G. (1954). Eye movement responses to a horizontally moving visual stimulus. *Archives of Ophthalmology*, **52**, 932–941.

Whiting, H. T. A., Gill, E. B., & Stephenson, J. M. (1970). Critical time intervals for taking in flight information in a ball-catching task. *Ergonomics*, **13**, 265–272.

Williams, H. G., & Woollacott, M. H. (1988). Characteristics of neuromuscular responses underlying posture control in clumsy children. *Neuroscience Abstracts*, **14**, 66.

Williams, H. G., Woollacott, M. H., & Ivry, R. (1989). Timing and motor control in clumsy children. *Neuroscience Abstracts*, **15**, 1334.

Zelaznik, H. N., Schmidt, R. A., & Gielen, S. C. (1986). Kinematic properties of aimed hand movements. *Journal of Motor Behavior*, **18**, 353-372..

■ AUTHOR INDEX

■ SUBJECT INDEX